DIABETIC DIET

After 50

210+ Healthy and Delicious Low-Carb, Low-Sugar, Low-Fat Recipes | Cookbook for Type 2 Diabetes and Newly Diagnosed with a 30-Day Meal Plan

Isabella Carr

Copyright © 2024 by Isabella Carr. All rights reserved.

This book is protected under international copyright law. No part of this book may be reproduced, stored in a retrieval system, or transmitted in any form or by any means, electronic, mechanical, photocopying, recording, or otherwise, without the prior written permission of the author, except in the case of brief quotations in reviews or articles. Unauthorized reproduction, distribution, or use of this book or its contents is legally prohibited.

Disclaimer:

This cookbook is intended for informational purposes only. The recipes and information provided in this book are not intended as a substitute for the advice of a medical professional. Individuals with diabetes or other health conditions should consult their healthcare provider before making dietary changes. The author and publisher are not responsible for any adverse effects or consequences resulting from using the recipes or suggestions in this book.

The nutritional information provided with the recipes is estimated and may vary depending on the ingredients and methods of preparation. The reader must ensure that the ingredients and processes suit their dietary needs and restrictions.

TABLE OF CONTENTS

Introduction..6

CHAPTER 1: UNDERSTANDING DIABETES.....................7

What is Diabetes...7
Diabetes After 50: Special Considerations......................7
The Connection Between Sleep and Diabetes................8

CHAPTER 2: THE IMPORTANCE OF DIET IN DIABETES MANAGEMENT..9

The Role of Nutrition in Blood Sugar Control...................9
Benefits of a Diabetic-Friendly Diet:.................................9
Understanding the Glycemic Index and Glycemic Load....10
Natural Sweeteners for Diabetics...................................10

CHAPTER 3: PRACTICAL TIPS FOR DIABETES-FRIENDLY COOKING...11

1. How to Use This Cookbook..11
2. Meal Planning and Preparation Tips..........................11
3. Smart Shopping for Diabetes-Friendly Ingredients....12
4. Creating a Diabetes-Friendly Kitchen........................12
5. Navigating Social Situations and Dining Out.............12

CHAPTER 4: BREAKFAST RECIPES................................14

1. Quick and Easy Breakfasts 14
Breakfast Tostada...14
Overnight Oats with Chia Seeds....................................14
Greek Yogurt with Fresh Berries and Nuts.....................15
Avocado Toast with Tomato Slices................................15
Apple Cinnamon Overnight Oats....................................16
Salad with Egg and Salsa Verde Vinaigrette.................16
Cottage Cheese with Pineapple Chunks.......................17
Creamy Scrambled Eggs with Smoked Salmon............17
Tomato and Basil Egg White Scramble.........................18
Avocado and Turkey Breakfast Roll-Ups.......................18

2. High-Protein Breakfasts..19
Spinach and Mushroom Egg Scramble.........................19
Tofu and Veggie Breakfast Bowl....................................19
Smoked Salmon and Avocado Plate..............................20
Greek Yogurt with Almonds and Honey.........................20
Egg and Cheese Breakfast Muffins................................21
Turkey Sausage and Egg Wrap.....................................21
Cottage Cheese and Veggie Stuffed Bell Peppers.......22
Cheese and Herb-Stuffed Omelette..............................22
Chicken Sausage and Kale Breakfast Skillet................23
Egg and Tofu Stir-Fry with Vegetables..........................23

3. Low-Carb Breakfasts..24
Veggie and Cheese Frittata..24
Low-Carb Pancakes with Berries..................................24
Zucchini and Tomato Omelette......................................25
Chia Seed Pudding with Almond Milk............................25
Cottage Cheese and Cucumber Bowl............................26
Cauliflower Hash Browns...26
Yogurt Parfait with Nuts and Seeds...............................27
Zucchini Noodles with Poached Eggs...........................27
Bacon-wrapped asparagus with Soft-Boiled Eggs........28
Portobello Mushroom and Spinach Breakfast Bake......28

CHAPTER 5: SMOOTHIES AND BEVERAGES.................29

1. Low-Glycemic Index Smoothies..............................29
Spinach and Blueberry Blast Smoothie.........................29
Kale and Green Apple Smoothie...................................29
Avocado Berry Delight Smoothie...................................30
Cucumber Mint Green Smoothie...................................30
Strawberry Spinach Smoothie.......................................31
Berry Bliss Smoothie with Chia Seeds..........................31
Creamy Avocado and Spinach Smoothie.....................32

2. Protein-Packed Smoothies 33
Chocolate Banana Protein Smoothie.............................33
Peanut Butter Berry Power Smoothie...........................33
Greek Yogurt and Almond Protein Shake.....................34
Spinach Almond Butter Protein Smoothie.....................34
Vanilla Strawberry Protein Smoothie.............................35
Peanut Butter and Greek Yogurt Power Shake............35
Almond-Coconut Protein Smoothie...............................36

3. Hydrating and Refreshing Beverages....................37
Cucumber Mint Infused Water.......................................37
Lemon Basil Infused Water..37
Ginger Lemon Herbal Tea..38
Watermelon Mint Cooler...38
Hibiscus Berry Iced Tea...39
Lemon-Lavender Sparkling Water.................................39
Cucumber Lime Electrolyte Drink..................................40

CHAPTER 6: LUNCH RECIPES..41

1. Salads and Bowls..41
Quinoa and Black Bean Salad.......................................41
Spinach and Strawberry Salad with Balsamic Vinaigrette 41
Grilled Chicken Caesar Salad..42

Mediterranean Chickpea Salad 42
Tuna and Avocado Salad Bowl 43
Kale and Roasted Beet Salad 43
Thai Peanut Chicken Salad...44
Lentil and Feta Salad..44
Cobb Salad with Turkey and Avocado 45
Salmon and Asparagus Salad....................................45

2. Sandwiches and Wraps **46**
Turkey and Avocado Whole Grain Wrap.....................46
Grilled Veggie and Hummus Sandwich......................46
Mediterranean Veggie and Hummus Wrap................47
Egg and Spinach Whole Wheat Sandwic...................47
Roast Beef Wrap with Mustard...................................48
Tuna Salad Whole Grain Sandwich............................48
Turkey and Spinach Wrap with Hummus...................49
Cucumber and Cream Cheese Sandwich..................49
Veggie and Tofu Wrap...50
Smoked Salmon and Avocado Sandwich..................50

3. Soups and Stews...**51**
Lentil and Vegetable Soup..51
Broccoli Cheddar Soup...51
Chicken and Kale Soup...52
Tomato Basil Soup..52
Spicy Lentil Stew...53
Minestrone Soup...53
Butternut Squash Soup...54
Beef and Vegetable Stew..54
Split Pea Soup with Ham 55
Moroccan Chickpea Stew...55

4. Vegetarian and Vegan Options...........................**56**
Roasted Veggie and Quinoa Bowl..............................56
Vegan Lentil Tacos..56
Stuffed Bell Peppers with Black Beans and Corn.......57
Chickpea and Spinach Curry......................................57
Zucchini Noodles with Pesto and Cherry Tomatoes...58
Sweet Potato and Black Bean Salad..........................58
Vegan Cauliflower Buffalo Wing..................................59
Tofu and Veggie Stir-Fry..59
Mushroom and Barley Pilaf...60
Eggplant and Tomato Stew 60

5. Pizza Recipes **61**
Whole Wheat Veggie Pizza with Pesto Sauce............61
Cauliflower Crust Margherita Pizza.............................61
Low-carb zucchini Crust Pizza with Fresh Herbs.......62
Grilled Chicken and Spinach Alfredo Pizza................62
Eggplant Mini Pizzas with Mozzarella.........................63
Spicy Shrimp and Garlic Pizza on a Cauliflower
Crust..63
Mushroom and Olive Pizza with Ricotta.....................64
Low-carb BBQ Chicken Pizza with Red Onion...........64

Keto-Friendly Broccoli and Cheese Pizza..................65
Low-carb zucchini Crust Pizza with Fresh Herbs.......65
Low-Carb Bell Pepper Crust Pizza with Fresh Herbs.....66

6. Fish and Seafood..**67**
Grilled Salmon and Avocado Salad............................67
Lemon-Dill Shrimp and Quinoa Bowl..........................67
Spicy Mackerel Salad with Cucumber and Tomato....68
Baked Cod with Garlic Spinach..................................68
Zucchini Noodles with Pesto Shrimp..........................69
Greek-Style Grilled Fish Tacos with Tzatziki...............69
Seared Scallops with Asparagus and Lemon.............70
Crispy Tilapia Lettuce Cups with Mango Salsa..........70
Sardine and Avocado Stuffed Bell Peppers................71
Ginger-Lime Grilled Shrimp with Cabbage Slaw........71
Low-Carb Salmon Patties with Cucumber Salad.......72
Blackened Fish and Cauliflower Rice Bowl................72

CHAPTER 7: DINNER RECIPES **73**

1. Lean Protein Dishes **73**
Lemon Herb Grilled Chicken......................................73
Chicken and Broccoli Stir-Fry.....................................73
Tofu and Vegetable Stir-Fry..74
Garlic Roasted Turkey Breast.....................................74
Baked Turkey Meatballs...75
Chicken and Spinach Stuffed Portobello
Mushrooms...75
Garlic and Rosemary Grilled Pork Tenderloin............76
Balsamic Glazed Pork Tenderloin...............................76
Herb-Rubbed Grilled Chicken Breasts.......................77
Lean Beef and Vegetable Stir-Fry...............................77

2. Low-Carb Dinner Ideas **78**
Spaghetti Squash Bolognese.....................................78
Cauliflower Fried Rice with Chicken...........................78
Zoodles with Pesto and Cherry Tomatoes.................79
Stuffed Bell Peppers with Ground Turkey..................79
Beef and Broccoli Stir-Fry...80
Herb-Roasted Chicken Thighs with Garlic and Vegetables
....80
Beef and Broccoli Stir-Fry with Cauliflower Rice........81
Eggplant Lasagna...81
Cauliflower Mashed Potatoes with Grilled
Chicken...82
Almond-Crusted Chicken Tenders 82

3. One-Pot and Slow Cooker Meals **83**
Slow Cooker Chicken and Vegetable Stew................83
One-pot beef and Vegetable Chili..............................83
Slow Cooker Beef and Vegetable Soup.....................84
One-Pot Mexican Quinoa...84
Slow Cooker Lentil and Spinach Curry......................85
One-pot garlic Parmesan Chicken with Broccoli.......85
Slow Cooker Turkey Chili...86

Slow Cooker BBQ Pulled Pork..................................86
One-Pot Ratatouille...87
One-Pot Creamy Mushroom Chicken......................87

4. International Cuisine...88
Greek Lemon Chicken with Tzatziki..........................88
Italian Stuffed Bell Peppers with Ground Turkey....88
Indian Spiced Chickpea Stew....................................89
Italian Stuffed Eggplant...89
Japanese Teriyaki Tofu with Broccoli.......................90
Moroccan Chicken Tagine with Vegetables............90
Mexican Chicken Fajitas with Bell Peppers.............91
Indian Chicken Curry with Cauliflower Rice............91
Middle Eastern Falafel with Tahini Sauce................92
Vietnamese Pho with Tofu and Vegetables.............92

CHAPTER 8: SNACKS AND APPETIZERS..............93

1. Healthy Snacking Tips..93
Greek Yogurt with Berries and Nuts.........................93
Apple Slices with Almond Butter..............................93
Carrot and Celery Sticks with Hummus...................94
Cottage Cheese with Pineapple...............................94
Mixed Nuts and Seeds..95
Bell Pepper Slices with Guacamole..........................95
Almond and Flaxseed Energy Bites.........................96
Roasted Chickpeas with Sea Salt and Paprika.......96
Greek Yogurt and Cucumber Dip with Veggie Sticks...........97
Celery Sticks with Cream Cheese and Walnuts......97

2. Quick and Easy Snacks......................................98
Spicy Roasted Chickpeas...98
Cucumber Slices with Hummus.................................98
Cheese and Cherry Tomato Skewers.......................99
Mixed Nuts and Seeds Trail Mix.................................99
Hard-Boiled Eggs with a Dash of Paprika..............100
Edamame with Sea Salt..100
Cottage Cheese and Tomato Stuffed Avocados...101
Hard-Boiled Eggs with Hummus...............................101
Rice Cake with Peanut Butter and Chia Seeds.....102
Zucchini Chips with Parmesan.................................102

3. Appetizers for Entertaining..............................103
Smoked Salmon Cucumber Bites............................103
Caprese Salad Skewers..103
Stuffed Mini Bell Peppers with Cream Cheese.....104
Zucchini and Feta Roll-Ups......................................104
Guacamole with Veggie Sticks................................105
Almond-Crusted Mozzarella Sticks 105

Spinach and Artichoke Dip with
Whole-Grain Crackers..106
Prosciutto-Wrapped Asparagus Spears................106
Garlic and Herb Stuffed Mushrooms......................107
Shrimp Cocktail with Avocado Salsa......................107

CHAPTER 9: DESSERTS AND TREATS.................108

1. Low-Sugar Desserts..108
Berry Greek Yogurt Parfait......................................108
Baked Apples with Cinnamon..................................108
Fresh Fruit Salad with Mint......................................109
Chia Seed Pudding with Mango..............................109
Strawberry Basil Sorbet...110
Orange and Almond Salad.......................................110
Berry Chia Seed Jam...111
Almond Butter Cookies...111
Coconut Flour Pancakes..112
Apple Cinnamon Chia Seed Pudding.....................112

2. Baking with Sugar Substitutes........................113
Almond Flour Chocolate Chip Cookies..................113
Sugar-Free Banana Bread.......................................113
Low-Carb Lemon Bars..114
Coconut Flour Brownies..114
Vanilla Almond Cupcakes...115
Pumpkin Spice Muffins..115
Lemon Blueberry Muffins...116
Chocolate Almond Brownies...................................116
Cinnamon Walnut Coffee Cake...............................117
Pumpkin Spice Bars..117

3. Special Occasion Treats..................................118
Dark Chocolate Covered Strawberries.................118
Pumpkin Spice Cheesecake Bites..........................118
Low-Carb Coconut Panna Cotta............................119
Raspberry Lemon Tart...119
Chocolate Avocado Mousse...................................120
Carrot Cake with Cream Cheese Frosting 120
Mini Berry Cheesecakes..121
Dark Chocolate Coconut Truffles...........................121
Almond Flour Lemon Bars.......................................122
Peanut Butter Chocolate Chip Cookies................122

30-Day Meal Plan..123
Recipe Index..126
Conclusion...139

INTRODUCTION

Welcome to the "Diabetic Diet Cookbook After 50," a book crafted to revolutionize your approach to managing diabetes while still enjoying the food you love. If you've been searching for a way to balance your health needs with a passion for delicious meals, you've come to the right place.

Why This Book Matters
As we age, our bodies change, and managing diabetes can become more challenging. But here's the good news: this book is designed to help you quickly navigate those challenges. Whether you're newly diagnosed or have been managing diabetes for years, this cookbook offers the tools, knowledge, and inspiration to take control of your health without sacrificing taste or variety.

What You'll Gain
By the end of this book, you'll have a solid understanding of using food as a powerful tool in your diabetes management toolkit. You'll discover:

- **Delicious and Diabetes-Friendly Recipes:** Enjoy a wide range of meals that stabilize your blood sugar while satisfying your palate.
- **Practical Nutritional Guidance:** Learn to make informed food choices that support your health goals, whether you're cooking for yourself or your entire family.
- **Personalized Strategies for Individuals Over 50:** Discover the unique nutritional requirements of those over 50 and how to modify your diet to meet those needs.
- **Lifestyle Tips:** Incorporate healthy practices into your daily routine to help manage diabetes and enhance overall well-being.

How to Make the Most of This Book
To make the most of this cookbook, read the introduction to diabetes and nutrition. This essential foundation will equip you to make well-informed choices in the kitchen. After that, explore the recipes, categorized by meal type, making it easy to find what you want—a quick breakfast or a satisfying dinner. Use the tips and advice throughout the book to tweak recipes, plan meals, and maintain a healthy lifestyle that supports diabetes management.

Embark on Your Health Journey Today
This book is more than just a collection of recipes; it's your guide to a healthier, happier life after 50. You can transform your relationship with food, take control of your diabetes, and enjoy every bite along the way. Let this book be your companion on this journey.

So, are you ready to take the first step towards better health? Let's get started!

CHAPTER 1
UNDERSTANDING DIABETES

Before diving into the recipes and dietary tips, it's essential to understand the fundamentals of diabetes, mainly how it affects those over 50. In this chapter, we'll cover the basics of diabetes, explore the different types, and discuss the unique challenges and considerations for managing the condition as you age. Understanding diabetes and its impact on the body will better equip you to make informed choices that support your health and well-being.

1. What is Diabetes

Type 1 Diabetes
- **Synopsis:** In type 1 diabetes, an autoimmune disease, the immune system assaults and kills the pancreatic beta cells that produce insulin. It often starts in the early years of life, but it may happen to anybody.
- **Management:** Insulin treatment is necessary to regulate blood sugar in individuals with Type 1 diabetes throughout their lives. To effectively manage, one must adhere to a nutritious diet, exercise regularly, and check blood sugar levels consistently.

Type 2 Diabetes
- **Generalization:** Type 2 diabetes accounts for most cases among people 50 and older. When insulin resistance develops, or pancreatic insulin production falls short of demand, diabetes sets in.
- **Synopsis:** Type 2 diabetes risk factors include a poor diet, insufficient physical activity, and being overweight. Another risk factor for getting diabetes is a personal or family history of the disease.
- **Management:** A healthy diet, frequent exercise, and oral medicine are the usual tools for controlling type 2 diabetes. Insulin treatment may also be required in some instances.

Gestational Diabetes
- **Overview:** Gestational diabetes develops during pregnancy and typically goes away after childbirth.
- **Management:** Controlling gestational diabetes requires following a balanced diet, maintaining regular physical activity, and in some cases, using insulin therapy. Consistent blood sugar monitoring is essential to prevent complications for the mother and baby.

Prediabetes
- **Overview:** Prediabetes occurs when blood sugar levels are elevated but not yet within the range for a diabetes diagnosis. It indicates a higher likelihood of progressing to Type 2 diabetes.
- **Management:** Lifestyle changes, such as adopting a healthier diet, engaging in more physical activity, and losing weight, can help reverse prediabetes and reduce the risk of progressing to Type 2 diabetes.

2. Diabetes After 50: Special Considerations

As you age, managing diabetes requires a more tailored approach. Your body's metabolism slows down, and you may experience changes in how you process foods and medications. Here are some critical considerations for managing diabetes effectively after 50:

Balanced Nutrition
- **Nutritional Requirements:** As you age past 50, your body requires fewer calories but a higher intake of essential nutrients to maintain good health. Emphasize a nutritious diet that incorporates a variety of whole grains, lean protein options, healthy fats, and various fruits and vegetables.
- **Dietary Adjustments:** To manage blood sugar levels effectively, you may need to adjust your carbohydrate intake, focus on portion control, and incorporate foods lower in the glycemic index.

Regular Physical Activity
- **The Advantages of Exercise:** Regular physical activity improves insulin sensitivity, supports healthy weight management, and boosts cardiovascular health. Walking, swimming, and strength training are great options for individuals over 50.
- **Staying Active:** Strive for at least 150 minutes of moderate exercise weekly, incorporating strength training twice-weekly to maintain muscle mass and bone density.

Regular Monitoring
- **Tracking Health Metrics:** Regularly monitoring your blood sugar, cholesterol, and blood pressure is key to managing diabetes. This helps you adjust your diet, exercise, or medications as needed.
- **Preventive Care:** Routine check-ups with your healthcare provider, eye exams, and foot care are crucial for preventing complications.

Unique Considerations for Women Over 50:
For women over 50, diabetes management can become more complex due to hormonal shifts during menopause, which may impact insulin sensitivity, body weight, and overall diabetes control.

Hormonal Changes and Diabetes
- **Impact of Menopause:** As estrogen levels drop during menopause, insulin sensitivity decreases, often causing higher blood sugar levels. Menopausal symptoms like hot flashes and night sweats can also disrupt sleep, making diabetes management more challenging.
- **Weight Management:** Hormonal shifts may lead to weight gain, especially around the abdomen, raising the risk of insulin resistance. Maintaining a balanced diet and a consistent exercise routine is essential during this period.

Nutritional Needs and Diet Adjustments
- **Calcium and Vitamin D:** Lower estrogen levels during menopause increase the risk of osteoporosis. To maintain bone health, ensure adequate calcium and vitamin D intake through diet or supplements.
- **Fiber:** A diet rich in fiber supports digestion, promotes reasonable weight control, and helps balance blood sugar. Eat more fruits, veggies, legumes, and whole grains.
- **Protein and Fats:** Maintaining lean muscle mass requires an adequate amount of protein, while the good fats found in foods like nuts, seeds, and fish aid heart health and general wellness.

3. The Connection Between Sleep and Diabetes:
Managing diabetes after 50 can be complicated by sleep disruptions. Poor sleep affects energy and mood and can worsen blood sugar control, creating a challenging cycle to break.

How Diabetes Affects Sleep
- **Blood Sugar Fluctuations:** High blood sugar levels can lead to frequent urination at night, while low blood sugar levels can cause symptoms like sweating and anxiety, disrupting sleep.
- **Diabetic Neuropathy:** Nerve pain, particularly in the legs and feet, can make it difficult to get comfortable and fall asleep.
- **Sleep Apnea:** Diabetics are at an increased risk of developing this sleep disorder, which is defined by episodes of disrupted breathing while sleeping. As a result, problems with controlling blood sugar levels and general health may worsen.

Improving Sleep Quality through Nutrition
- **Stabilize Blood Sugar Levels:** Eating healthily during the day may keep blood sugar levels steady, which in turn helps reduce the likelihood of dangerous spikes and crashes while you're trying to sleep.
- **Avoid Heavy Meals Before Bed:** Consuming a large meal right before sleep can lead to discomfort and indigestion, making it difficult to fall asleep. Instead, choose a light snack if you feel hungry before bedtime.
- **Incorporate Sleep Enhancing Nutrients:** Foods rich in magnesium (like leafy greens, nuts, and seeds) and tryptophan (found in turkey, eggs, and dairy) can promote relaxation and better sleep.

Understanding diabetes and its effects on your body, especially as you age, is the first step in taking control of your health. Whether you're managing Type 1, Type 2, or another form of diabetes, knowledge is power. By recognizing the unique challenges of diabetes after 50 and implementing the strategies discussed in this chapter, you can better manage your condition and live a healthier, more fulfilling life.

In the next chapter, we'll dive into the role of diet in diabetes management, exploring how the foods you eat can either help or hinder your blood sugar control. Let's continue this journey toward better health, one step at a time.

CHAPTER 2
THE IMPORTANCE OF DIET IN DIABETES MANAGEMENT

Managing diabetes effectively requires more than just medication—it involves making mindful choices about what you eat daily. In this chapter, we'll explore how your diet directly impacts your blood sugar levels, the benefits of a diabetes-friendly diet, and practical tools like the Glycemic Index that can help you make smarter food choices. Whether you're looking to lose weight, reduce your risk of complications, or feel more energetic, understanding the role of nutrition is crucial.

1. The Role of Nutrition in Blood Sugar Control

Your diet is one of the most powerful tools you have to manage diabetes. The foods you consume directly affect your blood sugar levels, and making the right choices can help you maintain stable glucose levels throughout the day. Here's how you can use nutrition to your advantage:

Carbohydrate Management: Choosing the Right Carbs

Carbohydrates have the most immediate impact on blood sugar levels, so it's essential to understand which ones to include in your diet:

- **Complex Carbohydrates:** Opt for whole grains, legumes, and non-starchy vegetables, which are digested slowly and cause a gradual rise in blood sugar.
- **Low-Glycemic Foods:** Foods with a low glycemic index (GI) release glucose more slowly, helping to prevent spikes in blood sugar.

The Importance of a Regular Eating Schedule

Skipping meals or eating irregularly can cause fluctuations in blood sugar levels, making diabetes more challenging to manage:

- **Regular Meals:** Eating at consistent times helps maintain stable blood sugar levels.
- **Balanced Snacks:** Incorporating small, balanced snacks between meals can prevent blood sugar dips.

Portion Control and Hydration

Understanding portion sizes and staying hydrated is vital to maintaining balanced blood sugar levels:

- **Portion Control:** Even nutritious foods can elevate blood sugar when consumed excessively. Paying attention to portion sizes is essential to prevent overeating.
- **Hydration:** Proper hydration is key for overall body function and can aid in maintaining stable blood sugar levels. Water is the best option; avoid sugary beverages that can lead to blood sugar spikes.

2. Benefits of a Diabetic-Friendly Diet:

A diet tailored to diabetes management does more than just regulate blood sugar. Here are some additional benefits:

Maintaining a healthy weight plays a key role in diabetes management:

- **Healthy Weight Loss:** Even a small amount of weight loss can significantly improve blood sugar control if you're overweight.
- **Steady Energy Levels:** A well-balanced diet helps prevent blood sugar fluctuations, providing consistent energy throughout the day.

Enhancing Mental Health and Well-being

What you eat affects not just your body but also your mind:

- **Cognitive Function:** A balanced diet of antioxidants, healthy fats, and whole foods supports brain health.
- **Emotional Balance:** Stabilizing blood sugar levels through diet can improve mood and reduce feelings of irritability or fatigue.

3. Understanding the Glycemic Index and Glycemic Load

Carbohydrates may be better planned for with knowledge of the glycaemic index (GI) and glycaemic load (GL). With these aids, you may find meals that regulate your blood sugar levels more consistently.

What is the Glycemic Index (GI)?

A food's ability to spike blood sugar levels in a short amount of time is quantified by its glycaemic index (GI):

- **High GI Foods:** Items such as white bread, rice, and potatoes cause a rapid spike in blood sugar and should be consumed in moderation.
- **Medium GI Foods:** Whole wheat products and sweet potatoes have a moderate effect on blood sugar.
- **Low GI Foods:** Foods like legumes, non-starchy vegetables, and most fruits result in a slower rise in blood sugar, making them better choices for managing diabetes.

What is Glycemic Load (GL)?

Glycemic Load (GL) takes into account both the Glycemic Index (GI) and the carbohydrate content in a serving, providing a clearer picture of how food influences blood sugar:

- **High GL:** Foods with a high glycemic load cause a substantial rise in blood sugar levels.
- **Medium GL:** These foods have a moderate effect and can be consumed in controlled portions.
- **Low GL:** Foods with a low glycemic load support stable blood sugar levels.

How to Use GI and GL in Your Diet:

Incorporating both GI and GL into meal planning can improve diabetes management:

- **Choose Low-GI Foods:** Include more low-GI foods to steady your blood sugar.
- **Combine Foods:** Pair high-GI foods with low-GI foods, proteins, and healthy fats to reduce the overall glycemic impact of your meal.
- **Watch Portions:** Even low-GI foods can raise blood sugar when consumed in large amounts, so be mindful of portion sizes.

4. Natural Sweeteners for Diabetics

For those managing diabetes, finding sugar alternatives is essential to keeping blood sugar levels in check. Below are some natural sweeteners that provide sweetness without causing significant blood sugar spikes:

Types of Natural Sweeteners

- **Stevia:** A zero-calorie sweetener made from the leaves of the Stevia plant. It doesn't elevate blood sugar and is safe for people with diabetes.
- **Monk Fruit:** A natural, calorie-free sweetener that is much sweeter than sugar and doesn't affect blood glucose levels.
- **Erythritol:** A sugar alcohol that offers about 70% of the sweetness of sugar, with minimal impact on blood sugar, and is generally well-tolerated.
- **Xylitol:** Another sugar alcohol with a low glycemic index, comparable in sweetness to sugar, but should be consumed in moderation due to potential digestive issues.
- **Yacon Syrup:** Derived from the yacon plant, this syrup contains fructooligosaccharides, which have little effect on blood sugar and may promote gut health.

Benefits and Potential Side Effects

Each natural sweetener has its own set of benefits and considerations:

- **Stevia:** Offers a natural sweetness without calories, but some people may find it has a slight aftertaste.
- **Monk Fruit:** Provides a sweet flavor with antioxidant properties, though it can be more expensive than other sweeteners.
- **Erythritol:** Generally well-tolerated but can cause digestive discomfort in large amounts.
- **Xylitol:** Helps prevent tooth decay but may cause digestive upset if consumed in excess. It's also toxic to pets, so caution is needed.
- **Yacon Syrup:** Supports digestive health but can cause gas or bloating in larger quantities.

Putting It All Together Understanding the role of nutrition in diabetes management is the first step toward better health. By making informed choices about your foods—choosing low-GI carbohydrates, incorporating natural sweeteners, and maintaining a balanced diet—you can effectively manage your diabetes and enjoy a high quality of life.

As you progress in this book, keep these principles in mind as you explore the recipes and practical tips designed to help you thrive. Remember, a well-planned diet is not just a way to manage diabetes; it's a way to live better, feel better, and embrace life after 50 with vitality and joy.

CHAPTER 3
PRACTICAL TIPS FOR DIABETES-FRIENDLY COOKING

Once you understand the basics of diabetes and the importance of nutrition, the next step is to apply that knowledge in your kitchen. This chapter is dedicated to helping you make the most of your culinary efforts, ensuring that every meal you prepare is delicious and supports your diabetes management. From selecting the right ingredients to mastering portion control, these practical tips will guide you in creating meals that keep your blood sugar levels stable and your taste buds satisfied.

1. How to Use This Cookbook

This cookbook is designed to be more than just a collection of recipes—it's a guide to help you create a sustainable, diabetes-friendly eating plan. Here's how to make the most of it:

Follow Portion Sizes

- **Why It Matters:** Managing portion sizes is key to controlling blood sugar. Even healthy foods can cause spikes if eaten in large amounts.
- **How to Do It:** Each recipe in this book provides recommended portion sizes. Use measuring cups, spoons, or a kitchen scale to ensure you eat correctly.

Balance Your Plate

- **Why It Matters:** A balanced meal that includes a mix of carbohydrates, proteins, and healthy fats helps stabilize blood sugar and provides lasting energy.
- **How to Do It:** Fill half your plate with non-starchy vegetables, a quarter with lean proteins, and the remaining quarter with whole grains or starchy vegetables. Add a small amount of healthy fats like olive oil or avocado.

Experiment with Flavors

- **Why It Matters:** Using a variety of herbs, spices, and seasonings enhances the flavor of your meals without adding extra calories or sugars, making it easier to stick to a diabetes-friendly diet.
- **How to Do It:** Be bold and experiment with new spices and combinations. This cookbook includes recipes with natural flavoring options to help you enjoy vibrant, satisfying meals without relying on added sugars or salt.

Read Labels Carefully

- **Why It Matters:** Many packaged foods contain hidden sugars, unhealthy fats, or excessive sodium, which can negatively impact blood sugar levels and overall health.
- **How to Do It:** When shopping, read nutrition labels. Look for hidden sugars (often listed under different names like sucrose, high-fructose corn syrup, or agave nectar) and choose products with minimal ingredients and no added sugars.

2. Meal Planning and Preparation Tips

Planning and preparing your meals ahead of time can significantly aid in managing diabetes. Careful planning ensures that nutritious options are always available, making it easier to stay on track with your dietary goals.

Plan Ahead

- **Why It's Important:** Meal planning reduces the likelihood of making impulsive, unhealthy food choices and streamlines your grocery shopping. It can also help you save time and money by minimizing waste and maximizing efficiency.
- **How to Do It:** Spend some time each week planning your meals. Use the recipes in this book to create a menu, then make a shopping list of the ingredients you'll need. Prepare meals or components (like chopping vegetables or cooking grains) beforehand.

Prep in Bulk

- **Why It Matters:** Cooking in more significant quantities allows you to have healthy, homemade meals ready throughout the week, reducing the temptation to reach for processed or fast foods.
- **How to Do It:** Double or triple your favorite recipes and store the extras in the refrigerator or freezer. Soups, stews, casseroles, and grain-based dishes often reheat well and can be portioned for quick meals.

Stay Flexible
- **Why It Matters:** Life can be unpredictable, and it's essential to have backup plans if your schedule changes. Flexibility with your meal plans helps you stay on track even on busy days.
- **How to Do It:** Keep a few quick and easy meal options on hand for days when you don't have time to cook. This could include pre-cooked proteins, frozen vegetables, or simple ingredients that can be thrown together for a healthy meal in minutes.

Monitor Your Progress
- **Why It Matters:** Regularly checking how your diet affects your blood sugar levels allows you to make informed adjustments and improve your overall diabetes management.
- **How to Do It:** Keep a food journal to track what you eat and how it affects your blood sugar. This can help you identify patterns and make changes if needed. Pair this with regular blood sugar monitoring and discuss your findings with your healthcare provider.

3. Smart Shopping for Diabetes-Friendly Ingredients

Creating diabetes-friendly meals starts with smart shopping. Choosing the right ingredients ensures you have the building blocks for nutritious, balanced meals.

Shop the Perimeter
- **Why It Matters:** Grocery stores' outer edges typically contain fresh produce, meats, dairy, and other whole foods, while the inner aisles often house processed and packaged items.
- **How to Do It:** Focus your shopping on the store's perimeter. Load up on fresh vegetables, fruits, lean proteins, and whole grains. When venturing into the aisles, stick to your list and choose minimally processed options.

Choose Whole Foods
- **Why It Matters:** Whole foods—as close to their natural state as possible—are more nutrient-dense and have a lower glycemic index than processed foods.
- **How to Do It:** Choose fresh or frozen vegetables over canned ones, whole fruits instead of fruit juices, and whole grains like quinoa, brown rice, or oats instead of refined grains.

Be Label-Savvy
- **Why It Matters:** Not all packaged foods are created equal. Some may seem healthy but contain hidden sugars, unhealthy fats, or other additives affecting blood sugar levels.
- **How to Do It:** Read the ingredient list first—if you can't pronounce it, it might not be the best choice. Look for products with high fiber content, low added sugars, and minimal processing.

4. Creating a Diabetes-Friendly Kitchen

A well-organized kitchen can make preparing diabetes-friendly meals more accessible and more enjoyable. Here's how to set up your kitchen for success:

Stock Up on Essentials
- **Why It Matters:** Having a well-stocked pantry with diabetes-friendly staples ensures you're always prepared to make a healthy meal.
- **How to Do It:** Keep items like whole grains (quinoa, brown rice, oats), canned beans, lentils, low-sodium broths, herbs, and spices on hand. Also, stock your fridge with fresh vegetables, lean proteins, and healthy fats like olive oil and avocados.

Organize Your Space
- **Why It Matters:** A clutter-free kitchen makes it easier to find what you need and encourages healthier cooking habits.
- **How to Do It:** Arrange your pantry, fridge, and countertop so that the healthiest options are easily accessible. Store less healthy items out of sight or eliminate them.

Invest in Quality Tools
- **Why It Matters:** The right kitchen tools can make meal preparation faster, easier, and more enjoyable, encouraging you to cook more often.
- **How to Do It:** Consider investing in quality kitchen tools, such as sharp knives, a good cutting board, measuring cups, and a food processor. These can help you prepare ingredients quickly and efficiently.

5. Navigating Social Situations and Dining Out

Managing diabetes doesn't mean missing out on social events or dining out. You can enjoy these occasions with some thoughtful strategies while staying aligned with your health goals.

Why INavigating Social Situations and Dining Out Managing diabetes doesn't mean missing out on social events or dining out. You can enjoy these occasions with thoughtful strategies while staying aligned with your health.

- **Goals.t Matters:** Being prepared allows you to make healthier decisions and resist temptations that could affect your blood sugar.

- **How to Do It:** If dining out, check the restaurant's menu online beforehand and decide what you'll order. At social events, offer to bring a diabetes-friendly dish you can enjoy with everyone else.

Be Mindful of Portions
- **Why It Matters:** Restaurant portions and buffet spreads are often more significant than you need, leading to overeating.
- **How to Do It:** Consider sharing an entrée, asking for a half-portion, or taking half of your meal home for later. At buffets, fill your plate once with healthy options and avoid returning for seconds.

Make Smart Choices
- **Why It Matters:** Not all menu items are equal when managing diabetes.
- **How to Do It:** Choose grilled or baked options instead of fried foods, dishes that feature vegetables or whole grains, and avoid sugary drinks and desserts. Feel free to ask your server to clarify an ingredient or preparation method.

CHAPTER 4
BREAKFAST RECIPES
1. Quick and Easy Breakfasts

Breakfast Tostada

 Yield: 2 servings   Preparation Time: 10 minutes
 Cooking Time: 5 minutes

Ingredients:
- 2 petite whole-grain tortillas (GI: 45)
- 1 ripe avocado (GI: 15)
- 2-large eggs (GI: 0)
- 1/2 teaspoon of salt and black pepper, if desired
- Half of a lime, squeezed (GI: less than 1)
- If you'd like some more protein, you may add 1/4 cup of crumbled feta cheese. (GI: 1)
- Olive oil or cooking spray, measuring 1 teaspoon (GI <1)

Optional toppings:
- Half a cup of cherry tomatoes (GI: 15)
- Fifteen milligrams of finely chopped red onion, 1/4 cup
- 1/4 cup of chopped fresh cilantro
- For taste, you may add 1/4 teaspoon of cumin

Instructions:
1. **Preheat the tortillas:** First, get the oven ready for the tortillas by heating it up to 375°F, or 190°C. Before placing the tortillas directly on the oven rack, coat them lightly with olive oil using a spray or brush. Bake for 5 minutes, or until they become crispy.
2. **Prepare the avocado:** While the tortillas are in the oven, split the avocado in half, scoop out the meat, and discard the pit. Add lime juice, salt, and pepper after mashing with a fork. Season with pepper to taste.
3. **Prepare the eggs:** Poach the eggs in a nonstick pan or saucepan until they are done (optional - scrambled or sunny side up) and add salt and pepper to taste.
4. **Assemble the tostada:** Distribute the mashed avocado equally across the crisp tortillas. Top with cooked eggs and optional toppings - if desired. Crumbled feta cheese, red onion, cherry tomatoes are optional toppings.
5. **If preferred, garnish** with chopped fresh cilantro and cumin. Add a side of mixed greens for extra fiber and nutrients.

Nutritional Information (Per Serving)
Calories: 280, Protein: 12g, Carbohydrates: 24g, Fats: 18g, Fiber: 8g, Cholesterol: 185mg,
Sodium: 350mg, Potassium: 600mg

Overnight Oats with Chia Seeds

 Yield: 2 servings   Preparation Time: 10 minutes
 Cooking Time: None (overnight soaking)

Ingredients:
- 1 cup rolled oats (GI: 55)
- 1 cup unsweetened almond milk (GI: 30)
- 1/2 cup Greek yogurt (plain, non-fat) (GI: 11)
- 2 tablespoons chia seeds (GI <1)
- 1/2 cup mixed berries (strawberries, blueberries, raspberries) (GI: 25-40)

Optional toppings:
- 1 tablespoon flaxseeds (for added fiber and omega-3s) (GI: <1)
- 1/2 teaspoon vanilla extract (for flavor) (GI <1)
- 1/2 teaspoon ground cinnamon (for flavor) (GI <1)
- 1 tablespoon honey or stevia (for sweetness) (GI: 50 for honey; <1 for stevia)

Instructions:
1. **Prepare the oatmeal:** Throw the rolled oats, unsweetened almond milk, Greek yogurt, chia seeds, flaxseeds (if using), ground cinnamon, and vanilla essence into a medium-sized bowl or mason jar.
2. **Stir:** Shake or stir the items until they are well combined. After adding the berries (some of the berries can be used for decoration), stir and add honey or sweetener if necessary.
3. **Let it brew:** To let the oats and chia seeds soak up the liquid, cover the dish or jar with a lid or plastic wrap and put it in the refrigerator for at least six hours, or overnight.
4. **Stir:** To proceed with serving, whisk the mixture well first thing in the morning. To adjust the thickness, just add more almond milk until you have the consistency you want. If desired, add some almonds or a couple additional fresh berries.

Nutritional Information (Per Serving)
Calories: 270, Protein: 12g, Carbohydrates: 35g, Fats: 9g, Fiber: 10g, Cholesterol: 5mg,
Sodium: 120mg, Potassium: 380mg

Greek Yogurt with Fresh Berries and Nuts

 Yield: 2 servings   Preparation Time: 5 minutes
Cooking Time: None

Ingredients:

- 1 cup Greek yogurt (plain, non-fat) (GI: 11)
- 1 cup mixed berries (strawberries, blueberries, raspberries) (GI: 25-40)
- 1/4 cup almonds, chopped (GI <1)
- 1 tablespoon chia seeds (GI <1)

Optional:

- 1 tablespoon flaxseeds (for added fiber and omega-3s) (GI <1)
- 1 teaspoon honey or stevia (GI: 50 for honey; <1 for stevia)
- 1/2 teaspoon vanilla extract (GI <1)

Instructions:

1. **Collect all the components:** In case it's still necessary, finely cut the almonds.
2. **Mix:** Mix the Greek yogurt, honey (or stevia, if using) and vanilla essence in a medium bowl. Mix thoroughly so that the honey is evenly distributed.
3. **Additives:** The next step is to add the nuts and berries. Gently mix in the chopped almonds, chia seeds, flaxseeds, and mixed berries.
4. **Serve:** To serve, spoon half of the mixture into each of two bowls and dig in! Serve cold. Add more fresh berries or extra nuts for crunch and nutrition.

Nutritional Information (Per Serving)

Calories: 230, Protein: 15g, Carbohydrates: 22g, Fats: 9g, Fiber: 6g, Cholesterol: 5mg, Sodium: 60mg, Potassium: 350mg

Avocado Toast with Tomato Slices

 Yield: 2 servings   Preparation Time: 5 minutes
 Cooking Time: None

Ingredients:

- 2 slices whole-grain bread (GI: 40)
- 1 ripe avocado (GI: 15)
- 1 medium tomato, sliced (GI: 15)
- 1 tablespoon lemon juice (GI <1)
- 1/4 teaspoon black pepper

Optional:

- 1/4 teaspoon salt
- 1/4 teaspoon red pepper flakes (for added flavor)
- 1 tablespoon extra virgin olive oil (GI <1)
- Fresh basil or cilantro leaves (optional for garnish)

Instructions:

1. **Prepare the bread:** Toast the pieces of whole-grain bread until they reach the crispiness you like.
2. **Get the avocado:** ready by halves it, removing the pit, and transferring the flesh to a dish while the bread is toasting. Use a fork to mash it until it's smooth. Toss in the lemon juice, black pepper, and salt, if using. Thoroughly combine.
3. **Put the Toast Together:** Evenly Distribute the Masked Avocado Between the Toast.
4. **Top with Slices of Tomato:** Place a slice of tomato on top of each avocado toast.
5. **For garnish**, you may top it off with red pepper flakes if you want. For an additional burst of flavor and nutritional value, drizzle with extra virgin olive oil and top with chopped fresh basil or cilantro.
6. **Serve** immediately while the toast is still warm. Pair with a side of mixed greens for extra fiber and nutrients.

Nutritional Information (Per Serving)

Calories: 250-280, Protein: 5g, Carbohydrates: 24g, Fats: 17g, Fiber: 8g, Cholesterol: 0mg, Sodium: 250mg, Potassium: 700mg

Apple Cinnamon Overnight Oats

 Yield: 2 servings Preparation Time: 10 minutes
 Cooking Time: None (overnight soaking)

Ingredients:

- 1 cup rolled oats (GI: 55)
- 1 cup unsweetened almond milk (GI: 30)
- 1/2 cup Greek yogurt (plain, non-fat) (GI: 11)
- 1 medium apple, diced (GI: 38)
- 1 tablespoon chia seeds (GI <1)

Optional:

- 1 tablespoon ground flaxseeds (for added fiber and omega-3s) (GI <1)
- 1 teaspoon ground cinnamon (GI <1)
- 1/2 teaspoon vanilla extract (optional for flavor) (GI <1) 1 tablespoon walnuts, chopped (for added crunch) (GI <1)
- 1 teaspoon honey or stevia (for sweetness) (GI: 50 for honey; <1 for stevia)

Instructions:

1. **Mix the ingredients:** First, mix all the ingredients in a medium-sized dish or mason jar. This should include the rolled oats, unsweetened almond milk, Greek yogurt, chia seeds, ground flaxseeds (if using), ground cinnamon, and vanilla extract.
2. **Sweetener:** Second, incorporate the sweetener by mixing in the apple dice. Here is where you add any sweeteners, such as honey or stevia, and stir to combine. Shake or stir the items until they are well combined.
3. **Let it brew:** To let the oats and chia seeds soak up the liquid, cover the dish or jar with a lid or plastic wrap and put it in the refrigerator for at least six hours, or overnight.
4. **Serve:** To proceed with serving, whisk the mixture well first thing in the morning. To adjust the thickness, just add more almond milk until you have the consistency you like. Add chopped walnuts on top if desired. To enhance the taste, you may add more apple slices or cinnamon.

Nutritional Information (Per Serving)

Calories: 350, Protein: 12g, Carbohydrates: 44g, Fats: 9g, Fiber: 9g, Cholesterol: 5mg, Sodium: 75mg, Potassium: 380mg

Salad with Egg and Salsa Verde Vinaigrette

 Yield: 2 servings Preparation Time: 10 minutes
Cooking Time: 10 minutes

Ingredients:
For the Salad:

- 4 large eggs (GI: 0)
- 4 cups mixed greens (such as spinach, arugula, and kale) (GI: 15)
- 1 avocado, diced (GI: 15)
- 1 cup cherry tomatoes, halved (GI: 15)
- 1/2 cucumber, sliced (GI: 15)
- 1/4 red onion, thinly sliced (GI: 15)

For the Salsa Verde Vinaigrette:

- Finely cut 1/4 cup fresh parsley (GI < 1)
- Finely cut 1/4 cup of fresh cilantro (GI < 1)
- Rinse and cut 2 tablespoons of capers (GI <1)
- Mince one tiny garlic clove (GI <1)
- Add 2 tablespoons lemon juice (GI <1)
- Use 1/4 cup extra virgin olive oil (GI <1)
- 1/4 teaspoon of black pepper
- 1/4 teaspoon salt (optional)

Instructions:

1. **Boil the eggs:** Boil some water and place the eggs in a saucepan. Bring the ingredients to a boil in a saucepan over medium high heat. After it boils, reduce the heat to low and simmer for around nine or ten minutes for a firmer yolk. To stop the eggs from cooking, put them in a basin of ice water. Once cold, peel and slice the eggs.
2. **Mix the ingredients:** In a large bowl, mix together the salad greens, avocado, cherry tomatoes, cucumber, and red onion to prepare.
3. **Prepare the dressing Salsa Verde Vinaigrette:** chopped parsley, cilantro, capers, minced garlic, lemon juice, olive oil, salt (if desired - salt can be omitted for lower sodium intake), and black pepper.
4. **Assemble the salad:** Toss the salad ingredients into two separate bowls. On top of every plate, layer sliced eggs. Drizzle the salsa verde vinaigrette over the salad just before serving.
5. **Serve:** Serve immediately as a fresh and nutritious breakfast option. If desired, add a side of whole-grain toast for extra fiber and carbohydrates.

Nutritional Information (Per Serving)

Calories: 320, Protein: 12g, Carbohydrates: 14g, Fats: 24g, Fiber: 8g, Cholesterol: 186mg, Sodium: 250mg, Potassium: 750mg

Cottage Cheese with Pineapple Chunks

Yield: 2 servings *Preparation Time: 10 minutes*
Cooking Time: None

Ingredients:

- 1 cup low-fat cottage cheese (GI: 30)
- 1 cup fresh pineapple chunks (GI: 66)
- 1 tablespoon chia seeds (GI <1)

Optional:

- 1/4 teaspoon ground cinnamon (for flavor) (GI <1)
- 1 tablespoon unsweetened shredded coconut (for added texture and flavor) (GI <1)

Instructions:

1. **Prepare all ingredients.** Combine cottage cheese and pineapple.
2. **Additives:** Add chia seeds, remaining and optional ingredients. Mix well.
3. **Serve:** Serve immediately for a quick and nutritious breakfast. This dish can be enjoyed independently or paired with a small handful of nuts for additional protein and healthy fats.

Nutritional Information (Per Serving)

Calories 210, Protein 15g, Carbohydrates 16g, Fats 5g, Sugars: 11g, Fiber 4g, Cholesterol 10mg, Sodium 400mg, Potassium 400mg

Creamy Scrambled Eggs with Smoked Salmon

Yield: 2 servings *Preparation Time: 5 minutes*
Cooking Time: 5 minutes

Ingredients:

- 4 large eggs (GI: 0)
- 2 tablespoons unsweetened almond milk (GI: 30)
- 2 ounces smoked salmon, chopped (GI: 0)
- 1 tablespoon cream cheese, softened (GI: 0)
- 1 tablespoon fresh chives, chopped (optional for garnish) (GI: 0)
- 1 tablespoon butter or olive oil (GI: 0)
- Salt and pepper to taste (GI: 0)
- 1/2 avocado, sliced (optional for Serving and nutritional impact) (GI: 15)

Instructions:

1. **Gather Ingredients:** Add the almond milk, pepper, and cracked eggs to a mixing dish and stir until well blended.
2. **Preheat the Pan:** Melt the butter or olive oil in a nonstick pan set over medium-low heat.
3. **Cook the Eggs:** Add the egg mixture to the pan. After a few seconds of sitting undisturbed, mix gently with a spatula. To ensure the eggs cook gently and evenly, toss them regularly while cooking. About two or three minutes should pass.
4. **Add the Cream Cheese:** When the eggs are nearly set but still slightly runny, add the softened cream cheese. Stir gently to incorporate the cream cheese into the eggs, creating a creamy texture.
5. **Add the Smoked Salmon:** Add the chopped smoked salmon once the eggs are almost fully cooked. Stir briefly to distribute the salmon throughout the eggs.
6. **Serve:** Divide the scrambled eggs between two plates. Garnish with fresh chives if desired. Serve immediately, optionally, with sliced avocado on the side for added healthy fats and fiber or a small salad of mixed greens for a balanced meal.

Nutritional Information (Per Serving)

Calories: 310, Protein: 21g, Carbohydrates: 3g, Fiber: 2g, Sugars: 1g, Fats: 23g, Cholesterol: 400mg, Sodium: 590mg, Potassium: 430mg

Tomato and Basil Egg White Scramble

 Yield: 2 servings   Preparation Time: 5 minutes

 Cooking Time: 5 minutes

Ingredients:

- 6 large egg whites (GI: 0)
- 1/2 cup cherry tomatoes, halved (GI: 15)
- 1/4 cup fresh basil leaves, chopped (GI: 0)
- 1 tablespoon olive oil (GI: 0)
- 1/4 teaspoon garlic powder (GI: 0)
- Salt and pepper to taste (GI: 0)
- 1 tablespoon grated Parmesan cheese (optional for added flavor) (GI: 0)
- 1/2 avocado, sliced (optional for Serving) (GI: 15)

Instructions:

1. **Get Everything Ready:** In a separate bowl, whisk the egg whites or use liquid egg whites. Reserve the whites. Chop the fresh basil leaves and cut the cherry tomatoes in half.
2. **Get the Pan Hot:** In a nonstick skillet, heat the olive oil over medium heat.
3. **Cook the Tomatoes:** Pinch of salt, pepper, and garlic powder should be added before the cherry tomatoes are sautéed for 2 minutes, or until they soften.
4. **Whisk in the Egg Whites:** Whisk the egg whites into the tomato-flavored skillet. The egg whites should be set but remain soft, which should take around two to three minutes of gentle cooking with intermittent stirring.
5. **Add the Basil:** Stir in the chopped basil once the egg whites are almost fully cooked. Continue to cook for another minute until the basil is wilted and the eggs are fully cooked.
6. **Serving:** Divide the scramble between two plates. If desired, sprinkle with a small amount of grated Parmesan cheese and serve with sliced avocado on the side.

Nutritional Information (Per Serving)
Calories: 50-60 (without optional avocado and Parmesan), Protein: 2g, Carbohydrates: 1g, Fiber: 1g, Sugars: 1g, Fat: 1g, Cholesterol: 0mg, Sodium: 50mg, Potassium: 70mg

Avocado and Turkey Breakfast Roll-Ups

 Yield: 2 servings   Preparation Time: 5 minutes

 Cooking Time: 5 minutes

Ingredients:

- 4 slices of deli turkey breast (preferably lowsodium) (GI: 0)
- 1/2 ripe avocado, sliced (GI: 15)
- 1/4 cup fresh baby spinach leaves (GI: 15)
- 1/4 cup shredded mozzarella or cheddar cheese (optional) (GI: 0)
- 1 tablespoon Dijon mustard or hummus (optional for added flavor) (GI: 0)
- Freshly ground black pepper to taste (GI: 0)

Instructions:

1. **Prepare Ingredients:** Slice the avocado and set aside the turkey slices, spinach leaves, and shredded cheese if using.
2. **Lay Out the Turkey Slices:** Place the turkey slices on a clean, flat surface. If using mustard or hummus, spread a thin layer on each slice of turkey.
3. **Add Fillings:** Place a few slices of avocado and a few spinach leaves on one end of each turkey slice. If desired, sprinkle some shredded cheese over the avocado and spinach.
4. **Roll Up:** Starting from the end with the fillings, carefully roll up each turkey slice, tucking in the fillings as you go to create a tight roll. Secure with a toothpick if needed.
5. **Serve:** Place the roll-ups on a plates and sprinkle with freshly ground black pepper to taste. Serve immediately.

Nutritional Information (Per Serving)
Calories: 170-200 (with optional cheese, without mustard and hummus), Protein: 15g, Carbohydrates: 5g, Fiber: 3g, Sugars: 1g, Fats: 12g, Cholesterol: 40mg, Sodium: 450mg (varies with the choice of turkey), Potassium: 360mg

2. High-Protein Breakfasts

Spinach and Mushroom Egg Scramble

Yield: 2 servings *Preparation Time: 5 minutes*
Cooking Time: 10 minutes

Ingredients:

- Four big eggs (GI: 0)
- 1 cup chopped fresh spinach (GI: 15)
- 1 cup sliced mushrooms (GI: 10)
- 1/4 cup sliced red bell pepper (GI: 15)
- 1/4 cup coarsely chopped onion (GI: 15)
- One tablespoon olive oil (GI <1)

Optional:
- 1/4 cup shredded low-fat cheese (GI: 0-10)
- Garnish with fresh parsley
- 1/4 teaspoon salt
- Add 1/4 teaspoon black pepper and 1/4 teaspoon garlic powder (for taste). (GI <1)

Instructions:

1. **Prepare the vegetables:** Wash and chop the red bell pepper, spinach, onion, and mushrooms.
2. **Heat the oil:** Heat olive oil in a nonstick skillet over medium heat. Add red bell pepper and onion; sauté for 2–3 minutes or until softened.
3. **Add mushrooms and spinach:** Add the mushrooms and sauté until browned and moisture is released (about 2–3 minutes). Stir in the spinach and cook for 1–2 minutes until wilted.
4. **Add eggs:** Whisk eggs with black pepper, salt, and garlic powder (if using). Pour the eggs over the vegetables in the skillet. Cook over medium-low heat, gently stirring every 2–3 minutes, until eggs are set but still slightly moist.
5. **If using cheese**, sprinkle it on top and cook for an additional minute until melted.
6. **Serve:** Divide into two servings and garnish with parsley if desired. Serve hot with whole-grain toast or a small serving of low-GI fruit.

Nutritional Information (Per Serving)

Calories: 200, Protein: 16g, Carbohydrates: 7g, Fats: 13g, Fiber: 2g, Cholesterol: 370mg, Sodium: 250mg, Potassium: 450mg

Tofu and Veggie Breakfast Bowl

Yield: 2 servings *Preparation Time: 10 minutes*
Cooking Time: 15 minutes

Ingredients:

- Drained and crumbled one block (14 oz) of firm tofu (GI <15)
- 1 cup chopped spinach (GI: 15)
- 1/2 cup chopped bell peppers (GI: 15)
- 1/2 cup cherry tomatoes halved (GI: 15)
- 1/4 cup coarsely chopped red onion (GI: 15)
- 1/4 cup shredded carrots (GI: 35)
- 1 tablespoon olive oil (GI <1)
- 1 tablespoon low-sodium soy sauce (GI <1)
- 1/2 teaspoon of turmeric (optional for color and health benefits). (GI <1)
- 1/4 teaspoon of black pepper

Optional:
- 1/4 teaspoon garlic powder (GI = <1)
- 1/4 teaspoon of salt
- Garnish with fresh parsley or cilantro

Instructions:

1. **Prepare the tofu:** Drain the tofu and crumble it into small pieces.
2. **Heat the oil:** Heat olive oil in a large nonstick pan over medium heat.
3. **Add vegetables:** Add red onion and bell peppers; sauté for 3–4 minutes until softened.
4. **Add the tofu:** Add the crumbled tofu to the pan. Sprinkle turmeric, garlic powder, black pepper, and salt (if using). Cook for 7–8 minutes, stirring occasionally, until the tofu is lightly browned.
5. **Add the remaining vegetables:** Add shredded carrots, cherry tomatoes, and spinach. Cook for 2–3 minutes, stirring occasionally, until the spinach wilts and vegetables soften. Drizzle soy sauce over the mixture and stir thoroughly. Cook for an additional 1–2 minutes.
6. **Serve:** Divide into two bowls and garnish with parsley or cilantro if desired. Serve hot, optionally paired with avocado slices or whole-grain toast.

Nutritional Information (Per Serving)

Calories: 235, Protein: 20g, Carbohydrates: 14g, Fats: 12g, Fiber: 7g, Cholesterol: 0mg, Sodium: 420mg, Potassium: 620mg

Smoked Salmon and Avocado Plate

 Yield: 2 servings   Preparation Time: 5 minutes
 Cooking Time: None

Ingredients:

- 4 oz (115g) smoked salmon, thinly sliced (GI: 0)
- 1 medium avocado, sliced (GI: 15)
- 1 cup baby spinach or mixed greens (GI <15)
- 1 small cucumber, thinly sliced (GI.: 15)
- 1 small tomato, diced (GI: 15)
- 2 tablespoons red onion, thinly sliced (GI: 10)
- 2 lemon wedges (GI < 15)
- 2 tablespoons of extra virgin olive oil (GI: 0)
- Season with salt and pepper to taste

Optional:
- Add 1 tablespoon chopped fresh dill (GI < 15)
- 1 tablespoon of drained capers (GI < 15)
- 1 tablespoon chia seeds (for additional fiber and omega-3) (GI: 1)

Instructions:

1. **Prepare the Ingredients:** Thinly slice the avocado, cucumber, and red onion. Dice the tomato into small pieces.
2. **Assemble the Plates:** Arrange the baby spinach or mixed greens evenly on two plates. Place the smoked salmon slices on top of the greens, dividing them evenly between the two plates. Distribute the sliced avocado, cucumber, and diced tomato around the smoked salmon. Sprinkle the sliced red onion and capers (if using) over the top.
3. **Season and Dress:** Drizzle each plate with 1 tablespoon of extra virgin olive oil. Squeeze the juice of a lemon wedge over each plate just before serving. Season with salt and pepper to taste.
4. **Serve:** Serve immediately while the ingredients are fresh. Garnish with fresh dill if desired. Pair with a side of whole grain or low-carb toast if desired (consider the additional carbohydrates if on a strict diabetic diet). A cup of green tea or black coffee makes a great beverage to accompany this dish.

Nutritional Information (Per Serving)

Calories: 320, Protein: 15g, Carbohydrates: 12g, Fats: 27g, Fiber: 8g, Cholesterol: 23mg, Sodium: 800mg, Potassium: 1000mg

Greek Yogurt with Almonds and Honey

 Yield: 2 servings   Preparation Time: 10 minutes
 Cooking Time: None

Ingredients:

- 1 cup plain Greek yogurt (non-fat or low-fat) (GI: 0)
- 2 tbsp sliced almonds (GI: 0)
- 1 tbsp honey (GI: 55), stevia or monk fruit for lower GI (GI <1)

Optional:
- 1 tbsp chia seeds (optional, for additional fiber) (GI: 1)
- 1 tbsp flaxseeds (optional, for additional fiber and omega-3s) (GI: 0)
- 1 tbsp unsweetened shredded coconut (optional) (GI: 0)
- 1/2 tsp cinnamon (optional, for flavor) (GI: 0)
- Fresh berries (e.g., blueberries, strawberries, or raspberries) (optional) (GI: 25-40)

Instructions:

1. **Prepare the Yogurt Base:** Evenly divide 1 cup of plain Greek yogurt between two serving bowls.
2. **Add Toppings:** Sprinkle 1 tablespoon of sliced almonds over each serving of yogurt.
3. **If using** chia seeds, flaxseeds, and unsweetened shredded coconut, sprinkle 1/2 tablespoon of each over the yogurt in each bowl.
4. **Sweeten and Flavor:** Drizzle 1/2 tablespoon of honey (or a low-GI alternative) over each serving of yogurt.
5. **Add a sprinkle of cinnamon** on top for additional flavor, if desired.

Optional:

1. **Add Fresh Berries:** If using berries, evenly divide about 1/4 cup (a small handful) between the two bowls.
2. **Serve:** Serve immediately, garnished with additional almonds or berries if desired. Pair with a glass of water or unsweetened herbal tea.

Nutritional Information (Per Serving)

Calories: 235-250, Protein: 16g, Carbohydrates: 20g, Fats: 8g, Fiber: 5g, Cholesterol: 0mg, Sodium: 60mg, Potassium: 360mg

Egg and Cheese Breakfast Muffins

Yield: 6 servings (12 muffins) *Preparation Time:* 5 minutes *Cooking Time:* None

Ingredients:
- 6 large eggs (GI: 0)
- 1 cup shredded low-fat cheddar cheese (GI: 0)
- 1/2 cup diced bell peppers (any color) (GI: 15)
- 1/2 cup finely chopped spinach (GI: 15)
- 1/4 cup chopped green onions (GI: 15)
- 1/4 cup chopped tomatoes (GI: 15)
- 1/4 cup milk (preferably low-fat or almond milk) (GI: 30 for cow's milk, GI: 30 for unsweetened almond milk)
- 1/2 tsp garlic powder (GI: 0)
- 1/2 tsp onion powder (GI: 0)
- 1/2 tsp black pepper (GI: 0)
- 1/4 tsp salt (optional) (GI: 0)
- Cooking spray or olive oil for greasing muffin tin (GI: 0)

Optional Ingredients (for additional flavor and nutrition)
- 1/4 cup diced mushrooms (GI: 10)
- 1/4 cup diced zucchini (GI: 15)
- 1/4 cup cooked and crumbled turkey bacon (GI: 0)

Instructions:
1. **Prepare the oven:** Preheat the oven to 350°F (175°C). Lightly grease a 12-cup muffin tin with olive oil or cooking spray.
2. **Combine ingredients:** In a large bowl, whisk together eggs, milk, garlic powder, onion powder, black pepper, and salt (if using).
3. **Add vegetables and cheese:** Fold in the shredded cheese, diced bell peppers, spinach, green onions, and optional ingredients (zucchini, mushrooms, or turkey bacon) if desired. Mix until evenly distributed.
4. **Bake:** Pour the mixture into the prepared muffin tin, filling each cup almost to the top. Bake for 18–20 minutes, or until muffins are set and golden brown on top. A toothpick inserted into the center should come out clean.
5. **Serve:** Allow the muffins to cool in the tin for 5 minutes before transferring them to a wire rack. Serve warm, or store in an airtight container in the refrigerator for up to 5 days.
6. **Optional Serving:** These Egg and Cheese Breakfast Muffins can be enjoyed independently or paired with a small serving of fresh fruit or a side salad for a complete meal. They are perfect for meal prep and quickly reheated in the microwave.

Nutritional Information (Per Serving) - 2 muffins

Calories: 165, Protein: 14g, Carbohydrates: 4g, Fats: 10g, Fiber: 1g, Cholesterol: 210mg, Sodium: 300mg, Potassium: 230mg

Turkey Sausage and Egg Wrap

Yield: 2 servings *Preparation Time:* 10 minutes *Cooking Time:* 10 minutes

Ingredients:
- 4 large eggs (GI: 0)
- 4 oz (113g) turkey sausage, crumbled (GI: 0)
- 1/2 cup diced bell peppers (any color) (GI: 15)
- 1/4 cup diced onions (GI: 10)
- 1/2 cup chopped spinach (GI: 15)
- 1/4 cup shredded low-fat cheddar cheese (GI: 0)
- 2 whole wheat tortillas (8-inch) (GI: 30) 1 tbsp olive oil (GI: 0)
- 1/2 tsp garlic powder (GI: 0)
- 1/2 tsp black pepper (GI: 0)
- 1/4 tsp salt (optional) (GI: 0)
- Cooking spray (GI: 0)

Optional Ingredients (for additional flavor and nutrition)
- 1/4 cup diced tomatoes (GI: 15)
- 1/4 avocado, sliced (GI: 15)
- Hot sauce (GI: 0)

Instructions:
1. **Heat the oil:** Heat 1 tablespoon of olive oil in a large nonstick pan over medium heat.
2. **Add ingredients:** Add diced bell peppers and onions; sauté for 3–4 minutes until softened. Add crumbled turkey sausage to the pan and cook for 5 minutes, stirring occasionally, until browned and cooked through.
3. **Whisk the eggs:** In a separate bowl, whisk the eggs with garlic powder, black pepper, and salt (if using).
4. **Prepare an omelette:** Push the sausage and veggie mixture to one side of the pan. Pour the eggs into the empty side, stirring frequently to scramble, until fully cooked (about 2–3 minutes).
5. **Mix the filling:** Combine the eggs with the sausage and veggies. Stir in spinach and cook for 1 minute until wilted.
6. **Warm the tortillas:** Warm the whole wheat tortillas in the microwave for 15–20 seconds to make them pliable.
7. **Assemble the dish:** Divide the egg mixture evenly between the two tortillas. Top each with 2 tablespoons of shredded cheddar cheese. Add optional diced tomatoes or avocado slices if desired.
8. **Serve:** Roll the tortillas into wraps and serve immediately, optionally with your favorite sauce.
9. **Tip:** These turkey sausage and egg wraps can be enjoyed alone, with fresh fruit, or in a small salad. They are perfect for a quick, nutritious breakfast that is easy to prepare.

Nutritional Information (Per Serving)

Calories: 365, Protein: 28g, Carbohydrates: 23g, Fats: 17g, Fiber: 5g, Cholesterol: 340mg, Sodium: 650mg, Potassium: 490mg

Cottage Cheese and Veggie Stuffed Bell Peppers

 Yield: 4 servings   Preparation Time: 10 minutes
Cooking Time: 20 minutes

Ingredients:

- 4 large bell peppers, tops cut off and seeds removed (GI: 15)
- 2 cups low-fat cottage cheese (GI: 10)
- 1 cup baby spinach, chopped (GI: 15)
- 1 small zucchini, diced (GI: 15)
- 1 small red onion, diced (GI: 15)
- 1 tablespoon olive oil (GI: 0)
- Salt and pepper to taste
- 1/4 cup shredded low-fat mozzarella cheese (optional) (GI: 30)
- Fresh basil leaves for garnish (optional) (GI: varies, minimal impact)

Instructions:

1. **Prepare the oven:** Preheat the oven to 375°F (190°C). Prepare the bell peppers by cutting off the tops, removing the seeds, and chopping the tops for the filling.
2. **Mix ingredients:** In a large bowl, combine the cottage cheese, chopped spinach, diced zucchini, diced red onion, and chopped bell pepper tops. Season with salt and pepper to taste.
3. **Prepare the peppers:** Fill each bell pepper with the cottage cheese and vegetable mixture. Lightly brush the outside of the peppers with olive oil.
4. **Bake:** Place the stuffed peppers in a baking dish and bake for 20 minutes, or until the peppers are tender.
5. **Add the cheese:** In the last 5 minutes of baking, sprinkle the shredded mozzarella cheese on top of the peppers and let it melt.
6. **Garnish and serve:** Remove from the oven and garnish with fresh basil leaves, if desired. Serve warm.
7. **Optional:** Serve the stuffed bell peppers warm, paired with a side of mixed greens or a simple cucumber salad for a light and refreshing meal. For a heartier option, accompany with a slice of whole-grain bread or quinoa. Garnish with extra fresh basil leaves or a drizzle of balsamic glaze for added flavor.

Nutritional Information (Per Serving)
Calories: 185, Protein: 15g, Carbohydrates: 13g, Fiber: 4g, Sugars: 8g, Fats: 9g, Saturated Fat: 2g, Unsaturated Fat: 7g, Cholesterol: 15mg, Sodium: 400mg, Potassium: 620mg

Cheese and Herb-Stuffed Omelette

 Yield: 2 servings   Preparation Time: 5 minutes
 Cooking Time: 5 minutes

Ingredients:

- 3 large eggs (GI: 0)
- 1/4 cup shredded mozzarella or cheddar cheese (GI: 0)
- 1 tablespoon fresh parsley, chopped (GI: 0)
- 1 tablespoon fresh chives, chopped (GI: 0)
- 1 tablespoon fresh basil, chopped (GI: 0)
- 1 tablespoon unsweetened almond milk (GI: 30)
- 1 tablespoon olive oil or butter (GI: 0)
- Salt and pepper to taste (GI: 0)
- Optional: 1/4 cup sautéed mushrooms or spinach (GI: 15 for spinach)

Instructions:

1. **Beat the eggs:** Crack the eggs into a bowl, add almond milk, and whisk until well combined. Season with salt and pepper to taste.
2. **Heat the pan:** Heat a nonstick pan over medium heat and add butter or olive oil.
3. **Cook the eggs:** Pour the egg mixture into the pan and let it cook undisturbed for 1–2 minutes, or until the edges begin to set.
4. **Add cheese and herbs:** Sprinkle shredded cheese evenly over one half of the omelette. Top with fresh basil, parsley, and chives. Optionally, add sautéed spinach or mushrooms at this stage.
5. **Assemble the omelette:** Gently fold the omelette in half and cook for another 1–2 minutes, or until the eggs are fully set and the cheese is melted.
6. **Serve:** Slide the omelette onto a plate and serve immediately.
7. **Optional:** Serve the Cheese and Herb-Stuffed Omelette with a side of crispy bacon or smoked salmon for added protein. Pair it with a fresh green salad or sautéed spinach for a light, balanced meal. For a heartier option, add a slice of toasted sourdough bread.

Nutritional Information (Per Serving)
Calories: 220 (without optional vegetables), Protein: 16g, Carbohydrates: 3g, Fiber: 0g, Sugars: 1g, Fats: 18g, Saturated Fat: 5g, Cholesterol: 375mg, Sodium: 200mg, Potassium: 240mg

Chicken Sausage and Kale Breakfast Skillet

 Yield: 4 servings   Preparation Time: 5 minutes
 Cooking Time: 15 minutes

Ingredients:

- 4 chicken sausage links, sliced (preferably low-sodium) (GI: 0)
- 2 cups fresh kale, chopped (GI: 15)
- 1/2 medium onion, diced (GI: 10)
- 1/2 red bell pepper, diced (GI: 15)
- 2 large eggs (GI: 0)
- 1 tablespoon olive oil (GI: 0)
- 1/4 teaspoon garlic powder (GI: 0)
- 1/4 teaspoon paprika (GI: 0)
- Salt and pepper to taste (GI: 0)
- Optional: 1/4 cup shredded cheese (mozzarella or cheddar) (GI: 0)

Instructions:

1. **Prepare the ingredients:** Slice the chicken sausage into bite-sized pieces. Wash and dry the kale. Dice the red bell pepper and onion.
2. **Heat the pan:** Heat olive oil in a large nonstick skillet over medium heat.
3. **Add ingredients:** Add the diced red bell pepper and onion to the skillet. Sauté for 3–4 minutes until softened. Add the sliced chicken sausage. Cook for an additional 3–4 minutes, turning occasionally, until browned. Add the chopped kale, garlic powder, paprika, salt, and pepper. Stir well to combine. Cook for 2–3 minutes until the kale is wilted.
4. **Add eggs:** Push the sausage and veggies to one side of the skillet. Crack the eggs directly into the pan on the other side. Scramble or fry them, as desired, until cooked to your preference.
5. **Optional:** Sprinkle shredded cheese on top during the final minute of cooking and let it melt.
6. **Serve:** Divide the mixture evenly between two plates and serve hot.
7. **Advice:** Serve with a side of sliced avocado or a dollop of sour cream for added creaminess. Pair with a slice of toasted sourdough or low-carb bread for a balanced breakfast. Garnish with freshly chopped parsley or a sprinkle of red chili flakes for an extra burst of flavor.

Nutritional Information (Per Serving)

Calories: 360 (with cheese), 340 (without cheese), Protein: 30g, Carbohydrates: 9g, Dietary Fiber: 3g, Sugars: 3g, Fats: 21g, Saturated Fat: 6g, Cholesterol: 230mg, Sodium: 600mg (varies with sausage choice), Potassium: 580mg

Egg and Tofu Stir-Fry with Vegetables

 Yield: 2 servings   Preparation Time: 10 minutes
 Cooking Time: 10 minutes

Ingredients:

- 4 large eggs (GI: 0)
- 1/2 block firm tofu, drained and cubed (approximately 200g) (GI: 15)
- 1/2 cup broccoli florets (GI: 10)
- 1/2 cup bell pepper, diced (GI: 15)
- 1/2 cup zucchini, sliced (GI: 15)
- 1/4 cup green onions, chopped (GI: 10)
- 1 tablespoon olive oil or sesame oil (GI: 0)
- 1 tablespoon low-sodium soy sauce or tamari (GI: 0)
- 1/2 teaspoon garlic powder (GI: 0)
- 1/2 teaspoon ground ginger (GI: 0)
- Salt and pepper to taste (GI: 0)
- Optional: 1/4 teaspoon red pepper flakes for a spicy kick (GI: 0)

Instructions:

1. **Prepare the ingredients:** Drain the tofu and cut it into small cubes. Wash and chop the broccoli, bell pepper, zucchini, and green onions. Crack the eggs into a bowl and whiskey until smooth.
2. **Heat the pan:** Heat olive or sesame oil in a large nonstick skillet or wok over medium heat.
3. **Add the tofu cubes** to the skillet. Sauté for 3–4 minutes, turning occasionally, until lightly browned. Season with a pinch of salt and pepper.
4. **Add the vegetables** (broccoli, bell pepper, zucchini, and green onions). Cook for 3–4 minutes, stirring frequently, until the vegetables are tender but still vibrant.
5. **Add spices:** Add ground ginger, garlic powder, and low-sodium soy sauce. Stir well to coat the tofu and vegetables evenly.
6. **Prepare:** Push the tofu and vegetables to one side of the skillet. Pour the whisked eggs into the empty side. Scramble gently until just cooked, then mix with the tofu and vegetables.
7. **Serve:** Divide into two portions. Serve hot, garnished with red pepper flakes if desired.
8. **Optional:** Serve the stir-fry over a bed of cauliflower rice or steamed white rice for a more filling meal. Garnish with freshly chopped cilantro or green onions for added freshness.

Nutritional Information (Per Serving)

Calories: 280 (without optional vegetables), Protein: 23g, Carbohydrates: 9g, Dietary Fiber: 3g, Sugars: 2g, Fats: 13g, Saturated Fat: 2g, Cholesterol: 220mg, Sodium: 450mg (using low-sodium soy sauce), Potassium: 580mg

3. Low-Carb Breakfasts

Veggie and Cheese Frittata

 Yield: 6 servings   Preparation Time: 15 minutes

 Cooking Time: 25 minutes

Ingredients:

- 8 big eggs (GI: 0)
- 1/4 cup skim milk (GI: 32)
- 1 cup chopped baby spinach (GI: 15)
- Dice one small zucchini (GI: 15)
- 1 chopped red bell pepper (GI: 15)
- Dice one small red onion (GI: 15)
- Halve 1/2 cup cherry tomatoes for a (GI: 15)
- Add 1/2 cup shredded low-fat mozzarella cheese (GI: 30)
- Add 1/4 cup grated Parmesan cheese (GI: 30)
- 2 tbsp olive oil (GI: 0)
- Salt and pepper to taste
- Optional: 1 teaspoon dried oregano (GI: 0)
- Optional: 1/2 teaspoon garlic powder (GI: 0)
- Garnish with fresh basil leaves (optional)

Instructions:

1. **Prepare the oven:** Preheat the oven to 375°F (190°C).
2. **Mix ingredients:** In a large bowl, whisk the eggs and skim milk. Add minced garlic, dried oregano, pepper, and salt. Set aside.
3. **Heat the oil:** Heat olive oil in a large oven-safe pan over medium heat. Saute the vegetables: Sauté the red bell pepper and diced red onion for 4–5 minutes until softened. Add the zucchini and cherry tomatoes. Cook for another 3-4 minutes until softened. Stir in the baby spinach and cook for 1-2 minutes until wilted.
4. **Add vegetables:** Remove the pan from heat and evenly pour the egg mixture over the vegetables. Add cheese: Sprinkle shredded mozzarella and gratified Parmesan cheese over the top.
5. **Bake:** Bake in the preheated oven for 20-25 minutes or until set and golden brown on top. To check doneness, insert a knife into the center; it should come out clean.
6. **Serve:** Allow the frittata to cool for a few minutes before slicing into 6 equal portions. Garnish with fresh basil leaves if desired. Serve warm or at room temperature.
7. **Optional:** Serve the Veggie and Cheese Frittata warm or at room temperature with a side of mixed greens or a simple salad. It pairs wonderfully with a dollop of sour cream or a light drizzle of olive oil. For an extra touch, sprinkle with fresh herbs like basil or parsley before serving.

Nutritional Information (Per Serving)

Calories: 180 (without optional vegetables), Protein: 12g, Carbohydrates: 5g, Dietary Fiber: 1g, Sugars: 0g, Fats: 12g, Saturated Fat: 8g, Cholesterol: 410mg, Sodium: 280mg, Potassium: 240mg

Low-Carb Pancakes with Berries

 Yield: 4 servings (makes about 8 pancakes)   Preparation Time: 10 minutes

Cooking Time: 15 minutes

Ingredients:

- 1 cup almond flour (GI: 0)
- 1/4 cup coconut flour (GI: 45)
- 1 teaspoon baking powder (GI: 0)
- 1/2 teaspoon baking soda (GI: 0)
- 1/4 teaspoon salt (GI: 0)
- 3 large eggs (GI: 0)
- 1/2 cup unsweetened almond milk (GI: 30)
- 2 tablespoons melted coconut oil (GI: 0)
- 1 teaspoon vanilla extract (optional) (GI: 0)
- 1/4 cup fresh blueberries (GI: 25)
- 1/4 cup fresh raspberries (GI: 26)
- Sugar-free maple syrup or Greek yogurt for serving (optional) (GI: varies)

Instructions:

1. **Mix dry ingredients:** In a medium bowl, whisk together almond flour, coconut flour, baking powder, baking soda, and salt.
2. **Beat the eggs:** In a separate bowl, beat the eggs with almond milk, melted coconut oil, and vanilla extract (if using).
3. **Mix the dough:** Gradually add the dry ingredients to the wet mixture. Stir until a thick but pourable batter forms. Add more almond milk if the batter is too thick.
4. **Heat the pan:** Heat a nonstick skillet or griddle over medium heat. Lightly grease with coconut oil.
5. **Bake the pancake:** Pour about 1/4 cup of batter onto the skillet for each pancake. Use the back of a spoon to spread into a circle.
6. **Fry:** Cook for 2-3 minutes or until bubbles form on the surface and the edges begin to set. Add a few blueberries and raspberries to the top of each pancake before flipping.
7. **Finish cooking:** Flip and cook for another 2–3 minutes until golden brown and cooked through. Repeat with the remaining batter, greasing the pan as necessary.
8. **Serve:** Serve warm with Greek yogurt, sugar-free maple syrup, or additional fresh berries (blueberries and raspberries)

Nutritional Information (Per Serving)

Calories: 200, Protein: 8g, Carbohydrates: 9g, Fiber: 4g, Sugars: 2g, Fats: 16g, Saturated Fat: 8g, Unsaturated Fat: 10g, Cholesterol: 110mg, Sodium: 300mg, Potassium: 150mg

Zucchini and Tomato Omelette

 Yield: 4 servings   Preparation Time: 10 minutes
Cooking Time: 10 minutes

Ingredients:

- 4 large eggs (GI: 0)
- 1/4 cup skim milk (GI: 32)
- 1 small zucchini, diced (GI: 15)
- 1/2 cup cherry tomatoes, halved (GI: 15)
- 1/4 cup grated Parmesan cheese (GI: 30)
- 1 tablespoon olive oil (GI: 0)
- 1/4 teaspoon garlic powder (optional) (GI: 0)
- Salt and pepper to taste
- Fresh basil leaves for garnish (optional) (GI: varies)

Instructions:

1. **Beat the eggs:** Whisk the eggs, skim milk, garlic powder, salt, and pepper in a bowl.
2. **Heat oil:** Heat olive oil in a nonstick skillet over medium heat. Saute the zucchini for 3–4 minutes until softened.
3. **Add the tomatoes:** Add the cherry tomatoes and cook for 2 more minutes until softened. Pour the egg mixture over the vegetables. Cook undisturbed over low heat for 3–4 minutes until the edges begin to set.
4. **Add cheese:** Sprinkle rated Parmesan cheese evenly over the top. Carefully lift the edges of the omelet with a spatula to allow uncooked egg to flow underneath.
5. **Finish cooking and serve:** When the omelet is almost set but slightly soft on top, fold it in half. Cook for 1 more minute until fully set. Transfer to a plate, garnish with fresh basil if desired, and serve immediately.
6. **Additionally:** Serve the Zucchini and Tomato Omelette with a side of fresh greens or a light salad. For an extra flavor boost, drizzle with a little balsamic vinegar or top with extra Parmesan cheese. Garnish with fresh basil leaves for a burst of color and fragrance. Enjoy as a wholesome breakfast or light lunch.

Nutritional Information (Per Serving)

Calories: 220, Protein: 16g, Carbohydrates: 6g, Fiber: 1g, Sugars: 3g, Fats: 15g, Saturated Fat: 4g, Unsaturated Fat: 11g, Cholesterol: 290mg, Sodium: 350mg, Potassium: 400mg

Chia Seed Pudding with Almond Milk

 Yield: 4 servings   Preparation Time: 10 minutes
 Cooking Time: 4 hours (chilling time)

Ingredients:

- 1 cup unsweetened almond milk (GI: 30)
- 1/4 cup chia seeds (GI: 1)
- 1 teaspoon vanilla extract (optional) (GI: 0)
- 1-2 tablespoons erythritol or other sugar-free sweetener (optional) (GI: 0)
- 1/4 cup fresh berries (blueberries, raspberries, strawberries) (GI: 25-40)
- 1/4 cup chopped nuts (almonds, walnuts) (optional) (GI: 15)

Instructions:

1. **Preparation:** Mix the almond milk, chia seeds, vanilla extract, and erythritol in a medium bowl. Stir well to ensure the chia seeds are evenly distributed.
2. **Chilling:** Cover the bowl and refrigerate for at least 4 hours or overnight. Stir the mixture after the first 30 minutes to prevent clumping.
3. **Serving:** Once the pudding has set and achieved a thick, creamy consistency, divide it into 4 servings. Top each Serving with fresh berries and chopped nuts if desired.

Nutritional Information (Per Serving)

Calories: 120, Protein: 4g, Carbohydrates: 8g, Fiber: 6g, Sugars: 2g, Fats: 8g, Saturated Fat: 1g, Unsaturated Fat: 7g, Cholesterol: 0mg, Sodium: 50mg, Potassium: 150mg

Cottage Cheese and Cucumber Bowl

Yield: 2 servings   Preparation Time: 10 minutes   Cooking Time: None

Ingredients:

- 1 cup low-fat cottage cheese (GI: 10)
- 1 medium cucumber, diced (GI: 15)
- 1 small avocado, diced (optional) (GI: 15)
- 1/4 cup cherry tomatoes, halved (GI: 15)
- 2 tablespoons chopped fresh dill (GI: 5)
- 1 tablespoon lemon juice (GI: 0)
- 1 teaspoon olive oil (GI: 0)

Instructions:

1. **Preparation:** Wash and dice the cucumber, avocado (if using), and cherry tomatoes. Chop the fresh dill.
2. **Mixing:** Combine the cottage cheese, diced cucumber, avocado, cherry tomatoes, and chopped dill in a medium bowl. Drizzle with lemon juice and olive oil. Season with salt and pepper to taste.
3. **Serving:** Divide the mixture into two serving bowls. Serve chilled for the best taste.
4. **Serve** as a refreshing snack, light lunch, or a side dish. It pairs well with grilled meats or as part of a salad spread. For added texture and flavor, you can top it with a sprinkle of sunflower seeds or a few olives. For a more filling option, serve with a side of whole-grain crackers or a slice of toasted bread.

Nutritional Information (Per Serving)
Calories: 180, Protein: 12g, Carbohydrates: 9g, Fiber: 4g, Sugars: 4g, Fats: 12g, Saturated Fat: 2g, Unsaturated Fat: 10g, Cholesterol: 15mg, Sodium: 320mg, Potassium: 400mg

Cauliflower Hash Browns

Yield: 4 servings   Preparation Time: 15 minutes   Cooking Time: 20 minutes

Ingredients:

- 1 medium head of cauliflower, grated (approximately 4 cups) (GI: 15)
- 1/4 cup almond flour (GI: 0)
- 1/4 cup grated Parmesan cheese (GI: 30)
- 2 large eggs, beaten (GI: 0)
- 1/4 cup chopped green onions (GI: 15)
- 1 teaspoon garlic powder (optional) (GI: 0)
- 1/2 teaspoon onion powder (optional) (GI: 0)
- Salt and pepper to taste 2 tablespoons olive oil (GI: 0)

Instructions:

1. **Prepare the oven:** To prepare, preheat the oven to 400°F (200°C) and line a baking sheet with parchment paper.
2. **Shred the cabbage:** Use a box grater or food processor to shred the cauliflower. Pour shredded cauliflower onto a clean kitchen towel and drain off excess moisture. This step is essential for crispy hash browns.
3. **Mix ingredients:** In a large bowl, mix the drained cauliflower, almond flour, grated Parmesan cheese, beaten eggs, sliced green onions, garlic powder, onion powder, salt, and pepper. Blend well.
4. **Prepare the patties:** Form 1/4 cup of ingredients into patties. Put each pattie on the prepared baking sheet. This combination should make 8 hash browns.
5. **Heat the pan:** Heat 1 tablespoon olive oil in a large non-stick pan over medium heat.
6. **Fry:** Cook the hash browns in batches for 3-4 minutes on each side until golden brown and crispy. Next batches may need extra olive oil.
7. **Or bake:** Another option is to bake the hash browns in the oven for 20 minutes, rotating halfway through.
8. **Serve:** Serve heated hash browns with chopped green onions if preferred, with a side of sour cream or your favorite dipping sauce. For extra flavor, top with additional gratified Parmesan, chopped green onions, or a sprinkle of red pepper flakes.
9. **Additionally:** These hash browns pair are wonderful with a fresh salad, eggs, or a protein of your choice. Enjoy them as a savory breakfast, snack, or side dish!

Nutritional Information (Per Serving)
Calories: 150-160 (without optional vegetables), Protein: 7g, Carbohydrates: 2g, Dietary Fiber: 2g, Sugars: 0g, Fats: 10g, Saturated Fat: 8g, Cholesterol: 410mg, Sodium: 350mg, Potassium: 120mg

Yogurt Parfait with Nuts and Seeds

 Yield: 4 servings   Preparation Time: 10 minutes
 Cooking Time: None

Ingredients:

- 2 cups plain Greek yogurt (GI: 11)
- 1/4 cup chia seeds (GI: 1)
- 1/4 cup flaxseeds (GI: 5)
- 1/4 cup sliced almonds (GI: 15)
- 1/4 cup chopped walnuts (GI: 15)
- 1/4 cup unsweetened coconut flakes (GI: 0)
- 1/2 cup fresh berries (strawberries (GI: 25), blueberries (GI: 40), or raspberries (GI: 32))
- 1 teaspoon vanilla extract (optional) (GI: 0)
- 1 tablespoon erythritol or other sugar-free sweetener (optional) (GI: 0)

Instructions:

1. **Preparation:** In a medium bowl, whisk the plain Greek yogurt with vanilla extract and erythritol until smooth (if using).
2. **Layering the Parfait:** Divide half of the yogurt evenly among four serving glasses or bowls. Layer with half the chia seeds, flaxseeds, sliced almonds, chopped walnuts, coconut flakes, and fresh berries. Repeat the layers with the remaining yogurt, seeds, nuts, and berries.
3. **Final Touches:** Top each parfait with a few extra berries and a sprinkle of nuts and seeds for garnish.
4. **Serve:** Serve the yogurt parfait chilled as a nutritious breakfast, snack, or dessert. It pairs well with a hot cup of coffee or herbal tea. For added sweetness, drizzle with honey or a sugar-free syrup. You can also customize the parfait by adding other fresh fruits or a dash of cinnamon for extra flavor.

Nutritional Information (Per Serving)

Calories: 260, Protein: 15g, Carbohydrates: 14g, Fiber: 10g, Sugars: 6g, Fats: 18g, Saturated Fat: 5g, Unsaturated Fat: 12g, Cholesterol: 0mg, Sodium: 60mg, Potassium: 400mg

Zucchini Noodles with Poached Eggs

 Yield: 2 servings   Preparation Time: 10 minutes
 Cooking Time: 10 minutes

Ingredients:

- 2 medium zucchinis, spiralized into noodles (GI: 15)
- 4 large eggs (GI: 0)
- 1 tablespoon olive oil (GI: 0)
- 1/4 cup cherry tomatoes, halved (GI: 15)
- 1 tablespoon fresh basil, chopped (GI: 0)
- 1 tablespoon grated Parmesan cheese (optional) (GI: 0)
- 1 tablespoon white vinegar (for poaching eggs) (GI: 0)

Instructions:

1. **Prepare the spaghetti:** Spiralize the zucchinis to create thin noodles. Set aside.
2. **To poach eggs:** Bring a medium saucepan of water to a gentle simmer. Add vinegar. Crack each egg into a small bowl, then slide it gently into the water. Cook for 3–4 minutes, or until the whites are set and the yolks are still soft. Remove with a slotted spoon and set aside.
3. **Heat the pan:** Heat olive oil in a large skillet over medium heat. Add zucchini noodles and sauté for 2–3 minutes until just tender. Toss in cherry tomatoes and fresh basil. Stir briefly, cooking for 1 minute.
4. **Serve:** Divide the zucchini noodles between two plates. Top each plate with two poached eggs. Garnish with grated Parmesan (if using) and extra basil. Serve immediately.

Nutritional Information (Per Serving)

Calories: 205 (without optional Parmesan cheese), Protein: 13g, Carbohydrates: 7g, Dietary Fiber: 3g, Sugars: 4g, Fats: 14g, Saturated Fat: 3g, Cholesterol: 370mg, Sodium: 200mg, Potassium: 580mg

Bacon-wrapped asparagus with Soft-Boiled Eggs

Yield: 2 servings **Preparation Time:** 5 minutes **Cooking Time:** 15 minutes

Ingredients:

- 8 asparagus spears (GI: 15)
- 4 slices of bacon (preferably low-sodium) (GI: 0)
- 4 large eggs (GI: 0)
- 1 tablespoon olive oil (GI: 0)
- Salt and pepper to taste (GI: 0)
- Optional: 1/4 teaspoon red pepper flakes for added heat (GI: 0)

Instructions:

1. **Preheat oven:** Preheat the oven to 400°F (200°C). Line a baking sheet with parchment paper or lightly grease it.
2. **Prepare the asparagus:** Wash and trim the asparagus by snapping off the woody ends. Divide into two bundles. Wrap each bundle with two slices of bacon. Arrange on the prepared baking sheet. Drizzle with olive oil and sprinkle with salt, pepper, and optional red pepper flakes.
3. **Bake:** Bake for 12–15 minutes or until the bacon is crispy and the asparagus is tender.
4. **Boil the eggs:** Meanwhile, bring a saucepan of water to a boil. Carefully lower the eggs into the water and cook for 6 minutes for soft-boiled or 7–8 minutes for firmer yolks. Transfer the eggs to an ice bath for 1–2 minutes, then peel.
5. **Serve:** Serve each plate with four bacon-wrapped asparagus spears and two soft-boiled eggs. Sprinkle eggs with salt and pepper.

Nutritional Information (Per Serving)

Calories: 280, Protein: 22g, Carbohydrates: 3g, Dietary Fiber: 1g, Sugars: 1g, Fats: 22g, Saturated Fat: 7g, Cholesterol: 370mg, Sodium: 500mg (varies with bacon choice), Potassium: 400mg

Portobello Mushroom and Spinach Breakfast Bake

Yield: 4 servings **Preparation Time:** 10 minutes **Cooking Time:** 25 minutes

Ingredients:

- 4 large Portobello mushrooms, stems removed (GI: 15)
- 4 large eggs (GI: 0)
- 2 cups fresh spinach, chopped (GI: 15)
- 1/2 cup cherry tomatoes, halved (GI: 15)
- 1/4 cup feta cheese, crumbled (optional) (GI: 0)
- 1/4 cup shredded mozzarella or cheddar cheese (GI: 0)
- 1 tablespoon olive oil (GI: 0)
- 1 clove garlic, minced (GI: 10)
- Salt and pepper to taste (GI: 0)
- Optional: 1/4 teaspoon red pepper flakes (GI: 0)

Instructions:

1. **Preheat oven:** Preheat the oven to 375°F (190°C). Line a baking sheet with parchment paper.
2. **Prepare the mushrooms:** Wash the Portobello mushrooms, remove stems, and brush both sides with olive oil. Place caps gill-side up on the prepared baking sheet.
3. **Heat the pan:** Heat olive oil in a skillet over medium heat. Fry the vegetables: Add garlic and spinach, cooking for 2–3 minutes until the spinach wilts. Season with salt and pepper.
4. **Stuff the mushrooms:** Fill each mushroom cap with a layer of sautéed spinach, followed by cherry tomatoes. Crack an egg into the center of each mushroom cap. Top with feta, mozzarella, or cheddar cheese and optional red pepper flakes.
5. **Bake:** Bake for 20–25 minutes, or until the eggs are set and the cheese is golden.
6. **Serve:** Serve hot, garnished with fresh herbs if desired or with a side of fresh avocado slices or a light salad for a complete meal. For extra flavor, drizzle with balsamic glaze or a sprinkle of fresh herbs like basil or parsley. Enjoy it with a cup of freshly brewed coffee or herbal tea to start your day on a delicious note.

Nutritional Information (Per Serving)

Calories: 190 (with optional cheese), Protein: 13g, Carbohydrates: 7g, Dietary Fiber: 3g, Sugars: 2g, Fats: 11g, Saturated Fat: 4g, Cholesterol: 175mg, Sodium: 300mg, Potassium: 550mg

CHAPTER 5
SMOOTHIES AND BEVERAGES
1. Low-Glycemic Index Smoothies

Spinach and Blueberry Blast Smoothie

 Yield: 2 servings   Preparation Time: 5 minutes
 Cooking Time: None

Ingredients:

- 1 cup fresh spinach (GI: 15)
- 1 cup unsweetened almond milk (GI: 30)
- 1/2 cup frozen blueberries (GI: 40)
- 1/2 cup Greek yogurt (GI: 11)
- 1 tablespoon chia seeds (GI: 1)
- 1 tablespoon flaxseeds (GI: 5)
- 1 teaspoon vanilla extract (optional) (GI: 0)
- 1/2 cup water or ice cubes (optional, for desired consistency) (GI: 0)

Instructions:

1. **Preparation:** Wash the fresh spinach thoroughly. Measure out all ingredients precisely.
2. **Blending:** Blend the spinach, unsweetened almond milk, frozen blueberries, Greek yogurt, chia seeds, flaxseeds, and vanilla extract. Blend on high speed until smooth and creamy for 1–2 minutes. If the smoothie is too thick, add water or ice cubes to reach your desired consistency and blend again.
3. **Serving:** Pour the smoothie into two serving glasses. Serve immediately. For added texture, top with a sprinkle of chia seeds or flaxseeds. You can also serve it with a side of protein-packed nuts or seeds to boost the meal's satiety.

Nutritional Information (Per Serving)
Calories: 155, Protein: 7g, Carbohydrates: 14g, Fiber: 7g, Sugars: 7g, Fats: 6g, Saturated Fat: 1g, Unsaturated Fat: 7g, Cholesterol: 3mg, Sodium: 80mg, Potassium: 350mg

Kale and Green Apple Smoothie

 Yield: 2 servings   Preparation Time: 5 minutes
 Cooking Time: None

Ingredients:

- 1 cup fresh kale, chopped (GI: 15)
- 1 green apple, cored and chopped (GI: 38)
- 1 cup unsweetened almond milk (GI: 30)
- 1/2 cup Greek yogurt (GI: 11)
- 1 tablespoon chia seeds (GI: 1)
- 1 tablespoon flaxseeds (GI: 5)
- 1/2 teaspoon ground cinnamon (optional) (GI: 0)
- 1/2 cup water or ice cubes (optional, for desired consistency) (GI: 0)

Instructions:

1. **Preparation:** Wash the fresh kale and green apple thoroughly. Core and chop the green apple.
2. **Blending:** Add the kale, green apple, unsweetened almond milk, Greek yogurt, chia seeds, flaxseeds, and ground cinnamon (if using) to a blender. Blend on high speed for 1–2 minutes until smooth and creamy. If the smoothie is too thick, add water or ice cubes to reach your desired consistency and blend again.
3. **Serving:** Pour the smoothie into two serving glasses. Serve is perfect for a refreshing, nutrient-packed start to your day. Serve it chilled with a sprinkle of cinnamon on top for extra flavor, or pair it with a light breakfast like a handful of nuts or a boiled egg for a balanced meal.

Nutritional Information (Per Serving)
Calories: 175, Protein: 7g, Carbohydrates: 18g, Fiber: 8g, Sugars: 9g, Fats: 7g, Saturated Fat: 1g, Unsaturated Fat: 7g, Cholesterol: 3mg, Sodium: 90mg, Potassium: 480mg

Avocado Berry Delight Smoothie

 Yield: 2 servings Preparation Time: 5 minutes
 Cooking Time: None

Ingredients:

- 1 ripe avocado, pitted and peeled (GI: 15)
- 1 cup mixed berries (strawberries, blueberries, raspberries) (GI: 25-40)
- 1 cup unsweetened almond milk (GI: 30)
- 1/2 cup Greek yogurt (GI: 11)
- 1 tablespoon chia seeds (GI: 1)
- 1 tablespoon flaxseeds (GI: 5)
- 1 teaspoon vanilla extract (optional) (GI: 0)
- 1/2 cup water or ice cubes (optional, for desired consistency) (GI: 0)

Instructions:

1. **Preparation:** Wash the mixed berries thoroughly. Pit and peel the avocado.
2. **Blending:** Add the avocado, mixed berries, unsweetened almond milk, Greek yogurt, chia seeds, flaxseeds, and vanilla extract (if using) to a blender. Blend until creamy, approximately 1-2 minutes.
3. **Serving:** Pour the smoothie into two serving glasses. Serve immediately. Serve as a refreshing breakfast or a light snack. For added texture, top with a few whole berries or a sprinkle of extra chia seeds. Enjoy it chilled for a refreshing treat!
4. **Note:** if necessary, adjust sweetness naturally (e.g., adding more berries or a pinch of stevia).

Nutritional Information (Per Serving)

Calories: 225, Protein: 9g, Carbohydrates: 16g, Fiber: 9g, Sugars: 8g, Fats: 15g, Saturated Fat: 2g, Unsaturated Fat: 13g, Cholesterol: 5mg, Sodium: 80mg, Potassium: 500mg

Cucumber Mint Green Smoothie

 Yield: 2 servings Preparation Time: 5 minutes
 Cooking Time: None

Ingredients:

- 1 cup fresh spinach (GI: 15)
- 1/2 medium cucumber, peeled and chopped (GI: 15)
- 1/2 avocado, pitted and peeled (GI: 15)
- 1/2 cup unsweetened almond milk (GI: 30)
- 1/2 cup Greek yogurt (GI: 11)
- 1 tablespoon chia seeds (GI: 1)
- 1 tablespoon flaxseeds (GI: 5)
- 1 tablespoon fresh mint leaves (GI: 0)
- 1 teaspoon lemon juice (optional) (GI: 0)
- 1/2 cup water or ice cubes (optional, for desired consistency) (GI: 0)

Instructions:

1. **Preparation:** Wash the fresh spinach, cucumber, and mint leaves thoroughly. Pit and peel the avocado.
2. **Blending:** Combine spinach, cucumber, avocado, unsweetened almond milk, Greek yogurt, chia seeds, flaxseeds, mint leaves, lemon juice. Blend on high speed until smooth, approximately 1-2 minutes. Adjust consistency with water or ice cubes.
3. **Serving:** Pour the smoothie into two serving glasses. Serve immediately. Serve chilled and garnish with a few extra mint leaves or a slice of cucumber for added flair. Pair it with a light snack like nuts or a small salad for a balanced meal.

Nutritional Information (Per Serving)

Calories: 200, Protein: 9g, Carbohydrates: 13g, Fiber: 8g, Sugars: 4g, Fats: 14g, Saturated Fat: 2g, Unsaturated Fat: 10g, Cholesterol: 5mg, Sodium: 60mg, Potassium: 550mg

Strawberry Spinach Smoothie

 Yield: 2 servings Preparation Time: 5 minutes
 Cooking Time: None

Ingredients:

- 1 cup fresh spinach (GI: 15)
- 1 cup strawberries, hulled and chopped (GI: 41)
- 1/2 avocado, pitted and peeled (GI: 15)
- 1 cup unsweetened almond milk (GI: 30)
- 1/2 cup Greek yogurt (GI: 11)
- 1 tablespoon chia seeds (GI: 1)
- 1 tablespoon flaxseeds (GI: 5)
- 1 teaspoon vanilla extract (optional) (GI: 0)
- 1/2 cup water or ice cubes (optional, for desired consistency) (GI: 0)

Instructions:

1. **Preparation:** Wash the fresh spinach and strawberries thoroughly. Pit and peel the avocado.
2. **Blending:** In a high-speed blender, combine spinach, strawberries, avocado, almond milk, Greek yogurt, chia seeds, flaxseeds, and vanilla extract. Blend on high speed until smooth, approximately 1–2 minutes. Add water or ice cubes gradually to adjust the consistency as desired.
3. **Serving:** Pour the smoothie into two serving glasses. Enjoy this refreshing smoothie as a nutritious breakfast or snack. Serve immediately in chilled glasses, and for an extra cooling effect use frozen strawberries. You can also customize the flavor with a drizzle of honey or a sprinkle of cinnamon if desired.

Nutritional Information (Per Serving)

Calories: 185, Protein: 8g, Carbohydrates: 14g, Fiber: 9g, Sugars: 5g, Fats: 12g, Saturated Fat: 2g, Unsaturated Fat: 10g, Cholesterol: 5mg, Sodium: 65mg, Potassium: 510mg

Berry Bliss Smoothie with Chia Seeds

 Yield: 2 servings Preparation Time: 5 minutes
 Cooking Time: None

Ingredients:

- 1 cup unsweetened almond milk (GI: 30)
- 1/2 cup frozen mixed berries (strawberries, blueberries, raspberries) (GI: 40)
- 1/4 cup plain Greek yogurt (GI: 11)
- 1 tablespoon chia seeds (GI: 1)
- 1/2 medium avocado (optional for creaminess and healthy fats) (GI: 15)
- 1/2 teaspoon vanilla extract (optional for flavor) (GI: 0)
- 1/2 teaspoon ground cinnamon (optional for flavor) (GI: 0)
- 1-2 ice cubes (optional for texture) (GI: 0)

Instructions:

1. **Prepare ingredients:** Gather all ingredients. If using fresh berries instead of frozen, add 1-2 ice cubes for a thicker consistency.
2. **Blend:** In a high-speed blender, combine the almond milk, mixed berries, Greek yogurt, chia seeds, and optional ingredients like avocado, vanilla extract, and cinnamon.
3. **Blend Until Smooth:** Start blending on low speed and gradually increase to high until the smoothie is completely smooth and creamy, approximately 1–2 minutes. Add more almond milk to reach your desired consistency if the smoothie is too thick.
4. **Serve:** Pour the smoothie into two glasses and serve immediately. Garnish with a few extra chia seeds or a few fresh berries for extra texture. Serve this berry-packed smoothie as a light, energizing breakfast or afternoon treat.

Nutritional Information (Per Serving)

Calories: 175 (with optional avocado), Protein: 7g, Carbohydrates: 13g, Dietary Fiber: 9g, Sugars: 6g, Fats: 11g, Saturated Fat: 1.5g, Cholesterol: 3mg, Sodium: 100mg, Potassium: 430mg

Creamy Avocado and Spinach Smoothie

 Yield: 2 servings   Preparation Time: 5 minutes   Cooking Time: None

Ingredients:

- 1 cup unsweetened almond milk (GI: 30)
- 1/2 medium avocado (GI: 15)
- 1 cup fresh spinach leaves (packed) (GI: 15)
- 1/4 cup plain Greek yogurt (GI: 11)
- 1 tablespoon chia seeds (GI: 1)
- 1/2 small green apple, cored and chopped (optional for sweetness) (GI: 39)
- 1/2 teaspoon vanilla extract (optional for flavor) (GI: 0)
- 1/2 teaspoon ground cinnamon (optional for flavor) (GI: 0)
- 1-2 ice cubes (optional for texture) (GI: 0)

Nutritional Information (Per Serving)
Calories: 190 (without optional green apple), Protein: 7g, Carbohydrates: 10g, Dietary Fiber: 7g, Sugars: 2g, Fats: 13g, Saturated Fat: 2g, Cholesterol: 3mg, Sodium: 60mg, Potassium: 510mg

Instructions:

1. **Prepare ingredients:** Gather all ingredients and chop the avocado and optional green apple.
2. **Blend:** In a high-speed blender, combine the almond milk, avocado, spinach, Greek yogurt, chia seeds, and optional ingredients like green apple, vanilla extract, and cinnamon.
3. **Blend Until Smooth:** Start blending on low speed and gradually increase to high until the smoothie is completely smooth and creamy, approximately 1–2 minutes. Add more almond milk or water to reach your desired consistency if the smoothie is too thick.
4. **Serve:** Pour the smoothie into two glasses and serve immediately. For a refreshing and nutrient-packed start to your day, enjoy this creamy avocado and spinach smoothie as a light breakfast or snack. It pairs well with a side of roasted nuts or a hard-boiled egg for added protein. You can also top it with a sprinkle of chia seeds or a few slices of fresh fruit for extra texture and flavor.

2. Protein-Packed Smoothies

Chocolate Banana Protein Smoothie

Yield: 2 servings *Preparation Time: 5 minutes* *Cooking Time: None*

Ingredients:
- 1 medium ripe banana, frozen (GI: 51)
- 1 cup unsweetened almond milk (GI: 30)
- 1 scoop chocolate whey protein powder (choose a low-carb option) (GI: 0)
- 1 tablespoon unsweetened cocoa powder (GI: 20)
- 1 tablespoon chia seeds (GI: 1)
- 1 tablespoon ground flaxseed (GI: 15)
- 1 teaspoon vanilla extract (GI: 0)
- 1/2 cup plain Greek yogurt (GI: 14)

Optional Ingredients:
- 1/2 avocado (for added creaminess and healthy fats) (GI: 15)
- 1 handful of spinach (for extra nutrients) (GI: 15)
- 1/2 teaspoon cinnamon (for flavor and blood sugar regulation) (GI: 0)
- 1 tablespoon almond butter (for added protein and healthy fats) (GI: 25)
- Ice cubes (for thicker texture) (GI: 0)
- Sweetener to taste (stevia or erythritol, both have GI: 0) (optional)

Instructions:
1. **Prepare Ingredients:** If necessary, slice and freeze the banana for at least 2 hours before making the smoothie.
2. **Blend Base Ingredients:** In a blender, combine the frozen banana, unsweetened almond milk, chocolate whey protein powder, unsweetened cocoa powder, chia seeds, ground flaxseed, vanilla extract, and Greek yogurt.
3. **Add Optional Ingredients:** If using, add the avocado, spinach, cinnamon, and/or almond butter to the blender.
4. **Blend Until Smooth:** Blend on high until all ingredients are well combined, and the smoothie reaches a creamy consistency, approximately 1–2 minutes.
5. **Sweeten if Necessary:** Taste the smoothie and add a small amount of stevia or erythritol if you prefer a sweeter flavor. Blend again briefly to mix.
6. **Serve:** Pour the smoothie into two glasses and serve immediately. Enjoy the smoothie as a nutritious breakfast or a post-workout snack. Garnish with a sprinkle of chia seeds or a dusting of cocoa powder for extra flair.

Nutritional Information (Per Serving)
Calories: 320 kcal, Protein: 24g, Carbohydrates: 18g, Fats: 10g, Fiber: 10g, Cholesterol: 15mg, Sodium: 190mg, Potassium: 650mg

Peanut Butter Berry Power Smoothie

Yield: 2 servings *Preparation Time: 5 minutes* *Cooking Time: None*

Ingredients:
- 1 cup unsweetened almond milk (GI: 30)
- 1/2 cup plain Greek yogurt (GI: 14)
- 1 scoop vanilla whey protein powder (choose a low-carb option) (GI: 0)
- 1/2 cup frozen mixed berries (strawberries, blueberries, raspberries) (GI: 40)
- 2 tablespoons natural peanut butter (no added sugar) (GI: 14)
- 1 tablespoon chia seeds (GI: 1)
- 1 tablespoon ground flaxseed (GI: 15)
- 1 teaspoon vanilla extract (GI: 0)

Optional Ingredients:
- Sweetener to taste (stevia or erythritol, both have GI: 0)
- Ice cubes (for thicker texture) (GI: 0)
- 1/2 avocado (for added creaminess and healthy fats) (GI: 15)
- 1 handful of spinach (for extra nutrients) (GI: 15)
- 1/2 teaspoon cinnamon (for flavor and blood sugar regulation) (GI: 0)

Instructions:
1. **Prepare Ingredients:** Gather all the ingredients and ensure the frozen berries are ready to use.
2. **Blend Base Ingredients:** In a blender, combine the unsweetened almond milk, plain Greek yogurt, vanilla whey protein powder, frozen mixed berries, natural peanut butter, chia seeds, ground flaxseed, and vanilla extract, approximately 1–2 minutes.
3. **Add Optional Ingredients:** If using, add the avocado, spinach, and/or cinnamon to the blender.
4. **Blend Until Smooth:** Blend on high until all ingredients are well combined, and the smoothie reaches a creamy consistency, tasting and adjusting sweetness.
5. **Sweeten if Necessary:** Taste the smoothie and add a small amount of stevia or erythritol if you prefer a sweeter flavor. Blend again briefly to mix.
6. **Serve:** Pour the smoothie into two glasses and serve immediately. Enjoy the smoothie as a nutritious breakfast or a post-workout snack. Garnish with a few fresh berries or a sprinkle of chia seeds for extra texture and visual appeal.

Nutritional Information (Per Serving)
Calories: 270 kcal, Protein: 20g, Carbohydrates: 15g, Fats: 14g, Fiber: 9g, Cholesterol: 12mg, Sodium: 170mg, Potassium: 500mg

Greek Yogurt and Almond Protein Shake

 Yield: 2 servings   Preparation Time: 10 minutes
 Cooking Time: None

Ingredients:
- 1 cup unsweetened almond milk (GI: 30)
- 1/2 cup plain Greek yogurt (GI: 14)
- 1 scoop vanilla whey protein powder (choose a low-carb
- option) (GI: 0)
- 1/4 cup raw almonds (GI: 15)
- 1 tablespoon almond butter (no added sugar) (GI: 25)
- 1 tablespoon chia seeds (GI: 1)
- 1 tablespoon ground flaxseed (GI: 15)
- 1 teaspoon vanilla extract (GI: 0)

Optional:
- Sweetener to taste (stevia or erythritol, both have GI: 0)
- Ice cubes (optional, for thicker texture) (GI: 0)
- 1/2 avocado (for added creaminess and healthy fats) (GI: 15)
- 1 handful of spinach (for extra nutrients) (GI: 15)
- 1/2 teaspoon cinnamon (for flavor and blood sugar regulation) (GI: 0)

Instructions:
1. **Prepare Ingredients:** Gather all the ingredients. For a smoother texture, soak the raw almonds in water overnight and drain them before use.
2. **Blend Base Ingredients:** In a blender, combine the unsweetened almond milk, plain Greek yogurt, vanilla whey protein powder, soaked almonds, almond butter, chia seeds, ground flaxseed, and vanilla extract.
3. **Add Optional Ingredients:** If using, add the avocado, spinach, and/or cinnamon to the blender.
4. **Blend Until Smooth:** Blend on high until all ingredients are completely smooth and creamy, approximately 1–2 minutes. If the shake is too thick, add more almond milk a tablespoon at a time until the desired consistency is achieved.
5. **Sweeten if Necessary:** Taste the shake and, if desired, add a small amount of stevia or erythritol. Blend again briefly to mix.
6. **Serve:** Pour the shake into two glasses and serve immediately. Enjoy the shake as a nutritious breakfast or a post-workout snack. Garnish with a sprinkle of chopped almonds or a dusting of cinnamon for extra flair.

Nutritional Information (Per Serving)
Calories: 300 kcal, Protein: 26g, Carbohydrates: 12g, Fats: 18g, Fiber: 7g, Cholesterol: 10mg, Sodium: 180mg, Potassium: 500mg

Spinach Almond Butter Protein Smoothie

 Yield: 2 servings   Preparation Time: 10 minutes
 Cooking Time: None

Ingredients:
- 1 cup unsweetened almond milk (GI: 30)
- 1/2 cup plain Greek yogurt (GI: 14)
- 1 scoop vanilla whey protein powder (choose a low-carb option) (GI: 0)
- 1 cup fresh spinach (GI: 15)
- 2 tablespoons almond butter (no added sugar) (GI: 25)
- 1 tablespoon chia seeds (GI: 1)
- 1 tablespoon ground flaxseed (GI: 15)
- 1 teaspoon vanilla extract (GI: 0)
- 1/2 small green apple, cored and sliced (GI: 38)

Optional:
- Sweetener to taste (stevia or erythritol, both have GI: 0)
- Ice cubes (optional, for thicker texture) (GI: 0)
- 1/2 avocado (for added creaminess and healthy fats) (GI: 15)
- 1/2 teaspoon cinnamon (for flavor and blood sugar regulation) (GI: 0)

Instructions:
1. **Prepare Ingredients:** Gather all the ingredients. Wash the spinach thoroughly and ensure the green apple is cored and sliced. If preferred, replace the green apple with ½ cup of frozen blueberries for a lower-GI option.
2. **Blend Base Ingredients:** In a blender, combine the unsweetened almond milk, plain Greek yogurt, vanilla whey protein powder, fresh spinach, almond butter, chia seeds, ground flaxseed, vanilla extract, and green apple slices (or substitute).
3. **Add Optional Ingredients:** If using, add the avocado and/or cinnamon to the blender.
4. **Blend Until Smooth:** Blend on high until all ingredients are well combined and the smoothie reaches a creamy consistency, approximately 1–2 minutes. If the smoothie is too thick, add a few tablespoons of almond milk and blend again. For a thicker texture, add a few ice cubes and blend until smooth.
5. **Sweeten if Necessary:** Taste the smoothie and, if needed, add a small amount of stevia or erythritol. Blend briefly to mix.
6. **Serve:** Pour the smoothie into two glasses and serve immediately. Garnish with a sprinkle of chia seeds or a dash of cinnamon for extra flavor and visual appeal.

Nutritional Information (Per Serving)
Calories: 290 kcal, Protein: 24g, Carbohydrates: 15g, Fats: 16g, Fiber: 9g, Cholesterol: 10mg, Sodium: 160mg, Potassium: 580mg

Vanilla Strawberry Protein Smoothie

Yield: 2 servings   Preparation Time: 10 minutes   Cooking Time: None

Ingredients:
- 1 cup unsweetened almond milk (GI: 30)
- 1/2 cup plain Greek yogurt (GI: 14)
- 1 scoop vanilla whey protein powder (choose a low-carb option) (GI: 0)
- 1 cup frozen strawberries (GI: 40)
- 1 tablespoon chia seeds (GI: 1)
- 1 tablespoon ground flaxseed (GI: 15)
- 1 teaspoon vanilla extract (GI: 0)

Optional Ingredients:
- Sweetener to taste (stevia or erythritol, both have GI: 0)
- Ice cubes (for thicker texture) (GI: 0)
- 1/2 avocado (for added creaminess and healthy fats) (GI: 15)
- 1 handful of spinach (for extra nutrients) (GI: 15)
- 1/2 teaspoon cinnamon (for flavor and blood sugar regulation) (GI: 0)

Instructions:
1. **Prepare Ingredients:** Gather all the ingredients. Ensure the frozen strawberries are ready to use. If desired, replace some of the strawberries with ½ cup of frozen raspberries or blueberries to reduce the overall GI.
2. **Blend Base Ingredients:** In a blender, combine the unsweetened almond milk, plain Greek yogurt, vanilla whey protein powder, frozen strawberries, chia seeds, ground flaxseed, and vanilla extract.
3. **Add Optional Ingredients:** If using, add the avocado, spinach, and/or cinnamon to the blender.
4. **Blend Until Smooth:** Blend on high until all ingredients are well combined, and the smoothie reaches a creamy consistency, approximately 1–2 minutes. If the texture is too thick, add a tablespoon of almond milk at a time and blend again.
5. **Sweeten if Necessary:** Taste the smoothie and add a small amount of stevia or erythritol, if needed, for a sweeter flavor. Blend again briefly to mix.
6. **Serve:** Pour the smoothie into two glasses and serve immediately. Garnish with a sprinkle of chia seeds or a dusting of cinnamon for extra flavor and visual appeal. Serve with a side of low-carb almond crackers for a satisfying snack. Pair with a boiled egg for a balanced breakfast option.

Nutritional Information (Per Serving)
Calories: 250 kcal, Protein: 22g, Carbohydrates: 13g, Fats: 18g, Fiber: 7g, Cholesterol: 10mg, Sodium: 140mg, Potassium: 450mg

Peanut Butter and Greek Yogurt Power Shake

Yield: 2 servings   Preparation Time: 5 minutes   Cooking Time: None

Ingredients:
- 1 cup unsweetened almond milk (GI: 30)
- 1/2 cup plain Greek yogurt (GI: 11)
- 2 tablespoons natural peanut butter (no added sugar) (GI: 14)
- 1 tablespoon chia seeds (GI: 1)

Optional Ingredients:
- 1/2 medium banana (for sweetness) (GI: 51)
- 1/2 teaspoon vanilla extract (for flavor) (GI: 0)
- 1/2 teaspoon ground cinnamon (for flavor) (GI: 0)
- 1-2 ice cubes (optional for texture) (GI: 0)

Instructions:
1. **Prepare Ingredients:** Gather all ingredients. If using a banana, slice it into small pieces for easier blending. Note that the banana is optional and can be substituted with ½ cup of frozen raspberries for a lower-GI option.
2. **Blend Base Ingredients:** In a blender, combine the unsweetened almond milk, plain Greek yogurt, peanut butter, chia seeds, and any optional ingredients like banana, vanilla extract, or cinnamon.
3. **Blend Until Smooth:** Start blending on low speed and gradually increase to high until the shake is smooth and creamy, approximately 1–2 minutes. If the shake is too thick, add more almond milk a tablespoon at a time to reach the desired consistency.
4. **Sweeten if Necessary:** Taste the shake and add a small amount of stevia or erythritol if needed for sweetness. Blend briefly to mix.
5. **Serve:** Pour the shake into two glasses and serve immediately. Garnish with a sprinkle of chia seeds or crushed peanuts for added texture.

Nutritional Information (Per Serving)
Calories: 240 (without optional banana), Protein: 16g, Carbohydrates: 8g, Dietary Fiber: 5g, Sugars: 4g, Fats: 14g, Saturated Fat: 3g, Cholesterol: 10mg, Sodium: 150mg, Potassium: 400mg

Almond-Coconut Protein Smoothie

 Yield: 2 servings   Preparation Time: 5 minutes   Cooking Time: None

Ingredients:

- 1 cup unsweetened almond milk (GI: 30)
- 1/2 cup plain Greek yogurt (GI: 11)
- 2 tablespoons unsweetened shredded coconut (GI: 45)
- 2 tablespoons almond butter (GI: 15)
- 1 tablespoon chia seeds (GI: 1)

Nutritional Information (Per Serving)
Calories: 260, Protein: 10g, Carbohydrates: 10g, Dietary Fiber: 7g, Sugars: 4g, Fats: 18g, Saturated Fat: 6g, Cholesterol: 10mg, Sodium: 140mg, Potassium: 500mg

Optional Ingredients:
- 1/2 teaspoon vanilla extract (optional for flavor) (GI: 0)
- 1/2 teaspoon ground cinnamon (optional for flavor) (GI: 0)
- 1/2 cup ice (optional for texture) (GI: 0)

Instructions:

1. **Prepare Ingredients:** Gather all ingredients. If using optional ingredients like avocado or green apple, ensure they are washed, peeled, and sliced as necessary.
2. **Blend Base Ingredients:** In a blender, combine the unsweetened almond milk, Greek yogurt, shredded coconut, almond butter, chia seeds, and vanilla extract.
3. **Add Optional Ingredients:** If desired, add the avocado, spinach, green apple, and/or cinnamon to the blender.
4. **Blend Until Smooth:** Start blending on low speed and gradually increase to high until the smoothie reaches a creamy consistency, approximately 1–2 minutes. If the texture is too thick, add a tablespoon of almond milk or water at a time and blend again.
5. **Serve:** Pour the smoothie into two glasses and serve immediately. Garnish with a sprinkle of shredded coconut or a dash of cinnamon for extra flavor and visual appeal. Pair it with a handful of mixed nuts or a boiled egg for a balanced snack. For an extra touch, garnish with a slice of green apple or a few spinach leaves. Enjoy as a refreshing breakfast or a midday energy boost.

3. Hydrating and Refreshing Beverages

Cucumber Mint Infused Water

 Yield: 2 servings   Preparation Time: 10 minutes
 Cooking Time: 2-4 hours

Ingredients:

- 1 medium cucumber, thinly sliced (GI: 15)
- 10-12 fresh mint leaves (GI: 0)
- 8 cups filtered water (GI: 0)
- 1 lemon, thinly sliced (optional, for added flavor) (GI: 20)
- 1/2 teaspoon stevia or erythritol (optional, for a touch of sweetness) (GI: 0)

Optional Ingredients:

- 1/2 teaspoon grated ginger (for added flavor and potential anti-inflammatory benefits) (GI: 15)
- A few basil leaves (for an additional layer of flavor) (GI: 0)

Instructions:

1. **Prepare Ingredients:** Wash the cucumber, mint leaves, and optional lemon thoroughly. Thinly slice the cucumber and lemon.
2. **Combine Ingredients:** In a large pitcher, add the cucumber slices, mint leaves, and optional lemon slices.
3. **Add Water:** Pour the filtered water into the pitcher to cover the ingredients.
4. **If using,** add grated ginger or basil leaves for additional flavor.
5. **Stir gently.** Add stevia or erythritol if desired for sweetness. Make sure the sweetener is completely dissolved.
6. **Infuse:** Cover the pitcher and refrigerate for 2-4 hours to allow flavors to infuse. For a stronger flavor, infuse overnight.
7. **Serve:** before serving. Pour into glasses over ice if desired. Serve chilled, garnished with additional cucumber slices or mint leaves for extra visual appeal. Enjoy this refreshing beverage as a hydrating drink throughout the day.

Nutritional Information (Per Serving)

Calories: 5, Protein: 0g, Carbohydrates: 1g, Fats: 0g, Fiber: 0g, Cholesterol: 0mg, Sodium: 2mg, Potassium: 12mg

Lemon Basil Infused Water

 Yield: 2 servings Preparation Time: 5 minutes
 Cooking Time: None

Ingredients:

- 1 large lemon, thinly sliced (GI: 20)
- 10-12 fresh basil leaves (GI: 0)
- 8 cups filtered water (GI: 0)
- 1/2 teaspoon stevia or erythritol (optional, for a touch of sweetness) (GI: 0)

Optional Ingredients:

- 1/2 cucumber, thinly sliced (for additional freshness) (GI: 15)
- 1/2 teaspoon grated ginger (for added flavor and potential anti-inflammatory benefits) (GI: 15)

Instructions:

1. **Prepare Ingredients:** Wash the lemon, basil leaves (slightly bruise basil leaves before adding to the pitcher for a more robust flavor), and optional cucumber and ginger thoroughly. Thinly slice the lemon and cucumber.
2. **Combine Ingredients:** In a large pitcher, add the lemon slices, basil leaves, and optional cucumber slices.
3. **Add Water:** Pour the filtered water into the pitcher to cover the ingredients.
4. **Optional Add-ins:** If using, add the grated ginger.
5. **Sweeten if Desired:** Add stevia or erythritol to taste if you prefer a slightly sweet flavor. Make sure the sweetener is completely dissolved.
6. **Infuse:** Cover and refrigerate for 2-4 hours to infuse the flavors. For a stronger flavor, infuse overnight.
7. **Serve:** Stir before serving. Pour into glasses over ice if desired. Serve chilled, garnished with additional lemon slices or basil leaves for extra visual appeal. Enjoy this refreshing beverage as a hydrating drink throughout the day.

Nutritional Information (Per Serving)

Calories: 5, Protein: 0g, Carbohydrates: 1g, Fats: 0g, Fiber: 0g, Cholesterol: 0mg, Sodium: 1mg, Potassium: 10mg

Ginger Lemon Herbal Tea

 Yield: 2 servings   *Preparation Time: 10 minutes*
 Cooking Time: 2-4 hours

Ingredients:

- 4 cups water (GI: 0)
- 1 tablespoon fresh ginger, grated (GI: 15)
- 1 large lemon, thinly sliced (GI: 20)
- 1 tablespoon fresh lemon juice (GI: 20)
- 2-3 sprigs fresh mint (optional, for added flavor) (GI: 0)
- 1-2 teaspoons stevia or erythritol (optional, for sweetness) (GI: 0)

Optional Ingredients:

- 1/2 teaspoon ground cinnamon (for added flavor and potential blood sugar regulation) (GI: 0)
- 1 green tea bag (for added antioxidants and slight caffeine boost) (GI: 0)

Instructions:

1. **Prepare Ingredients:** Wash the lemon and mint leaves thoroughly. Thinly slice the lemon and grate the ginger.
2. **Boil Water:** Bring 4 cups of water to a boil in a medium saucepan.
3. **Add Ginger and Lemon:** Add the grated ginger and lemon slices once the water is boiling. Reduce the heat and let it simmer for about 10 minutes.
4. **Optional Add-ins:** Add the mint sprigs and/or ground cinnamon to the saucepan. For a green tea option: If using a green tea bag, steep separately in boiled water for 3–5 minutes to avoid bitterness before combining with ginger tea.
5. **Strain and Serve:** Strain the tea into a teapot or directly into serving cups after simmering. Add the fresh lemon juice and stir.
6. **Sweeten if Desired:** If you prefer a sweeter flavor, add stevia or erythritol to taste. Stir well to combine.
7. **Serve:** Enjoy this tea hot to soothe and relax, or serve it chilled over ice for a refreshing drink. Garnish with a slice of lemon or a sprig of mint for extra flavor and visual appeal.

Nutritional Information (Per Serving)

Calories: 5, Protein: 0g, Carbohydrates: 1g, Fats: 0g, Fiber: 0g, Cholesterol: 0mg, Sodium: 5mg, Potassium: 20mg

Watermelon Mint Cooler

 Yield: 2 servings   *Preparation Time: 5 minutes*
 Cooking Time: None

Ingredients:

- 1 large lemon, thinly sliced (GI: 20)
- 10-12 fresh basil leaves (GI: 0)
- 8 cups filtered water (GI: 0)
- 1/2 teaspoon stevia or erythritol (optional, for a touch of sweetness) (GI: 0)

Optional Ingredients:

- 1/2 cucumber, peeled and sliced (for added freshness) (GI: 15)
- 1/2 teaspoon grated ginger (for added flavor and potential anti-inflammatory benefits) (GI: 15)

Instructions:

1. **Prepare Ingredients:** Gather all the ingredients and ensure the watermelon is cubed and chilled (at least 2 hours before cooking). Use watermelon with firm flesh and a lower sugar content for better GI control.
2. **Blend Base Ingredients:** In a blender, combine the watermelon cubes, cold water, fresh mint leaves, and fresh lime juice.
3. **Optional Add-ins:** Add the cucumber slices and/or grated ginger to the blender.
4. **Blend Until Smooth:** Blend on high until all ingredients are well combined and smooth. Strain the mixture through a fine mesh sieve if you prefer a softer texture.
5. **Sweeten if Desired:** Taste the cooler and add stevia or erythritol if you prefer a sweeter flavor. Blend again briefly to mix.
6. **Serve:** Pour the watermelon mint cooler into glasses. Serve chilled, garnished with a mint sprig and a lime slice for extra flavor and visual appeal. Enjoy as a refreshing beverage on a hot day or as a hydrating drink after exercise.

Nutritional Information (Per Serving)

Calories: 30, Protein: 0.6g, Carbohydrates: 7g, Fats: 0g, Fiber: 0.5g, Cholesterol: 0mg, Sodium: 1mg, Potassium: 85mg

Hibiscus Berry Iced Tea

 Yield: 2 servings   Preparation Time: 15 minutes

 Cooking Time: 1 hour

Ingredients:

- 4 cups water (GI: 0)
- 4 hibiscus tea bags (GI: 0)
- 1/2 cup mixed berries (strawberries, blueberries, raspberries), fresh or frozen (GI: 40-53)
- 1 tablespoon fresh lemon juice (GI: 20)
- 1/2 teaspoon stevia or erythritol (optional, for sweetness) (GI: 0)
- Ice cubes (GI: 0)

Optional Ingredients:
- 1/2 teaspoon grated ginger (for added flavor and potential anti-inflammatory benefits) (GI: 15)
- Fresh mint leaves for garnish (GI: 0)
- Additional lemon slices for garnish (GI: 20)

Instructions:

1. **Boil Water:** Bring 4 cups of water to a boil in a medium saucepan.
2. **Steep Hibiscus Tea:** Remove the saucepan from the heat and add the hibiscus tea bags. Let the tea steep for about 10 minutes.
3. **Prepare Berries:** Mash the mixed berries slightly while the tea steeps to release their juices. For a clearer tea, strain the mixture through a fine mesh sieve before refrigerating
4. **Combine Ingredients:** Remove the tea bags and add the mashed berries to the hibiscus tea. Stir in the fresh lemon juice.
5. **Sweeten if Desired:** If you prefer a sweeter flavor, add stevia or erythritol to taste. Stir well to combine.
6. **Optional Add-ins:** If using, add the grated ginger for added flavor.
7. **Cool the Tea:** Let the mixture cool to room temperature, then refrigerate for at least 1 hour to chill.
8. **Serve:** Fill glasses with ice cubes and pour the chilled hibiscus berry tea over the ice. Serve chilled, garnished with fresh mint leaves and lemon slices for extra flavor and visual appeal. Enjoy as a refreshing beverage on a hot day or as a hydrating drink throughout the day.

Nutritional Information (Per Serving)

Calories: 10, Protein: 0g, Carbohydrates: 2g, Fats: 0g, Fiber: 0.5g, Cholesterol: 0mg, Sodium: 2mg, Potassium: 30mg

Lemon-Lavender Sparkling Water

 Yield: 2 servings   Preparation Time: 5 minutes

 Cooking Time: 15 minutes (optional for stronger flavor)

Ingredients:

- 4 cups sparkling water (GI: 0)
- 1 medium lemon, thinly sliced (GI: 20)
- 1 teaspoon dried culinary lavender (GI: 0)
- 1 tablespoon fresh lemon juice (GI: 20)
- Ice cubes (optional for Serving) (GI: 0)
- Fresh mint leaves (optional for garnish) (GI: 0)

Instructions:

1. **Prepare Ingredients:** Thinly slice the lemon and measure the dried culinary lavender. Use only food-grade culinary lavender for safety and quality.
2. **Combine Ingredients:** Add the lemon slices, dried lavender, and fresh lemon juice to a large pitcher. Pour the sparkling water over the ingredients.
3. **Infuse (Optional):** Allow the mixture to sit for about 15 minutes to let the flavors infuse. If you prefer a stronger lavender flavor, let it infuse for up to an hour in the refrigerator.
4. **Strain (Optional):** If you prefer not to have the lavender and lemon slices in your drink, strain the sparkling water mixture into another pitcher. Recommend in any case removing lemon slices after 1 hour to prevent bitterness.
5. **Serve:** Add ice cubes to four glasses, pour the Lemon-Lavender Sparkling Water over the ice, and garnish with fresh mint leaves if desired. Serve immediately.

Nutritional Information (Per Serving)

Calories: 5, Protein: 0g, Carbohydrates: 1g, Dietary Fiber: 0g, Sugars: 0g, Fats: 0g, Cholesterol: 0mg, Sodium: 5mg, Potassium: 15mg

Cucumber Lime Electrolyte Drink

 Yield: 4 servings Preparation Time: 10 minutes Cooking Time: None

Ingredients:

- 4 cups water (GI: 0)
- 1 medium cucumber, thinly sliced (GI: 15)
- 2 limes, thinly sliced (GI: 20)
- 1/4 teaspoon salt (preferably sea salt or Himalayan pink salt) (GI: 0)
- 1 tablespoon fresh mint leaves (optional for flavor) (GI: 0)
- 1/2 teaspoon chia seeds (optional for added fiber and electrolytes) (GI: 1)
- Ice cubes (optional for Serving) (GI: 0)

Nutritional Information (Per Serving)
Calories: 5, Protein: 0g, Carbohydrates: 1g, Dietary Fiber: 0g, Sugars: 0g, Fats: 0g, Cholesterol: 0mg, Sodium: 150mg, Potassium: 50mg

Instructions:

1. **Prepare Ingredients:** Thinly slice the cucumber and limes. If using, chop the mint leaves, mash them and measure the chia seeds.
2. **Combine Ingredients:** Add the cucumber slices, lime slices, salt, optional mint leaves, and chia seeds to a large pitcher.
3. **Add Water:** Pour 4 cups of water into the pitcher and stir gently to mix the ingredients.
4. **Infuse:** Let the mixture sit for at least 10 minutes to allow the flavors to meld. For a more intense flavor, refrigerate for up to 1 hour.
5. **Serve:** Fill four glasses with ice cubes if desired, and pour the Cucumber Lime Electrolyte Drink over the ice. Stir before serving to ensure the salt is evenly distributed. Serve the Cucumber Lime Electrolyte Drink chilled over ice for a refreshing boost. Garnish each glass with an extra lime wedge or cucumber slice for visual appeal. For added flair, rim the glasses with salt or sugar before serving.

CHAPTER 6
LUNCH RECIPES
1. Salads and Bowls

Quinoa and Black Bean Salad

 Yield: 4 servings   Preparation Time: 15 minutes

 Cooking Time: 15 minutes

Ingredients:
- 1 cup washed quinoa (GI: 53)
- 2 cups water (GI: 0)
- One (15-ounce) can of rinsed and drained black beans (GI: 30)
- Halve 1 cup cherry tomatoes (GI: 15)
- Diced red bell pepper (GI: 10)
- Finely cut one tiny red onion (GI: 10)
- 1 diced avocado (GI: 15)
- 1/4 cup chopped fresh cilantro (GI: 0)
- 1/4 cup fresh lime juice (GI: 0)
- 2 tbsp olive oil (GI: 0)
- 1 tsp ground cumin (GI: 0)
- Add salt and pepper to taste (GI: 0)

Optional Ingredients:
- 1/4 cup crumbled feta cheese (GI: 0) (Serve)
- 1/2 teaspoon smoked paprika (GI: <1)
- 1 jalapeño, finely chopped (GI: 15)
- 1/4 cup corn kernels, fresh or frozen and thawed (GI: 55)

Instructions:
1. **Cook the Quinoa:** Bring 2 cups of water to a boil in a medium saucepan. Add the washed quinoa, reduce the heat to low, cover, and simmer for 15 minutes or until the quinoa is cooked and water is absorbed. Remove from heat, cover, and let sit for 5 minutes. Fluff with a fork and let cool.
2. **Prepare the Vegetables:** Dice the red bell pepper, finely chop the red onion, halve the cherry tomatoes, and dice the avocado. Chop the cilantro.
3. **Mix the Dressing:** In a small bowl, whisk together lime juice, olive oil, ground cumin, salt, and black pepper.
4. **Combine Ingredients:** In a large mixing bowl, combine the cooked quinoa, black beans, cherry tomatoes, red bell pepper, red onion, avocado, and cilantro.
5. **If using, add optional ingredients** such as smoked paprika, jalapeño, or corn.
6. **Toss the Salad:** Pour the dressing over the salad and gently toss to combine.
7. **Serve:** Serve immediately as a main dish for a light, healthy meal or refrigerate for 30 minutes to allow flavors to meld. Garnish with crumbled feta cheese, if desired.

Nutritional Information (Per Serving)
Calories: 325 (without optional ingredients), Protein: 13g, Carbohydrates: 45g, Fats: 12g, Fiber: 10g, Cholesterol: 0mg, Sodium: 300mg, Potassium: 750mg

Spinach and Strawberry Salad with Balsamic Vinaigrette

 Yield: 4 servings   Preparation Time: 15 minutes

 Cooking Time: 15 minutes

Ingredients:
Salad:
- 6 cups baby spinach leaves, washed and dried (GI: 15)
- 1 cup strawberries, hulled and sliced (GI: 41)
- 1/4 cup red onion, thinly sliced (GI: 10)
- 1/4 cup feta cheese, crumbled (GI: 0)
- 1/4 cup walnuts, chopped (GI: 15)

Optional Ingredients:
- 1 avocado, sliced (GI: 15)
- 1/2 cup blueberries (GI: 53)
- 1 tablespoon chia seeds (GI: 1)

Balsamic Vinaigrette:
- 1/4 cup balsamic vinegar (GI: 0)
- 2 tablespoons extra virgin olive oil (GI: 0)
- 1 tablespoon Dijon mustard (GI: 35)
- 1 teaspoon honey or stevia (optional for sweetness) (GI: 55 for honey, GI: 0 for stevia)
- Salt and pepper to taste (GI: 0)

Instructions:
1. **Prepare the Salad Base:** In a large bowl, combine the baby spinach, sliced strawberries, red onion, crumbled feta cheese, and walnuts.
2. **If using optional ingredients**, add sliced avocado, blueberries, or chia seeds to the bowl.
3. **Make the Dressing:** In a small bowl, whisk together balsamic vinegar, olive oil, Dijon mustard, honey (or stevia), salt, and black pepper until emulsified.
4. **Assemble the Salad:** Drizzle the balsamic vinaigrette over the salad ingredients. Toss gently to combine and ensure the dressing coats all components.
5. **Serve:** Serve immediately as a light, refreshing meal or a side dish. Optionally pair with grilled chicken or fish for added protein.

Nutritional Information (Per Serving)
Calories: 190, Protein: 5g, Carbohydrates: 12g, Fats: 14g, Fiber: 4g, Cholesterol: 10mg, Sodium: 180mg, Potassium: 450mg

Grilled Chicken Caesar Salad

 Yield: 4 servings   Preparation Time: 20 minutes
 Cooking Time: 15 minute

Ingredients:

For the Salad:
- 4 boneless, skinless chicken breasts (about 1 pound total) (GI: 0)
- 1 tablespoon olive oil (GI: 0)
- Salt and pepper to taste (GI: 0)
- 8 cups romaine lettuce, chopped (GI: 15)
- 1/2 cup grated Parmesan cheese (GI: 0)

Optional toppings:
- 1 cup cherry tomatoes, halved (for added flavor and color) (GI: 15)
- 1/4 cup red onion, thinly sliced (GI: 10)
- 1/2 avocado, sliced (for added creaminess and healthy fats)(GI: 15)

For the Dressing:
- 1/4 cup plain Greek yogurt (GI: 14)
- 2 tablespoons grated Parmesan cheese (GI: 0)
- 1 tablespoon Dijon mustard (GI: 35)
- 1 tablespoon lemon juice (GI: 0)
- 1 teaspoon Worcestershire sauce (GI: 0)
- 1 clove garlic, minced (GI: 0)
- 1 teaspoon anchovy paste (optional, for traditional Caesar flavor) (GI: 0)

Instructions:

1. **Prepare the Chicken:** Preheat a grill or grill pan to medium-high heat. Brush the chicken breasts with olive oil and season with salt and black pepper. Grill the chicken for 6-7 minutes per side, or until the internal temperature reaches 165°F (74°C). Let the chicken rest for 5 minutes before slicing into strips.
2. **Make the Dressing:** In a small bowl, whisk together the Greek yogurt, Parmesan cheese, Dijon mustard, lemon juice, Worcestershire sauce, garlic, and anchovy paste (if using). Season with salt and black pepper to taste.
3. **Assemble the Salad:** In a large salad bowl, combine the chopped romaine lettuce and grated Parmesan cheese. If using optional toppings, add cherry tomatoes, red onion, and avocado slices. Add the grilled chicken strips on top.
4. **Dress the Salad:** Drizzle the dressing over the salad and toss gently to combine all ingredients thoroughly.
5. **Serve:** Serve immediately as a main course. For a balanced meal, pair with a small portion of whole-grain bread or quinoa.

Nutritional Information (Per Serving)

Calories: 320, Protein: 36g, Carbohydrates: 8g, Fats: 16g, Fiber: 3g, Cholesterol: 85mg, Sodium: 400mg, Potassium: 600mg

---

Mediterranean Chickpea Salad

 Yield: 4 servings   Preparation Time: 15 minutes
 Cooking Time: None

Ingredients:

- 1 (15-ounce) can chickpeas, rinsed and drained (GI: 28)
- 1 cup cherry tomatoes, halved (GI: 15)
- 1 cucumber, diced (GI: 15)
- 1 red bell pepper, diced (GI: 10)
- 1/4 red onion, finely chopped (GI: 10)
- 1/4 cup Kalamata olives, pitted and sliced (GI: 15)
- 1/4 cup feta cheese, crumbled (GI: 0)
- 1/4 cup fresh parsley, chopped (GI: 0)

For the Dressing:
- 3 tablespoons extra virgin olive oil (GI: 0)
- 2 tablespoons lemon juice (GI: 0)
- 1 teaspoon dried oregano (GI: 0)
- 1 clove garlic, minced (GI: 0)
- Salt and pepper to taste (GI: 0)

Optional Ingredients:
- 1/2 avocado, diced (for added creaminess and healthy fats) (GI: 15)
- 1/2 cup cooked quinoa (GI: 53)
- 1 tablespoon capers (GI: 0)

Instructions:

1. **Prepare the Salad Base:** In a large bowl, combine the chickpeas, cherry tomatoes, cucumber, red bell pepper, red onion, Kalamata olives, and feta cheese. If using optional ingredients, add diced avocado, cooked quinoa, or capers.
2. **Make the Dressing:** In a small bowl, whisk together olive oil, lemon juice, dried oregano, minced garlic, salt, and black pepper.
3. **Toss the Salad:** Pour the dressing over the salad ingredients. Toss gently to combine and ensure the dressing coats all components.
4. **Serve:** Serve immediately as a light and refreshing main dish or refrigerate for 30 minutes to allow the flavors to meld. Optionally pair with grilled chicken or fish for added protein.

Nutritional Information (Per Serving)

Calories: 220, Protein: 7g, Carbohydrates: 22g, Fats: 12g, Fiber: 6g, Cholesterol: 10mg, Sodium: 430mg, Potassium: 450mg

Tuna and Avocado Salad Bowl

Yield: 4 servings   *Preparation Time: 20 minutes*
Cooking Time: 15 minute

Ingredients:

- 1 (5-ounce) can of tuna in water, drained (GI: 0)
- 1 avocado, diced (GI: 15)
- 1 cup cherry tomatoes, halved (GI: 15)
- 1/2 cucumber, diced (GI: 15)
- 1/4 red onion, finely chopped (GI: 10)
- 2 cups mixed greens (such as spinach, arugula, and romaine) (GI: 15)
- 2 tablespoons fresh lemon juice (GI: 0)
- 2 tablespoons extra virgin olive oil (GI: 0)
- 1 tablespoon fresh parsley, chopped (GI: 0)
- Salt and pepper to taste (GI: 0)

Optional Ingredients:

- 1/4 cup feta cheese, crumbled (GI: 0)
- 1 tablespoon capers (GI: 0)
- 1/2 cup cooked quinoa (GI: 53)
- 1/2 teaspoon dried oregano (GI: 0)
- 1 boiled egg, sliced (GI: 0)

Instructions:

1. **Prepare the Salad Base:** In a large mixing bowl, combine mixed greens, cherry tomatoes, cucumber, and red onion.
2. **Add Protein and Fats:** Gently fold in the drained tuna and diced avocado. Be careful not to mash the avocado.
3. **Make the Dressing:** In a small bowl, whisk together lemon juice, olive oil, parsley, salt, and black pepper. Add dried oregano if desired.
4. **Assemble the Salad:** Pour the dressing over the salad and toss gently to coat all ingredients evenly.
5. **If using optional ingredients**, sprinkle feta cheese, capers, or add sliced boiled egg and quinoa on top.
6. **Serve:** Divide the salad into two bowls and serve immediately. Optionally, pair with whole-grain crackers or a small portion of whole-grain bread for added fiber. This salad is best served fresh but can be stored in the refrigerator for up to 1 day.

Nutritional Information (Per Serving)

Calories: 320 (without optional ingredients), Protein: 22g, Carbohydrates: 12g, Fats: 22g, Fiber: 7g, Cholesterol: 35mg, Sodium: 350mg, Potassium: 750mg

Kale and Roasted Beet Salad

Yield: 4 servings   *Preparation Time: 15 minutes*
Cooking Time: 40 minutes

Ingredients:

- 4 medium beets, peeled and cut into wedges (GI: 64)
- 2 tablespoons olive oil (GI: 0)
- 1/2 teaspoon salt (GI: 0)
- 1/4 teaspoon black pepper (GI: 0)
- 6 cups kale, chopped and massaged (GI: 15)
- 1/4 cup red onion, thinly sliced (GI: 10)
- 1/4 cup feta cheese, crumbled (GI: 0)
- 1/4 cup walnuts, chopped (GI: 15)

Optional Ingredients:

- 1/2 avocado, sliced (GI: 15)
- 1/4 cup pomegranate seeds (GI: 35)

For the Dressing:

- 3 tablespoons balsamic vinegar (GI: 0)
- 2 tablespoons olive oil (GI: 0)
- 1 tablespoon Dijon mustard (GI: 35)
- 1 teaspoon honey or stevia (optional for sweetness) (GI: 55 for honey, GI: 0 for stevia)
- 1 clove garlic, minced (GI: 0)
- Salt and pepper to taste (GI: 0)

Instructions:

1. **Roast the Beets:** Preheat the oven to 400°F (200°C). Toss the beet wedges with olive oil, salt, and black pepper. Spread them evenly on a baking sheet. Roast for 35-40 minutes or until tender and caramelized, flipping halfway through.
2. **Prepare the Kale:** While the beets are roasting, massage the chopped kale with a small drizzle of olive oil to soften it. Set aside.
3. **Make the Dressing:** In a small bowl, whisk together balsamic vinegar, olive oil, Dijon mustard, honey (or stevia), garlic, salt, and black pepper until well combined.
4. **Assemble the Salad:** In a large salad bowl, combine the massaged kale, roasted beets, red onion, feta cheese, and walnuts.
5. **If using optional garnishes**, add sliced avocado and pomegranate seeds.
6. **Dress the Salad:** Drizzle the dressing over the salad and toss gently to combine all ingredients evenly.
7. **Serve:** Divide the salad among plates and serve immediately as a nutritious main dish or side.

Nutritional Information (Per Serving)

Calories: 250, Protein: 6g, Carbohydrates: 20g, Fats: 18g, Fiber: 6g, Cholesterol: 10mg, Sodium: 300mg, Potassium: 750mg

Thai Peanut Chicken Salad

 Yield: 4 servings   Preparation Time: 20 minutes
 Cooking Time: 15 minute

Ingredients:

For the Salad:
- 2 boneless, skinless chicken breasts (about 1 pound total) (GI: 0)
- 1 tablespoon olive oil (GI: 0)
- 4 cups mixed greens (spinach, romaine, arugula) (GI: 15)
- 1 cup red cabbage, shredded (GI: 10)
- 1 cup carrots, shredded (GI: 35)
- 1 red bell pepper, thinly sliced (GI: 10)
- 1/4 cup cilantro, chopped (GI: 0)
- 1/4 cup green onions, thinly sliced (GI: 10)
- 1/4 cup peanuts, chopped (GI: 14)

For the Peanut Dressing:
- 1/4 cup natural peanut butter (no added sugar) (GI: 14)
- 2 tablespoons soy sauce (low sodium) (GI: 0)
- 1 tablespoon rice vinegar (GI: 0)
- 1 tablespoon lime juice (GI: 0)
- 1 tablespoon honey or stevia (optional for sweetness) (GI: 55 for honey, GI: 0 for stevia)
- 1 teaspoon sesame oil (GI: 0)
- 1 clove garlic, minced (GI: 0)
- 1 teaspoon fresh ginger, grated (GI: 15)
- 2-3 tablespoons water (as needed to thin the dressing) (GI: 0)

Optional Ingredients:
- 1/2 avocado, sliced (GI: 15)
- 1/2 cup edamame, shelled (GI: 18)

Instructions:

1. **Cook the Chicken:** Preheat a skillet or grill to medium-high heat. Brush the chicken breasts with olive oil and season with salt and pepper. Cook for 6-7 minutes on each side, or until the internal temperature reaches 165°F (74°C). Let the chicken rest for 5 minutes, then slice into thin strips.
2. **Prepare the Salad Base:** In a large salad bowl, combine mixed greens, shredded red cabbage, carrots, bell pepper, cilantro, and green onions.
3. **Make the Dressing:** In a small bowl, whisk together peanut butter, soy sauce, rice vinegar, lime juice, sesame oil, garlic, ginger, and honey (or stevia). Add water a tablespoon at a time until the dressing reaches your desired consistency.
4. **Assemble the Salad:** Top the salad base with sliced chicken and sprinkle with chopped peanuts.
5. **If using optional ingredients**, add sliced avocado or edamame.
6. **Dress and Serve:** Drizzle the peanut dressing over the salad and toss gently to combine.
7. **Serve** immediately as a main dish for lunch or dinner.

Nutritional Information (Per Serving)

Calories: 350, Protein: 28g, Carbohydrates: 18g, Fats: 20g, Fiber: 6g, Cholesterol: 55mg, Sodium: 470mg, Potassium: 750mg

Lentil and Feta Salad

 Yield: 4 servings   Preparation Time: 15 minutes
Cooking Time: 30 minutes

Ingredients:

- 1 cup green or brown lentils, rinsed (GI: 32)
- 3 cups water (GI: 0)
- 1 cup cherry tomatoes, halved (GI: 15)
- 1 cucumber, diced (GI: 15)
- 1/4 red onion, finely chopped (GI: 10)
- 1/4 cup Kalamata olives, pitted and sliced (GI: 15)
- 1/2 cup feta cheese, crumbled (GI: 0)
- 1/4 cup fresh parsley, chopped (GI: 0)
- 1/4 cup fresh mint, chopped (optional) (GI: 0)

For the Dressing:
- 3 tablespoons extra virgin olive oil (GI: 0)
- 2 tablespoons lemon juice (GI: 0)
- 1 tablespoon red wine vinegar (GI: 0)
- 1 teaspoon Dijon mustard (GI: 35)
- 1 clove garlic, minced (GI: 0)
- Salt and pepper to taste (GI: 0)

Optional Ingredients:
- 1 avocado, diced (GI: 15)
- 1/4 cup toasted pine nuts (GI: 15)

Instructions:

1. **Cook the Lentils:** In a medium saucepan, bring 3 cups of water to a boil. Add rinsed lentils, reduce the heat to medium, and simmer for 25–30 minutes until tender but not mushy. Drain and let the lentils cool to room temperature.
2. **Prepare the Vegetables:** In a large mixing bowl, combine the cooled lentils, cherry tomatoes, cucumber, red onion, Kalamata olives, feta cheese, parsley, and mint (if using).
3. **Make the Dressing:** In a small bowl, whisk together olive oil, lemon juice, red wine vinegar, Dijon mustard, minced garlic, salt, and black pepper until well combined.
4. **Assemble the Salad:** Pour the dressing over the lentil and vegetable mixture. Toss gently to coat all ingredients evenly.
5. **Serve:** Add optional diced avocado and toasted pine nuts on top, if desired. Serve immediately or refrigerate for 30 minutes to allow the flavors to meld.

Nutritional Information (Per Serving)

Calories: 300, Protein: 12g, Carbohydrates: 30g, Fats: 15g, Fiber: 10g, Cholesterol: 15mg, Sodium: 400mg, Potassium: 650mg

Cobb Salad with Turkey and Avocado

 Yield: 4 servings   Preparation Time: 20 minutes
 Cooking Time: None

Ingredients:

- 6 cups mixed greens (romaine, spinach, arugula) (GI: 15)
- 1 cup cooked turkey breast, diced (GI: 0)
- 4 slices turkey bacon, cooked and crumbled (GI: 0)
- 1 avocado, diced (GI: 15)
- 1 cup cherry tomatoes, halved (GI: 15)
- 1/2 cucumber, diced (GI: 15)
- 1/4 red onion, thinly sliced (GI: 10)
- 1/2 cup blue cheese, crumbled (GI: 0)
- 2 hard-boiled eggs, sliced (GI: 0)

For the Dressing:

- 1/4 cup extra virgin olive oil (GI: 0)
- 2 tablespoons red wine vinegar (GI: 0)
- 1 tablespoon Dijon mustard (GI: 35)
- 1 teaspoon honey or stevia (optional for sweetness) (GI: 55 for honey, GI: 0 for stevia)
- 1 clove garlic, minced (GI: 0)
- Salt and pepper to taste (GI: 0)

Optional Ingredients:

- 1/4 cup chopped fresh parsley (GI: 0)
- 1/4 cup toasted walnuts (GI: 15)

Instructions:

1. **Prepare Salad Ingredients:** In a large salad bowl, combine the mixed greens, diced cooked turkey breast, crumbled turkey bacon, diced avocado, halved cherry tomatoes, diced cucumber, and thinly sliced red onion.
2. **Add Eggs and Cheese:** Top the salad with crumbled blue cheese and sliced hard-boiled eggs.
3. **Prepare the Dressing:** In a small bowl, whisk together the extra virgin olive oil, red wine vinegar, Dijon mustard, honey or stevia (if using), and minced garlic. Season with salt and pepper to taste.
4. **Dress the Salad:** Pour the dressing over the salad and toss gently to combine all ingredients thoroughly.
5. **Add Optional Ingredients:** If using, sprinkle the chopped fresh parsley and toasted walnuts over the salad for added flavor and texture.
6. **Serve:** Divide the salad among four plates and serve immediately. Serve as a nutritious main dish for lunch or dinner. Pair with a side of whole-grain bread or quinoa for added fiber.

Nutritional Information (Per Serving)

Calories: 350, Protein: 25g, Carbohydrates: 12g, Fats: 25g, Fiber: 7g, Cholesterol: 200mg, Sodium: 600mg, Potassium: 750mg

Salmon and Asparagus Salad

 Yield: 4 servings   Preparation Time: 15 minutes
 Cooking Time: 15 minutes

Ingredients:

- 4 (4-ounce) salmon fillets (GI: 0)
- 1 tablespoon olive oil (GI: 0)
- Salt and pepper to taste (GI: 0)
- 1 bunch asparagus, trimmed and cut into 2-inch pieces (GI: 15)
- 6 cups mixed greens (spinach, arugula, romaine) (GI: 15)
- 1 cup cherry tomatoes, halved (GI: 15)
- 1/2 red onion, thinly sliced (GI: 10)
- 1 avocado, diced (GI: 15)
- 1/4 cup feta cheese, crumbled (GI: 0)

For the Dressing:

- 1/4 cup extra virgin olive oil (GI: 0)
- 2 tablespoons lemon juice (GI: 0)
- 1 tablespoon Dijon mustard (GI: 35)
- 1 teaspoon honey or stevia (optional for sweetness) (GI: 55 for honey, GI: 0 for stevia)
- 1 clove garlic, minced (GI: 0)
- Salt and pepper to taste (GI: 0)

Optional Ingredients:

- 1/4 cup toasted almonds (GI: 15)
- 1/4 cup fresh dill, chopped (GI: 0)

Instructions:

1. **Prepare the Salmon:** Preheat a nonstick skillet over medium heat. Brush the salmon fillets with olive oil and season with salt and pepper. Cook for 4–5 minutes per side until the salmon is cooked through and flakes easily with a fork. Set aside to rest.
2. **Cook the Asparagus:** In the same skillet, add the asparagus and sauté for 3–4 minutes until tender but still crisp. Season with a pinch of salt and pepper.
3. **Prepare the Salad Base:** In a large salad bowl, combine the mixed greens, cherry tomatoes, red onion, avocado, and feta cheese.
4. **Make the Dressing:** In a small bowl, whisk together olive oil, lemon juice, Dijon mustard, garlic, and honey or stevia (if using). Season with salt and pepper to taste.
5. **Assemble the Salad:** Add the cooked salmon and asparagus to the salad bowl. Drizzle the dressing over the top and gently toss to combine.
6. **Optional Garnish:** Sprinkle with toasted almonds and fresh dill for added crunch and flavor.
7. **Serve:** Divide the salad into four bowls and serve immediately. Pair with a side of whole-grain bread or quinoa for a balanced meal if desired.

Nutritional Information (Per Serving)

Calories: 350, Protein: 30g, Carbohydrates: 12g, Fats: 22g, Fiber: 6g, Cholesterol: 55mg, Sodium: 400mg, Potassium: 850mg

2. Sandwiches and Wraps

Turkey and Avocado Whole Grain Wrap

 Yield: 4 servings   Preparation Time: 10 minutes
 Cooking Time: None

Ingredients:

- 4 whole grain tortillas (8-inch) (GI: 50)
- 8 ounces cooked turkey breast, sliced (GI: 0)
- 1 avocado, sliced (GI: 15)
- 1 cup mixed greens (spinach, arugula, romaine) (GI: 15)
- 1/2 cucumber, sliced (GI: 15)
- 1/2 red bell pepper, thinly sliced (GI: 10)
- 1/4 red onion, thinly sliced (GI: 10)
- 1/4 cup feta cheese, crumbled (GI: 0)
- 1 tablespoon Dijon mustard (GI: 35)
- 2 tablespoons Greek yogurt (GI: 14)
- Salt and pepper to taste (GI: 0)

Optional Ingredients:
- 1/4 cup fresh parsley, chopped (GI: 0)
- 1/4 cup shredded carrots (GI: 35)
- 1 tablespoon hummus (GI: 6)

Instructions:

1. **Make the spread:** Mix Dijon mustard and Greek yogurt in a small bowl until smooth
2. **Make filling:** Divide turkey breast slices, avocado, mixed greens, cucumber, red bell pepper, red onion, crumbled feta cheese, fresh parsley, shredded carrots, and hummus.
3. **Assemble wraps:** Spread yogurt-mustard mixture on each tortilla, then spread filling.
4. **Roll wraps** by folding sides in and from the bottom up.
5. **Serve:** Serve by slicing wraps diagonally and serving immediately with fresh fruit or a small green salad if desired for a complete meal.
6. **Storage:** Wrap each tortilla tightly in plastic wrap to keep fresh and prevent moisture loss for stored in the refrigerator for up to 24 hours.

Nutritional Information (Per Serving)

Calories: 290, Protein: 20g, Carbohydrates: 28g, Fats: 12g, Fiber: 8g, Cholesterol: 35mg, Sodium: 450mg, Potassium: 600mg

Grilled Veggie and Hummus Sandwich

 Yield: 4 servings   Preparation Time: 10 minutes
 Cooking Time: 15 minutes

Ingredients:

- 8 slices whole grain bread (GI: 50)
- 1 cup hummus (GI: 6)
- 1 zucchini, sliced lengthwise (GI: 15)
- 1 red bell pepper, sliced into strips (GI: 10)
- 1 yellow bell pepper, sliced into strips (GI: 10)
- 1 red onion, sliced into rings (GI: 10)
- 1 eggplant, sliced into rounds (GI: 15)
- 2 tablespoons olive oil (GI: 0)
- 1 tablespoon balsamic vinegar (GI: 0)
- Salt and pepper to taste (GI: 0)
- 1/4 cup fresh basil leaves (optional) (GI: 0)

Optional Ingredients:
- 1/4 cup feta cheese, crumbled (GI: 0)
- 1 avocado, sliced (GI: 15)
- 1/4 cup shredded carrots (GI: 35)

Instructions:

1. **Prepare the grill:** Preheat grill to medium-high heat.
2. **Prepare the vegetables:** Toss vegetables with olive oil, balsamic vinegar, salt, and pepper.
3. **Fry the vegetables:** Grill for 5-7 minutes per side or until tender. Remove from grill and set aside.
4. **Prepare the bread:** Toast whole grain bread slices on grill for 1-2 minutes per side.
5. **Assemble sandwiches:** Spread hummus evenly on one side of toasted bread slices before layering other ingredients. Arrange the grilled vegetables, fresh basil leaves, feta cheese, avocado, and carrots.
6. **Finish sandwiches** with another slice of hummus-spread bread.
7. **Serve** immediately. Serve with fresh fruit or a small green salad for a complete meal.
8. **Storage:** Sandwiches can be wrapped tightly in plastic and stored in the refrigerator for up to 24 hours.

Nutritional Information (Per Serving)

Calories: 320, Protein: 10g, Carbohydrates: 38g, Fats: 15g, Fiber: 9g, Cholesterol: 0mg, Sodium: 350mg, Potassium: 750mg

Mediterranean Veggie and Hummus Wrap

 Yield: 2 servings   Preparation Time: 10 minutes

Cooking Time: None

Ingredients:

- 2 low-carb whole wheat tortillas or lettuce leaves (GI: 30 for whole wheat)
- 1/2 cup hummus (GI: 6)
- 1/4 cup crumbled feta cheese (GI: 0)
- 1/2 cup cucumber, sliced (GI: 15)
- 1/4 cup roasted red peppers, sliced (GI: 15)
- 1/4 cup red onion, thinly sliced (GI: 15)
- 1/4 cup spinach leaves (GI: 15)
- 1 tablespoon olive oil (optional, for added healthy fats) (GI: 0)
- 1 teaspoon balsamic vinegar (GI: 0)
- 1 tablespoon fresh parsley, chopped (optional) (GI: 0)
- Salt and pepper to taste (GI: 0)

Instructions:

1. **Prepare the Vegetables:** Slice the cucumber, roasted red peppers, and red onion. Set aside.
2. **Assemble the Wrap:** Lay the tortilla or lettuce leaf flat. Divide the hummus, spreading 2 tablespoons on each wrap. Layer the spinach, cucumber, roasted red peppers, red onion, and feta cheese. Drizzle with olive oil and balsamic vinegar if using. Sprinkle with parsley, salt, and pepper.
3. **Wrap and Serve:** Fold the sides of the tortilla or lettuce leaf and roll it up tightly. Slice the wrap in half if desired and serve immediately.
4. **Additional Serve:**

- Pair with a side of mixed greens drizzled with olive oil and lemon juice for a light and refreshing meal.
- Alternatively, enjoy with a small bowl of lentil soup for added warmth and protein.
- For a snack-like option, serve alongside crispy baked pita chips or fresh veggie sticks such as carrots and celery.

Nutritional Information (Per Serving)
Calories: 310, Protein: 11g, Carbohydrates: 28g, Fiber: 6g, Sugars: 4g, Fats: 12g, Cholesterol: 15mg, Sodium: 470mg, Potassium: 260mg

Egg and Spinach Whole Wheat Sandwich

 Yield: 2 servings   Preparation Time: 10 minutes

 Cooking Time: 10 minutes

Ingredients:

- 4 slices whole wheat bread (GI: 69)
- 4 large eggs (GI: 0)
- 1 cup fresh spinach leaves (GI: 15)
- 1/2 avocado, sliced (GI: 15)
- 1/4 cup cherry tomatoes, halved (GI: 15)
- 1/4 red onion, thinly sliced (GI: 10)
- 1 tablespoon olive oil (GI: 0)
- Salt and pepper to taste (GI: 0)

Optional Ingredients:
- 1/4 cup feta cheese, crumbled (GI: 0)
- 1 tablespoon Dijon mustard (GI: 35)

Instructions:

1. **Prepare the Bread:** Toast the whole wheat bread slices until lightly browned.
2. **Cook the eggs** in olive oil.
3. **Sauté the Spinach:** Add the spinach leaves to the same skillet and sauté spinach should specify the amount of time or when it is done.
4. **Assemble the Sandwiches:** Place a layer of spinach on two slices of toasted bread. Top the spinach with the cooked eggs. Add the sliced avocado, cherry tomatoes, and red onion. If using, sprinkle with crumbled feta cheese and spread Dijon mustard on the other two slices of bread.
5. **Finish the Sandwiches:** Place the remaining slices of bread on top of the sandwiches, pressing down gently.
6. **Serve:** Cut each sandwich in half and serve immediately. Serve with mixed greens or a small salad for a complete meal. Optionally, pair with fresh fruit or a low-sugar yogurt for a balanced breakfast or lunch.

Nutritional Information (Per Serving)
Calories: 340, Protein: 18g, Carbohydrates: 28g, Fats: 18g, Fiber: 7g, Cholesterol: 185mg, Sodium: 320mg, Potassium: 650mg

Roast Beef Wrap with Mustard

 Yield: 2 servings   Preparation Time: 10 minutes
 Cooking Time: None

Ingredients:

- 4 large lettuce leaves (butter lettuce or romaine) (GI: 15)
- 6 ounces roast beef, thinly sliced (GI: 0)
- 1/2 avocado, sliced (GI: 15)
- 1/4 cup red bell pepper, thinly sliced (GI: 10)
- 1/4 cup cucumber, thinly sliced (GI: 15)
- 1/4 cup red onion, thinly sliced (GI: 10)
- 2 tablespoons Dijon mustard (GI: 35)
- 2 tablespoons Greek yogurt (GI: 14)
- Salt and pepper to taste (GI: 0)

Optional Ingredients:
- 1/4 cup shredded carrots (GI: 35)
- 1 tablespoon fresh parsley, chopped (GI: 0)
- 1 tablespoon capers, drained (GI: 0)

Instructions:

1. **Make the spread:** Mix Dijon mustard and Greek yogurt.
2. **Add seasonings:** Season with salt and pepper.
3. **Lay** lettuce leaves on clean surface.
4. **Assemble wraps:** Layer mustard and yogurt mixture, roast beef, avocado, red bell pepper, cucumber, red onion, shredded carrots, parsley, capers.
5. **Roll the roll:** Roll wraps from bottom up, secure with toothpick.
6. **Serving and Storage:** Serve immediately or store in refrigerator for up to 4 hours. Serve with fresh fruit or a small green salad for a complete meal. These wraps can also be enjoyed as a snack or a light lunch.

Nutritional Information (Per Serving)

Calories: 220, Protein: 22g, Carbohydrates: 8g, Fats: 12g, Fiber: 5g, Cholesterol: 60mg, Sodium: 450mg, Potassium: 650mg

Tuna Salad Whole Grain Sandwich

 Yield: 2 servings   Preparation Time: 10 minutes
 Cooking Time: 10 minutes

Ingredients:

- 1 (5-ounce) can of tuna in water, drained (GI: 0)
- 1/4 cup plain Greek yogurt (GI: 14)
- 1 tablespoon Dijon mustard (GI: 35)
- 1 tablespoon lemon juice (GI: 0)
- 1 tablespoon fresh parsley, chopped (GI: 0)
- 1/4 cup celery, finely chopped (GI: 0)
- 1/4 cup red onion, finely chopped (GI: 10)
- 1/4 avocado, diced (GI: 15)
- Salt and pepper to taste (GI: 0)
- 4 slices whole grain bread (GI: 50)
- 1 cup mixed greens (spinach, arugula, romaine) (GI: 15)

Optional Ingredients:
- 1/4 cup shredded carrots (GI: 35)
- 1 tablespoon capers, drained (GI: 0)
- 1 hard-boiled egg, sliced (GI: 0)

Instructions:

1. **Make the spread:** Combine drained tuna, Greek yogurt, Dijon mustard, lemon juice, parsley, celery, and red onion.
2. **Add avocado:** Gently fold diced avocado into the tuna mixture to avoid mashing, season with salt and pepper, and add shredded carrots and capers.
3. **Prepare the bread:** Toast whole grain bread until lightly browned.
4. **Assemble sandwiches** by spreading tuna salad mixture on two slices of bread, top with mixed greens.
5. **Finish sandwiches** with remaining bread slices and sliced hard-boiled egg. Cut each sandwich in half and serve immediately.
6. **Serving and Storage:** with fresh fruit or a small green salad for a complete meal. These sandwiches can be wrapped tightly and stored in the refrigerator for 24 hours.

Nutritional Information (Per Serving)

Calories: 320, Protein: 25g, Carbohydrates: 32g, Fats: 12g, Fiber: 7g, Cholesterol: 40mg, Sodium: 450mg, Potassium: 600mg

Turkey and Spinach Wrap with Hummus

 Yield: 2 servings Preparation Time: 10 minutes
Cooking Time: None

Ingredients:

- 2 whole grain tortillas (8-inch) (GI: 50)
- 4 ounces cooked turkey breast, thinly sliced (GI: 0)
- 1/2 cup hummus (GI: 6)
- 1 cup fresh spinach leaves (GI: 15)
- 1/4 red bell pepper, thinly sliced (GI: 10)
- 1/4 cucumber, thinly sliced (GI: 15)
- 1/4 red onion, thinly sliced (GI: 10)
- 1 tablespoon fresh lemon juice (GI: 0)
- Salt and pepper to taste (GI: 0)

Optional Ingredients:
- 1/4 avocado, sliced (GI: 15)
- 1/4 cup shredded carrots (GI: 35)
- 1 tablespoon fresh parsley, chopped (GI: 0)

Instructions:

1. **Preparation:** Wash spinach leaves, slice red bell pepper, cucumber, red onion, and optional ingredients.
2. **Spreading:** Lay whole-grain tortillas on clean surface, spread 1/4 cup hummus.
3. **Layering:** Evenly layer turkey, spinach leaves, red bell pepper, cucumber, red onion, avocado, shredded carrots, fresh parsley across the tortillas.
4. **Seasoning:** Drizzle with lemon juice, season with salt and pepper, roll tortillas.
5. **Serving and Storage:** Cut wraps in half, serve immediately. Serve with fresh fruit or a small green salad for a complete meal. If wrapped tightly, these wraps can be stored in the refrigerator for up to 24 hours.

Nutritional Information (Per Serving)

Calories: 320, Protein: 22g, Carbohydrates: 36g, Fats: 12g, Fiber: 10g, Cholesterol: 30mg, Sodium: 450mg, Potassium: 750mg

Cucumber and Cream Cheese Sandwich

 Yield: 2 servings Preparation Time: 10 minutes
 Cooking Time: None

Ingredients:

- 4 slices whole grain bread (GI: 50)
- 4 ounces low-fat cream cheese (GI: 0)
- 1/2 cucumber, thinly sliced (GI: 15)
- 1 tablespoon fresh dill, chopped (GI: 0)
- 1 tablespoon fresh chives, chopped (GI: 0)
- 1/4 teaspoon garlic powder (GI: 0)
- Salt and pepper to taste (GI: 0)
- 1 tablespoon lemon juice (GI: 0)

Optional Ingredients:
- 1/4 avocado, thinly sliced (GI: 15)
- 1/4 cup alfalfa sprouts (GI: 15)
- 1/4 cup shredded carrots (GI: 35)

Instructions:

1. **Prepare the Cream Cheese Spread:** In a small bowl, mix the low-fat cream cheese with the chopped dill, chives, garlic powder, lemon juice, salt, and pepper until well combined.
2. **Prepare the Bread:** Toast the whole grain bread slices until lightly browned.
3. **Assemble the Sandwiches:** Spread an even layer of the cream cheese mixture on each slice of toasted bread. Layer the cucumber slices evenly over two slices of the bread. Add thinly sliced avocado, alfalfa sprouts, and shredded carrots.
4. **If using optional ingredients**, layer them with the cucumber slices.
5. **Finish the sandwiches:** Top each with the remaining bread and cream cheese slices.
6. **Serving and Storage:** Cut each sandwich in half and serve immediately. Serve with fresh fruit or a small green salad for a complete meal. If wrapped tightly, these sandwiches can be stored in the refrigerator for up to 24 hours.

Nutritional Information (Per Serving)

Calories: 250, Protein: 8g, Carbohydrates: 30g, Fats: 12g, Fiber: 5g, Cholesterol: 30mg, Sodium: 300mg, Potassium: 350mg

Veggie and Tofu Wrap

 Yield: 4 servings   **Preparation Time:** 20 minutes
 Cooking Time: 15 minutes

Ingredients:

- 1 block (14 oz) extra-firm tofu, drained and pressed (GI: 15)
- 1 tablespoon olive oil (GI: 0)
- 1 teaspoon garlic powder (GI: 0)
- 1 teaspoon onion powder (GI: 0)
- 1 teaspoon smoked paprika (GI: 0)
- 1 tablespoon low-sodium soy sauce (GI: 0)
- 4 whole-grain tortillas (GI: 30)
- 1 cup shredded carrots (GI: 39)
- 1 cup sliced bell peppers (any color) (GI: 15)
- 1 cup cucumber, thinly sliced (GI: 15)
- 1 cup spinach leaves (GI: 15)
- 1/2 avocado, sliced (optional for added creaminess and healthy fats) (GI: 15)
- 1/4 cup hummus (optional for additional flavor) (GI: 6)

Instructions:

1. **Prepare the Tofu:** Cut tofu into thin strips. Press tofu for 10 minutes to remove excess moisture before slicing. Heat olive oil in non-stick skillet. Add tofu strips, season with garlic, onion, paprika, and soy sauce. Cook for 8-10 minutes, turning occasionally. Remove from heat and set aside.
2. **Prepare the Vegetables:** While the tofu is cooking, wash and slice the vegetables. Shred the carrots and slice the bell peppers, cucumber, and avocado (if using).
3. **Assemble the Wraps:** Lay out the whole-grain tortillas on a clean surface. If using hummus, spread a thin layer onto each tortilla. Arrange the spinach leaves evenly across each tortilla. Distribute the tofu strips evenly among the tortillas. Top with shredded carrots, sliced bell peppers, cucumber, and avocado slices. Roll up each tortilla tightly to form a wrap.
4. **Serve:** Cut each wrap in half diagonally. Serve immediately or wrap in foil to enjoy later. Serve with fresh mixed greens or a small bowl of vegetable soup. Enjoy with a refreshing glass of unsweetened iced tea or infused water with lemon and mint.

Nutritional Information (Per Serving)

Calories: 265, Protein: 12g, Carbohydrates: 30g, Fats: 12g, Fiber: 8g, Cholesterol: 0mg, Sodium: 250mg, Potassium: 530mg

Smoked Salmon and Avocado Sandwich

 Yield: 2 servings   **Preparation Time:** 10 minutes
 Cooking Time: None

Ingredients:

- 4 slices whole-grain bread (GI: 40)
- 4 oz smoked salmon (GI: 0)
- 1 avocado, thinly sliced (GI: 15)
- 1/4 cup Greek yogurt (GI: 0)
- 1 teaspoon lemon juice (GI: 20)
- 1/4 teaspoon black pepper (GI: 0)
- 1/4 teaspoon dried dill (optional for added flavor) (GI: 0)
- 1/2 cup spinach leaves (GI: 15)
- 1/4 cup red onion, thinly sliced (GI: 10)
- 1/2 cucumber, thinly sliced (GI: 15)
- 1 tablespoon capers (optional for added flavor) (GI: 0)

Instructions:

1. **Prepare the Greek Yogurt Spread:** In a small bowl, mix the Greek yogurt with lemon juice, black pepper, and dried dill (if using).
2. **Assemble the Sandwich:** Lay out the whole-grain bread slices on a clean surface. Spread the Greek yogurt mixture evenly on one side of each bread slice. Layer the spinach leaves evenly on two of the bread slices. Distribute the smoked salmon evenly over the spinach leaves. Add the avocado slices on top of the smoked salmon. Sprinkle the red onion slices and cucumber slices evenly over the avocado. Sprinkle capers evenly over the cucumber slices, if using.
3. **Complete the Sandwich:** Place the remaining bread slices on top, yogurt spread side down, to form the sandwiches. Cut each sandwich in half diagonally for easier handling.
4. **Serve:** Serve immediately or wrap tightly in parchment paper for later consumption. Pair with a side salad of mixed greens with a light vinaigrette. Enjoy a glass of sparkling water with a slice of lemon or lime.

Nutritional Information (Per Serving)

Calories: 350, Protein: 20g, Carbohydrates: 30g, Fats: 18g, Fiber: 8g, Cholesterol: 35mg, Sodium: 500mg, Potassium: 700mg

3. Soups and Stews

Lentil and Vegetable Soup

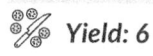 *Yield: 6 servings* *Preparation Time: 15 minutes*
Cooking Time: 45 minutes

Ingredients:
- 1 cup lentils (green or brown) (GI: 32)
- 1 tablespoon olive oil (GI: 0)
- 1 medium onion, diced (GI: 10)
- 2 cloves garlic, minced (GI: 10)
- 2 medium carrots, diced (GI: 39)
- 2 celery stalks, diced (GI: 15)
- 1 medium zucchini, diced (GI: 15)
- 1 bell pepper, diced (GI: 15)
- 1 can (14.5 oz) diced tomatoes, no salt added (GI: 15)
- 6 cups low-sodium vegetable broth (GI: 15)
- 1 teaspoon ground cumin (GI: 5)
- 1 teaspoon dried thyme (GI: 5)
- 1 teaspoon paprika (GI: 5)
- 1 bay leaf (GI: 0)
- 1/2 teaspoon black pepper (GI: 0)
- 1/2 teaspoon salt (optional) (GI: 0)
- 2 cups fresh spinach, roughly chopped (GI: 15)
- Juice of 1 lemon (GI: 0)

Optional Ingredients for Additional Flavor and Nutrition:
- 1 teaspoon turmeric (GI: 5)
- 1/4 teaspoon red pepper flakes (GI: 0)
- 1/4 cup chopped fresh parsley (GI: 5)

Instructions:
1. **Prepare the lentils:** Rinse lentils under cold water.
2. **Sauté the vegetables in the skillet:** Heat olive oil over medium heat. Sauté the onion and garlic until fragrant (about 2–3 minutes). Add carrots, celery, zucchini, and bell pepper; sauté for another 5 minutes.
3. **Add the tomatoes and lentils:** Stir in lentils and tomatoes, ensuring they are evenly combined.
4. **Make the soup:** Transfer the vegetables to the pan. Pour in broth, spices, and salt. Boil mixture over high heat.
5. **Simmer the soup:** Reduce heat to low, cover, and simmer for 30–35 minutes until lentils are tender. About 5 minutes before doneness, stir in spinach, lemon juice, bay leaf, and optional ingredients.
6. **Serve** this soup hot, garnished with a sprinkle of fresh parsley or a lemon wedge. Adjust seasoning and remove bay leaf before serving. Pair it with a small side salad or a slice of whole-grain bread (optional, ensure it's suitable for diabetic diets).

Nutritional Information (Per Serving)
Calories: 180, Protein: 10g, Carbohydrates: 28g, Fats: 3g, Fiber: 10g, Cholesterol: 0mg, Sodium: 250mg, Potassium: 700mg

Broccoli Cheddar Soup

 Yield: 6 servings *Preparation Time: 15 minutes*
Cooking Time: 30 minutes

Ingredients:
- 1 tablespoon olive oil (GI: 0)
- 1 medium onion, diced (GI: 10)
- 2 cloves garlic, minced (GI: 10)
- 4 cups broccoli florets, chopped (GI: 10)
- 1 medium carrot, grated (GI: 39)
- 4 cups low-sodium vegetable broth (GI: 15)
- 1 cup unsweetened almond milk (GI: 30)
- 1 cup shredded sharp cheddar cheese (GI: 0)
- 1/2 teaspoon ground nutmeg (GI: 5)
- 1/2 teaspoon black pepper (GI: 0)
- 1/4 teaspoon salt (optional) (GI: 0)
- 2 tablespoons whole wheat flour (GI: 45)
- 1/2 cup plain Greek yogurt (GI: 0)

Optional Ingredients for Additional Flavor and Nutrition:
- 1/4 teaspoon red pepper flakes (GI: 0)
- 1/4 teaspoon smoked paprika (GI: 5)
- 2 tablespoons nutritional yeast (GI: 0)
- 2 tablespoons chopped fresh parsley (GI: 5)

Instructions:
1. **Prepare the aromatics:** Heat olive oil over medium heat. Sauté the diced onion and minced garlic for 5 minutes until softened.
2. **Cook the vegetables:** Add broth and broccoli florets and gratified carrots to the pot. Stir well and cook for 5–7 minutes. Reduce heat to low and simmer for 10–15 minutes until the vegetables are tender.
3. **Prepare the dressing mixture:** In a separate bowl, whisk together almond milk and whole wheat flour until smooth. Gradually stir this mixture into the soup. Cook for 2–3 minutes to thicken.
4. **Blend the soup:** Use an immersion blender to partially or fully blend the soup, depending on your desired consistency.
5. **Add the cheese and yogurt:** Stir in shredded cheddar cheese until melted, followed by the Greek yogurt for added creaminess.
6. **Serve:** Taste and adjust seasoning. Garnish with fresh parsley, additional cheddar, or smoked paprika if desired. Serve hot, optionally paired with a small side salad or whole-grain bread.

Nutritional Information (Per Serving)
Calories: 220, Protein: 11g, Carbohydrates: 12g, Fats: 12g, Fiber: 4g, Cholesterol: 20mg, Sodium: 320mg, Potassium: 450mg

Chicken and Kale Soup

 Yield: 6 servings   Preparation Time: 30 minutes
 Cooking Time: 15 minutes

Ingredients:

- 1 tablespoon olive oil (GI: 0)
- 1 medium onion, diced (GI: 10)
- 3 cloves garlic, minced (GI: 10)
- 2 medium carrots, diced (GI: 39)
- 2 celery stalks, diced (GI: 15)
- 1 medium zucchini, diced (GI: 15)
- 1 pound boneless, skinless chicken breast cut into bite-sized pieces (GI: 0)
- 6 cups low-sodium chicken broth (GI: 0)
- 4 cups chopped kale, stems removed (GI: 3)
- 1 teaspoon dried thyme (GI: 5)
- 1 teaspoon dried oregano (GI: 5)
- 1 teaspoon paprika (GI: 5)
- 1 bay leaf (GI: 0)
- 1/2 teaspoon black pepper (GI: 0)
- 1/2 teaspoon salt (optional) (GI: 0)
- 1/2 cup quinoa, rinsed (GI: 53)

Optional Ingredients for Additional Flavor and Nutrition:

- 1/4 teaspoon red pepper flakes (GI: 0)
- 1/4 cup chopped fresh parsley (GI: 5)
- Juice of 1 lemon (GI: 0)

Instructions:

1. **Sauté the aromatics:** Heat olive oil in a large pot over medium heat. Sauté the diced onion and minced garlic until fragrant, about 3 minutes.
2. **Cook the vegetables:** Add diced carrots, celery, and zucchini. Stir well and cook for 5 minutes.
3. **Cook the chicken:** Add the chicken pieces to the pot and cook for 5–7 minutes until lightly browned.
4. **Make the soup:** Pour in the chicken broth and add quinoa, thyme, oregano, paprika, bay leaf, black pepper, and salt. Bring the mixture to a boil, then reduce heat to low and simmer for 20 minutes.
5. **Add kale and finish:** Stir in the chopped kale and let it wilt for 3–5 minutes. Add red pepper flakes, parsley, and lemon juice. Taste and adjust seasoning as needed.
6. **Serve:** Remove the bay leaf before serving. Serve hot with a garnish of fresh parsley. Optionally, pair it with a slice of whole-grain bread or a side salad.

Nutritional Information (Per Serving)

Calories: 220, Protein: 22g, Carbohydrates: 18g, Fats: 7g, Fiber: 4g, Cholesterol: 45mg, Sodium: 300mg, Potassium: 650mg

Tomato Basil Soup

 Yield: 6 servings   Preparation Time: 10 minutes
 Cooking Time: 35 minutes

Ingredients:

- 1 tablespoon olive oil (GI: 0)
- 1 medium onion, diced (GI: 10)
- 3 cloves garlic, minced (GI: 10)
- 1 medium carrot, diced (GI: 39)
- 1 celery stalk, diced (GI: 15)
- 2 cans (28 oz each) whole peeled tomatoes, no added salt (GI: 15)
- 4 cups low-sodium vegetable broth (GI: 15)
- 1 cup fresh basil leaves, chopped (GI: 5)
- 1 teaspoon dried oregano (GI: 5)
- 1 teaspoon dried thyme (GI: 5)
- 1 teaspoon black pepper (GI: 0)
- 1/2 teaspoon salt (optional) (GI: 0)

Optional Ingredients for Additional Flavor and Nutrition:

- 1/4 cup grated Parmesan cheese (GI: 0)
- 1 tablespoon balsamic vinegar (GI: 0)
- 1/4 cup chopped fresh parsley (GI: 5)

Instructions:

1. **Sauté Aromatics:** Heat olive oil over medium heat. Sauté onion and garlic for 2–3 minutes until fragrant.
2. **Cook Vegetables:** Add carrot and celery. Cook for 5 minutes, stirring occasionally.
3. **Add Base Ingredients:** Stir in whole peeled tomatoes with their juice and vegetable broth.
4. **Simmer:** Reduce heat, cover, and simmer for 20 minutes until vegetables are tender.
5. **Blend Soup:** Puree the soup with an immersion blender or in batches using a blender, then return to the pot.
6. **Add Herbs and Seasoning:** Stir in basil, oregano, thyme, black pepper, and salt. Mix well.
7. **Add Creaminess:** Stir in Greek yogurt for creaminess. Cook for 2–3 minutes.
8. **Adjust Flavor:** Taste and adjust seasoning. Add optional smoked paprika or balsamic vinegar if desired.
9. **Serve Hot:** Garnish with fresh basil or a drizzle of olive oil. Pair with a side salad or whole-grain bread (optional, ensure diabetic-friendly).

Nutritional Information (Per Serving)

Calories: 120, Protein: 4g, Carbohydrates: 16g, Fats: 5g, Fiber: 4g, Cholesterol: 0mg, Sodium: 320mg, Potassium: 700mg

Spicy Lentil Stew

 Yield: 6 servings *Preparation Time: 15 minutes*

 Cooking Time: 40 minutes

Ingredients:
- 1 tablespoon olive oil (GI: 0)
- 1 medium onion, diced (GI: 10)
- 3 cloves garlic, minced (GI: 10)
- 2 medium carrots, diced (GI: 39)
- 2 celery stalks, diced (GI: 15)
- 1 red bell pepper, diced (GI: 15)
- 1 cup dried lentils, rinsed (GI: 32)
- 1 can (14.5 oz) diced tomatoes, no salt added (GI: 15)
- 4 cups low-sodium vegetable broth (GI: 15)
- 2 cups water (GI: 0)
- 1 tablespoon tomato paste (GI: 15)
- 1 teaspoon ground cumin (GI: 5)
- 1 teaspoon ground coriander (GI: 5)
- 1 teaspoon smoked paprika (GI: 5)
- 1/2 teaspoon turmeric (GI: 5)
- 1/2 teaspoon ground black pepper (GI: 0)
- 1/2 teaspoon salt (optional) (GI: 0)
- 1/4 teaspoon cayenne pepper (optional, adjust to taste) (GI: 0)
- 3 cups fresh spinach, roughly chopped (GI: 15)
- 1/4 cup chopped fresh cilantro (GI: 5)
- Juice of 1 lemon (GI: 0)

Optional Ingredients for Additional Flavor and Nutrition:
- 1/4 teaspoon red pepper flakes (GI: 0)
- 1 teaspoon grated fresh ginger (GI: 10)
- 1 cup diced zucchini (GI: 15)

Instructions:
1. **Sauté Aromatics:** Heat olive oil over medium heat. Cook onion and garlic for 2–3 minutes until fragrant.
2. **Cook Vegetables:** Add carrots, celery, red bell pepper, ginger, and zucchini. Cook for 5 minutes, stirring occasionally.
3. **Add Spices and Lentils:** Stir in lentils, cumin, coriander, smoked paprika, turmeric, black pepper, salt, and cayenne. Mix well.
4. **Add Liquids and Tomatoes:** Add tomato paste, water, broth, and tomatoes. Bring to a boil.
5. **Simmer:** Reduce heat, cover, and simmer for 25–30 minutes, stirring occasionally, until lentils are tender.
6. **Add Greens and Citrus:** Stir in spinach, lemon juice, and cilantro. Cook for 2–3 minutes until spinach wilts.
7. **Adjust Seasoning:** Taste and adjust as needed.
8. **Serve Hot:** Garnish with extra fresh cilantro and a lemon wedge. Pair with a small side salad or a slice of whole-grain bread (optional, ensure diabetic-friendly).

Nutritional Information (Per Serving)
Calories: 180, Protein: 10g, Carbohydrates: 28g, Fats: 4g, Fiber: 10g, Cholesterol: 0mg, Sodium: 300mg, Potassium: 600mg

Minestrone Soup

 Yield: 6 servings *Preparation Time: 15 minutes*

Cooking Time: 40 minutes

Ingredients:
- 1 tablespoon olive oil (GI: 0)
- 1 medium onion, diced (GI: 10)
- 3 cloves garlic, minced (GI: 10)
- 2 medium carrots, diced (GI: 39)
- 2 celery stalks, diced (GI: 15)
- 1 medium zucchini, diced (GI: 15)
- 1 red bell pepper, diced (GI: 15)
- 1 cup green beans, trimmed and cut into 1-inch pieces (GI: 15)
- 1 can (14.5 oz) diced tomatoes, no salt added (GI: 15)
- 4 cups low-sodium vegetable broth (GI: 15)
- 1 cup water (GI: 0)
- 1 can (15 oz) kidney beans, rinsed and drained (GI: 29)
- 1 teaspoon dried oregano (GI: 5)
- 1 teaspoon dried basil (GI: 5)
- 1 teaspoon dried thyme (GI: 5)
- 1/2 teaspoon black pepper (GI: 0)
- 1/2 teaspoon salt (optional) (GI: 0)
- 1/2 cup whole-grain pasta, such as rotini or penne (GI: 45)
- 2 cups fresh spinach, roughly chopped (GI: 15)
- 1/4 cup chopped fresh parsley (GI: 5)
- Juice of 1 lemon (GI: 0)

Optional Ingredients for Additional Flavor and Nutrition:
- 1/4 teaspoon red pepper flakes (GI: 0)
- 1 teaspoon grated Parmesan cheese per serving (GI: 0)

Instructions:
1. **Sauté Aromatics:** Heat olive oil over medium heat. Sauté onion and garlic for 2–3 minutes until softened.
2. **Cook Vegetables:** Add carrots, celery, zucchini, red bell pepper, and green beans. Cook for 5–7 minutes until slightly softened.
3. **Add Liquids and Seasonings:** Stir in diced tomatoes, vegetable broth, and water. Add oregano, basil, thyme, black pepper, and salt. Bring to a boil.
4. **Cook Pasta and Beans:** Add kidney beans and whole-grain pasta. Reduce heat and simmer for 12–15 minutes, until pasta is al dente.
5. **Add Greens:** Stir in spinach, parsley, and lemon juice. Cook for 2–3 minutes until spinach wilts.
6. **Serve Hot:** Adjust seasoning as needed. Garnish with Parmesan (if using). Pair with a side salad or whole-grain bread.

Nutritional Information (Per Serving)
Calories: 180, Protein: 7g, Carbohydrates: 29g, Fats: 4g, Fiber: 5g, Cholesterol: 0mg, Sodium: 320mg, Potassium: 600mg

Butternut Squash Soup

 Yield: 6 servings   Preparation Time: 15 minutes

 Cooking Time: 35 minutes

Ingredients:

- 1 tablespoon olive oil (GI: 0)
- 1 medium onion, diced (GI: 10)
- 3 cloves garlic, minced (GI: 10)
- 1 medium carrot, diced (GI: 39)
- 1 medium butternut squash, peeled, seeded, and cubed (about 4 cups) (GI: 51)
- 4 cups low-sodium vegetable broth (GI: 15)
- 1 cup water (GI: 0)
- 1 teaspoon ground cumin (GI: 5)
- 1 teaspoon ground cinnamon (GI: 5)
- 1/2 teaspoon ground nutmeg (GI: 5)
- 1/2 teaspoon ground black pepper (GI: 0)
- 1/2 teaspoon salt (optional) (GI: 0)
- 1/4 cup plain Greek yogurt (GI: 0)
- 2 tablespoons chopped fresh parsley (GI: 5)

Optional Ingredients for Additional Flavor and Nutrition:

- 1/4 teaspoon red pepper flakes (GI: 0)
- 1 tablespoon grated fresh ginger (GI: 10)
- 1/4 cup chopped fresh cilantro (GI: 5)

Instructions:

1. **Sauté Aromatics:** Heat olive oil over medium heat. Sauté onion and garlic for 2–3 minutes until fragrant.
2. **Cook Vegetables:** Add carrot and butternut squash. Stir and cook for 5–7 minutes.
3. **Add Liquids and Spices:** Pour in vegetable broth and water. Stir in cumin, cinnamon, nutmeg, black pepper, and salt. Bring to a boil.
4. **Simmer Soup:** Reduce heat, cover, and simmer for 20–25 minutes until squash and carrots are tender.
5. **Blend Soup:** Cool slightly, then puree with an immersion blender or in batches using a blender until smooth.
6. **Add Creaminess:** Stir in Greek yogurt and mix well.
7. **Serve Hot:** Adjust seasoning as needed. Garnish with parsley or cilantro. Pair with a side salad or whole-grain bread (optional, diabetic-friendly).

Nutritional Information (Per Serving)

Calories: 110, Protein: 3g, Carbohydrates: 20g, Fats: 3g, Fiber: 4g, Cholesterol: 0mg, Sodium: 200mg, Potassium: 600mg

Beef and Vegetable Stew

 Yield: 6 servings   Preparation Time: 15 minutes

 Cooking Time: 40 minutes

Ingredients:

- 1 tablespoon olive oil (GI: 0)
- 1 pound lean beef stew meat, cut into 1-inch cubes (GI: 0)
- 1 medium onion, diced (GI: 10)
- 3 cloves garlic, minced (GI: 10)
- 2 medium carrots, sliced (GI: 39)
- 2 celery stalks, sliced (GI: 15)
- 1 medium turnip, peeled and diced (GI: 72)
- 1 cup green beans, trimmed and cut into 1-inch pieces (GI: 15)
- 1 cup diced tomatoes, no salt added (GI: 15)
- 4 cups low-sodium beef broth (GI: 0)
- 1 cup water (GI: 0)
- 1 teaspoon dried thyme (GI: 5)
- 1 teaspoon dried rosemary (GI: 5)
- 1 bay leaf (GI: 0)
- 1/2 teaspoon black pepper (GI: 0)
- 1/2 teaspoon salt (optional) (GI: 0)
- 1/4 teaspoon red pepper flakes (optional) (GI: 0)
- 1 cup baby spinach, roughly chopped (GI: 15)
- 1/4 cup chopped fresh parsley (GI: 5)

Optional Ingredients for Additional Flavor and Nutrition:

- 1/4 teaspoon smoked paprika (GI: 5)
- 1 tablespoon balsamic vinegar (GI: 0)
- 1 cup sliced mushrooms (GI: 15)

Instructions:

1. **Brown the Beef:** Heat olive oil in a large pot over medium-high heat. Brown beef cubes on all sides for 5–7 minutes. Remove and set aside.
2. **Sauté Aromatics:** Add onion and garlic to the pot. Sauté for 2–3 minutes until fragrant.
3. **Cook Vegetables:** Stir in carrots, celery, turnip, and green beans. Cook for 5 minutes until slightly softened.
4. **Make the Stew:** Return beef to the pot. Add diced tomatoes, beef broth, water, thyme, rosemary, bay leaf, black pepper, and salt. Bring to a boil, reduce heat, and simmer for 1 hour.
5. **Add Greens and Finish:** Stir in spinach and parsley. Let wilt for 3–5 minutes, then stir in balsamic vinegar.
6. **Serve:** Taste and adjust seasoning. Remove the bay leaf before serving. Serve hot, optionally paired with a side salad.

Nutritional Information (Per Serving)

Calories: 240, Protein: 25g, Carbohydrates: 18g, Fats: 9g, Fiber: 4g, Cholesterol: 60mg, Sodium: 300mg, Potassium: 700mg

Split Pea Soup with Ham

 Yield: 6 servings  Preparation Time: 15 minutes

 Cooking Time: 1 hour 30 minutes

Ingredients:
- 1 tablespoon olive oil (GI: 0)
- 1 medium onion, diced (GI: 10)
- 3 cloves garlic, minced (GI: 10)
- 2 medium carrots, diced (GI: 39)
- 2 celery stalks, diced (GI: 15)
- 1 medium turnip, peeled and diced (GI: 72)
- 1 cup dried split peas, rinsed (GI: 32)
- 1 cup cooked ham, diced (preferably lowsodium) (GI: 0)
- 6 cups low-sodium chicken or vegetable broth (GI: 15)
- 1 bay leaf (GI: 0)
- 1 teaspoon dried thyme (GI: 5)
- 1/2 teaspoon black pepper (GI: 0)
- 1/2 teaspoon salt (optional) (GI: 0)
- 1/4 teaspoon ground cumin (optional) (GI: 5)
- 2 tablespoons chopped fresh parsley (GI: 5)

Optional Ingredients for Additional Flavor and Nutrition:
- 1/4 teaspoon red pepper flakes (GI: 0)
- 1 teaspoon smoked paprika (GI: 5)
- 1 tablespoon apple cider vinegar (GI: 0)

Instructions:
1. **Heat the oil and fry the vegetables:** Heat olive oil in a large pot over medium heat. Add onion and garlic, and sauté for 2-3 minutes until fragrant. Add diced carrots, celery, and turnip. Cook for 5 minutes, stirring occasionally.
2. **Add ham:** Add split peas and ham to the pot. Stir well to combine.
3. **Add broth:** Pour in the low-sodium broth, and add the bay leaf, thyme, black pepper, salt (if using). Stir to mix.
4. **Bring the soup** to a boil, then reduce heat to low. Cover and simmer for 1-1 ½ hours, stirring occasionally, until the split peas are tender and the soup thickens.
5. **Serve:** Taste and adjust seasoning as needed. Remove and discard the bay leaf before serving. Serve with small diabetic croutons.

Nutritional Information (Per Serving)

Calories: 220, Protein: 15g, Carbohydrates: 25g, Fats: 5g, Fiber: 8g, Cholesterol: 20mg, Sodium: 350mg, Potassium: 550mg

Moroccan Chickpea Stew

 Yield: 6 servings   Preparation Time: 15 minutes

 Cooking Time: 35 minutes

Ingredients:
- 1 tablespoon olive oil (GI: 0)
- 1 medium onion, diced (GI: 10)
- 3 cloves garlic, minced (GI: 10)
- 2 medium carrots, diced (GI: 39)
- 2 celery stalks, diced (GI: 15)
- 1 red bell pepper, diced (GI: 15)
- 1 can (14.5 oz) diced tomatoes, no salt added (GI: 15)
- 1 can (15 oz) chickpeas, drained and rinsed (GI: 28)
- 4 cups low-sodium vegetable broth (GI: 15)
- 1 cup water (GI: 0)
- 2 tablespoons tomato paste (GI: 15)
- 1 teaspoon ground cumin, coriander, cinnamon (each) (GI: 5)
- 1/2 teaspoon ground turmeric (GI: 5)
- 1/2 teaspoon ground black pepper (GI: 0)
- 1/2 teaspoon salt (optional) (GI: 0)
- 1/4 teaspoon cayenne pepper (optional) (GI: 0)
- 1 medium zucchini, diced (GI: 15)
- 1 cup baby spinach, roughly chopped (GI: 15)
- 1/4 cup chopped fresh cilantro (GI: 5)
- Juice of 1 lemon (GI: 0)

Optional Ingredients for Additional Flavor and Nutrition:
- 1/4 cup raisins (GI: 64)
- 1/4 cup sliced almonds (GI: 0)

Instructions:
1. **Sauté Vegetables:** Heat olive oil in a large pot over medium heat. Sauté onion and garlic for 2-3 minutes until softened. Add carrots, celery, and bell pepper, and cook for 5 minutes, stirring occasionally.
2. **Add Tomato and Spices:** Stir in diced tomatoes, chickpeas, tomato paste, cumin, coriander, cinnamon, turmeric, black pepper, and cayenne. Mix well.
3. **Add Broth and Simmer:** Pour in vegetable broth and water. Bring to a boil, reduce heat to low, cover, and simmer for 20-25 minutes.
4. **Add Zucchini and Spinach:** Stir in zucchini and spinach. Cook for 5-7 minutes until zucchini is tender and spinach wilts.
5. **Add Dressing:** Stir in lemon juice and cilantro. Adjust seasoning as needed.
6. **Serve:** Serve hot, garnished with extra cilantro if desired.

Nutritional Information (Per Serving)

Calories: 180, Protein: 7g, Carbohydrates: 28g, Fats: 4g, Fiber: 8g, Cholesterol: 0mg, Sodium: 320mg, Potassium: 550mg

4. Vegetarian and Vegan Options

Roasted Veggie and Quinoa Bowl

Yield: 4 servings *Preparation Time: 15 minutes*
Cooking Time: 40 minutes

Ingredients:
- 1 cup quinoa, rinsed (GI: 53)
- 2 cups low-sodium vegetable broth (GI: 15)
- 1 medium sweet potato, diced (GI: 44)
- 1 medium zucchini, diced (GI: 15)
- 1 red bell pepper, diced (GI: 15)
- 1 yellow bell pepper, diced (GI: 15)
- 1 small red onion, diced (GI: 10)
- 1 cup broccoli florets (GI: 15)
- 2 tablespoons olive oil (GI: 0)
- 1 teaspoon dried oregano, thyme, cumin (each) (GI: 5)
- 1/2 teaspoon black pepper (GI: 0)
- 1/2 teaspoon salt (optional) (GI: 0)
- 1 can (15 oz) chickpeas, drained and rinsed (GI: 28)
- 1/4 cup chopped fresh parsley (GI: 5)
- Juice of 1 lemon (GI: 0)
- 1/4 cup crumbled feta cheese (optional) (GI: 0)

Optional Ingredients for Additional Flavor and Nutrition:
- 1/4 teaspoon red pepper flakes (GI: 0)
- 1 tablespoon tahini (GI: 0)
- 1 tablespoon balsamic vinegar (GI: 0)

Instructions:
1. **Preheat Oven:** Preheat to 400°F (200°C) and line a baking sheet with parchment paper.
2. **Cook Quinoa:** Bring vegetable broth to a boil. Add rinsed quinoa, reduce heat, cover, and simmer for 15 minutes. Fluff with a fork and set aside.
3. **Roast Sweet Potatoes:** Place diced sweet potato on the baking sheet and roast for 10 minutes.
4. **Add Vegetables:** Add zucchini, bell peppers, red onion, and broccoli to the sheet. Drizzle with olive oil, sprinkle with oregano, thyme, cumin, black pepper, and salt. Toss to coat.
5. **Finish Roasting:** Roast vegetables for 20–25 minutes, stirring halfway through, until tender and caramelized.
6. **Optional Chickpeas:** Roast chickpeas separately for 10–15 minutes at 400°F (200°C) for extra texture.
7. **Combine Ingredients:** In a large bowl, mix cooked quinoa, roasted vegetables, chickpeas, parsley, lemon juice, tahini, and balsamic vinegar.
8. **Serve:** Divide into four bowls and top with optional feta cheese or other garnishes. Serve warm.

Nutritional Information (Per Serving)
Calories: 320, Protein: 10g, Carbohydrates: 48g, Fats: 10g, Fiber: 10g, Cholesterol: 5mg, Sodium: 300mg, Potassium: 700mg

Vegan Lentil Tacos

Yield: 6 servings *Preparation Time: 15 minutes*
Cooking Time: 30 minutes

Ingredients:
- 1 tablespoon olive oil (GI: 0)
- 1 medium onion, diced (GI: 10)
- 3 cloves garlic, minced (GI: 10)
- 1 cup dried green or brown lentils, rinsed (GI: 32)
- 2 cups low-sodium vegetable broth (GI: 15)
- 1 cup water (GI: 0)
- 1 teaspoon ground cumin (GI: 5)
- 1 teaspoon ground coriander (GI: 5)
- 1 teaspoon smoked paprika (GI: 5)
- 1/2 teaspoon chili powder (GI: 5)
- 1/2 teaspoon black pepper (GI: 0)
- 1/2 teaspoon salt (optional) (GI: 0)
- 1/4 teaspoon cayenne pepper (optional) (GI: 0)
- 1 cup diced tomatoes, no salt added (GI: 15)
- 1/4 cup chopped fresh cilantro (GI: 5)
- Juice of 1 lime (GI: 0)
- 12 small whole-grain tortillas (GI: 45)
- 1 cup shredded lettuce (GI: 10)
- 1/2 cup diced red onion (GI: 10)
- 1 avocado, diced (GI: 15)

Optional Ingredients for Additional Flavor and Nutrition:
- 1/4 cup vegan sour cream (GI: 0)
- 1/2 cup salsa (GI: 15)
- 1/4 cup chopped fresh jalapeños (GI: 15)

Instructions:
1. **Sauté Aromatics:** Heat olive oil in a skillet over medium heat. Sauté onion and garlic for 2–3 minutes until softened.
2. **Add Broth and Spices:** Add lentils, vegetable broth, and water. Stir in cumin, coriander, smoked paprika, chili powder, black pepper, salt (if using), and cayenne. Mix well.
3. **Simmer Lentils:** Bring to a boil, reduce heat, cover, and simmer for 20–25 minutes, stirring occasionally, until lentils are tender and liquid is absorbed.
4. **Add Tomatoes:** Stir in diced tomatoes and cook for 3–5 minutes. Remove from heat, mix in cilantro and lime juice, and adjust seasoning as needed.
5. **Warm Tortillas:** Heat whole-grain tortillas in a dry skillet for 30–60 seconds per side.
6. **Assemble tacos** by dividing the lentil mixture among tortillas. Top with shredded lettuce, chopped red onion, avocado, vegan sour cream, salsa, and jalapeños as desired. Serve immediately.

Nutritional Information (Per Serving)
Calories: 320, Protein: 12g, Carbohydrates: 50g, Fats: 9g, Fiber: 15g, Cholesterol: 0mg, Sodium: 300mg, Potassium: 700mg

Stuffed Bell Peppers with Black Beans and Corn

 Yield: 6 servings   Preparation Time: 20 minutes

Cooking Time: 35 minutes

Ingredients:
- 6 large bell peppers, any color (GI: 15)
- 1 tablespoon olive oil (GI: 0)
- 1 medium onion, diced (GI: 10)
- 3 cloves garlic, minced (GI: 10)
- 1 cup cooked quinoa (GI: 53)
- 1 can (15 oz) black beans, drained and rinsed (GI: 28)
- 1 cup corn kernels, fresh or frozen (GI: 55)
- 1 can (14.5 oz) diced tomatoes, no salt added (GI: 15)
- 1 teaspoon ground cumin (GI: 5)
- 1 teaspoon smoked paprika (GI: 5)
- 1/2 teaspoon chili powder (GI: 5)
- 1/2 teaspoon black pepper (GI: 0)
- 1/2 teaspoon salt (optional) (GI: 0)
- 1/4 cup chopped fresh cilantro (GI: 5)
- Juice of 1 lime (GI: 0)

Optional Ingredients for Additional Flavor and Nutrition:
- 1/4 cup shredded low-fat cheese (GI: 0)
- 1/4 cup chopped fresh jalapeños (GI: 15)
- 1/4 cup salsa (GI: 15)
- 1 avocado, diced (GI: 15)

Instructions:
1. **Preheat the skillet:** Preheat oven to 375°F (190°C).
2. **Prepare the peppers:** Slice the tops off the bell peppers and remove seeds and membranes. Arrange the peppers upright in a baking dish.
3. **Toast the aromatics:** Heat olive oil in a skillet over medium heat. Add diced onion and garlic, and sauté for 2-3 minutes until fragrant.
4. **Prepare the quinoa:** Cook the quinoa according to package directions.
5. **Mix the ingredients:** In a large bowl, combine cooked quinoa, black beans, corn, diced tomatoes, cumin, smoked paprika, chili powder, black pepper, and salt (if using). Stir well.
6. **Add the herbs and lemon:** Add fresh cilantro and lime juice to the mixture. Spoon the filling into the prepared bell peppers.
7. **Bake:** Cover the baking dish with foil and bake for 25 minutes. Remove the foil, sprinkle with shredded low-fat cheese (if using), and bake for an additional 10 minutes.
8. **Garnish and Serve:** Garnish with optional toppings like jalapeños, salsa, or avocado. Serve hot.

Nutritional Information (Per Serving)

Calories: 220, Protein: 7g, Carbohydrates: 35g, Fats: 5g, Fiber: 10g, Cholesterol: 0mg, Sodium: 320mg, Potassium: 600mg

Chickpea and Spinach Curry

 Yield: 4 servings Preparation Time: 15 minutes

Cooking Time: 25 minutes

Ingredients:
- 1 tablespoon olive oil (GI: 0)
- 1 medium onion, diced (GI: 10)
- 3 cloves garlic, minced (GI: 10)
- 1 tablespoon fresh ginger, grated (GI: 10)
- 1 can (15 oz) chickpeas, drained and rinsed (GI: 28)
- 1 can (14.5 oz) diced tomatoes, no salt added (GI: 15)
- 1 can (13.5 oz) light coconut milk (GI: 41)
- 4 cups fresh spinach, roughly chopped (GI: 15)
- 1 tablespoon curry powder (GI: 5)
- 1 teaspoon ground cumin (GI: 5)
- 1 teaspoon ground coriander (GI: 5)
- 1/2 teaspoon turmeric (GI: 5)
- 1/2 teaspoon ground black pepper (GI: 0)
- 1/2 teaspoon salt (optional) (GI: 0)
- 1/4 teaspoon cayenne pepper (optional) (GI: 0)
- Juice of 1 lemon (GI: 0)
- 1/4 cup chopped fresh cilantro (GI: 5)

Optional Ingredients for Additional Flavor and Nutrition:
- 1/2 cup diced bell peppers (GI: 15)
- 1/2 cup diced carrots (GI: 39)

Instructions:
1. **Toast the aromatics:** Heat olive oil in a large skillet over medium heat. Add diced onion, garlic, and grated ginger, and sauté for 2-3 minutes until fragrant.
2. **Add spices:** Stir in curry powder, cumin, coriander, turmeric, black pepper, salt (if using), and cayenne. Cook for 1-2 minutes until the spices are aromatic.
3. **Add vegetables:** Add chickpeas, diced tomatoes, and light coconut milk to the skillet. Stir well and bring to a simmer.
4. **Cook with spinach:** Reduce heat to low and cook for 10-15 minutes, stirring occasionally. Add spinach and cook for 2-3 minutes until wilted. Stir in lemon juice and fresh cilantro.
5. **Taste** and adjust seasoning as needed.
6. **Serve:** Serve this chickpea and spinach curry hot over a bed of quinoa or brown rice (optional, to ensure it's suitable for diabetic diets). Garnish with additional fresh cilantro and a wedge of lemon, if desired.

Nutritional Information (Per Serving)

Calories: 250, Protein: 8g, Carbohydrates: 29g, Fats: 12g, Fiber: 9g, Cholesterol: 0mg, Sodium: 350mg, Potassium: 600mg

Zucchini Noodles with Pesto and Cherry Tomatoes

 Yield: 4 servings   *Preparation Time: 15 minutes*
 Cooking Time: 10 minutes

Ingredients:
- 4 medium zucchinis, spiralized into noodles (GI: 15)
- 1 cup cherry tomatoes, halved (GI: 15)
- 1 tablespoon olive oil (GI: 0)
- 2 cloves garlic, minced (GI: 10)
- 1/4 cup grated Parmesan cheese (optional) (GI: 0)
- 1/4 cup pine nuts, toasted (optional) (GI: 15)
- 1/4 cup fresh basil leaves for garnish (GI: 5)

For the Pesto:
- 2 cups fresh basil leaves (GI: 5)
- 1/4 cup pine nuts (GI: 15)
- 1/4 cup grated Parmesan cheese (GI: 0)
- 2 cloves garlic (GI: 10)
- 1/4 cup olive oil (GI: 0)
- 1 tablespoon lemon juice (GI: 0)
- 1/4 teaspoon salt (optional) (GI: 0)
- 1/4 teaspoon black pepper (GI: 0)

Optional Ingredients for Additional Flavor and Nutrition:
- 1/4 cup sun-dried tomatoes, chopped (GI: 35)
- 1/4 cup feta cheese, crumbled (GI: 0)
- 1 tablespoon nutritional yeast (GI: 0)

Instructions:
1. **Prepare the pesto:** In a food processor, combine basil leaves, pine nuts, Parmesan cheese (if using), garlic, olive oil, lemon juice, salt, and black pepper. Blend until smooth.
2. **Prepare the noodles:** Spiralize zucchinis into noodles. Place the noodles on paper towels to absorb excess moisture for 5–10 minutes.
3. **Heat the oil and fry the vegetables:** Heat olive oil in a large skillet over medium heat. Add minced garlic and cook for 1 minute until fragrant. Add zucchini noodles to the skillet and cook for 2–3 minutes until slightly softened but still firm. Stir in halved cherry tomatoes and cook for 1–2 minutes until slightly tender.
4. **Finish cooking:** Remove skillet from heat and toss noodles with prepared pesto. Mix in gratified Parmesan and toasted pine nuts (if using).
5. **Serve:** Serve warm, garnished with fresh basil leaves and optional toppings like sun-dried tomatoes or nutritional yeast.

Nutritional Information (Per Serving)
Calories: 200, Protein: 5g, Carbohydrates: 9g, Fats: 17g, Fiber: 3g, Cholesterol: 5mg, Sodium: 150mg, Potassium: 500mg

Sweet Potato and Black Bean Salad

 Yield: 4 servings   *Preparation Time: 15 minutes*
 Cooking Time: 25 minutes

Ingredients:
- 2 medium sweet potatoes, peeled and cubed (GI: 44)
- 1 tablespoon olive oil (GI: 0)
- 1 teaspoon ground cumin (GI: 5)
- 1/2 teaspoon smoked paprika (GI: 5)
- 1/2 teaspoon black pepper (GI: 0)
- 1/2 teaspoon salt (optional) (GI: 0)
- 1 can (15 oz) black beans, drained and rinsed (GI: 28)
- 1 red bell pepper, diced (GI: 15)
- 1 yellow bell pepper, diced (GI: 15)
- 1 small red onion, diced (GI: 10)
- 1 avocado, diced (GI: 15)
- 1/4 cup chopped fresh cilantro (GI: 5)
- Juice of 2 limes (GI: 0)
- 1 tablespoon balsamic vinegar (GI: 0)
- 1 teaspoon honey or agave nectar (optional) (GI: 19-54)

Optional Ingredients for Additional Flavor and Nutrition:
- 1/2 cup crumbled feta cheese (GI: 0)
- 1/4 cup toasted pumpkin seeds (GI: 10)
- 1/4 teaspoon red pepper flakes (GI: 0)

Instructions:
1. **Roast Sweet Potatoes:** Preheat oven to 400°F (200°C). Toss cubed sweet potatoes with olive oil, cumin, smoked paprika, black pepper, and salt (if using). Spread evenly on a baking sheet and roast for 20–25 minutes, turning halfway through, until tender and lightly browned.
2. **Prepare Salad Base:** In a large bowl, combine black beans, diced red bell pepper, yellow bell pepper, and red onion.
3. **Prepare Dressing:** Whisk together olive oil, lime juice, and any optional seasonings (e.g., red pepper flakes) in a small bowl.
4. **Combine Ingredients:** Add roasted sweet potatoes to the salad base. Toss with the prepared dressing until evenly coated.
5. **Add Fresh Herbs and Optional Ingredients:** Fold in diced avocado and chopped fresh cilantro. Gently mix to avoid mashing the avocado.

Nutritional Information (Per Serving)
Calories: 280, Protein: 7g, Carbohydrates: 45g, Fats: 10g, Fiber: 12g, Cholesterol: 0mg, Sodium: 320mg, Potassium: 900mg

Vegan Cauliflower Buffalo Wings

 Yield: 4 servings   Preparation Time: 15 minutes
 Cooking Time: 30 minutes

Ingredients:
- 1 large head of cauliflower, cut into bite-sized florets (GI: 15)
- 1 cup chickpea flour (GI: 35)
- 1 cup water (GI: 0)
- 1 teaspoon garlic powder (GI: 5)
- 1 teaspoon onion powder (GI: 5)
- 1 teaspoon smoked paprika (GI: 5)
- 1/2 teaspoon black pepper (GI: 0)
- 1/2 teaspoon salt (optional) (GI: 0)
- 1 cup hot sauce (GI: 0)
- 2 tablespoons olive oil (GI: 0)

Optional Ingredients for Additional Flavor and Nutrition:
- 1 teaspoon nutritional yeast (GI: 0)
- 1/4 teaspoon red pepper flakes (GI: 0)
- 1/4 cup chopped fresh parsley (GI: 5)

Instructions:
1. **Preheat Oven:** Preheat oven to 400°F (200°C) and line a baking sheet with parchment paper.
2. **Prepare Batter:** In a large bowl, whisk together chickpea flour, water, garlic powder, onion powder, smoked paprika, black pepper, and salt until smooth.
3. **Coat Cauliflower:** Dip each cauliflower floret into the batter, ensuring it is fully coated. Shake off any excess batter and place on the prepared baking sheet.
4. **Bake:** Bake for 20 minutes, flipping the florets halfway through for even cooking.
5. **Prepare Buffalo Sauce:** In a small bowl, whisk together hot sauce and olive oil.
6. **Coat with Sauce:** Remove cauliflower from the oven and toss in the buffalo sauce until evenly coated. Return to the baking sheet.
7. **Finish Baking:** Bake for an additional 10 minutes until cauliflower is crispy and lightly browned.
8. **Serve:** Garnish with parsley (if using) and serve hot with celery sticks and a healthy dip like hummus or dairy-free ranch dressing.

Nutritional Information (Per Serving)

Calories: 180, Protein: 6g, Carbohydrates: 18g, Fats: 10g, Fiber: 6g, Cholesterol: 0mg, Sodium: 960mg, Potassium: 400mg

Tofu and Veggie Stir-Fry

 Yield: 4 servings   Preparation Time: 15 minutes
 Cooking Time: 20 minutes

Ingredients:
- 1 block (14 oz) firm tofu, pressed and cubed (GI: 15)
- 2 tablespoons soy sauce (low sodium) (GI: 15)
- 1 tablespoon rice vinegar (GI: 0)
- 1 tablespoon sesame oil (GI: 0)
- 1 tablespoon olive oil (GI: 0)
- 1 medium onion, sliced (GI: 10)
- 3 cloves garlic, minced (GI: 10)
- 1 tablespoon fresh ginger, grated (GI: 10)
- 1 red bell pepper, sliced (GI: 15)
- 1 yellow bell pepper, sliced (GI: 15)
- 1 medium zucchini, sliced (GI: 15)
- 1 cup broccoli florets (GI: 15)
- 1 cup snow peas (GI: 15)
- 1 carrot, julienned (GI: 39)
- 2 tablespoons low-sodium vegetable broth (GI: 15)
- 1 tablespoon cornstarch (optional for thickening) (GI: 85)
- 1/4 teaspoon black pepper (GI: 0)
- 1/4 cup chopped fresh cilantro (GI: 5)
- 1/4 cup chopped green onions (GI: 15)
- Juice of 1 lime (GI: 0)
- 1 tablespoon sesame seeds (optional) (GI: 15)

Optional Ingredients for Additional Flavor and Nutrition:
- 1/4 teaspoon red pepper flakes (GI: 0)
- 1 tablespoon hoisin sauce (GI: 20)

Instructions:
1. **Marinate Tofu:** Press tofu to remove excess water and cut into cubes. Marinate with soy sauce and rice vinegar for 5–10 minutes.
2. **Cook Tofu:** Heat olive oil in a non-stick skillet over medium heat. Add tofu and cook until golden brown on all sides, about 5–7 minutes. Remove and set aside.
3. **Sauté Aromatics:** In the same skillet, heat sesame oil. Add onion, garlic, and ginger, and sauté for 2–3 minutes until fragrant.
4. **Stir-Fry Vegetables:** Add bell peppers, zucchini, broccoli, snow peas, and carrot. Cook for 5–7 minutes, stirring frequently, until vegetables are tender but still crisp.
5. **Add Sauce:** Mix remaining soy sauce, vegetable broth, and cornstarch in a small bowl. Pour over tofu and vegetables, stirring well. Cook for 2–3 minutes until the sauce thickens slightly.
6. **Season and Garnish:** Add black pepper, cilantro, green onions, lime juice, and sesame seeds. Stir in red pepper flakes or hoisin sauce, if desired.

Nutritional Information (Per Serving)

Calories: 200, Protein: 12g, Carbohydrates: 18g, Fats: 11g, Fiber: 5g, Cholesterol: 0mg, Sodium: 380mg, Potassium: 600mg

Mushroom and Barley Pilaf

Yield: 4 servings   *Preparation Time: 15 minutes*
Cooking Time: 40 minutes

Ingredients:
- 1 tablespoon olive oil (GI: 0)
- 1 medium onion, diced (GI: 10)
- 3 cloves garlic, minced (GI: 10)
- 2 cups mushrooms, sliced (such as cremini or button) (GI: 15)
- 1 cup pearl barley, rinsed (GI: 25)
- 3 cups low-sodium vegetable broth (GI: 15)
- 1 teaspoon dried thyme (GI: 5)
- 1 teaspoon dried oregano (GI: 5)
- 1/2 teaspoon black pepper (GI: 0)
- 1/2 teaspoon salt (optional) (GI: 0)
- 1 cup spinach, roughly chopped (GI: 15)
- 1/4 cup chopped fresh parsley (GI: 5)
- Juice of 1 lemon (GI: 0)

Optional Ingredients for Additional Flavor and Nutrition:
- 1/4 cup grated Parmesan cheese (GI: 0)
- 1/4 cup toasted pine nuts (GI: 15)
- 1/4 teaspoon red pepper flakes (GI: 0)

Instructions:
1. **Heat the oil:** Heat olive oil in a large skillet over medium heat. Add diced onion and sauté for 2–3 minutes until softened.
2. **Sauté aromatics:** Add minced garlic and cook for 1 minute until fragrant.
3. **Add mushrooms:** Stir in mushrooms and cook for 5 minutes until they release moisture and soften.
4. **Add pearl barley:** Add pearl barley and cook for 2 minutes, stirring to coat in oil and aromatics.
5. **Add broth and spices:** Pour in the vegetable broth, thyme, oregano, black pepper, and salt (if using). Bring to a boil.
6. **Cook:** Reduce heat to low, cover, and simmer for 30–35 minutes, stirring occasionally, until the barley is tender and liquid is absorbed.
7. **Add greens:** Stir in spinach and cook for 2–3 minutes until wilted. Add parsley and lemon juice, and toss to combine.
8. **Optional:** Top with Parmesan cheese, pine nuts, or red pepper flakes before serving.
9. **Serve** hot as a main dish or side. Pair with a green salad or steamed vegetables for a balanced meal. Avoid high-carb sides like bread; opt for leafy greens instead.

Nutritional Information (Per Serving)
Calories: 180, Protein: 5g, Carbohydrates: 30g, Fats: 4g, Fiber: 6g, Cholesterol: 0mg, Sodium: 250mg, Potassium: 400mg

Eggplant and Tomato Stew

Yield: 4 servings   *Preparation Time: 15 minutes*
Cooking Time: 40 minutes

Ingredients:
- 1 tablespoon olive oil (GI: 0)
- 1 medium onion, diced (GI: 10)
- 3 cloves garlic, minced (GI: 10)
- 1 large eggplant, diced (about 4 cups) (GI: 15)
- 2 medium zucchinis, diced (GI: 15)
- 1 red bell pepper, diced (GI: 15)
- 1 yellow bell pepper, diced (GI: 15)
- 1 can (14.5 oz) diced tomatoes, no salt added (GI: 15)
- 1 cup low-sodium vegetable broth (GI: 15)
- 1 teaspoon dried oregano (GI: 5)
- 1 teaspoon dried basil (GI: 5)
- 1/2 teaspoon dried thyme (GI: 5)
- 1/2 teaspoon black pepper (GI: 0)
- 1/2 teaspoon salt (optional) (GI: 0)
- 1/4 teaspoon red pepper flakes (optional) (GI: 0)
- 2 tablespoons tomato paste (GI: 15)
- 1/4 cup chopped fresh parsley (GI: 5)
- Juice of 1 lemon (GI: 0)

Optional Ingredients for Additional Flavor and Nutrition:
- 1/2 cup cooked chickpeas (GI: 28)
- 1 teaspoon smoked paprika (GI: 5)
- 1/4 cup chopped fresh basil (GI: 5)

Instructions:
1. **Sauté aromatics:** Heat olive oil in a large pot over medium heat. Sauté onion for 2–3 minutes until translucent, then add garlic and cook for 1 minute.
2. **Cook vegetables:** Add eggplant, zucchini, red, and yellow bell peppers. Cook for 10 minutes, stirring occasionally.
3. **Add tomatoes and spices:** Stir in diced tomatoes, tomato paste, broth, and spices. Mix well, bring to a boil, reduce heat, cover, and simmer for 20–25 minutes.
4. **Add chickpeas:** Stir in chickpeas (if using) and cook for 5 minutes.
5. **Finish with herbs:** Remove from heat, stir in parsley, basil (if using), and lemon juice.
6. **Serve:** Garnish with herbs and serve hot with a slice of whole-grain bread (limit ~15g carbs) or quinoa.

Nutritional Information (Per Serving)
Calories: 140, Protein: 4g, Carbohydrates: 22g (with chickpeas: ~25g), Fats: 4g, Fiber: 8g, Cholesterol: 0mg, Sodium: 210mg, Potassium: 500mg

5. Pizza Recipes

Whole Wheat Veggie Pizza with Pesto Sauce

Yield: 4 servings   Preparation Time: 20 minutes   Cooking Time: 15 minutes

Ingredients:

For the Whole Wheat Pizza Crust:
- 1 1/2 cups whole wheat flour (GI: 45)
- 1/2 cup warm water (110°F) (GI: 0)
- 1 tablespoon olive oil (GI: 0)
- 1 teaspoon active dry yeast (GI: 0)
- 1/2 teaspoon salt (optional) (GI: 0)
- 1/2 teaspoon honey or a sugar substitute like stevia (optional, for yeast activation) (GI: 50 for honey, 0 for stevia)

For the Pesto Sauce:
- 1 cup fresh basil leaves (GI: 0)
- 1/4 cup walnuts (GI: 15)
- 1/4 cup grated Parmesan cheese (GI: 0)
- 2 cloves garlic, minced (GI: 10)
- 2 tablespoons olive oil (GI: 0)
- 1 tablespoon lemon juice (GI: 0)
- Salt and pepper to taste (optional) (GI: 0)

For the Toppings:
- 1/2 cup sliced bell peppers (red, yellow, or green) (GI: 15)
- 1/2 cup sliced zucchini (GI: 15)
- 1/2 cup cherry tomatoes, halved (GI: 15)
- 1/4 cup red onion, thinly sliced (GI: 10)
- 1/2 cup fresh spinach leaves (GI: 15)
- 1/2 cup part-skim mozzarella cheese, shredded (GI: 0)
- 1/4 cup crumbled feta cheese (optional) (GI: 0)

Optional Toppings for Additional Flavor:
- Sliced black olives (GI: 15)
- Sliced mushrooms (GI: 15)
- Fresh herbs like oregano or basil (GI: 0)
- Crushed red pepper flakes (GI: 0)

Instructions:

1. **Preheat oven:** Set oven to 425°F (220°C).
2. **Prepare the crust:** Combine water, yeast, and sweetener. Rest 5 minutes. Add flour, olive oil, and salt; knead until smooth. Let dough rest 10–15 minutes.
3. **Shape the dough:** Roll dough into a 1/4-inch circle; transfer to a baking sheet.
4. **Make pesto:** Blend basil, walnuts, Parmesan, garlic, olive oil, and lemon juice; season to taste.
5. **Assemble pizza:** Spread pesto on dough; add vegetables, mozzarella, and feta.
6. **Bake:** Cook for 12–15 minutes until crust is golden and cheese melts.
7. **Serve:** Cool 2–3 minutes, slice, garnish with herbs, and enjoy.

Nutritional Information (Per Serving)

Calories: 320, Protein: 14g, Carbohydrates: 30g, Fiber: 7g, Fats: 15g, Cholesterol: 20mg, Sodium: 380mg, Potassium: 480mg

Cauliflower Crust Margherita Pizza

Yield: 4 servings   Preparation Time: 20 minutes   Cooking Time: 25 minutes

Ingredients:

For the Cauliflower Crust:
- 1 medium head of cauliflower, chopped into florets (about 4 cups) (GI: 15)
- 1/4 cup grated Parmesan cheese (GI: 0)
- 1/4 cup part-skim mozzarella cheese, shredded (GI: 0)
- 1 large egg (GI: 0)
- 1 teaspoon dried oregano (GI: 0)
- 1 teaspoon garlic powder (GI: 0)
- 1/4 teaspoon salt (optional) (GI: 0)
- 1/4 teaspoon black pepper (GI: 0)

For the Margherita Topping:
- 1/2 cup low-sugar tomato sauce or crushed tomatoes (GI: 15)
- 1 cup part-skim mozzarella cheese, shredded (GI: 0)
- 1/2 cup fresh cherry tomatoes, sliced in half (GI: 15)
- 1/4 cup fresh basil leaves (GI: 0)
- 1 tablespoon olive oil (GI: 0)
- Salt and pepper to taste (optional) (GI: 0)

Instructions:

1. **Preheat oven:** Set to 425°F (220°C) and line a baking sheet with parchment paper.
2. **Prepare cauliflower:** Process florets into rice, steam or microwave for 4–5 minutes, cool, and squeeze out moisture.
3. **Mix ingredients:** Combine cauliflower, Parmesan, mozzarella, egg, oregano, garlic powder, salt, and pepper.
4. **Form crust:** Press mixture onto baking sheet into a 1/4-inch-thick circle.
5. **Bake crust:** Cook for 15–20 minutes until golden and firm.
6. **Add toppings:** Spread tomato sauce, top with mozzarella, cherry tomatoes, and basil.
7. **Bake again:** Cook for 5–7 minutes until cheese melts and bubbles.
8. **Finish and serve:** Drizzle with olive oil, garnish with basil, and enjoy.
9. **Additionally:** Serve the pizza with a side salad of mixed greens, cherry tomatoes, and a light vinaigrette to keep the meal balanced and full of fiber. Add extra vegetables as toppings, such as mushrooms, spinach, or bell peppers, for additional flavor and nutrients.

Nutritional Information (Per Serving)

Calories: 210, Protein: 14g, Carbohydrates: 8g, Fiber: 3g, Fats: 14g, Cholesterol: 65mg, Sodium: 380mg, Potassium: 460mg

Low-carb Zucchini Crust Pizza with Fresh Herbs

 Yield: 4 servings    Preparation Time: 20 minutes

 Cooking Time: 15 minutes

Ingredients:

For the Zucchini Crust:
- 2 medium zucchinis, grated (about 2 cups) (GI: 15)
- 1/4 cup grated Parmesan cheese (GI: 0)
- 1/4 cup part-skim mozzarella cheese, shredded (GI: 0)
- 1 large egg (GI: 0)
- 1/2 teaspoon garlic powder (GI: 0)
- 1 teaspoon dried oregano (GI: 0)
- 1/4 teaspoon salt (optional) (GI: 0)
- 1/4 teaspoon black pepper (GI: 0)

Optional toppings:
- 1/2 cup homemade tomato sauce (GI: 30-45)
- 1 cup cooked chicken breast, sliced (GI: 0)
- 1/4 cup red onion, thinly sliced (GI: 10)
- 1 cup mushrooms, sliced (such as cremini or button) (GI: 15)

Instructions:

1. **Preheat oven:** Set to 400°F (200°C) and line a baking sheet or pizza stone with parchment paper.
2. **Prepare zucchini:** Grate zucchini, then squeeze out excess moisture using a kitchen towel.
3. **Mix ingredients:** Combine zucchini, Parmesan, egg, garlic powder, oregano, salt, and pepper in a bowl.
4. **Form crust:** Spread mixture into a 1/4-inch-thick circle on the prepared baking sheet.
5. **Bake crust:** Cook for 15-20 minutes until golden and firm.
6. **Add Optional toppings (if you use):** Spread tomato sauce, sprinkle mozzarella, and add optional toppings like mushrooms or bell peppers.
7. **Bake pizza:** Cook for another 5-7 minutes until cheese melts and bubbles.
8. **Serve** the pizza cut the pizza into portions, cool for 5 minutes with mixed greens and a simple vinaigrette to add fiber and nutrients.

Nutritional Information (Per Serving)

Calories: 210 (without optional toppings), Protein: 14g, Carbohydrates: 8g, Fiber: 3g, Fats: 14g, Cholesterol: 65mg, Sodium: 320mg, Potassium: 460mg

Grilled Chicken and Spinach Alfredo Pizza

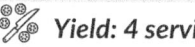 Yield: 4 servings   Preparation Time: 20 minutes

 Cooking Time: 20 minutes

Ingredients:

For the Whole Wheat Pizza Crust:
- 1 1/2 cups whole wheat flour (GI: 45)
- 1/2 cup warm water (110°F) (GI: 0)
- 1 tablespoon olive oil (GI: 0)
- 1 teaspoon active dry yeast (GI: 0)
- 1/2 teaspoon salt (optional) (GI: 0)
- 1/2 teaspoon honey or sugar substitute (optional, for yeast activation) (GI: 50 for honey, 0 for stevia)

For the Alfredo Sauce:
- 1/2 cup plain Greek yogurt (unsweetened) (GI: 0)
- 1/4 cup grated Parmesan cheese (GI: 0)
- 1/4 cup part-skim mozzarella cheese, shredded (GI: 0)
- 1 clove garlic, minced (GI: 10)
- 1 tablespoon olive oil (GI: 0)
- 1/4 teaspoon black pepper (GI: 0)
- 1/4 teaspoon salt (optional) (GI: 0)

For the Toppings:
- 1 cup grilled chicken breast, sliced (GI: 0)
- 1 cup fresh spinach leaves (GI: 15)
- 1/4 cup red onion, thinly sliced (GI: 10)
- 1/2 cup part-skim mozzarella cheese, shredded (GI: 0)
- 1 tablespoon fresh basil, chopped (GI: 0)
- 1 tablespoon olive oil for drizzling (GI: 0)

Instructions:

1. **Preheat oven:** Set to 400°F (200°C) and line a baking sheet or pizza stone with parchment.
2. **Activate the yeast:** Mix warm water, yeast, and honey (or sugar substitute) in a small bowl. Let sit for 5-10 minutes until frothy.
3. **Make the dough:** In a large bowl, combine flour and salt (if using). Add the yeast mixture and olive oil, then stir until dough forms. Knead on a floured surface for 5-7 minutes until smooth. Place dough in an oiled bowl, cover, and let rest for 10-15 minutes.
4. **Shape the dough:** Roll into a 1/4-inch-thick circle.
5. **Grill chicken:** Place the chicken on the grill and cook for 4-6 minutes on each side, depending on thickness, until the internal temperature reaches 165°F (74°C).
6. **Prepare Alfredo sauce:** Sauté garlic in olive oil for 1 minute. Add Greek yogurt, Parmesan, mozzarella, salt, and pepper, stirring until smooth. Set aside.
7. **Assemble pizza:** Spread sauce on the crust, top with grilled chicken slices, spinach, red onion and sprinkle with mozzarella and feta (if using).
8. **Bake pizza:** Bake for 5-7 minutes until cheese melts and bubbles.
9. **Garnish and serve:** Sprinkle with basil or mixed greens, or a simple cucumber-tomato salad and serve warm

Nutritional Information (Per Serving)

Calories: 310, Protein: 26g, Carbohydrates: 24g, Fiber: 5g, Fats: 14g, Cholesterol: 60mg, Sodium: 420mg, Potassium: 500mg

Eggplant Mini Pizzas with Mozzarella

 Yield: 4 servings   Preparation Time: 15 minutes
Cooking Time: 20 minutes

Ingredients:

- 1 large eggplant, sliced into 1/2-inch rounds (GI: 15)
- 1 tablespoon olive oil (GI: 0)
- 1/2 teaspoon salt (optional) (GI: 0)
- 1/4 teaspoon black pepper (GI: 0)
- 1/2 teaspoon dried oregano (GI: 0)
- 1/2 teaspoon garlic powder (GI: 0)
- 1/2 cup low-sugar tomato sauce or marinara sauce (GI: 15)
- 1 cup part-skim mozzarella cheese, shredded (GI: 0)
- 1/4 cup grated Parmesan cheese (optional) (GI: 0)
- 1/4 cup fresh basil leaves, chopped (GI: 0)
- Optional toppings: sliced cherry tomatoes (GI: 15), sliced black olives (GI: 15), sliced mushrooms (GI: 15)

Instructions:

1. **Prepare the oven:** Preheat oven to 400°F (200°C). Line a baking sheet with parchment paper.
2. **Prepare the eggplants and bake:** Brush eggplant slices with olive oil on both sides and season with salt, pepper, oregano, and garlic powder. Arrange the eggplant slices on the baking sheet and bake for 10 minutes, flipping halfway through, until softened and lightly browned.
3. **Assemble the pizza:** Remove from oven and spread 1 tablespoon of low-sugar tomato sauce over each eggplant slice. Sprinkle shredded mozzarella cheese evenly over the slices.
4. **If using** Parmesan, sprinkle lightly on top. Add optional toppings such as cherry tomatoes, olives, or mushrooms, if using.
5. **Finish cooking:** Return to the oven and bake for 8–10 minutes, or until the cheese is melted and bubbly.
6. **Serve:** Remove from oven, garnish with fresh basil leaves, and serve hot. Or with mixed greens or a simple cucumber-tomato salad to add fiber and nutrients. Consider pairing with a lean protein, such as grilled chicken or turkey, to create a more balanced meal.

Nutritional Information (Per Serving)

Calories: 180, Protein: 10g, Carbohydrates: 10g, Fiber: 4g, Fats: 12g, Cholesterol: 25mg, Sodium: 350mg, Potassium: 400mg

Spicy Shrimp and Garlic Pizza on a Cauliflower Crust

 Yield: 4 servings Preparation Time: 25 minutes
Cooking Time: 25 minutes

Ingredients:

For the Cauliflower Crust:
- 1 medium head of cauliflower, chopped into florets (about 4 cups) (GI: 15)
- 1/4 cup grated Parmesan cheese (GI: 0)
- 1/4 cup part-skim mozzarella cheese, shredded (GI: 0)
- 1 large egg (GI: 0)
- 1 teaspoon dried oregano (GI: 0)
- 1 teaspoon garlic powder (GI: 0)
- 1/4 teaspoon salt (optional) (GI: 0)
- 1/4 teaspoon black pepper (GI: 0)

For the Spicy Shrimp Topping:
- 1/2 lb (about 20 medium) shrimp, peeled and deveined (GI: 0)
- 1 tablespoon olive oil (GI: 0)
- 2 cloves garlic, minced (GI: 10)
- 1/2 teaspoon red pepper flakes (adjust to taste) (GI: 0)
- 1/2 teaspoon paprika (GI: 0)
- 1/2 teaspoon black pepper (GI: 0)
- 1/4 teaspoon salt (optional) (GI: 0)
- 1/2 cup low-sugar tomato sauce or marinara sauce (GI: 15)
- 1/2 cup part-skim mozzarella cheese, shredded (GI: 0)
- 1/4 cup fresh parsley or basil, chopped (GI: 0)

Instructions:

1. **Preheat oven:** Set to 400°F (200°C) and line a baking sheet with parchment paper.
2. **Prepare the crust:** Process cauliflower into rice-like granules, microwave for 5 minutes, cool, and squeeze out moisture. Mix with Parmesan, mozzarella, egg, oregano, garlic powder, salt, and pepper.
3. **Bake the crust:** Shape into a 1/4-inch-thick circle on the baking sheet and bake for 15–20 minutes until golden and firm.
4. **Prepare the shrimp:** Toss shrimp with olive oil, garlic, paprika, red pepper flakes, salt, and pepper.
5. **Fry the shrimp:** Sauté in a skillet over medium heat for 3–4 minutes until cooked. Set aside.
6. **Assemble the pizza:** Spread tomato sauce on the crust, top with shrimp and mozzarella.
7. **Finish cooking:** Bake for 7–8 minutes until cheese melts and bubbles.
8. **Serve:** Garnish with fresh parsley or basil. Serve immediately with a side of mixed greens or a simple cucumber-tomato salad.

Nutritional Information (Per Serving)

Calories: 240, Protein: 22g, Carbohydrates: 8g, Fiber: 3g, Fats: 14g, Cholesterol: 145mg, Sodium: 480mg, Potassium: 500mg

Mushroom and Olive Pizza with Ricotta

 Yield: 4 servings   Preparation Time: 20 minutes

Cooking Time: 20 minutes

Ingredients:

For the Whole Wheat Pizza Crust:
- 1 1/2 cups whole wheat flour (GI: 45)
- 1/2 cup warm water (110°F) (GI: 0)
- 1 tablespoon olive oil (GI: 0)
- 1 teaspoon active dry yeast (GI: 0)
- 1/2 teaspoon salt (optional) (GI: 0)
- 1/2 teaspoon honey or sugar substitute (optional, for yeast activation) (GI: 50 for honey, 0 for stevia)

For the Toppings:
- 1/2 cup low-sugar tomato sauce or marinara sauce (GI: 15)
- 1 cup mushrooms, sliced (GI: 15)
- 1/2 cup black olives, sliced (GI: 15)
- 1/2 cup part-skim ricotta cheese (GI: 0)
- 1/2 cup part-skim mozzarella cheese, shredded (GI: 0)
- 1/4 cup grated Parmesan cheese (optional) (GI: 0)
- 1 teaspoon dried oregano (GI: 0)
- 1/2 teaspoon garlic powder (GI: 0)
- 1/4 teaspoon red pepper flakes (optional, for spice) (GI: 0)
- 1 tablespoon fresh basil or parsley, chopped (GI: 0)

Instructions:

1. **Prepare the dough:** In a bowl, mix warm water, yeast, and stevia. Stir gently and let sit for 5 minutes to activate the yeast. Add olive oil, salt, and whole wheat flour. Knead the mixture for 7–10 minutes until smooth and elastic.
2. **Let the dough rise:** Lightly oil a bowl, place the dough inside, cover with a clean kitchen towel, and let rise for 1 hour or until doubled in size.
3. **Preheat the oven:** Preheat the oven to 425°F (220°C). Place a baking sheet or pizza stone in the oven to heat.
4. **Roll out the dough:** On a floured surface, roll out the dough to your desired thickness. Transfer to the preheated baking sheet or pizza stone.
5. **Assemble the pizza:** Spread tomato sauce evenly over the crust. Add mushrooms, olives, ricotta cheese, mozzarella, Parmesan, oregano, garlic powder, and red pepper flakes evenly across the surface.
6. **Bake the pizza:** Bake for 12–15 minutes until the crust is golden and the cheese is melted and bubbly.
7. **Garnish and serve:** Remove the pizza from the oven and garnish with fresh parsley or basil. Slice and serve hot.

Nutritional Information (Per Serving)
Calories: 310, Protein: 16g, Carbohydrates: 30g, Fiber: 6g, Fats: 14g, Cholesterol: 30mg, Sodium: 480mg, Potassium: 450mg

---

Low-carb BBQ Chicken Pizza with Red Onion

 Yield: 4 servings   Preparation Time: 20 minutes

Cooking Time: 20 minutes

Ingredients:

For the Cauliflower Crust:
- 1 medium head of cauliflower, chopped into florets (about 4 cups) (GI: 15)
- 1/4 cup grated Parmesan cheese (GI: 0)
- 1/4 cup part-skim mozzarella cheese, shredded (GI: 0)
- 1 large egg (GI: 0)
- 1 teaspoon dried oregano (GI: 0)
- 1 teaspoon garlic powder (GI: 0)
- 1/4 teaspoon salt (optional) (GI: 0)
- 1/4 teaspoon black pepper (GI: 0)

For the Toppings:
- 1/2 cup sugar-free BBQ sauce (GI: varies, usually low)
- 1 cup cooked chicken breast, shredded (GI: 0)
- 1/2 cup red onion, thinly sliced (GI: 10)
- 1 cup part-skim mozzarella cheese, shredded (GI: 0)
- 1/4 cup fresh cilantro, chopped (GI: 0)
- 1 tablespoon olive oil (GI: 0)
- Optional: 1/2 teaspoon red pepper flakes for added spice (GI: 0)

Instructions:

1. **Prepare the oven:** Preheat the oven to 400°F (200°C). Line a baking sheet or pizza stone with parchment paper.
2. **Prepare the cauliflower crust:** Pulse cauliflower florets in a food processor until rice-like, or grate them using a box grater. Microwave for 5 minutes or steam until tender. Let cool slightly, then squeeze out excess moisture using a clean towel or cheesecloth.
3. **Mix the crust ingredients:** In a bowl, combine the cooked cauliflower, Parmesan, mozzarella, egg, oregano, garlic powder, salt, and pepper. Mix well.
4. **Form the crust:** Press the mixture onto the prepared baking sheet into a circle about 1/4-inch thick.
5. **Bake the crust:** Bake for 15–20 minutes until golden and firm.
6. **Add the toppings:** Spread sugar-free BBQ sauce evenly over the crust. Distribute shredded chicken, sliced red onion, and mozzarella cheese evenly.
7. **Bake the pizza:** Return the pizza to the oven and bake for 5–7 minutes until the cheese is melted and bubbly.
8. **Garnish and serve:** Remove from the oven, garnish with fresh cilantro and optional red pepper flakes, and serve hot. Pair the pizza with a side salad of mixed greens dressed in light vinaigrette to add fiber and nutrients. For added protein, serve with grilled chicken or tofu.

Nutritional Information (Per Serving)
Calories: 260, Protein: 23g, Carbohydrates: 12g, Fiber: 5g, Fats: 14g, Cholesterol: 90mg, Sodium: 480mg, Potassium: 550mg

Keto-Friendly Broccoli and Cheese Pizza

Yield: 4 servings Preparation Time: 15 minutes
Cooking Time: 25 minutes

Ingredients:

For the Broccoli Crust:
- 1 large head of broccoli, chopped into florets (about 3 cups) (GI: 15)
- 1/2 cup grated Parmesan cheese (GI: 0)
- 1/2 cup part-skim mozzarella cheese, shredded (GI: 0)
- 2 large eggs (GI: 0)
- 1 teaspoon garlic powder (GI: 0)
- 1 teaspoon dried oregano (GI: 0)
- 1/4 teaspoon salt (optional) (GI: 0)
- 1/4 teaspoon black pepper (GI: 0)

For the Toppings:
- 1 cup part-skim mozzarella cheese, shredded (GI: 0)
- 1/2 cup ricotta cheese (GI: 0)
- 1/2 cup cooked broccoli florets, chopped (GI: 15)
- 1/4 cup grated Parmesan cheese (GI: 0)
- 1 tablespoon olive oil (GI: 0)
- 1 teaspoon red pepper flakes (optional, for spice) (GI: 0)
- 1/4 cup fresh basil or parsley, chopped (GI: 0)

Instructions:

For the Broccoli Crust:
1. Preheat the oven to 400°F (200°C) and line a pizza stone or baking sheet with parchment paper.
2. Process broccoli in a food processor or grate it into rice-sized pieces.
3. Microwave the riced broccoli for 4–5 minutes until softened, then let it cool slightly. Transfer to a clean kitchen towel and squeeze thoroughly to remove as much moisture as possible.
4. In a mixing bowl, combine broccoli, Parmesan, mozzarella, eggs, garlic powder, oregano, salt, and pepper.
5. Spread the mixture on the prepared sheet into a 1/4-inch thick circle.
6. Bake for 15–20 minutes until golden and firm. Cool for 5 minutes before adding toppings.

For the Toppings:
1. Spread ricotta over the crust, then sprinkle with mozzarella.
2. Distribute cooked broccoli florets and sprinkle Parmesan on top.
3. Bake the pizza for another 5–7 minutes until cheese is melted and bubbling.
4. Drizzle with olive oil, then garnish with fresh basil and red pepper flakes if desired. Let cool for 2–3 minutes before slicing.
5. Serve with a mixed greens salad for added fiber.

Nutritional Information (Per Serving)

Calories: 280, Protein: 18g, Carbohydrates: 6g, Fiber: 3g, Fats: 20g, Cholesterol: 125mg, Sodium: 450mg, Potassium: 450mg

Grilled Veggie Pizza with a Cauliflower Crust

Yield: 4 servings Preparation Time: 25 minutes
Cooking Time: 30 minutes

Ingredients:

For the Cauliflower Crust:
- 1 medium head of cauliflower, chopped into florets (about 4 cups) (GI: 15)
- 1/4 cup grated Parmesan cheese (GI: 0)
- 1/4 cup part-skim mozzarella cheese, shredded (GI: 0)
- 1 large egg (GI: 0)
- 1 teaspoon garlic powder (GI: 0)
- 1 teaspoon dried oregano (GI: 0)
- 1/4 teaspoon salt (optional) (GI: 0)
- 1/4 teaspoon black pepper (GI: 0)

For the Grilled Veggie Toppings:
- 1 small zucchini, sliced into rounds (GI: 15)
- 1 small eggplant, sliced into rounds (GI: 15)
- 1/2 red bell pepper, sliced (GI: 15)
- 1/2 yellow bell pepper, sliced (GI: 15)
- 1/2 red onion, thinly sliced (GI: 10)
- 1 tablespoon olive oil (GI: 0)
- 1/2 teaspoon dried oregano (GI: 0)
- 1/2 teaspoon garlic powder (GI: 0)
- 1/4 teaspoon salt (optional) (GI: 0)
- 1/4 teaspoon black pepper (GI: 0)
- 1/2 cup part-skim mozzarella cheese, shredded (GI: 0)
- 1/4 cup crumbled feta cheese (optional) (GI: 0)
- 1/4 cup fresh basil leaves, chopped (GI: 0)

Instructions:

Cauliflower Crust:
1. Preheat oven to 400°F (200°C). Line a baking sheet with parchment paper.
2. Process or grate cauliflower into rice-like granules, microwave for 5 minutes, cool slightly, and squeeze out water.
3. Combine cauliflower, Parmesan, mozzarella, egg, garlic powder, oregano, salt (optional), and black pepper.
4. Shape into a 1/4-inch-thick circle on the baking sheet and bake for 15–20 minutes until golden and firm.

Grilled Veggies:
1. Toss zucchini, eggplant, bell peppers, and red onion with olive oil, oregano, garlic powder, salt (optional), and pepper.
2. Grill 3–4 minutes per side until tender and charred.

Assemble Pizza:
1. Spread veggies on the crust, top with mozzarella and feta (optional). Bake 5–7 minutes until cheese melts. Garnish with fresh basil.

Serving
1. Pair with mixed greens or a cucumber-tomato salad. Add grilled chicken or tofu for extra protein.

Nutritional Information (Per Serving)

Calories: 210, Protein: 14g, Carbohydrates: 8g, Fiber: 3g, Fats: 14g, Cholesterol: 65mg, Sodium: 320mg, Potassium: 460mg

Low-Carb Bell Pepper Crust Pizza with Fresh Herbs

 Yield: 4 servings   Preparation Time: 15 minutes   Cooking Time: 20 minutes

Ingredients:

For the Bell Pepper Crust:
- 4 large bell peppers, halved and deseeded (GI: 15)
- 1/4 cup grated Parmesan cheese (GI: 0)
- 1/4 cup part-skim mozzarella cheese, shredded (GI: 0)
- 1 large egg (GI: 0)
- 1/2 teaspoon garlic powder (GI: 0)
- 1/2 teaspoon dried oregano (GI: 0)
- 1/4 teaspoon salt (optional) (GI: 0)
- 1/4 teaspoon black pepper (GI: 0)

For the Toppings:
- 1/2 cup no-sugar-added marinara or pizza sauce (GI: 35)
- 1/2 cup shredded mozzarella cheese (GI: 0)
- 1/4 cup grated Parmesan cheese (GI: 0)
- 1/4 cup cherry tomatoes, halved (GI: 15)
- 2 tablespoons black olives, sliced (GI: 15)
- 1 tablespoon olive oil (GI: 0)
- 1 teaspoon red pepper flakes (optional, for spice) (GI: 0)
- 1/4 cup fresh basil or parsley, chopped (GI: 0)

Instructions:

1. **Prepare the Bell Peppers:** Preheat the oven to 400°F (200°C) and line a baking sheet with parchment paper. Halve and deseed the bell peppers, ensuring a flat base for each half.
2. **Make the Crust Mixture:** In a mixing bowl, combine Parmesan, mozzarella, egg, garlic powder, oregano, salt, and black pepper.
3. **Fill the Bell Peppers:** Spoon the crust mixture evenly into each bell pepper half, pressing gently to create a flat surface.
4. **Bake the Crust:** Arrange the filled bell peppers on the prepared baking sheet. Bake for 10–12 minutes, or until the cheese mixture is golden and slightly firm.
5. **Add the Toppings:** Remove the peppers from the oven and spread a thin layer of marinara sauce over each. Sprinkle mozzarella and Parmesan cheeses over the sauce, followed by cherry tomatoes and olives.
6. **Final Bake:** Return the peppers to the oven and bake for an additional 7–8 minutes, or until the cheese is melted and bubbling.
7. **Finish and Serve:** Drizzle olive oil over the finished pizzas and garnish with fresh basil or parsley. Add red pepper flakes for extra spice if desired. Allow to cool for 2–3 minutes before serving. To add fiber and nutrients, serve the pizza with mixed greens or a simple cucumber-tomato salad. For extra protein, add grilled chicken or tofu as an additional topping.

Nutritional Information (Per Serving)

Calories: 220, Protein: 14g, Carbohydrates: 10g, Fiber: 4g, Fats: 14g, Cholesterol: 55mg, Sodium: 340mg, Potassium: 460mg

6. Fish and Seafood

Grilled Salmon and Avocado Salad

Yield: 4 servings *Preparation Time: 15 minutes*
Cooking Time: 10 minutes

Ingredients:

For the Salmon:
- 4 salmon fillets (4-6 oz each) (GI: 0)
- 1 tablespoon olive oil (GI: 0)
- 1 tablespoon fresh lemon juice (GI: 0)
- 1 teaspoon garlic powder (GI: 0)
- 1 teaspoon dried dill (GI: 0)
- 1/2 teaspoon salt (optional) (GI: 0)
- 1/4 teaspoon black pepper (GI: 0)

For the Salad:
- 1 large avocado, diced (GI: 15)
- 4 cups mixed salad greens (spinach, arugula, romaine) (GI: 0-15)
- 1 cup cherry tomatoes, halved (GI: 15)
- 1/2 cucumber, sliced (GI: 15)
- 1/4 red onion, thinly sliced (GI: 10)
- 2 tablespoons fresh cilantro, chopped (GI: 0)

For the Dressing:
- 2 tablespoons olive oil (GI: 0)
- 1 tablespoon fresh lemon juice (GI: 0)
- 1 teaspoon Dijon mustard (GI: 0)
- 1 teaspoon honey or sugar substitute (optional) (GI: 55 for honey, 0 for stevia)
- 1 clove garlic, minced (GI: 10)
- Salt and pepper to taste (optional) (GI: 0)

Instructions:

1. **Prepare the Salmon:** Mix olive oil, lemon juice, garlic powder, dried dill, salt (if using), and black pepper in a bowl. Brush marinade over salmon fillets and let rest for 10 minutes. Preheat grill to medium-high heat. Grill salmon for 4–5 minutes per side until opaque and flaky. Rest for 3–5 minutes.
2. **Prepare the Salad:** Combine greens, avocado, cherry tomatoes, cucumber, red onion, and cilantro in a large bowl.
3. **Make the Dressing:** Whisk olive oil, lemon juice, Dijon mustard, sugar substitute, minced garlic, salt, and pepper.
4. **Assemble:** Drizzle dressing over salad and toss gently. Place grilled salmon on top, whole or flaked.
5. **Serve** immediately with quantified sides (e.g., 1 slice whole-grain bread or ½ cup quinoa).

Nutritional Information (Per Serving)

Calories: 400, Protein: 28g, Carbohydrates: 10g, Fiber: 6g, Fats: 30g, Cholesterol: 70mg, Sodium: 320mg, Potassium: 1100mg

Lemon-Dill Shrimp and Quinoa Bowl

Yield: 4 servings *Preparation Time: 15 minutes*
Cooking Time: 20 minutes

Ingredients:

For the Quinoa:
- 1 cup quinoa, rinsed (GI: 53)
- 2 cups water or low-sodium vegetable broth (GI: 0)
- 1/4 teaspoon salt (optional) (GI: 0)

For the Shrimp:
- 1 lb large shrimp, peeled and deveined (GI: 0)
- 2 tablespoons olive oil (GI: 0)
- 2 tablespoons fresh lemon juice (GI: 0)
- 2 cloves garlic, minced (GI: 10)
- 1 tablespoon fresh dill, chopped (GI: 0)
- 1/4 teaspoon salt (optional) (GI: 0)
- 1/4 teaspoon black pepper (GI: 0)
- 1/2 teaspoon red pepper flakes (optional for spice) (GI: 0)

For the Bowl:
- 2 cups baby spinach leaves (GI: 15)
- 1/2 cup cucumber, diced (GI: 15)
- 1/2 cup cherry tomatoes, halved (GI: 15)
- 1/4 cup red onion, thinly sliced (GI: 10)
- 1/4 cup feta cheese, crumbled (optional) (GI: 0)

For the Dressing:
- 2 tablespoons olive oil (GI: 0)
- 1 tablespoon fresh lemon juice (GI: 0)
- 1 teaspoon Dijon mustard (GI: 0)
- 1 teaspoon honey or a sugar substitute (optional) (GI: 50 for honey, 0 for stevia)
- Salt and pepper to taste (optional) (GI: 0)

Instructions:

1. **Prepare the Quinoa:** Rinse quinoa thoroughly. Boil in water or broth with salt for 15 minutes, then fluff with a fork.
2. **Prepare the Shrimp:** Mix olive oil, lemon juice, garlic, dill, salt, black pepper, and red pepper flakes. Toss shrimp in marinade; let rest for 10 minutes. Heat a skillet and cook shrimp 2–3 minutes per side until pink.
3. **Prepare the Bowl:** Divide spinach into bowls. Add ½ cup cooked quinoa to each. Top with shrimp, cucumber, tomatoes, red onion, and feta (if using).
4. **Make the Dressing:** Whisk olive oil, lemon juice, Dijon mustard, sugar substitute, salt, and pepper. Drizzle dressing over bowls.
5. **Serving:** Serve with a side of roasted vegetables or ½ cup quinoa for controlled carb intake.

Nutritional Information (Per Serving)

Calories: 360, Protein: 26g, Carbohydrates: 24g, Fiber: 5g, Fats: 19g, Cholesterol: 190mg, Sodium: 360mg, Potassium: 700mg

Spicy Mackerel Salad with Cucumber and Tomato

 Yield: 4 servings    Preparation Time: 5 minutes

Cooking Time: 5 minutes (if mackerel needs to be cooked)

Ingredients:

For the Salad:
- 2 cups cooked or canned mackerel fillets, flaked (GI: 0)
- 1 cup cucumber, diced (GI: 15)
- 1 cup cherry tomatoes, halved (GI: 15)
- 1/4 cup red onion, thinly sliced (GI: 10)
- 1/4 cup fresh cilantro, chopped (GI: 0)
- 1/2 avocado, diced (optional) (GI: 15)
- 1 small jalapeño pepper, finely chopped (optional, for spice) (GI: 0)
- 4 cups mixed salad greens (GI: 0-15)

For the Dressing:
- 2 tablespoons olive oil (GI: 0)
- 1 tablespoon fresh lime juice (GI: 0)
- 1 teaspoon Dijon mustard (GI: 0)
- 1/2 teaspoon ground cumin (GI: 0)
- 1/4 teaspoon red pepper flakes (optional, for additional spice) (GI: 0)
- Salt and pepper to taste (optional) (GI: 0)

Instructions:

1. **Prepare the Mackerel:** Drain canned mackerel or cook fresh fillets. Flake into bite-sized pieces.
2. **Prepare the Salad Base:** Combine cucumber, tomatoes, onion, cilantro, and avocado in a bowl.
3. **Make the Dressing:** Whisk olive oil, lime juice, Dijon mustard, cumin, red pepper flakes, salt, and pepper.
4. **Assemble:** Toss mackerel with salad ingredients and dressing. Plate over mixed greens.
5. **Serving:** Serve immediately with a small side of quinoa or whole-grain crackers.

Nutritional Information (Per Serving)

Calories: 300, Protein: 25g, Carbohydrates: 8g, Fiber: 4g, Fats: 18g, Cholesterol: 60mg, Sodium: 220mg, Potassium: 800mg

---

Baked Cod with Garlic Spinach

 Yield: 4 servings   Preparation Time: 10 minutes

 Cooking Time: 20 minutes

Ingredients:

For the Baked Cod:
- 4 cod fillets (4-6 oz each) (GI: 0)
- 2 tablespoons olive oil (GI: 0)
- 2 tablespoons fresh lemon juice (GI: 0)
- 2 cloves garlic, minced (GI: 10)
- 1 teaspoon dried thyme (GI: 0)
- 1 teaspoon dried parsley (GI: 0)
- 1/4 teaspoon salt (optional) (GI: 0)
- 1/4 teaspoon black pepper (GI: 0)
- Lemon wedges for Serving (optional) (GI: 0)

For the Garlic Spinach:
- 1 tablespoon olive oil (GI: 0)
- 3 cloves garlic, minced (GI: 10)
- 8 cups fresh spinach leaves (GI: 15)
- 1/4 teaspoon salt (optional) (GI: 0)
- 1/4 teaspoon black pepper (GI: 0)
- 1/4 teaspoon red pepper flakes (optional) (GI: 0)

Instructions:

1. **Prepare the Cod:** Preheat oven to 400°F. Line a baking dish. Mix olive oil, lemon juice, garlic, thyme, parsley, salt, and pepper. Brush cod fillets. Bake for 12–15 minutes.
2. **Prepare the Spinach:** Heat olive oil in a skillet. Add garlic; sauté for 1 minute. Toss in spinach, cooking until wilted (2–3 minutes). Season to taste.
3. **Serve:** Plate spinach, top with cod, and garnish with lemon. Serve with ½ cup quinoa or steamed broccoli for fiber and with lemon wedges on the side for an extra flavor, if desired.

Nutritional Information (Per Serving)

Calories: 220, Protein: 30g, Carbohydrates: 5g, Fiber: 2g, Fats: 9g, Cholesterol: 65mg, Sodium: 320mg, Potassium: 1100mg

Zucchini Noodles with Pesto Shrimp

Yield: 4 servings **Preparation Time:** 15 minutes **Cooking Time:** 10 minutes

Ingredients:

For the Pesto:
- 2 cups fresh basil leaves (GI: 0)
- 1/4 cup pine nuts (GI: 15)
- 1/4 cup grated Parmesan cheese (GI: 0)
- 2 cloves garlic, minced (GI: 10)
- 1/3 cup olive oil (GI: 0)
- 1 tablespoon fresh lemon juice (GI: 0)
- Salt and pepper to taste (optional) (GI: 0)

For the Zucchini Noodles:
- 4 medium zucchinis, spiralized into noodles (GI: 15)
- 1 tablespoon olive oil (GI: 0)
- 1/4 teaspoon salt (optional) (GI: 0)
- 1/4 teaspoon black pepper (GI: 0)

For the Shrimp:
- 1 lb large shrimp, peeled and deveined (GI: 0)
- 1 tablespoon olive oil (GI: 0)
- 2 cloves garlic, minced (GI: 10)
- 1/4 teaspoon red pepper flakes (optional, for spice) (GI: 0)
- 1/4 teaspoon salt (optional) (GI: 0)
- 1/4 teaspoon black pepper (GI: 0)
- 1 tablespoon fresh lemon juice (GI: 0)

Optional Garnish:
- Freshly grated Parmesan cheese (GI: 0)
- Fresh basil leaves, chopped (GI: 0)

Instructions:

1. **Prepare the Pesto:** Blend basil, pine nuts, Parmesan, and garlic in a food processor until finely chopped. Gradually add olive oil and lemon juice while blending until smooth. Season with salt and pepper.
2. **Prepare the Zucchini Noodles:** Spiralize zucchini. Heat olive oil in a skillet, add zucchini noodles, and cook for 2–3 minutes. Season with salt and pepper.
3. **Prepare the Shrimp:** Clean and devein shrimp. Heat olive oil in a skillet, sauté garlic and red pepper flakes for 30 seconds, then add shrimp. Cook 2–3 minutes per side until pink. Squeeze lemon juice on top.
4. **Combine:** Toss zucchini noodles and shrimp with pesto in the skillet. Serve with Parmesan and basil.
5. **Serving:** Pair with a small mixed greens salad or ½ cup cooked quinoa for fiber.

Nutritional Information (Per Serving)
Calories: 320, Protein: 25g, Carbohydrates: 8g, Fiber: 3g, Fats: 22g, Cholesterol: 220mg, Sodium: 360mg, Potassium: 700mg

Greek-Style Grilled Fish Tacos with Tzatziki

Yield: 4 servings (8 tacos) **Preparation Time:** 20 minutes **Cooking Time:** 10 minutes

Ingredients:

For the Fish:
- 1 lb white fish fillets (such as cod, tilapia, or haddock) (GI: 0)
- 2 tablespoons olive oil (GI: 0)
- 2 tablespoons fresh lemon juice (GI: 0)
- 2 cloves garlic, minced (GI: 10)
- 1 teaspoon dried oregano (GI: 0)
- 1/2 teaspoon ground cumin (GI: 0)
- 1/4 teaspoon salt (optional) (GI: 0)
- 1/4 teaspoon black pepper (GI: 0)

For the Tzatziki:
- 1 cup plain Greek yogurt, unsweetened (GI: 0)
- 1/2 cucumber, grated and excess water squeezed out (GI: 15)
- 1 clove garlic, minced (GI: 10)
- 1 tablespoon fresh lemon juice (GI: 0)
- 1 tablespoon fresh dill, chopped (GI: 0)
- Salt and pepper to taste (optional) (GI: 0)

For the Tacos:
- 8 small whole wheat tortillas (GI: 30-40)
- 1 cup cherry tomatoes, halved (GI: 15)
- 1/2 red onion, thinly sliced (GI: 10)
- 1/2 cup shredded lettuce (GI: 10)
- 1/4 cup crumbled feta cheese (optional) (GI: 0)
- 1/4 cup fresh parsley or cilantro, chopped (GI: 0)
- Lemon wedges for Serving (optional) (GI: 0)

Instructions:

1. **Prepare the Fish:** Marinate fish with olive oil, lemon juice, garlic, oregano, cumin, salt, and pepper for 10–15 minutes. Grill 3–4 minutes per side until flaky.
2. **Prepare the Tzatziki:** Grate cucumber and squeeze out excess water. Mix with yogurt, garlic, lemon juice, dill, salt, and pepper.
3. **Assemble the Tacos:** Warm tortillas, then fill with fish, tzatziki, tomatoes, onion, lettuce, and feta (if using). Garnish with parsley or cilantro.
4. **Serving:** Serve with a side Greek salad or roasted vegetables. Limit to 2 tacos per serving for carb control.

Nutritional Information (Per Serving)
Calories: 320, Protein: 25g, Carbohydrates: 24g, Fiber: 5g, Fats: 15g, Cholesterol: 55mg, Sodium: 400mg, Potassium: 650mg

Seared Scallops with Asparagus and Lemon

 Yield: 4 servings   Preparation Time: 10 minutes

 Cooking Time: 15 minutes

Ingredients:

- 1 lb large sea scallops (GI: 0)
- 1 bunch asparagus, trimmed and cut into 2-inch pieces (about 2 cups) (GI: 15)
- 2 tablespoons olive oil, divided (GI: 0)
- 2 cloves garlic, minced (GI: 10)
- 1 tablespoon fresh lemon juice (GI: 0)
- 1 teaspoon lemon zest (GI: 0)
- 1/4 teaspoon salt (optional) (GI: 0)
- 1/4 teaspoon black pepper (GI: 0)
- 1 tablespoon fresh parsley, chopped (optional) (GI: 0)

Instructions:

1. **Prepare the Asparagus:** Heat olive oil in a skillet, sauté asparagus for 4–5 minutes. Add garlic and cook 1 more minute. Season to taste.
2. **Prepare the Scallops:** Remove the side muscle from scallops. Pat dry and season with salt and pepper. Heat olive oil in a skillet, sear scallops 2–3 minutes per side until golden. Add garlic and lemon zest in the last minute. Squeeze lemon juice over scallops.
3. **Serve:**

- Plate the Dish: Divide the cooked asparagus among four plates. Place the seared scallops on top of the asparagus.
- Garnish: If desired, garnish with chopped fresh parsley. Serve immediately with an extra wedge of lemon on the side for an additional flavor

Nutritional Information (Per Serving)

Calories: 210, Protein: 22g, Carbohydrates: 6g, Fiber: 3g, Fats: 11g, Cholesterol: 35mg, Sodium: 310mg, Potassium: 600mg

Crispy Tilapia Lettuce Cups with Mango Salsa

 Yield: 4 servings   Preparation Time: 15 minutes

 Cooking Time: 10 minutes

Ingredients:

For the Tilapia:
- 4 tilapia fillets (about 4 oz each) (GI: 0)
- 1/2 cup whole wheat flour (GI: 45)
- 1/2 teaspoon garlic powder (GI: 0)
- 1/2 teaspoon paprika (GI: 0)
- 1/4 teaspoon salt (optional) (GI: 0)
- 1/4 teaspoon black pepper (GI: 0)
- 1 tablespoon olive oil (GI: 0)
- 1 tablespoon fresh lemon juice (GI: 0)

For the Mango Salsa:
- 1 ripe mango, diced (GI: 51)
- 1/4 red onion, finely chopped (GI: 10)
- 1/2 red bell pepper, diced (GI: 15)
- 1/2 jalapeño, seeded and finely chopped (optional) (GI: 0)
- 2 tablespoons fresh cilantro, chopped (GI: 0)
- 1 tablespoon fresh lime juice (GI: 0)
- Salt and pepper to taste (optional) (GI: 0)

For the Lettuce Cups:
- 8 large lettuce leaves, such as romaine or butter lettuce (GI: 0)

Instructions:

1. **Prepare the Mango Salsa:** Combine diced mango, onion, bell pepper, jalapeño, and cilantro. Toss with lime juice, salt, and pepper.
2. **Prepare the Tilapia:** Season flour with garlic powder, paprika, salt, and pepper. Dredge tilapia in flour, then pan-fry 3–4 minutes per side in olive oil. Add lemon juice.
3. **Assemble the Lettuce Cups:** Fill lettuce leaves with tilapia and salsa.
4. **Serving:** Limit mango salsa to 2 tbsp per lettuce cup. Pair with black beans or quinoa for a balanced meal.

Nutritional Information (Per Serving)

Calories: 280, Protein: 22g, Carbohydrates: 18g, Fiber: 4g, Fats: 12g, Cholesterol: 50mg, Sodium: 200mg, Potassium: 450mg

Sardine and Avocado Stuffed Bell Peppers

Yield: 4 servings *Preparation Time: 15 minutes*
Cooking Time: 0 minutes

Ingredients:

- 4 large bell peppers, any color (GI: 15)
- 2 ripe avocados, diced (GI: 15)
- 2 cans (4 oz each) of sardines in water or olive oil, drained and flaked (GI: 0)
- 1/4 cup red onion, finely chopped (GI: 10)
- 1/4 cup cherry tomatoes, diced (GI: 15)
- 2 tablespoons fresh cilantro or parsley, chopped (GI: 0)
- 2 tablespoons fresh lemon or lime juice (GI: 0)
- 1 tablespoon olive oil (GI: 0)
- 1/4 teaspoon black pepper (GI: 0)
- 1/4 teaspoon salt (optional) (GI: 0)
- Optional: 1/2 jalapeño, finely chopped for spice (GI: 0)

Instructions:

1. **Prepare the Bell Peppers:** Slice off the tops of the bell peppers and remove seeds and membranes. If peppers don't stand upright, carefully trim the bottom to level them.
2. **Prepare the Stuffing:** In a medium bowl, mash avocados, leaving some chunks. Add flaked sardines, red onion, cherry tomatoes, cilantro, lemon juice, olive oil, and seasonings. Mix gently to combine.
3. **Assemble the Peppers:** Stuff each bell pepper with the mixture, pressing gently to fill completely.
4. **Serve** these stuffed bell peppers as a light lunch or dinner. Pair them with mixed greens or a cucumber salad for additional fiber and nutrients. Consider serving the stuffed peppers with quinoa or brown rice for added protein.

Nutritional Information (Per Serving)

Calories: 280, Protein: 14g, Carbohydrates: 14g, Fiber: 8g, Fats: 19g, Cholesterol: 45mg, Sodium: 320mg, Potassium: 800mg

Ginger-Lime Grilled Shrimp with Cabbage Slaw

Yield: 4 servings *Preparation Time: 20 minutes*
Cooking Time: 10 minutes

Ingredients:

For the Ginger-Lime Grilled Shrimp:
- 1 lb large shrimp, peeled and deveined (GI: 0)
- 2 tablespoons fresh lime juice (GI: 0)
- 1 tablespoon olive oil (GI: 0)
- 1 tablespoon fresh ginger, grated (GI: 0)
- 2 cloves garlic, minced (GI: 10)
- 1 tablespoon soy sauce (low sodium) (GI: 0)
- 1 teaspoon honey or sugar substitute (optional) (GI: 55 for honey, 0 for stevia)
- 1/4 teaspoon black pepper (GI: 0)
- 1/4 teaspoon red pepper flakes (optional, for spice) (GI: 0)

For the Cabbage Slaw:
- 3 cups shredded green cabbage (GI: 10)
- 1 cup shredded red cabbage (GI: 10)
- 1 large carrot, shredded (GI: 35)
- 1/4 cup fresh cilantro, chopped (GI: 0)
- 2 tablespoons fresh lime juice (GI: 0)
- 1 tablespoon olive oil (GI: 0)
- 1 teaspoon apple cider vinegar (GI: 5)
- 1 teaspoon honey or sugar substitute (optional) (GI: 55 for honey, 0 for stevia)
- Salt and pepper to taste (optional) (GI: 0)

Instructions:

1. **Prepare the Shrimp:** Whisk lime juice, olive oil, ginger, garlic, soy sauce, honey (or substitute), black pepper, and red pepper flakes in a bowl. Add shrimp and marinate for 10–15 minutes. Preheat grill to medium-high. Thread shrimp onto skewers and grill 2–3 minutes per side.
2. **Prepare the Slaw:** Combine green and red cabbage, carrot, and cilantro in a large bowl. Whisk lime juice, olive oil, apple cider vinegar, honey (or substitute), salt, and pepper. Toss with slaw just before serving.
3. **Serve:** Plate the slaw and top with grilled shrimp. Garnish with lime wedges and cilantro. Pair with a side of steamed vegetables or ½ cup quinoa for fiber. Serve this dish as a light and refreshing lunch or dinner. Pair it with steamed vegetables or a small portion of brown rice or quinoa for added fiber and nutrients. Add a sprinkle of sesame seeds or crushed peanuts for an extra flavor.

Nutritional Information (Per Serving)

Calories: 220, Protein: 22g, Carbohydrates: 10g, Fiber: 4g, Fats: 10g, Cholesterol: 170mg, Sodium: 350mg, Potassium: 500mg

Low-Carb Salmon Patties with Cucumber Salad

 Yield: 4 servings   Preparation Time: 15 minutes

 Cooking Time: 15 minutes

Ingredients:

For the Salmon Patties:
- 1 can (14.75 oz) wild-caught salmon, drained and flaked (GI: 0)
- 1/4 cup almond flour (GI: 0)
- 1 large egg, beaten (GI: 0)
- 2 tablespoons mayonnaise (preferably avocado oilbased) (GI: 0)
- 1 tablespoon Dijon mustard (GI: 0)
- 1/4 cup red onion, finely chopped (GI: 10)
- 2 tablespoons fresh parsley, chopped (GI: 0)
- 1 clove garlic, minced (GI: 10)
- 1/2 teaspoon paprika (GI: 0)
- 1/4 teaspoon salt (optional) (GI: 0)
- 1/4 teaspoon black pepper (GI: 0)
- 2 tablespoons olive oil for frying (GI: 0)

For the Cucumber Salad:
- 1 large cucumber, thinly sliced (GI: 15)
- 1/4 red onion, thinly sliced (GI: 10)
- 1/4 cup fresh dill, chopped (GI: 0)
- 2 tablespoons olive oil (GI: 0)
- 1 tablespoon apple cider vinegar (GI: 5)
- 1 tablespoon fresh lemon juice (GI: 0)
- 1/4 teaspoon salt (optional) (GI: 0)
- 1/4 teaspoon black pepper (GI: 0)

Instructions:

1. **Prepare the Salmon Patties:** Combine salmon, almond flour, egg, mayonnaise, Dijon mustard, red onion, parsley, garlic, paprika, salt, and pepper. Mix until combined. If the mixture is too loose, add more almond flour or egg. Divide into 8 equal portions and shape into patties.
2. **Cook the Patties:** Heat olive oil in a skillet over medium heat. Fry patties 3–4 minutes per side until golden and cooked through.
3. **Prepare the Cucumber Salad:** Combine cucumber, red onion, and dill in a bowl. Whisk olive oil, apple cider vinegar, lemon juice, salt, and pepper; pour over the salad.
4. **Serve:** Plate two salmon patties with a side of cucumber salad. Pair with roasted sweet potatoes or a small portion of quinoa.

Nutritional Information (Per Serving)

Calories: 310, Protein: 22g, Carbohydrates: 8g, Fiber: 3g, Fats: 22g, Cholesterol: 75mg, Sodium: 400mg, Potassium: 650mg

Blackened Fish and Cauliflower Rice Bowl

 Yield: 4 servings   Preparation Time: 15 minutes

 Cooking Time: 20 minutes

Ingredients:

For the Blackened Fish:
- 4 fillets of firm white fish such as tilapia, cod, or catfish (Glycemic Index: 0)
- 1 tablespoon olive oil (GI: 0)
- 1 teaspoon paprika (GI: 0)
- 1 teaspoon garlic powder (GI: 0)
- 1 teaspoon onion powder (GI: 0)
- 1/2 teaspoon dried thyme (GI: 0)
- 1/2 teaspoon dried oregano (GI: 0)
- 1/2 teaspoon cayenne pepper (optional for heat) (GI: 0)
- 1/4 teaspoon black pepper (GI: 0)
- 1/4 teaspoon salt (GI: 0)

For the Cauliflower Rice:
- 1 medium head of cauliflower, riced (about 4 cups) (GI: 15)
- 1 tablespoon olive oil (GI: 0)
- 1 clove garlic, minced (GI: 10)
- 1/4 teaspoon salt (GI: 0)
- 1/4 teaspoon black pepper (GI: 0)

Optional Toppings (for added flavor and nutrition):
- 1/2 avocado, sliced (GI: 15)
- 1/4 cup chopped fresh cilantro (GI: 0)
- 1/2 cup cherry tomatoes, halved (GI: 15)
- 1/4 cup diced red onion (GI: 10)
- 1 tablespoon lime juice (GI: 0)

Instructions:

1. **Prepare the Fish:** Mix paprika, garlic powder, onion powder, thyme, oregano, cayenne, black pepper, and salt. Coat fish with olive oil and season with spice mixture. Heat a skillet over medium-high heat. Cook fish 3–4 minutes per side until blackened.
2. **Prepare the Cauliflower Rice:** Pulse cauliflower florets in a food processor until rice-sized. Heat olive oil in a skillet, sauté garlic for 1 minute, and add cauliflower rice. Cook for 4–5 minutes, stirring occasionally. Season with salt and pepper.
3. **Assemble the Bowl:** Divide cauliflower rice into bowls. Top with fish and optional toppings like 2 tbsp avocado, 1 tbsp lime juice, and ¼ cup cherry tomatoes.
4. **Serve** with a side of mixed greens or roasted vegetables.

Nutritional Information (Per Serving)

Calories: 280, Protein: 25g, Carbohydrates: 10g, Dietary Fiber: 4g, Sugars: 2g, Fats: 16g, Saturated Fat: 2.5g, Cholesterol: 55mg, Sodium: 450mg, Potassium: 800mg

CHAPTER 7
DINNER RECIPES
1. Lean Protein Dishes

Lemon Herb Grilled Chicken

Yield: 4 servings Preparation Time: 15 minutes
Marinade Time: 15 minutes Cooking Time: 15 minutes

Ingredients:

- 4 boneless, skinless chicken breasts (approximately 4 oz each) (GI: 0)
- 2 tablespoons olive oil (GI: 0)
- 1/4 cup fresh lemon juice (GI: 0)
- 1 tablespoon lemon zest (GI: 0)
- 3 cloves garlic, minced (GI: 10)
- 2 teaspoons dried oregano (GI: 5)
- 2 teaspoons dried thyme (GI: 5)
- 1 teaspoon dried rosemary (GI: 5)
- 1/2 teaspoon black pepper (GI: 0)
- 1/2 teaspoon salt (optional) (GI: 0)
- 1/4 cup fresh parsley, chopped (GI: 5)

Optional Ingredients for Additional Flavor and Nutrition:

- 1 teaspoon red pepper flakes (GI: 0)
- 1 tablespoon Dijon mustard (GI: 15)
- 1 tablespoon honey (optional) (GI: 58)

Instructions:

1. **Prepare Marinade:** In a large bowl, mix olive oil, lemon juice, lemon zest, minced garlic, oregano, thyme, rosemary, black pepper, and salt (if using). Stir until combined. For extra flavor, add red pepper flakes, Dijon mustard, or honey (optional).
2. **Marinate Chicken:** Place chicken breasts in the bowl and coat evenly with marinade. Cover and refrigerate for 15–30 minutes. (Do not marinate longer than 2 hours for safety with acidic marinades.)
3. **Preheat Grill:** Heat grill to medium-high. Oil the grates lightly to prevent sticking.
4. **Grill Chicken:** Remove chicken from the marinade, letting excess drip off. Discard remaining marinade. Grill for 6–8 minutes per side until internal temperature reaches 165°F (74°C).
5. **Garnish and Serve:** Let chicken rest for 5 minutes before serving. Garnish with fresh parsley and serve hot. Pair with steamed broccoli or a mixed green salad. For a balanced meal, add ½ cup of quinoa (GI: 53) or roasted vegetables (e.g., carrots, zucchini).

Nutritional Information (Per Serving)

Calories: 180, Protein: 24g, Carbohydrates: 2g, Fats: 8g, Fiber: 0g, Cholesterol: 65mg, Sodium: 220mg, Potassium: 350mg

Chicken and Broccoli Stir-Fry

Yield: 4 servings Preparation Time: 15 minutes
Cooking Time: 15 minutes

Ingredients:

- 1 lb boneless, skinless chicken breasts, thinly sliced (GI: 0)
- 1 tbsp olive oil (GI: 0)
- 3 cups broccoli florets (GI: 10)
- 1 red bell pepper, thinly sliced (GI: 30)
- 3 cloves garlic, minced (GI: 0)
- 1 tbsp fresh ginger, grated (GI: 0)
- 1/4 cup low-sodium soy sauce (GI: 0)
- 1 tbsp rice vinegar (GI: 0)
- 1 tbsp sesame oil (GI: 0)
- 1 tbsp cornstarch mixed with 2 tbsp water (optional for thickening) (GI: 85, but used in small amounts)
- 1/4 tsp black pepper (GI: 0)
- 1/4 tsp red pepper flakes (optional for heat) (GI: 0)
- 2 tbsp chopped green onions or cilantro for garnish (optional) (GI: 0)

Instructions:

1. **Prepare Chicken and Vegetables:** Thinly slice chicken breasts. Cut broccoli into small florets and slice red bell pepper thinly.
2. **Cook Chicken:** Heat olive oil in a skillet over medium-high heat. Cook chicken slices for 5–6 minutes until browned and fully cooked. Remove and set aside.
3. **Stir-Fry Vegetables:** In the same skillet, sauté garlic and ginger for 1 minute until fragrant. Add broccoli and bell pepper. Stir-fry for 4–5 minutes until tender-crisp.
4. **Combine Chicken and Sauce:** Return chicken to the skillet. Add soy sauce, rice vinegar, sesame oil, and black pepper. Stir and cook for 2–3 minutes. For a thicker sauce, mix cornstarch with water and add during this step, stirring until the sauce thickens (optional).
5. **Serve:** Garnish with green onions or cilantro if desired. Serve hot. Pair with cauliflower rice (GI: 15) for a low-carb meal. Optionally, add a side salad or steamed green beans for extra fiber.

Nutritional Information (Per Serving)

Calories: 240, Protein: 28 g, Carbohydrates: 10 g, Fats: 10 g, Fiber: 3g, Cholesterol: 65 mg, Sodium: 480 mg, Potassium: 600 mg

Low-Carb Salmon Patties with Cucumber Salad

 Yield: 4 servings   Preparation Time: 15 minutes
Cooking Time: 15 minutes

Ingredients:

For the Salmon Patties:
- 1 block (14 oz) firm tofu, pressed and cubed (GI: 15)
- 2 tablespoons soy sauce (low sodium) (GI: 15)
- 1 tablespoon rice vinegar (GI: 0)
- 1 tablespoon sesame oil (GI: 0)
- 1 tablespoon olive oil (GI: 0)
- 1 medium onion, sliced (GI: 10)
- 3 cloves garlic, minced (GI: 10)
- 1 tablespoon fresh ginger, grated (GI: 10)
- 1 red bell pepper, sliced (GI: 15) 1 yellow bell pepper, sliced (GI: 15)
- 1 medium zucchini, sliced (GI: 15)
- 1 cup broccoli florets (GI: 15)
- 1 cup snow peas (GI: 15)
- 1 carrot, julienned (GI: 39)
- 2 tablespoons low-sodium vegetable broth (GI: 15)
- 1 tablespoon cornstarch (optional for thickening) (GI: 85)
- 1/4 teaspoon black pepper (GI: 0)
- 1/4 cup chopped fresh cilantro (GI: 5)
- 1/4 cup chopped green onions (GI: 15)
- Juice of 1 lime (GI: 0)
- 1 tablespoon sesame seeds optional) (GI: 15)

Optional Ingredients for Additional Flavor and Nutrition:
- 1/4 teaspoon red pepper flakes (GI: 0)
- 1 tablespoon hoisin sauce (GI: 20)

Instructions:

1. **Prepare Salmon Patties:** Use canned salmon (14 oz, drained) or fresh salmon (cooked and flaked). In a bowl, mix salmon with almond flour, a lightly beaten egg, minced garlic, chopped parsley, salt, and pepper. For added flavor, include a teaspoon of Dijon mustard or lemon zest. Form the mixture into 4–6 patties, about 1 inch thick. Chill in the refrigerator for 15 minutes to help them hold their shape.
2. **Cook Patties:** Heat olive oil in a skillet over medium heat. Fry patties for 3–4 minutes per side until golden brown and cooked through. Remove and keep warm.
3. **Prepare Cucumber Salad:** Slice cucumber thinly and mix with a small amount of olive oil, lemon juice, salt, and pepper. For more flavor, add fresh dill or a dollop of Greek yogurt.
4. **Serve:** Plate the salmon patties with cucumber salad on the side. Garnish with fresh parsley or a wedge of lemon. Pair with a side of roasted asparagus or steamed broccoli for extra fiber. If more carbohydrates are needed, serve with a small portion of quinoa or brown rice (½ cup).

Nutritional Information (Per Serving)

Calories: 280, Protein: 30g, Carbohydrates: 6g, Fats: 15g, Fiber: 2g, Cholesterol: 75mg, Sodium: 320mg, Potassium: 600mg

Garlic Roasted Turkey Breast

 Yield: 4 servings   Preparation Time: 15 minutes
 Cooking Time: 1 hour 30 min

Ingredients:
- 2 pounds boneless, skinless turkey breast (GI: 0)
- 2 tablespoons olive oil (GI: 0)
- 6 cloves garlic, minced (GI: 10)
- 2 teaspoons dried thyme (GI: 5)
- 2 teaspoons dried rosemary (GI: 5)
- 1 teaspoon paprika (GI: 5)
- 1/2 teaspoon black pepper (GI: 0)
- 1/2 teaspoon salt (optional) (GI: 0)
- Juice of 1 lemon (GI: 0)
- 1/4 cup fresh parsley, chopped (GI: 5)

Optional Ingredients for Additional Flavor and Nutrition:
- 1/2 teaspoon red pepper flakes (GI: 0)
- 1 tablespoon Dijon mustard (GI: 15)
- 1 teaspoon lemon zest (GI: 0)

Instructions:

1. **Prepare Turkey Breast:** Preheat oven to 375°F (190°C). Pat the turkey breast dry with paper towels. Mix olive oil, minced garlic, thyme, rosemary, paprika, black pepper, and salt (if using). Optionally, mix in Dijon mustard and lemon zest for added flavor. Rub the herb mixture over the turkey breast, ensuring an even coating.
2. **Roast Turkey:** Place turkey breast in a roasting pan. Pour ½ cup of water or chicken broth into the pan to keep the turkey moist. Roast for 1 hour 15 minutes to 1 hour 30 minutes, basting with pan juices every 30 minutes. Use a meat thermometer to ensure the internal temperature reaches 165°F (74°C).
3. **Rest and Serve:** Remove turkey from the oven and let it rest for 10 minutes before slicing. Garnish with fresh parsley before serving. Serve with steamed green beans or roasted Brussels sprouts. For additional carbs, pair with a small portion of sweet potato mash or wild rice (½ cup) or a mixed green salad.

Nutritional Information (Per Serving)

Calories: 220, Protein: 35g, Carbohydrates: 2g, Fats: 8g, Fiber: 0g, Cholesterol: 90mg, Sodium: 200mg, Potassium: 450mg

Baked Turkey Meatballs

 Yield: 4 servings (Makes 16 meatballs)   Preparation Time: 15 minutes

Cooking Time: 15 minutes

Ingredients:

- 1 lb lean ground turkey (93% lean)
- 1/4 cup almond flour (GI: 0)
- 1/4 cup grated Parmesan cheese (optional) (GI: 0)
- 1 large egg (GI: 0)
- 2 cloves garlic, minced (GI: 0)
- 1/4 cup finely chopped onion (GI: 15)
- 1 tsp dried Italian seasoning (GI: 0
- 1/2 tsp dried basil (GI: 0)
- 1/2 tsp dried oregano (GI: 0)
- 1/4 tsp black pepper (GI: 0)
- 1/4 tsp salt (optional) (GI: 0)
- Cooking spray or 1 tbsp olive oil (GI: 0) for greasing the baking sheet

Instructions:

1. **Prepare the Turkey Mixture:** Preheat oven to 375°F (190°C). In a large bowl, mix ground turkey, almond flour, Parmesan (if using), egg, minced garlic, onion, Italian seasoning, basil, oregano, black pepper, and salt (if using).
2. **Form the Meatballs:** Roll the mixture into 16 even-sized meatballs (approximately 1 inch in diameter). Place meatballs on a parchment-lined baking sheet, ensuring they are evenly spaced.
3. **Bake the Meatballs:** Bake for 20–25 minutes, turning the meatballs halfway through. Use a meat thermometer to check for an internal temperature of 165°F (74°C).
4. **Serve:** Remove meatballs from the oven and let them rest for 5 minutes before serving. Pair with a low-carb marinara sauce or on a bed of sautéed spinach or zucchini noodles, or with a side of roasted vegetables, such as Brussels sprouts (GI: 15), or a green salad with a light vinaigrette.

Nutritional Information (Per Serving)

Calories: 200, Protein: 24 g, Carbohydrates: 4 g, Fats: 10 g, Fiber: 1g, Cholesterol: 95 mg, Sodium: 220 mg, Potassium: 350 mg

Chicken and Spinach Stuffed Portobello Mushrooms

 Yield: 4 servings   Preparation Time: 15 minutes

Cooking Time: 25 minutes

Ingredients:

- 4 large Portobello mushrooms, stems removed and gills scraped out (GI: 15)
- 1 tablespoon olive oil (GI: 0)
- 1 pound ground chicken breast (GI: 0)
- 1 medium onion, diced (GI: 10)
- 3 cloves garlic, minced (GI: 10)
- 5 cups fresh spinach, roughly chopped (GI: 15)
- 1/4 cup sun-dried tomatoes, chopped (GI: 35)
- 1/2 cup part-skim mozzarella cheese, shredded (optional) (GI: 0)
- 1/4 cup grated Parmesan cheese (optional) (GI: 0)
- 1 teaspoon dried oregano (GI: 5)
- 1 teaspoon dried basil (GI: 5)
- 1/2 teaspoon black pepper (GI: 0)
- 1/2 teaspoon salt (optional) (GI: 0)
- Juice of 1 lemon (GI: 0)
- 1/4 cup fresh parsley, chopped (GI: 5)

Optional Ingredients for Additional Flavor and Nutrition:

- 1/4 teaspoon red pepper flakes (GI: 0)
- 1 tablespoon balsamic vinegar (GI: 0)
- 1/4 cup chopped fresh basil (GI: 5)

Instructions:

1. **Prepare the Mushrooms:** Preheat oven to 375°F (190°C). Brush Portobello mushroom caps with olive oil and place them gill-side up on a baking sheet.
2. **Cook the Filling:** Heat olive oil in a skillet over medium heat. Sauté diced onion for 5 minutes until softened. Add garlic and cook for 1 minute. Stir in ground chicken, cooking for 7–8 minutes until browned. Add spinach and cook for 2–3 minutes until wilted. Stir in sun-dried tomatoes, oregano, basil, black pepper, and salt. Cook for 1 minute, then remove from heat.
3. **Stuff the Mushrooms:** Fill each mushroom cap with the chicken and spinach mixture. Top with mozzarella and Parmesan (if using).
4. **Bake**: Bake stuffed mushrooms for 15–20 minutes, until the mushrooms are tender and the cheese is melted and bubbly.
5. **Serve**: Drizzle with balsamic vinegar (if using) and garnish with fresh parsley or basil. Serve with a side salad or steamed asparagus. Add cauliflower rice or quinoa for additional carbohydrates if needed.

Nutritional Information (Per Serving)

Calories: 250, Protein: 28g, Carbohydrates:10g, Fats: 12g, Fiber: 4g, Cholesterol: 75mg, Sodium: 280mg, Potassium: 800mg

Garlic and Rosemary Grilled Pork Tenderloin

 Yield: 4 servings   *Preparation Time: 10 minutes*
 Cooking Time: 20-25 minutes

Ingredients:

- 1 lb pork tenderloin (GI: 0)
- 2 tbsp olive oil (GI: 0)
- 3 cloves garlic, minced (GI: 0)
- 1 tbsp fresh rosemary, finely chopped (or 1 tsp dried rosemary) (GI: 0)
- 1 tbsp fresh lemon juice (GI: 0)
- 1 tsp Dijon mustard (GI: 0)
- 1/2 tsp black pepper (GI: 0)
- 1/4 tsp salt (optional) (GI: 0)
- Fresh parsley for garnish (optional) (GI: 0)

Instructions:

1. **Prepare the Marinade:** In a small bowl, whisk together olive oil, minced garlic, chopped rosemary, lemon juice, Dijon mustard, black pepper, and salt (if using). Add optional liquid smoke for enhanced flavor.
2. **Marinate the Pork:** Pat the pork tenderloin dry with paper towels. Place the pork in a resealable plastic bag or shallow dish and pour the marinade over it, ensuring even coating. Seal the bag or cover the dish and refrigerate for at least 30 minutes or up to 2 hours.
3. **Preheat the Grill:** Preheat the grill to medium-high heat (~375–400°F/190–200°C).
4. **Grill the Pork:** Remove the pork from the marinade, letting excess drip off. Place the pork on the grill and cook for 10–12 minutes per side, or until the internal temperature reaches 145°F (63°C) for medium-rare or 160°F (71°C) for well-done.
5. **Rest and Serve:** Remove the pork from the grill and let it rest for 5 minutes before slicing. Garnish with fresh parsley if desired. Serve the Garlic and Rosemary Grilled Pork Tenderloin with roasted Brussels sprouts (GI: 15) or steamed asparagus (GI: 15). A small portion of quinoa (GI: 53) or cauliflower mash (GI: 15) pairs well with the dish for a complete, balanced meal.

Nutritional Information (Per Serving)
Calories: 220, Protein: 25 g, Carbohydrates: 2 g, Fats: 12 g, Fiber: 0 g, Cholesterol: 70 mg, Sodium: 220 mg, Potassium: 350 mg

Balsamic Glazed Pork Tenderloin

 Yield: 4 servings   *Preparation Time: 10 minutes*
 Cooking Time: 25 minutes

Ingredients:

- 1 pound pork tenderloin (GI: 0)
- 2 tablespoons olive oil (GI: 0)
- 1/4 cup balsamic vinegar (GI: 0)
- 2 tablespoons Dijon mustard (GI: 15)
- 2 tablespoons honey (optional) (GI: 58)
- 3 cloves garlic, minced (GI: 10)
- 1 teaspoon dried thyme (GI: 5)
- 1 teaspoon dried rosemary (GI: 5)
- 1/2 teaspoon black pepper (GI: 0)
- 1/2 teaspoon salt (optional) (GI: 0)

Optional Ingredients for Additional Flavor and Nutrition:
- 1/2 teaspoon red pepper flakes (GI: 0)
- 1 tablespoon fresh parsley, chopped (GI: 5)

Instructions:

1. **Prepare the Marinade:** In a small bowl, whisk together balsamic vinegar, Dijon mustard, honey (or sugar substitute), minced garlic, thyme, rosemary, black pepper, and salt.
2. **Optionally**, add red pepper flakes for a touch of heat.
3. **Marinate the Pork:** Place the pork tenderloin in a shallow dish or resealable bag. Pour the marinade over the pork, turning to coat evenly. Let it marinate for at least 15 minutes, turning occasionally.
4. **Preheat the Oven:** Preheat the oven to 400°F (200°C).
5. **Sear the Pork:** Heat olive oil in an oven-safe skillet over medium-high heat. Remove the pork from the marinade (reserve the marinade) and sear on all sides for 2–3 minutes per side until browned.
6. **Roast the Pork:** Pour the reserved marinade over the seared pork. Transfer the skillet to the oven and roast for 15–20 minutes, or until the internal temperature reaches 145°F (63°C).
7. **Rest and Slice:** Remove the pork from the oven and let it rest for 5 minutes before slicing.
8. **Garnish and Serve:** Garnish with fresh parsley and, if desired, sprinkle with additional red pepper flakes.

Nutritional Information (Per Serving)
Calories: 240, Protein: 28g, Carbohydrates: 6g, Fats: 10g, Fiber: 0g, Cholesterol: 80mg, Sodium: 300mg, Potassium: 450mg

Herb-Rubbed Grilled Chicken Breasts

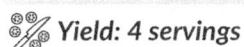 Yield: 4 servings   Preparation Time: 10 minutes
Marinade Time: 15 minutes   Cooking Time: 15 minutes

Ingredients:

- 4 boneless, skinless chicken breasts (approximately 6 oz each) (GI: 0)
- 2 tablespoons olive oil (GI: 0)
- 2 tablespoons fresh lemon juice (GI: 0)
- 3 cloves garlic, minced (GI: 10)
- 2 teaspoons dried oregano (GI: 5)
- 2 teaspoons dried thyme (GI: 5)
- 1 teaspoon dried rosemary (GI: 5)
- 1 teaspoon paprika (GI: 5)
- 1/2 teaspoon black pepper (GI: 0)
- 1/2 teaspoon salt (optional) (GI: 0)
- 1/4 cup fresh parsley, chopped (GI: 5)
- 1 tablespoon fresh basil, chopped (optional) (GI: 5)

Optional Ingredients for Additional Flavor and Nutrition:

- 1/4 teaspoon red pepper flakes (GI: 0)
- 1 tablespoon Dijon mustard (GI: 15)
- 1 tablespoon balsamic vinegar (GI: 0)

Instructions:

1. **Prepare the Marinade:** In a bowl, mix olive oil, lemon juice, minced garlic, dried oregano, thyme, rosemary, paprika, black pepper, and salt (if using). For additional flavor, whisk in Dijon mustard and balsamic vinegar.
2. **Marinate the Chicken:** Place chicken breasts in a resealable bag or shallow dish. Pour the marinade over the chicken, ensuring even coating. Seal and refrigerate for at least 30 minutes, up to 2 hours.
3. **Preheat the Grill:** Preheat the grill to medium-high heat (~375-400°F/190-200°C).
4. **Grill the Chicken:** Remove the chicken from the marinade, letting excess drip off. Grill for 6-7 minutes per side, or until the internal temperature reaches 165°F (74°C).
5. **Rest and Garnish:** Remove the chicken from the grill and let it rest for 5 minutes. Garnish with fresh parsley or basil before serving. Pair with roasted vegetables like Brussels sprouts or asparagus. Add a small portion of quinoa or wild rice if needed for extra carbohydrates. For a complete meal, pair it with a serving of quinoa or brown rice (optional, ensure it's suitable for diabetic diets).

Nutritional Information (Per Serving)

Calories: 210, Protein: 32g, Carbohydrates: 2g, Fats: 9g, Fiber: 0g, Cholesterol: 85mg, Sodium: 250mg, Potassium: 400mg

Lean Beef and Vegetable Stir-Fry

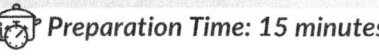 Yield: 4 servings   Preparation Time: 15 minutes
Cooking Time: 15 minutes

Ingredients:

- 1 lb lean beef sirloin or flank steak, thinly sliced (GI: 0) 1 tbsp olive oil (GI: 0)
- 2 cloves garlic, minced (GI: 0)
- 1 tbsp fresh ginger, grated (GI: 0)
- 1 red bell pepper, thinly sliced (GI: 30)
- 1 green bell pepper, thinly sliced (GI: 30)
- 1 medium zucchini, sliced into half-moons (GI: 15)
- 1 cup broccoli florets (GI: 10)
- 1/4 cup low-sodium soy sauce (GI: 0)
- 1 tbsp rice vinegar (GI: 0)
- 1 tbsp sesame oil (GI: 0)
- 1/4 tsp black pepper (GI: 0)
- 1/4 tsp red pepper flakes (optional, for a bit of heat) (GI: 0)
- 2 tbsp chopped fresh cilantro or green onions for garnish (optional) (GI: 0)

Instructions:

1. **Prepare the Beef:** Slice beef into thin strips against the grain for tenderness. Toss with half the soy sauce and let marinate for 10 minutes.
2. **Stir-Fry the Beef:** Heat 1 tablespoon olive oil in a large skillet or wok over medium-high heat. Stir-fry beef in a single layer for 3-4 minutes until browned. Remove and set aside.
3. **Cook the Vegetables:** Add remaining olive oil to the skillet. Stir-fry garlic and ginger for 1 minute until fragrant. Add broccoli, bell peppers, and zucchini. Stir-fry for 4-5 minutes until tender-crisp.
4. **Combine and Flavor:** Return beef to the skillet with the vegetables. Stir in remaining soy sauce, rice vinegar, sesame oil, and black pepper. Cook for 2-3 minutes to meld flavors. If using, add red pepper flakes for heat.
5. **Serve:** Garnish with chopped cilantro and sesame seeds, if desired. Serve over a bed of cauliflower rice (GI: 15) or with a small portion of quinoa (GI: 53) to keep the dish low in carbohydrates. For extra fiber, add steamed green beans (GI: 15) or a mixed green salad (GI: 0).

Nutritional Information (Per Serving)

Calories: 280, Protein: 28 g, Carbohydrates: 8 g, Fats: 14 g, Fiber: 3 g, Cholesterol: 65 mg, Sodium: 480 mg, Potassium: 750 mg

2. Low-Carb Dinner Ideas

Spaghetti Squash Bolognese

Yield: 4 servings   *Preparation Time: 15 minutes*
Cooking Time: 50 minutes

Ingredients:
- 1 large spaghetti squash (GI: 20)
- 1 tablespoon olive oil (GI: 0)
- 1 pound lean ground beef or turkey (GI: 0)
- 1 medium onion, diced (GI: 10)
- 3 cloves garlic, minced (GI: 10)
- 1 carrot, finely diced (GI: 39)
- 1 celery stalk, finely diced (GI: 15)
- 1 can (14.5 oz) diced tomatoes, no salt added (GI: 15)
- 1 can (6 oz) tomato paste (GI: 15)
- 1/2 cup low-sodium beef or chicken broth (GI: 15)
- 1 teaspoon dried oregano (GI: 5)
- 1 teaspoon dried basil (GI: 5)
- 1/2 teaspoon dried thyme (GI: 5)
- 1/2 teaspoon black pepper (GI: 0)
- 1/2 teaspoon salt (optional) (GI: 0)
- 1/4 cup fresh parsley, chopped (GI: 5)
- 1/4 cup grated Parmesan cheese (optional) (GI: 0)

Optional Ingredients for Additional Flavor and Nutrition:
- 1/4 teaspoon red pepper flakes (GI: 0)
- 1 tablespoon balsamic vinegar (GI: 0)
- 1/4 cup chopped fresh basil (GI: 5)

Instructions:
1. **Prepare the Spaghetti Squash:** Preheat the oven to 400°F (200°C). Cut the squash in half lengthwise and scoop out the seeds. Brush the cut sides with olive oil and season with salt and pepper. Place cut side down on a baking sheet and roast for 35–40 minutes, or until tender. Once cool enough to handle, use a fork to scrape out the strands into a bowl.
2. **Cook the Meat Sauce:** Heat olive oil in a large skillet over medium heat. Add diced onion, carrot, and celery. Sauté for 5 minutes until softened. Add minced garlic and cook for 1 minute. Stir in ground turkey or beef, breaking it apart, and cook until browned (7–8 minutes). Mix in diced tomatoes, tomato paste, broth, oregano, basil, thyme, black pepper, and salt. **Optionally,** add red pepper flakes and balsamic vinegar for extra flavor. Simmer on low heat for 15–20 minutes until thickened.
3. **Assemble and Serve:** Divide the spaghetti squash strands among four plates. Top with the meat sauce. Garnish with fresh parsley, grated Parmesan, and optional fresh basil.
4. **Serving:** Pair with a side of steamed vegetables or a fresh green salad with a light vinaigrette.

Nutritional Information (Per Serving)
Calories: 260, Protein: 24g, Carbohydrates: 10g, Fats: 15g, Fiber: 5g, Cholesterol: 65mg, Sodium: 42mg, Potassium: 900mg

Cauliflower Fried Rice with Chicken

Yield: 4 servings   *Preparation Time: 15 minutes*
Cooking Time: 20 minutes

Ingredients:
- 1 medium head cauliflower, riced (GI: 15)
- 2 tablespoons olive oil (GI: 0)
- 1 pound boneless, skinless chicken breast, diced (GI: 0)
- 1 medium onion, diced (GI: 10)
- 3 cloves garlic, minced (GI: 10)
- 1 cup frozen peas and carrots mix (GI: 39 for carrots, 22 for peas)
- 1 red bell pepper, diced (GI: 15)
- 2 large eggs, lightly beaten (GI: 0)
- 3 tablespoons low-sodium soy sauce (GI: 15)
- 1 tablespoon sesame oil (GI: 0)
- 2 green onions, sliced (GI: 15)
- 1/4 cup fresh cilantro, chopped (GI: 5)
- 1 tablespoon fresh ginger, grated (GI: 10)
- 1/4 teaspoon black pepper (GI: 0)
- 1/2 teaspoon salt (optional) (GI: 0)

Optional Ingredients for Additional Flavor and Nutrition:
- 1/4 teaspoon red pepper flakes (GI: 0)
- 1 tablespoon rice vinegar (GI: 0)
- 1/4 cup chopped fresh basil (GI: 5)

Instructions:
1. **Prepare the Cauliflower Rice:** Remove leaves and core from the cauliflower. Cut into florets and pulse in a food processor until it resembles rice. Set aside.
2. **Cook the Chicken:** Heat 1 tablespoon olive oil in a large skillet over medium-high heat. Add diced chicken and cook for 5–7 minutes until browned and cooked through. Remove and set aside.
3. **Cook the Vegetables:** In the same skillet, heat the remaining olive oil. Sauté onion for 3–4 minutes until translucent. Add minced garlic and grated ginger, cooking for 1 minute until fragrant. Stir in the peas, carrots, and bell pepper. Cook for 3–4 minutes until tender-crisp.
4. **Add the Cauliflower Rice:** Push the vegetables to the side of the skillet and add the cauliflower rice. Cook for 5 minutes, stirring frequently, until tender.
5. **Scramble the Eggs:** Move everything to the sides of the skillet, creating a well in the center. Pour in the beaten eggs and scramble until cooked. Mix with the vegetables.
6. **Combine and Flavor:** Return the chicken to the skillet. Add soy sauce, sesame oil, rice vinegar, and black pepper. Optionally, sprinkle with red pepper flakes for heat. Stir to combine.
7. **Finish and Serve:** Garnish with sliced green onions and chopped cilantro. Serve as a standalone meal or with a simple cucumber salad for added freshness.

Nutritional Information (Per Serving)
Calories: 280, Protein: 30g, Carbohydrates: 12g, Fats: 12g, Fiber: 5g, Cholesterol: 110mg, Sodium: 450mg, Potassium: 800mg

Zoodles with Pesto and Cherry Tomatoes

Yield: 4 servings   Preparation Time: 15 minutes   Cooking Time: 10 minutes

Ingredients:
- 4 medium zucchinis, spiralized into noodles (GI: 15)
- 1 cup cherry tomatoes, halved (GI: 15)
- 1 tablespoon olive oil (GI: 0)
- 2 cloves garlic, minced (GI: 10)
- 1/4 cup grated Parmesan cheese (optional) (GI: 0)
- 1/4 cup pine nuts, toasted (optional) (GI: 15)
- 1/4 cup fresh basil leaves for garnish (GI: 5)

For the Pesto:
- 2 cups fresh basil leaves (GI: 5)
- 1/4 cup pine nuts (GI: 15)
- 1/4 cup grated Parmesan cheese (GI: 0)
- 2 cloves garlic (GI: 10)
- 1/4 cup olive oil (GI: 0)
- 1 tablespoon lemon juice (GI: 0)
- 1/4 teaspoon salt (optional) (GI: 0)
- 1/4 teaspoon black pepper (GI: 0)

Optional Ingredients for Additional Flavor and Nutrition:
- 1/4 cup sun-dried tomatoes, chopped (GI: 35)
- 1/4 cup feta cheese, crumbled (GI: 0)
- 1 tablespoon nutritional yeast (GI: 0)

Instructions:
1. **Prepare the Pesto:** In a food processor, combine basil leaves, pine nuts, Parmesan cheese, garlic, olive oil, lemon juice, salt, and pepper. Blend until smooth, scraping down the sides as needed. Add more olive oil, a tablespoon at a time, if the consistency is too thick.
2. **Prepare the Zoodles:** Spiralize the zucchinis into noodles. Place them on paper towels to remove excess moisture. Heat olive oil in a large skillet over medium heat. Add minced garlic and sauté for 30 seconds until fragrant. Add the zoodles and cook for 2–3 minutes, stirring frequently, until tender but still firm. Avoid overcooking to prevent sogginess.
3. **Combine with Pesto:** Remove the skillet from heat. Add cherry tomatoes and the prepared pesto to the zoodles. Toss until evenly coated.
4. **Optional Toppings:** Stir in sun-dried tomatoes or sprinkle feta cheese and nutritional yeast on top for added flavor.
5. **Serve:** Divide the zoodles onto four plates. Garnish with fresh basil and pine nuts, if desired. Serve as a light main dish with grilled chicken or salmon for added protein. Pair with a mixed green salad for additional fiber.

Nutritional Information (Per Serving)
Calories: 200, Protein: 5g, Carbohydrates: 9g, Fats: 17g, Fiber: 3g, Cholesterol: 5mg, Sodium: 150mg, Potassium: 500mg

Stuffed Bell Peppers with Ground Turkey

Yield: 4 servings   Preparation Time: 15 minutes   Cooking Time: 40 minutes

Ingredients:
- 4 large bell peppers, any color, tops cut off and seeds removed (GI: 15)
- 1 pound ground turkey (GI: 0)
- 1 tablespoon olive oil (GI: 0)
- 1 medium onion, diced (GI: 10)
- 3 cloves garlic, minced (GI: 10)
- 1 medium zucchini, diced (GI: 15)
- 1 cup diced tomatoes, no salt added (GI: 15)
- 1/2 cup quinoa, cooked (GI: 53)
- 1 teaspoon dried oregano (GI: 5)
- 1 teaspoon dried basil (GI: 5)
- 1/2 teaspoon dried thyme (GI: 5)
- 1/2 teaspoon black pepper (GI: 0)
- 1/2 teaspoon salt (optional) (GI: 0)
- 1/4 cup grated Parmesan cheese (optional) (GI: 0)
- 1/4 cup fresh parsley, chopped (GI: 5)
- 1/4 cup fresh basil, chopped (optional) (GI: 5)

Optional Ingredients for Additional Flavor and Nutrition:
- 1/4 teaspoon red pepper flakes (GI: 0)
- 1 tablespoon balsamic vinegar (GI: 0)
- 1/4 cup crumbled feta cheese (GI: 0)

Instructions:
1. **Prepare the Bell Peppers:** Preheat the oven to 375°F (190°C). Cut the tops off the bell peppers and remove seeds. Trim bottoms slightly if needed to make them stand upright.
2. **Cook the Filling:** Heat olive oil in a skillet over medium heat. Add diced onion and sauté for 5 minutes until softened. Add minced garlic and cook for 1 minute. Stir in ground turkey, breaking it apart as it cooks. Cook for 7–8 minutes until browned. Add diced zucchini, diced tomatoes, quinoa, oregano, basil, salt, pepper, and optional balsamic vinegar and red pepper flakes. Simmer for 5 minutes to blend flavors.
3. **Stuff the Peppers:** Place the bell peppers upright in a baking dish. Spoon the filling into the peppers, packing it down slightly.
4. **Bake:** Cover the baking dish with aluminum foil and bake for 30 minutes. Remove the foil, sprinkle Parmesan cheese on top (if using), and bake for an additional 10 minutes until the cheese melts and the peppers are tender.
5. **Serve:** Garnish with fresh parsley or basil. Pair with steamed broccoli or a mixed green salad for a complete meal. For added carbohydrates, serve with a small portion of brown rice.

Nutritional Information (Per Serving)
Calories: 270, Protein: 25g, Carbohydrates: 20g, Fats: 10g, Fiber: 6g, Cholesterol: 70mg, Sodium: 300mg, Potassium: 800mg

Beef and Broccoli Stir-Fry

Yield: 4 servings **Preparation Time:** 15 minutes **Cooking Time:** 15 minutes

Ingredients:
- 1 pound beef sirloin, thinly sliced (GI: 0)
- 4 cups broccoli florets (GI: 15)
- 1 red bell pepper, thinly sliced (GI: 15)
- 1 medium onion, thinly sliced (GI: 10)
- 3 cloves garlic, minced (GI: 10)
- 1 tablespoon fresh ginger, grated (GI: 10)
- 3 tablespoons soy sauce (low sodium) (GI: 15)
- 2 tablespoons oyster sauce (GI: 0)
- 1 tablespoon sesame oil (GI: 0)
- 1 tablespoon olive oil (GI: 0)
- 1 tablespoon rice vinegar (GI: 0)
- 1 tablespoon cornstarch (optional for thickening) (GI: 85)
- 1/4 teaspoon black pepper (GI: 0)
- 1/4 cup water (GI: 0)

Optional Ingredients for Additional Flavor and Nutrition:
- 1 teaspoon red pepper flakes (GI: 0)
- 1 tablespoon hoisin sauce (GI: 35)
- 1 tablespoon sesame seeds (GI: 15)
- 1/4 cup chopped fresh cilantro (GI: 5)

Instructions:
1. **Prepare the Beef:** Thinly slice beef against the grain. In a small bowl, toss beef with 1 tablespoon soy sauce, 1 tablespoon oyster sauce, and 1 tablespoon cornstarch. Marinate for 10 minutes.
2. **Prepare the Sauce:** In a separate bowl, whisk together the remaining soy sauce, oyster sauce, rice vinegar, sesame oil, and water. If using, stir in hoisin sauce and red pepper flakes.
3. **Cook the Beef:** Heat olive oil in a large skillet or wok over medium-high heat. Add marinated beef in a single layer and stir-fry for 2-3 minutes until browned. Remove and set aside.
4. **Cook the Vegetables:** In the same skillet, add broccoli and onion. Stir-fry for 3-4 minutes until tender-crisp. Add garlic, ginger, and red bell pepper, cooking for 2 minutes until fragrant.
5. **Combine and Thicken Sauce:** Return beef to the skillet. Pour the sauce over the beef and vegetables. Stir and cook for 2-3 minutes. If a thicker sauce is desired, mix 1 tablespoon cornstarch with 2 tablespoons water and add to the skillet. Stir until the sauce thickens.
6. **Serve:** Garnish with sesame seeds, chopped cilantro, and optional green onions. Serve over cauliflower rice for a low-carb option. Pair with a cucumber salad or steamed green beans for added fiber.

Nutritional Information (Per Serving)
Calories: 280, Protein: 28g, Carbohydrates: 12g, Fats: 12g, Fiber: 4g, Cholesterol: 70mg, Sodium: 450mg, Potassium: 700mg

Herb-Roasted Chicken Thighs with Garlic and Vegetables

Yield: 4 servings **Preparation Time:** 15 minutes **Cooking Time:** 35-40 minutes

Ingredients:
- 8 bone-in, skin-on chicken thighs (about 2.5 lbs) (GI: 0)
- 2 tbsp olive oil (GI: 0)
- 4 cloves garlic, minced (GI: 0)
- 1 tbsp fresh rosemary, chopped (or 1 tsp dried rosemary) (GI: 0)
- 1 tbsp fresh thyme, chopped (or 1 tsp dried thyme) (GI: 0)
- 1 tsp paprika (GI: 0)
- 1/2 tsp black pepper (GI: 0)
- 1/2 tsp salt (optional) (GI: 0)
- 1 lb Brussels sprouts, halved (GI: 15)
- 1 large red onion, cut into wedges (GI: 15)
- 2 medium zucchinis, sliced into thick rounds (GI: 15)
- Juice of 1 lemon (GI: 0)
- Fresh parsley for garnish (optional) (GI: 0)

Instructions:
1. **Prepare the Garlic Herb Mixture:** In a small bowl, mix olive oil, minced garlic, rosemary, thyme, paprika, black pepper, and salt (if using).
2. **Prepare the Chicken Thighs:** Pat the chicken thighs dry with paper towels. Rub the garlic herb mixture all over the chicken, ensuring even coating.
3. **Prepare the Vegetables:** Spread Brussels sprouts, red onion, and zucchini on a baking sheet. Drizzle with olive oil and season with salt and pepper. Toss to coat evenly.
4. **Roast the Chicken and Vegetables:** Place chicken thighs on top of the vegetables. Roast in a preheated oven at 400°F (200°C) for 35-40 minutes. Toss vegetables halfway through for even roasting.
5. **Serve:** Once cooked, garnish with fresh parsley and squeeze lemon juice over the dish for added flavor. Serve with a side of cauliflower mash or a cucumber salad for additional nutrients. A small portion with a side of cauliflower mash (GI: 15) or a mixed green salad (GI: 0) can be included for those requiring more carbohydrates. Add roasted carrots (GI: 39) to the vegetable mix for added fiber and texture.

Nutritional Information (Per Serving)
Calories: 380, Protein: 28 g, Carbohydrates: 10 g, Fats: 26 g, Fiber: 4 g, Cholesterol: 120 mg, Sodium: 320 mg, Potassium: 700 mg

Beef and Broccoli Stir-Fry with Cauliflower Rice

🌀 *Yield: 4 servings*   🍲 *Preparation Time: 15 minutes*
🍽 *Cooking Time: 15 minutes*

Ingredients:
- 1 pound beef sirloin, thinly sliced (GI: 0)
- 4 cups broccoli florets (GI: 15)
- 1 red bell pepper, thinly sliced (GI: 15)
- 1 medium onion, thinly sliced (GI: 10)
- 3 cloves garlic, minced (GI: 10)
- 1 tablespoon fresh ginger, grated (GI: 10)
- 3 tablespoons soy sauce (low sodium) (GI: 15)
- 2 tablespoons oyster sauce (GI: 0)
- 1 tablespoon sesame oil (GI: 0)
- 1 tablespoon olive oil (GI: 0)
- 1 tablespoon rice vinegar (GI: 0)
- 1 tablespoon cornstarch (optional for thickening) (GI: 85)
- 1/4 teaspoon black pepper (GI: 0)
- 1/4 cup water (GI: 0)

Optional Ingredients for Additional Flavor and Nutrition:
- 1 teaspoon red pepper flakes (GI: 0)
- 1 tablespoon hoisin sauce (GI: 35)
- 1 tablespoon sesame seeds (GI: 15)
- 1/4 cup chopped fresh cilantro (GI: 5)

Instructions:
1. **Prepare the Beef:** Slice the beef thinly against the grain for tenderness. Toss with 1 tablespoon soy sauce, 1 tablespoon oyster sauce, and 1 tablespoon cornstarch in a bowl. Marinate for 10–15 minutes.
2. **Prepare the Sauce:** In a small bowl, whisk together remaining soy sauce, oyster sauce, sesame oil, rice vinegar, and water. Add red pepper flakes if desired.
3. **Cook the Beef:** Heat 1 tablespoon olive oil in a large skillet or wok over medium-high heat. Add the marinated beef and stir-fry for 2–3 minutes until browned. Remove from the skillet and set aside.
4. **Cook the Vegetables:** Add another tablespoon of olive oil to the skillet. Add broccoli and onion, stir-frying for 3–4 minutes until tender-crisp. Add garlic and ginger, and cook for 1–2 minutes until fragrant.
5. **Combine and Thicken Sauce:** Return the cooked beef to the skillet. Pour in the sauce and stir to coat. If a thicker sauce is desired, dissolve 1 tablespoon cornstarch in 2 tablespoons water and stir into the skillet. Cook for 2–3 minutes until the sauce thickens.
6. **Prepare the Cauliflower Rice:** Heat olive oil in a separate skillet over medium heat. Add riced cauliflower and stir-fry for 5–7 minutes until tender. Season with salt and pepper to taste.
7. **Serve:** Serve the beef and broccoli stir-fry over the cauliflower rice. Garnish with sesame seeds, chopped cilantro, and optional green onions. For extra fiber and nutrients, serve the dish with steamed green beans (GI: 15) or a mixed green salad (GI: 0). If you want a heartier meal, add a small portion of quinoa (GI: 53) on the side.

Nutritional Information (Per Serving)

Calories: 320, Protein: 28 g, Carbohydrates: 12 g, Fats: 18 g, Fiber: 5 g, Cholesterol: 65 mg, Sodium: 520 mg, Potassium: 750 mg

---

Eggplant Lasagna

🌀 *Yield: 6 servings*   🍲 *Preparation Time: 30 minutes*
🍽 *Cooking Time: 60 minutes*

Ingredients:
- 8 bone-in, skin-on chicken thighs (about 2.5 lbs) (GI: 0)
- 2 tbsp olive oil (GI: 0)
- 4 cloves garlic, minced (GI: 0)
- 1 tbsp fresh rosemary, chopped (or 1 tsp dried rosemary) (GI: 0)
- 1 tbsp fresh thyme, chopped (or 1 tsp dried thyme) (GI: 0)
- 1 tsp paprika (GI: 0)
- 1/2 tsp black pepper (GI: 0)
- 1/2 tsp salt (optional) (GI: 0)
- 1 lb Brussels sprouts, halved (GI: 15)
- 1 large red onion, cut into wedges (GI: 15)
- 2 medium zucchinis, sliced into thick rounds (GI: 15)
- Juice of 1 lemon (GI: 0)
- Fresh parsley for garnish (optional) (GI: 0)

Instructions:
1. **Prepare the Eggplant:** Preheat oven to 400°F (200°C). Slice eggplants lengthwise into 1/4-inch slices. Sprinkle slices with salt and let sit for 15 minutes to remove excess moisture and bitterness. Pat dry with paper towels. Brush slices with olive oil, place on a baking sheet, and roast for 15–20 minutes, flipping halfway, until tender and golden.
2. **Cook the Meat Sauce:** Heat olive oil in a skillet over medium heat. Add diced onion and garlic, cooking until softened. Add ground turkey or beef, breaking it apart and cooking until browned. Stir in diced tomatoes, tomato sauce, oregano, basil, salt, pepper, and red pepper flakes. Simmer for 15 minutes.
3. **Prepare the Cheese Mixture:** In a bowl, combine ricotta, 1/2 cup mozzarella, Parmesan, egg, and parsley. Mix until smooth.
4. **Assemble the Lasagna:** Reduce oven temperature to 375°F (190°C). Spread a thin layer of meat sauce in a 9x13-inch baking dish. Layer roasted eggplant slices, half the ricotta mixture, and a portion of the meat sauce. Repeat the layers, ending with meat sauce on top. Sprinkle with the remaining mozzarella cheese.
5. **Bake:** Cover with foil and bake for 30 minutes. Remove foil and bake for an additional 10–15 minutes until cheese is bubbly and golden.
6. **Serve:** Let cool slightly before slicing. Garnish with fresh basil if desired. Pair with a mixed green salad and a light vinaigrette. For additional protein, serve with grilled chicken or salmon.

Nutritional Information (Per Serving)

Calories: 280, Protein: 22g, Carbohydrates: 12g, Fats: 18g, Fiber: 5g, Cholesterol: 90mg, Sodium: 600mg, Potassium: 700mg

Cauliflower Mashed Potatoes with Grilled Chicken

Yield: 4 servings   Preparation Time: 20 minutes
Cooking Time: 30 minutes

Ingredients:

- 4 boneless, skinless chicken breasts (GI: 0)
- 2 tablespoons olive oil (GI: 0)
- 2 cloves garlic, minced (GI: 10)
- 1 teaspoon dried rosemary (GI: 5)
- 1 teaspoon dried thyme (GI: 5)
- 1/2 teaspoon salt (optional, GI: 0)
- 1/4 teaspoon black pepper (GI: 0)
- 1 tablespoon lemon juice (GI: 0)

For the Cauliflower Mashed Potatoes:
- 1 large head of cauliflower, cut into florets (GI: 15)
- 2 tablespoons unsalted butter (GI: 0)
- 1/4 cup grated Parmesan cheese (GI: 0)
- 1/4 cup plain Greek yogurt (GI: 0)
- 2 cloves garlic, minced (GI: 10)
- 1/2 teaspoon salt (optional, GI: 0)
- 1/4 teaspoon black pepper (GI: 0)
- 1 tablespoon chopped fresh chives (optional, GI: 5)

Optional Ingredients for Additional Flavor or Nutritional Benefits:
- 1 tablespoon chopped fresh parsley (GI: 5)
- 1/4 cup shredded cheddar cheese (GI: 0)
- 1 teaspoon lemon zest (GI: 0)

Instructions:

1. **Prepare the chicken marinade:** In a small bowl, mix olive oil, minced garlic, rosemary, thyme, salt, black pepper, and lemon juice.
2. **Marinate the chicken:** Place the chicken breasts in a resealable plastic bag or shallow dish. Pour marinade over the chicken, ensuring full coverage. Refrigerate for at least 15 minutes or up to 2 hours.
3. **Grill the chicken:** Preheat grill or grill pan over medium-high heat. Remove chicken from the marinade, shake off excess, and grill for 6–7 minutes per side, or until the internal temperature reaches 165°F (75°C). Let rest for 5 minutes before slicing.
4. **Prepare the cauliflower:** Bring a large pot of water to a boil. Add cauliflower florets and cook for 10–12 minutes until tender. Drain thoroughly to remove excess water.
5. **Make mashed cauliflower:** In a food processor, combine cooked cauliflower, butter, Parmesan, Greek yogurt, garlic, salt, and black pepper. Blend until smooth and creamy. Taste and adjust seasoning. Stir in chopped chives, if using.
6. **Optional garnish:** Sprinkle parsley, cheddar cheese, or lemon zest over the mash, if desired.
7. **Serve:** Plate mashed cauliflower, top with grilled chicken slices, and serve with 1/2 cup steamed green beans or a fresh garden salad. Serve this low-carb cauliflower mashed potatoes. A glass of sparkling water with a slice of lemon or lime complements the meal nicely.

Nutritional Information (Per Serving)

Calories: 300, Protein: 35g, Carbohydrates: 8g, Fats: 15g, Fiber: 3g, Cholesterol: 100mg, Sodium: 450mg, Potassium: 900mg

Almond-Crusted Chicken Tenders

Yield: 6 servings   Preparation Time: 30 minutes
Cooking Time: 60 minutes

Ingredients:

For the Chicken Tenders:
- 1 lb chicken tenders (GI: 0)
- 1 cup almond flour (GI: 0)
- 1/2 cup grated Parmesan cheese (GI: 0)
- 1 teaspoon paprika (GI: 5)
- 1 teaspoon garlic powder (GI: 0)
- 1 teaspoon dried oregano (GI: 5)
- 1/2 teaspoon salt (optional, GI: 0)
- 1/4 teaspoon black pepper (GI: 0)
- 2 large eggs, beaten (GI: 0)
- 2 tablespoons olive oil (GI: 0)

Optional Ingredients for Additional Flavor or Nutritional Benefits:
- 1 teaspoon lemon zest (GI: 0)
- 1 tablespoon chopped fresh parsley (GI: 5)
- 1/4 teaspoon cayenne pepper for a spicy kick (GI: 0)

Instructions:

1. **Preheat the oven:** Preheat oven to 400°F (200°C). Line a baking sheet with parchment paper or lightly grease it with cooking spray.
2. **Prepare the breading mixture:** In a shallow bowl, mix almond flour, Parmesan, paprika, garlic powder, oregano, salt, and black pepper. Add lemon zest, parsley, and cayenne pepper if desired.
3. **Prepare the egg wash:** In another shallow bowl, beat eggs until smooth. Optionally season with a pinch of salt and black pepper.
4. Bread the chicken tenders: Dip each tender in the egg wash, ensuring full coating. Then dredge in the almond flour mixture, pressing to adhere the coating. Place tenders on the prepared baking sheet.
5. **Bake the chicken tenders:** Drizzle olive oil over the breaded chicken or spray lightly with cooking spray. Bake for 20–25 minutes, flipping halfway through, until golden brown and cooked through. Use a meat thermometer to confirm an internal temperature of 165°F (75°C).
6. **Serve:** Let chicken rest for 3–5 minutes before serving. Plate with 1 cup steamed broccoli or a garden salad with light vinaigrette. Optionally offer a sugar-free dipping sauce like garlic aioli or lemon herb yogurt dip.

Nutritional Information (Per Serving)

Calories: 320, Protein: 30g, Carbohydrates: 5g, Fats: 20g, Fiber: 3g, Cholesterol: 120mg, Sodium: 400mg, Potassium: 500mg

3. One-Pot and Slow Cooker Meals

Slow Cooker Chicken and Vegetable Stew

Yield: 6 servings *Preparation Time: 15 minutes*
Cooking Time: 6-8 hours on low or 3-4 hours on high

Ingredients:
- 1 large spaghetti squash (GI: 20)
- 1 tablespoon olive oil (GI: 0)
- 1 pound lean ground beef or turkey (GI: 0)
- 1 medium onion, diced (GI: 10)
- 3 cloves garlic, minced (GI: 10)
- 1 carrot, finely diced (GI: 39)
- 1 celery stalk, finely diced (GI: 15)
- 1 can (14.5 oz) diced tomatoes, no salt added (GI: 15)
- 1 can (6 oz) tomato paste (GI: 15)
- 1/2 cup low-sodium beef or chicken broth (GI: 15)
- 1 teaspoon dried oregano (GI: 5)
- 1 teaspoon dried basil (GI: 5)
- 1/2 teaspoon dried thyme (GI: 5)
- 1/2 teaspoon black pepper (GI: 0)
- 1/2 teaspoon salt (optional) (GI: 0)
- 1/4 cup fresh parsley, chopped (GI: 5)
- 1/4 cup grated Parmesan cheese (optional) (GI: 0)

Optional Ingredients for Additional Flavor and Nutrition:
- 1/4 teaspoon red pepper flakes (GI: 0)
- 1 tablespoon balsamic vinegar (GI: 0)
- 1/4 cup chopped fresh basil (GI: 5)

Instructions:
1. **Prepare the Ingredients:** Wash and chop all vegetables as needed. Dice chicken into 1-inch pieces.
2. **Assemble in Slow Cooker:** Add chicken pieces, chicken broth, onions, garlic, carrots, celery, bell peppers, zucchini, and diced tomatoes into a 6-quart slow cooker. Sprinkle with thyme, oregano, basil, smoked paprika, black pepper, and salt.
3. **Cook the Stew:** Cover and cook on low for 6-8 hours or high for 3-4 hours until chicken is cooked and vegetables are tender.
4. **Add Greens:** Stir in 2 cups chopped kale or spinach during the last 30 minutes of cooking.
5. **Finish:** Add 1 tablespoon lemon juice and garnish with parsley or cilantro.
6. **Serve** hot, with whole-grain bread or a small mixed green salad if desired.

Nutritional Information (Per Serving)
Calories: 230, Protein: 30g, Carbohydrates: 18g, Fat: 4g, Fiber: 5g, Cholesterol: 75mg, Sodium: 450mg, Potassium: 960mg

One-pot beef and Vegetable Chili

Yield: 6 servings *Preparation Time: 15 minutes*
Cooking Time: 1 hour (or 4-6 hours in a slow cooker)

Ingredients:
- 1 lb lean ground beef (90% lean) (GI: 0)
- 1 medium onion, diced (GI: 15)
- 3 cloves garlic, minced (GI: 0)
- 1 red bell pepper, diced (GI: 30)
- 1 green bell pepper, diced (GI: 30)
- 2 medium zucchini, diced (GI: 15)
- 1 cup chopped celery (GI: 15)
- 1 can (14.5 oz) diced tomatoes, no added salt (GI: 15)
- 1 can (14.5 oz) tomato sauce, no added sugar (GI: 45)
- 1 can (15 oz) kidney beans, drained and rinsed (optional) (GI: 28)
- 2 tbsp chili powder (GI: 0)
- 1 tbsp ground cumin (GI: 0)
- 1 tsp smoked paprika (GI: 0)
- 1 tsp dried oregano (GI: 0)
- 1/2 tsp black pepper (GI: 0)
- 1/4 tsp cayenne pepper (optional for heat) (GI: 0)
- 2 cups low-sodium beef broth (GI: 0)
- 2 tbsp olive oil (GI: 0)
- Fresh cilantro or parsley for garnish (optional) (GI: 0)

Instructions:
1. **Prepare the Ingredients:** Dice onion, bell peppers, zucchini, and celery. Mince garlic.
2. **Cook the Beef:** Heat olive oil in a pot. Brown lean ground beef, breaking it into crumbles for 5-7 minutes. Drain excess fat if using higher-fat meat.
3. **Add Vegetables:** Stir in onions, garlic, bell peppers, zucchini, and celery. Cook for 5-7 minutes until softened.
4. **Season the Chili:** Add chili powder, cumin, smoked paprika, oregano, black pepper, and cayenne (optional). Stir to coat.
5. **Add Liquids and Simmer:** Mix in diced tomatoes, tomato paste, broth, and kidney beans (optional). Simmer for 1 hour on low heat or cook in a slow cooker on low for 4-6 hours.
6. **Serve:** For a low-carb meal, serve the chili with a side of cauliflower rice (GI: 15) or a mixed green salad (GI: 0). You can also top the chili with a dollop of Greek yogurt (GI: 0) or avocado slices (GI: 15) for added creaminess and healthy fats.

Nutritional Information (Per Serving)
Calories: 290, Protein: 22g, Carbohydrates: 14g, Fats: 15g, Fiber: 6g, Cholesterol: 55mg, Sodium: 350mg, Potassium: 850mg

Slow Cooker Beef and Vegetable Soup

Yield: 6 servings **Preparation Time:** 15 minutes
Cooking Time: 6-8 hours on low or 3-4 hours on high

Ingredients:

- 1.5 lbs lean beef stew meat, trimmed of excess fat, cut into 1-inch pieces (GI: 0)
- 1 tablespoon olive oil (GI: 0)
- 1 medium onion, chopped (GI: 10)
- 3 cloves garlic, minced (GI: 10)
- 4 cups low-sodium beef broth (GI: 0)
- 1 can (14.5 oz) diced tomatoes, no salt added (GI: 15)
- 2 cups chopped carrots (GI: 39)
- 2 cups chopped celery (GI: 15)
- 1 cup chopped green beans (GI: 15)
- 1 cup chopped zucchini (GI: 15)
- 1 cup sliced mushrooms (GI: 15)
- 1 teaspoon dried thyme (GI: 0)
- 1 teaspoon dried oregano (GI: 0)
- 1 teaspoon smoked paprika (GI: 0)
- 1 teaspoon black pepper (GI: 0)
- 1/2 teaspoon salt, or to taste (GI: 0)
- 2 bay leaves (GI: 0)
- 1/4 cup fresh parsley, chopped (GI: 0)

Optional Ingredients:
- 1 tablespoon Worcestershire sauce (GI: 0) for depth of flavor
- 1 cup chopped spinach or kale (GI: 15) for added nutrition

Instructions:

1. **Prepare Ingredients:** Trim excess fat from beef and cut into 1-inch pieces. Chop onion, garlic, carrots, celery, green beans, zucchini, and mushrooms.
2. **Sear the Beef:** Heat olive oil in a skillet over medium-high heat. Sear beef in batches for 2-3 minutes per side until browned. Transfer to the slow cooker.
3. **Assemble in the Slow Cooker:** Sauté onion and garlic in the same skillet for 2 minutes, then transfer to the slow cooker. Add beef broth, diced tomatoes, carrots, celery, green beans, zucchini, mushrooms, thyme, oregano, smoked paprika, black pepper, and salt. Add bay leaves.
4. **Cook:** Cover and cook on low for 6-8 hours or high for 3-4 hours until the beef is tender and vegetables are cooked through.
5. **Optional Greens:** During the last 30 minutes of cooking, stir in 1 cup chopped spinach or kale, if desired.
6. **Finishing Touches:** Remove bay leaves. Stir in Worcestershire sauce (if using) and garnish with parsley.
7. **Serve:** Serve hot with a side of whole-grain bread or brown rice, if desired.

Nutritional Information (Per Serving)
Calories: 300, Protein: 30g, Carbohydrates: 15g, Fat: 13g, Fiber: 4g, Cholesterol: 75mg, Sodium: 450mg, Potassium: 800mg

---

One-Pot Mexican Quinoa

Yield: 6 servings **Preparation Time:** 15 minutes
Cooking Time: 1 hour (or 4-6 hours in a slow cooker)

Ingredients:

- 1 tablespoon olive oil (GI: 0)
- 1 small onion, diced (GI: 10)
- 3 cloves garlic, minced (GI: 10)
- 1 cup quinoa, rinsed (GI: 53)
- 1 can (14.5 oz) diced tomatoes, no salt added (GI: 15)
- 1 cup low-sodium vegetable broth (GI: 0)
- 1 can (15 oz) black beans, drained and rinsed (GI: 30)
- 1 cup corn kernels, fresh or frozen (GI: 55)
- 1 teaspoon chili powder (GI: 0)
- 1 teaspoon cumin (GI: 0)
- 1/2 teaspoon smoked paprika (GI: 0)
- 1/2 teaspoon salt (or to taste) (GI: 0)
- 1/4 teaspoon black pepper (GI: 0)
- 1 cup chopped bell peppers (any color) (GI: 15)
- 1 medium zucchini, diced (GI: 15)
- 1/4 cup fresh cilantro, chopped (GI: 0)
- 1 lime, juiced (GI: 20)

Optional Ingredients:
- 1 avocado, diced (GI: 15) for healthy fats
- 1/4 cup crumbled feta or cotija cheese (GI: 0) for extra flavor
- 1 jalapeño, sliced (GI: 15) for added heat
- 1/4 cup pumpkin seeds or sunflower seeds (GI: 0) for extra crunch

Instructions:

1. **Prepare Ingredients:** Dice onion, bell peppers, and zucchini. Mince garlic. Rinse quinoa under cold water.
2. **Sauté Aromatics:** Heat olive oil in a pot over medium heat. Sauté onion and garlic for 2-3 minutes until translucent.
3. **Add Quinoa and Liquid:** Add quinoa, diced tomatoes (drain excess liquid if needed), and vegetable broth. Stir well and bring to a simmer.
4. **Add Vegetables and Spices:** Stir in black beans, corn, chili powder, cumin, smoked paprika, salt, and pepper. Add bell peppers and zucchini.
5. **Cook the Quinoa:** Cover the pot and reduce heat to low. Cook for 20-25 minutes, stirring occasionally, until the quinoa is tender, and liquid is absorbed. Adjust cooking time as needed.
6. **Finish with Fresh Ingredients:** Remove from heat and stir in cilantro and lime juice. Adjust seasoning to taste.
7. **Serve:** Serve hot, garnished with avocado, cheese, jalapeños, or seeds, if desired.

Nutritional Information (Per Serving)
Calories: 320, Protein: 12g, Carbohydrates: 50g, Fat: 8g, Fiber: 12g, Cholesterol: 0mg, Sodium: 380mg, Potassium: 750mg

One-pot garlic Parmesan Chicken with Broccoli

Yield: 6 servings   **Preparation Time:** 10 minutes   **Cooking Time:** 25 minutes

Ingredients:
- 1 tablespoon olive oil (GI: 0)
- 1.5 lbs boneless, skinless chicken breasts cut into bite-sized pieces (GI: 0)
- 4 cloves garlic, minced (GI: 10)
- 1 teaspoon dried Italian herbs (GI: 0)
- 1/2 teaspoon salt (or to taste) (GI: 0)
- 1/4 teaspoon black pepper (GI: 0)
- 1 cup low-sodium chicken broth (GI: 0)
- 1/4 cup grated Parmesan cheese (GI: 0)
- 1 large head of broccoli, cut into florets (about 4 cups) (GI: 15)
- 1 tablespoon lemon juice (GI: 20)
- 2 tablespoons fresh parsley, chopped (GI: 0)

Optional Ingredients:
- 1/2 teaspoon red pepper flakes (GI: 0) for added heat
- 1/4 cup sun-dried tomatoes, chopped (GI: 35) for additional flavor
- 1/4 cup slivered almonds (GI: 0) for extra crunch and healthy fats

Instructions:
1. **Prepare the Ingredients:** Cut chicken into bite-sized pieces. Mince garlic and chop broccoli into florets.
2. **Cook the Chicken:** Heat olive oil in a large skillet over medium-high heat. Season chicken with salt, pepper, and Italian herbs. Cook for 5-7 minutes until browned and cooked through. Remove chicken from skillet and set aside.
3. **Steam or Sauté Broccoli:** In the same skillet, sauté garlic for 30 seconds. Add broccoli florets and 1/4 cup water. Cover and steam for 3-4 minutes until tender-crisp.
4. **Combine Ingredients:** Return the cooked chicken to the skillet. Stir in Parmesan cheese and lemon juice. Cook for 2-3 minutes to heat through. Adjust seasoning as needed.
5. **Serve:** Serve hot, garnished with parsley. Pair with cauliflower rice for a low-carb option or quinoa for additional carbohydrates. Pair with mixed greens or a simple salad for extra fiber and nutrients. Serve over whole-grain quinoa or brown rice for those who need more carbohydrates.

Nutritional Information (Per Serving)
Calories: 320, Protein: 40g, Carbohydrates: 10g, Fat: 15g, Fiber: 4g, Cholesterol: 95mg, Sodium: 340mg, Potassium: 850mg

Slow Cooker Lentil and Spinach Curry

Yield: 6 servings   **Preparation Time:** 15 minutes   **Cooking Time:** 6-8 hours on low or 3-4 hours on high

Ingredients:
- 1 1/2 cups dry green or brown lentils, rinsed and drained (GI: 30)
- 1 tablespoon olive oil (GI: 0)
- 1 large onion, chopped (GI: 10)
- 3 cloves garlic, minced (GI: 10)
- 1 tablespoon fresh ginger, grated (GI: 10)
- 1 tablespoon curry powder (GI: 0)
- 1 teaspoon ground cumin (GI: 0)
- 1 teaspoon ground coriander (GI: 0)
- 1 teaspoon turmeric (GI: 0)
- 1/2 teaspoon cayenne pepper (optional) (GI: 0)
- 1 can (14.5 oz) diced tomatoes, no salt added (GI: 15)
- 4 cups low-sodium vegetable broth (GI: 0)
- 1 cup coconut milk, unsweetened (GI: 31)
- 5 cups fresh spinach, roughly chopped (GI: 15)
- Salt and pepper to taste (GI: 0)
- 1/4 cup fresh cilantro, chopped (GI: 0)
- Juice of 1 lime (GI: 20)

Optional Ingredients:
- 1 cup chopped carrots (GI: 39) for added sweetness and nutrition
- 1 bell pepper, chopped (GI: 15) for extra flavor and color
- 1 teaspoon garam masala (GI: 0) for a deeper spice profile
- 1/4 cup Greek yogurt (GI: 0) as a topping for creaminess

Instructions:
1. **Prepare the Ingredients:** Rinse and drain lentils. Chop onion and garlic. Grate ginger. Roughly chop spinach.
2. **Sauté Aromatics:** Heat olive oil in a skillet over medium heat. Add onion and sauté for 3-4 minutes until translucent. Stir in garlic and ginger. Cook for 1 minute.
3. **Toast Spices:** Add curry powder, cumin, coriander, turmeric, and cayenne (optional). Toast spices for 1-2 minutes.
4. **Assemble in Slow Cooker:** Transfer sautéed mixture to the slow cooker. Add lentils, diced tomatoes, vegetable broth, and optional carrots. Stir to combine.
5. **Cook the Curry:** Cover and cook on low for 6-8 hours or high for 3-4 hours until lentils are tender but not mushy.
6. **Add Spinach:** Stir in chopped spinach during the last 15 minutes of cooking to wilt.
7. **Finish:** Season with salt, pepper, and lime juice. Garnish with cilantro before serving.
8. **Serve:** Serve over a small portion of brown rice or quinoa for additional carbohydrates if needed. Pair with a side salad or steamed vegetables for extra fiber and nutrients.

Nutritional Information (Per Serving)
Calories: 280, Protein: 14g, Carbohydrates: 40g, Fat: 9g, Fiber: 15g, Cholesterol: 0mg, Sodium: 320mg, Potassium: 860mg

Slow Cooker Turkey Chili

Yield: 6 servings **Preparation Time:** 10 minutes
Cooking Time: 1 hour (or 4-6 hours in a slow cooker)

Ingredients:
- 1 tablespoon olive oil (GI: 0)
- 1.5 lbs boneless, skinless chicken breasts cut into 1 tablespoon olive oil (GI: 0)
- 1 lb ground turkey (lean, 93% or 99%) (GI: 0)
- 1 large onion, chopped (GI: 10)
- 3 cloves garlic, minced (GI: 10)
- 1 red bell pepper, chopped (GI: 15)
- 1 green bell pepper, chopped (GI: 15)
- 1 can (15 oz) black beans, drained and rinsed (GI: 30)
- 1 can (15 oz) kidney beans, drained and rinsed (GI: 28)
- 1 can (14.5 oz) diced tomatoes, no salt added (GI: 15)
- 1 can (6 oz) tomato paste (GI: 15)
- 2 cups low-sodium chicken or vegetable broth (GI: 0)
- 2 tablespoons chili powder (GI: 0)
- 1 tablespoon ground cumin (GI: 0)
- 1 teaspoon smoked paprika (GI: 0)
- 1/2 teaspoon cayenne pepper (optional) (GI: 0)
- 1 teaspoon dried oregano (GI: 0)
- 1/2 teaspoon salt (or to taste) (GI: 0)
- 1/4 teaspoon black pepper (GI: 0)
- 1 zucchini, diced (GI: 15)
- 1/4 cup fresh cilantro, chopped (GI: 0)
- Juice of 1 lime (GI: 20)

Optional Ingredients:
- 1/2 teaspoon ground cinnamon (GI: 0) for a hint of warmth
- 1 tablespoon unsweetened cocoa powder (GI: 20) for depth of flavor
- 1 avocado, diced (GI: 15) for topping
- 1/4 cup shredded low-fat cheese (GI: 0) for topping
- 1/4 cup plain Greek yogurt (GI: 0) for topping

Instructions:
1. **Prepare the Ingredients:** Dice onion, bell peppers, and zucchini. Mince garlic. Rinse black beans and kidney beans.
2. **Cook the Turkey:** Heat olive oil in a skillet, cook ground turkey for 5-7 minutes until browned, and drain excess fat.
3. **Sauté Vegetables:** Add onion, garlic, and bell peppers; sauté for 3-4 minutes until softened.
4. **Assemble the Chili:** Combine turkey, vegetables, beans, diced tomatoes, tomato paste, zucchini, and broth in a slow cooker. Stir well.
5. **Add Seasonings:** Mix in chili powder, cumin, paprika, cayenne (optional), oregano, salt, and pepper.
6. **Cook:** Cover and cook on low for 6-8 hours or high for 4 hours, stirring occasionally.
7. **Finish:** Stir in lime juice and cilantro before serving. Adjust seasoning to taste.
8. **Serve:** Enjoy hot with toppings like avocado, cheese, or Greek yogurt. Pair with mixed greens, whole-grain bread, or cauliflower rice.

Nutritional Information (Per Serving)
Calories: 310, Protein: 27g, Carbohydrates: 35g, Fat: 9g, Fiber: 12g, Cholesterol: 50mg, Sodium: 420mg, Potassium: 950mg

Slow Cooker BBQ Pulled Pork

Yield: 8 servings **Preparation Time:** 15 minutes
Cooking Time: 8 hours on low or 4 hours on high

Ingredients:
- 3 lbs pork shoulder, trimmed of excess fat (GI: 0)
- 1 tablespoon olive oil (GI: 0)
- 1 medium onion, sliced (GI: 10)
- 3 cloves garlic, minced (GI: 10)
- 1 teaspoon smoked paprika (GI: 0)
- 1 teaspoon ground cumin (GI: 0)
- 1 teaspoon chili powder (GI: 0)
- 1/2 teaspoon salt (or to taste) (GI: 0)
- 1/4 teaspoon black pepper (GI: 0)
- 1/4 teaspoon cayenne pepper (optional) (GI: 0)
- 1/2 cup low-sugar ketchup (GI: 55)
- 1/4 cup apple cider vinegar (GI: 5)
- 2 tablespoons Worcestershire sauce (GI: 0)
- 2 tablespoons Dijon mustard (GI: 0)
- 1 tablespoon liquid smoke (optional) (GI: 0)
- 1/4 cup water (GI: 0)
- 2 tablespoons erythritol or another sugar substitute (optional) (GI: 0)

Optional Ingredients:
- 1 teaspoon garlic powder (GI: 0) for additional flavor
- 1 teaspoon onion powder (GI: 0) for extra seasoning
- 1 tablespoon hot sauce (GI: 0) for added heat

Instructions:
1. **Prepare the Ingredients:** Trim excess fat from the pork shoulder. Pat the pork dry with paper towels. Slice the onion and mince the garlic.
2. **Season the Pork:**
3. In a small bowl, mix smoked paprika, cumin, chili powder, salt, pepper, and cayenne pepper (if using). Rub the mixture evenly over the pork.
4. **Sear the Pork:** Heat olive oil in a skillet over medium-high heat. Sear the pork on all sides for 3-4 minutes per side. Remove the pork and set aside.
5. **Prepare the Slow Cooker:** Layer the sliced onion and minced garlic at the bottom of the slow cooker. Place the seared pork on top.
6. **Make the Sauce:** In a bowl, whisk together low-sugar ketchup, apple cider vinegar, Worcestershire sauce, Dijon mustard, liquid smoke (if using), water, and erythritol. Pour the sauce over the pork.
7. **Cook the Pork:** Cover the slow cooker and cook on low for 8 hours or on high for 4 hours, until the pork is tender and easily shredded with a fork.
8. **Shred the Pork:** Remove the pork from the slow cooker and shred it with two forks. Return the shredded pork to the sauce and stir to coat.
9. **Serve:** Serve hot with coleslaw, steamed vegetables, or lettuce wraps for a low-carb option.

Nutritional Information (Per Serving)
Calories: 320, Protein: 28g, Carbohydrates: 6g, Fat: 21g, Fiber: 1g, Cholesterol: 95mg, Sodium: 480mg, Potassium: 570mg

One-Pot Ratatouille

 Yield: 4 servings   Preparation Time: 15 minutes
Cooking Time: 45 minutes

Ingredients:
- 3 lbs pork shoulder, trimmed of excess fat (GI: 0)
- 2 tablespoons olive oil (GI: 0)
- 1 medium onion, chopped (GI: 10)
- 3 cloves garlic, minced (GI: 10)
- 1 medium eggplant, diced (GI: 15)
- 1 zucchini, sliced (GI: 15)
- 1 yellow squash, sliced (GI: 15)
- 1 red bell pepper, chopped (GI: 15)
- 1 green bell pepper, chopped (GI: 15)
- 1 can (14.5 oz) diced tomatoes, no salt added (GI: 15)
- 1 tablespoon tomato paste (GI: 15)
- 1 teaspoon dried thyme (GI: 0)
- 1 teaspoon dried oregano (GI: 0)
- 1/2 teaspoon dried basil (GI: 0)
- 1/4 teaspoon red pepper flakes (optional) (GI: 0)
- Salt and pepper to taste (GI: 0)
- 1/4 cup fresh basil, chopped (GI: 0)
- 2 tablespoons fresh parsley, chopped (GI: 0)

Optional Ingredients:
- 1/4 cup grated Parmesan cheese (GI: 0) for topping
- 1/4 cup black olives, sliced (GI: 15) for additional flavor

Instructions:

1. **Prepare the Ingredients:** Dice the eggplant, zucchini, squash, and bell peppers. Chop the onion and mince the garlic. Sprinkle eggplant with salt, let sit for 20 minutes, then rinse and pat dry.
2. **Sauté Aromatics:** Heat olive oil in a large pot over medium heat. Sauté onion for 3-4 minutes until translucent, then add garlic and cook 1 minute.
3. **Cook the Vegetables:** Add eggplant and cook for 5 minutes, stirring occasionally. Stir in zucchini, squash, and bell peppers, cooking for 5 more minutes.
4. **Add Tomatoes and Seasonings:** Mix in diced tomatoes, tomato paste, thyme, oregano, basil, red pepper flakes (if using), salt, and pepper.
5. **Simmer the Ratatouille:** Reduce heat to low, cover, and simmer for 30 minutes, stirring occasionally.
6. **Finish and Serve:** Stir in fresh basil and parsley. Adjust seasoning. Serve hot with grilled chicken, fish, or a side of quinoa or brown rice.

Nutritional Information (Per Serving)
Calories: 180, Protein: 4g, Carbohydrates: 25g, Fat: 8g, Fiber: 7g, Cholesterol: 0mg, Sodium: 320mg, Potassium: 750mg

One-Pot Creamy Mushroom Chicken

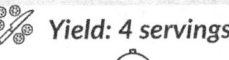 Yield: 4 servings    Preparation Time: 15 minutes
Cooking Time: 45 minutes

Ingredients:
- 1 tablespoon olive oil (GI: 0)
- 1.5 lbs boneless, skinless chicken breasts, cut into pieces (GI: 0)
- Salt and pepper to taste (GI: 0)
- 1 medium onion, chopped (GI: 10)
- 3 cloves garlic, minced (GI: 10)
- 8 oz cremini or button mushrooms, sliced (GI: 15)
- 1 teaspoon dried thyme (GI: 0)
- 1 teaspoon dried oregano (GI: 0)
- 1 cup low-sodium chicken broth (GI: 0)
- 1/2 cup plain Greek yogurt (GI: 0)
- 1/4 cup grated Parmesan cheese (GI: 0)
- 1 tablespoon lemon juice (GI: 20)
- 1/4 cup fresh parsley, chopped (GI: 0)

Optional Ingredients:
- 1/2 teaspoon red pepper flakes (GI: 0) for a touch of heat
- 1/4 cup sun-dried tomatoes, chopped (GI: 35) for added flavor
- 1/4 cup slivered almonds (GI: 0) for extra crunch

Instructions:

1. **Prepare the Ingredients:** Cut chicken into bite-sized pieces, mince garlic, chop onion, and slice mushrooms.
2. **Cook the Chicken:** Heat olive oil in a skillet over medium-high heat. Season chicken with salt and pepper. Cook for 5-7 minutes until browned and cooked through. Remove and set aside.
3. **Sauté the Vegetables:** In the same skillet, sauté onion for 2-3 minutes, then add garlic and mushrooms. Cook for 3-4 minutes until tender.
4. **Add Spices and Broth:** Stir in thyme, oregano, and chicken broth. Simmer, scraping browned bits from the skillet.
5. **Make the Creamy Sauce:** Reduce heat to low. Whisk in Greek yogurt and Parmesan until smooth. Stir in lemon juice.
6. **Combine and Finish:** Return chicken to the skillet and coat with the sauce. Add red pepper flakes or sun-dried tomatoes if desired. Cook for 2-3 minutes.
7. **Garnish and Serve:** Garnish with parsley and optional almonds. Serve hot with broccoli or cauliflower rice.

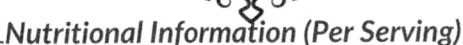

Nutritional Information (Per Serving)
Calories: 320, Protein: 35g, Carbohydrates: 10g, Fat: 15g, Fiber: 2g, Cholesterol: 95mg, Sodium: 340mg, Potassium: 750mg

4. International Cuisine

Greek Lemon Chicken with Tzatziki

Yield: 4 servings **Preparation Time:** 15 minutes
Marinade Time: 1 hour (optional, for enhanced flavor) **Cooking Time:** 25 minutes

Ingredients:

For the Greek Lemon Chicken:
- 1.5 lbs boneless, skinless chicken breasts (GI: 0)
- 2 tablespoons olive oil (GI: 0)
- 1/4 cup lemon juice (freshly squeezed) (GI: 20)
- Zest of 1 lemon (GI: 20)
- 3 cloves garlic, minced (GI: 10)
- 1 teaspoon dried oregano (GI: 0)
- 1 teaspoon dried thyme (GI: 0)
- 1 teaspoon ground cumin (GI: 0)
- Salt and pepper to taste (GI: 0)
- 1 tablespoon fresh parsley, chopped (GI: 0)
- 1 tablespoon fresh dill, chopped (optional) (GI: 0)

For the Tzatziki Sauce:
- 1 cup Greek yogurt (plain, low-fat or full-fat) (GI: 0)
- 1/2 cucumber, grated and drained (GI: 15)
- 2 cloves garlic, minced (GI: 10)
- 1 tablespoon olive oil (GI: 0)
- 1 tablespoon lemon juice (GI: 20)
- 1 tablespoon fresh dill, chopped (GI: 0)
- Salt and pepper to taste (GI: 0)

Optional Ingredients:
- 1 teaspoon smoked paprika (GI: 0) for a smoky flavor in the chicken marinade
- 1/4 cup feta cheese, crumbled (GI: 0) for topping
- Kalamata olives, sliced (GI: 15) for garnish

Instructions:

1. **Marinate the Chicken:** In a bowl, mix olive oil, lemon juice, zest, minced garlic, oregano, thyme, cumin, salt, and pepper. Add chicken and coat evenly. Cover and refrigerate for 1 hour or overnight.
2. **Cook the Chicken:** Preheat grill/skillet over medium-high heat. Remove chicken from marinade and discard excess. Grill 6-7 minutes per side, or until internal temperature reaches 165°F (74°C). Let rest before slicing.
3. **Prepare Tzatziki Sauce:** Mix yogurt, grated (and drained) cucumber, garlic, olive oil, lemon juice, dill, salt, and pepper in a bowl. Chill until serving.
4. **Serve:** Slice chicken. Plate with tzatziki sauce and optional garnishes: parsley, dill, feta, or olives.

Nutritional Information (Per Serving)
Calories: 320, Protein: 35g, Carbohydrates: 8g, Fat: 18g, Fiber: 1g, Cholesterol: 85mg, Sodium: 300mg, Potassium: 520mg

Italian Stuffed Bell Peppers with Ground Turkey

Yield: 4 servings **Preparation Time:** 20 minutes
Cooking Time: 45 minutes

Ingredients:
- 4 large bell peppers (Glycemic Index (GI): 15)
- 1 lb (450g) ground turkey (93% lean) (GI: 0)
- 1/2 cup quinoa, uncooked (GI: 53)
- 1 medium onion, finely chopped (GI: 10)
- 2 cloves garlic, minced (GI: 0)
- 1 can (14.5 oz) diced tomatoes, no salt added (GI: 15)
- 1/2 cup tomato sauce, no added sugar (GI: 15)
- 1 tsp dried oregano (GI: 0)
- 1 tsp dried basil (GI: 0)
- 1/2 tsp ground black pepper (GI: 0)
- 1/2 tsp salt (optional for those monitoring sodium)
- 1/4 tsp crushed red pepper flakes (optional, for heat)
- 1/2 cup low-fat mozzarella cheese, shredded (optional, for topping) (GI: 0)
- 1 tbsp olive oil (GI: 0)
- Fresh parsley or basil for garnish (optional) (GI: 0)

Instructions:

1. **Preheat the Oven:** Preheat oven to 375°F (190°C).
2. **Prepare Bell Peppers:** Cut tops, remove seeds/membranes, and trim bottoms if needed. Arrange peppers upright in a baking dish.
3. **Cook Quinoa:** Rinse quinoa. Boil 1 cup of water with a pinch of salt. Add quinoa, reduce heat, cover, and simmer for 15 minutes. Fluff and set aside.
4. **Prepare the Filling:** Heat olive oil in a skillet. Sauté onion for 5 minutes, then add garlic and cook 1 minute. Add turkey, cook until browned (~7-8 minutes). Stir in quinoa, tomatoes, tomato sauce, oregano, basil, salt, and pepper. Cook for 5 minutes to blend flavors. Let cool slightly.
5. **Stuff the Peppers:** Spoon filling into bell peppers, packing lightly.
6. **Bake:** Cover with foil and bake for 30 minutes. If using mozzarella, sprinkle on top and bake uncovered for 10 minutes more until cheese is bubbly.
7. **Serve:** Garnish with parsley or basil. Serve warm with steamed vegetables or a side salad.

Nutritional Information (Per Serving)
Calories: 250 kcal, Protein: 26g, Carbohydrates: 22g, Dietary Fiber: 6g, Sugars: 6g, Fat: 9g, Saturated Fat: 2g, Cholesterol: 60mg, Sodium: 420mg (less if salt is omitted), Potassium: 800mg

Indian Spiced Chickpea Stew

🌀 **Yield:** 4 servings 🍲 **Preparation Time:** 10 minutes
🍽 **Cooking Time:** 30 minutes

Ingredients:

- 1 tablespoon olive oil (GI: 0)
- 1 medium onion, chopped (GI: 10)
- 3 cloves garlic, minced (GI: 10)
- 1 tablespoon fresh ginger, grated (GI: 10)
- 1 teaspoon cumin seeds (GI: 0)
- 1 teaspoon ground coriander (GI: 0)
- 1 teaspoon ground cumin (GI: 0)
- 1 teaspoon turmeric (GI: 0)
- 1/2 teaspoon garam masala (GI: 0)
- 1/2 teaspoon chili powder (optional) (GI: 0)
- 1 can (14.5 oz) diced tomatoes, no salt added (GI: 15)
- 1 can (15 oz) chickpeas, drained and rinsed (GI: 28)
- 1 cup low-sodium vegetable broth (GI: 0)
- 2 cups spinach or kale, roughly chopped (GI: 15)
- Salt and pepper to taste (GI: 0)
- 1/4 cup fresh cilantro, chopped (GI: 0)
- Juice of 1/2 lemon (GI: 20)

Optional Ingredients:
- 1/2 cup coconut milk (GI: 31) for creaminess
- 1/2 teaspoon fenugreek seeds (GI: 0) for added flavor
- 1/2 cup diced sweet potato (GI: 70) for a sweeter profile

Instructions:

1. **Prepare Ingredients:** Chop onion, mince garlic and ginger, and prepare diced sweet potato (if using). Rinse and drain chickpeas.
2. **Sauté Aromatics:** Heat olive oil in a pot over medium heat. Toast cumin seeds for 1 minute. Add onion, sauté for 3-4 minutes, then add garlic and ginger for 1 minute.
3. **Add Spices:** Stir in coriander, cumin, turmeric, garam masala, and chili powder. Toast spices for 1-2 minutes.
4. **Add Tomatoes and Chickpeas:** Add diced tomatoes, chickpeas, broth, and fenugreek seeds (if using). If using sweet potato, add now. Simmer for 15 minutes.
5. **Add Greens:** Stir in spinach or kale. Cook until wilted, about 5 minutes.
6. **Finish:** Stir in lemon juice and cilantro. Add coconut milk (optional) and season to taste.
7. **Serve:** Garnish with cilantro. Pair with a small serving of brown rice or quinoa for added fiber.

Nutritional Information (Per Serving)

Calories: 250, Protein: 10g, Carbohydrates: 38g, Fat: 8g, Fiber: 10g, Cholesterol: 0mg, Sodium: 300mg, Potassium: 700mg

Italian Stuffed Eggplant

🌀 **Yield:** 4 servings 🍲 **Preparation Time:** 15 minutes
🍽 **Cooking Time:** 40 minutes

Ingredients:

- 2 large eggplants, halved lengthwise (GI: 15)
- 2 tablespoons olive oil (GI: 0)
- 1 medium onion, chopped (GI: 10)
- 3 cloves garlic, minced (GI: 10)
- 1 red bell pepper, diced (GI: 15)
- 1 can (14.5 oz) diced tomatoes, no salt added (GI: 15)
- 1 pound ground turkey or chicken (GI: 0)
- 1 teaspoon dried oregano (GI: 0)
- 1 teaspoon dried basil (GI: 0)
- 1/2 teaspoon red pepper flakes (optional) (GI: 0)
- 1/2 teaspoon salt (or to taste) (GI: 0)
- 1/4 teaspoon black pepper (GI: 0)
- 1/4 cup grated Parmesan cheese (GI: 0)
- 1/2 cup shredded mozzarella cheese (GI: 0)
- 1/4 cup fresh parsley, chopped (GI: 0)

Optional Ingredients:
- 1/4 cup chopped black olives (GI: 15) for extra flavor
- 1 tablespoon capers (GI: 0) for added tanginess
- 1/4 cup sun-dried tomatoes, chopped (GI: 35) for additional depth

Instructions:

1. **Prepare Eggplants:** Preheat oven to 375°F (190°C). Halve eggplants lengthwise, scoop out flesh, leaving 1/2-inch shells. Dice flesh. Brush shells with olive oil and bake for 15 minutes.
2. **Cook Filling:** Heat oil in a skillet. Sauté onion for 3 minutes. Add garlic for 1 minute. Stir in diced eggplant and bell pepper; cook 5-7 minutes.
3. **Add Protein and Seasonings:** Add ground turkey or chicken. Cook until browned. Stir in diced tomatoes, oregano, basil, red pepper flakes, salt, and black pepper. Simmer for 10 minutes.
4. **Stuff Eggplants:** Remove shells from the oven. Fill with mixture. Top with grated Parmesan and shredded mozzarella.
5. **Bake:** Return stuffed eggplants to the oven. Bake 20-25 minutes until cheese is melted and bubbly.
6. **Serve:** Garnish with parsley. Add olives or capers for extra flavor if desired.

Nutritional Information (Per Serving)

Calories: 320, Protein: 28g, Carbohydrates: 20g, Fat: 17g, Fiber: 8g, Cholesterol: 70mg, Sodium: 460mg, Potassium: 900mg

Japanese Teriyaki Tofu with Broccoli

Yield: 4 servings   *Preparation Time: 15 minutes*
Cooking Time: 20 minutes

Ingredients:

- 14 oz firm tofu, drained and pressed (GI: 15)
- 2 tablespoons cornstarch (GI: 85)
- 2 tablespoons olive oil (GI: 0)
- 4 cups broccoli florets (GI: 15)

For the Teriyaki Sauce:
- 1/4 cup low-sodium soy sauce (GI: 0)
- 2 tablespoons mirin (optional) (GI: 35)
- 1 tablespoon rice vinegar (GI: 0)
- 1 tablespoon sesame oil (GI: 0)
- 1 tablespoon honey or a sugar substitute like erythritol (optional) (GI: 30)
- 2 cloves garlic, minced (GI: 10)
- 1 teaspoon fresh ginger, grated (GI: 10)
- 1 tablespoon sesame seeds (GI: 0)
- 1/4 cup water (GI: 0)

Optional Ingredients:
- 1 tablespoon sesame seeds (GI: 0)
- 2 tablespoons chopped green onions (GI: 10)
- 1 tablespoon chopped fresh cilantro (GI: 0)

Instructions:

1. **Prepare Tofu:** Press tofu for 10 minutes to remove moisture. Dice into cubes and toss in cornstarch.
2. **Cook Tofu:** Heat oil in a skillet. Fry tofu for 4-5 minutes per side until golden. Remove and set aside.
3. **Cook Broccoli:** In the same skillet, sauté broccoli for 5-7 minutes. Remove and set aside.
4. **Make Sauce:** Whisk soy sauce, rice vinegar, sesame oil, honey (or substitute), garlic, ginger, and water.
5. **Combine:** Return tofu and broccoli to skillet. Pour sauce and cook for 2-3 minutes, stirring until thickened.
6. **Garnish:** Top with sesame seeds, green onions, and cilantro. Serve with a low-carb base like cauliflower rice.

Nutritional Information (Per Serving)

Calories: 250, Protein: 10g, Carbohydrates: 38g, Fat: 8g, Fiber: 10g, Cholesterol: 0mg, Sodium: 300mg, Potassium: 700mg

Moroccan Chicken Tagine with Vegetables

Yield: 4 servings   *Preparation Time: 15 minutes*
Cooking Time: 45 minutes

Ingredients:

- 1.5 lbs chicken thighs, skinless and boneless, cut into chunks (GI: 0)
- 2 tablespoons olive oil (GI: 0)
- 1 large onion, sliced (GI: 10)
- 3 cloves garlic, minced (GI: 10)
- 1 teaspoon ground cumin (GI: 0)
- 1 teaspoon ground coriander (GI: 0)
- 1 teaspoon ground cinnamon (GI: 0)
- 1/2 teaspoon ground turmeric (GI: 0)
- 1/2 teaspoon ground ginger (GI: 0)
- 1/2 teaspoon paprika (GI: 0)
- 1/4 teaspoon cayenne pepper (optional) (GI: 0)
- 1 cup low-sodium chicken broth (GI: 0)
- 1 can (14.5 oz) diced tomatoes, no salt added (GI: 15)
- 1 large carrot, sliced (GI: 39)
- 1 medium zucchini, sliced (GI: 15)
- 1 red bell pepper, sliced (GI: 15)
- 1/2 cup dried apricots, chopped (GI: 57)
- 1/4 cup green olives, pitted and halved (GI: 0)
- Salt and pepper to taste (GI: 0)
- 1/4 cup fresh cilantro, chopped (GI: 0)
- 1 tablespoon lemon juice (GI: 20)

Optional Ingredients:
- 1/4 cup almonds, toasted (GI: 0) for added crunch
- 1 tablespoon harissa paste (GI: 0) for additional heat
- 1/4 cup raisins (GI: 64) for extra sweetness

Instructions:

1. **Prepare Chicken:** Season chicken with salt and pepper. Heat 1 tablespoon olive oil in a pot and brown chicken for 5-7 minutes. Remove and set aside.
2. **Cook Aromatics:** In the same pot, add remaining olive oil. Sauté onion for 3-4 minutes until translucent. Stir in garlic, cumin, coriander, cinnamon, turmeric, ginger, paprika, and cayenne (if using). Cook for 1-2 minutes.
3. **Add Vegetables:** Return chicken to the pot. Add chicken broth, tomatoes, carrots, zucchini, bell pepper, apricots, and olives. Mix well.
4. **Simmer:** Cover and simmer for 30 minutes, stirring occasionally, until chicken is cooked and vegetables are tender.
5. **Finish:** Stir in lemon juice and cilantro. Adjust seasoning as needed. If using, stir in harissa paste and toasted almonds.
6. **Serve:** Serve hot with a small portion of quinoa, couscous, or cauliflower rice. Garnish with additional cilantro and raisins, if desired.

Nutritional Information (Per Serving)

Calories: 380, Protein: 28g, Carbohydrates: 28g, Fat: 17g, Fiber: 6g, Cholesterol: 95mg, Sodium: 320mg, Potassium: 920mg

Mexican Chicken Fajitas with Bell Peppers

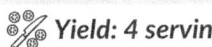 Yield: 4 servings  Preparation Time: 15 minutes
 Cooking Time: 20 minutes

Ingredients:

- 1.5 lbs boneless, skinless chicken breasts, sliced into thin strips (GI: 0)
- 2 tablespoons olive oil (GI: 0)
- 1 red bell pepper, sliced (GI: 15)
- 1 yellow bell pepper, sliced (GI: 15)
- 1 green bell pepper, sliced (GI: 15)
- 1 large onion, sliced (GI: 10)
- 3 cloves garlic, minced (GI: 10)
- 1 teaspoon ground cumin (GI: 0)
- 1 teaspoon chili powder (GI: 0)
- 1 teaspoon smoked paprika (GI: 0)
- 1/2 teaspoon dried oregano (GI: 0)
- 1/4 teaspoon cayenne pepper (optional) (GI: 0)
- Salt and pepper to taste (GI: 0)
- 1 lime, juiced (GI: 20)
- 1/4 cup fresh cilantro, chopped (GI: 0)

Optional Ingredients:

- 1 avocado, sliced (GI: 15) for healthy fats
- 1/4 cup salsa (GI: 20) for added flavor
- Whole-grain tortillas (GI: 50) for serving

Instructions:

1. **Prepare Chicken:** Combine sliced chicken, olive oil, cumin, chili powder, smoked paprika, oregano, cayenne (if using), salt, and pepper in a bowl. Mix well.
2. **Cook Chicken:** Heat a skillet over medium-high heat. Cook chicken for 6-8 minutes until fully cooked. Remove and set aside.
3. **Cook Vegetables:** Add olive oil to the skillet. Sauté onions and bell peppers for 5-7 minutes until tender-crisp. Add garlic for the last minute.
4. **Combine:** Return chicken to the skillet with vegetables. Stir in lime juice and cilantro. Cook for 2 minutes.
5. **Serve:** Serve hot with optional avocado slices and salsa. Use lettuce wraps or serve over a bed of greens for a low-carb option. For a traditional approach, use whole-grain tortillas.

Nutritional Information (Per Serving)

Calories: 280, Protein: 35g, Carbohydrates: 12g, Fat: 16g, Fiber: 4g, Cholesterol: 95mg, Sodium: 320mg, Potassium: 780mg

Indian Chicken Curry with Cauliflower Rice

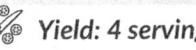 Yield: 4 servings Preparation Time: 15 minutes
 Cooking Time: 30 minutes

Ingredients:

- 1 lb (450g) boneless, skinless chicken breast, cut into bite-sized pieces (GI: 0)
- 1 medium onion, finely chopped (GI: 10)
- 2 cloves garlic, minced (GI: 0)
- 1-inch piece of ginger, minced (GI: 0)
- 1 can (14.5 oz) diced tomatoes, no salt added (GI: 15)
- 1/2 cup plain Greek yogurt, low-fat (GI: 14)
- 1 tbsp olive oil or avocado oil (GI: 0)
- 1 tsp cumin seeds (GI: 0)
- 1 tsp ground coriander (GI: 0)
- 1 tsp turmeric powder (GI: 0)
- 1 tsp garam masala (GI: 0)
- 1/2 tsp ground cumin (GI: 0)
- 1/2 tsp ground cinnamon (GI: 0)
- 1/2 tsp cayenne pepper (optional, for heat) (GI: 0)
- 1/4 tsp salt (optional for those monitoring sodium)
- 1/4 cup fresh cilantro, chopped (for garnish) (GI: 0)

For the Cauliflower Rice:

- 1 medium head of cauliflower, riced (GI: 15)
- 1 tbsp olive oil (GI: 0)
- 1/4 tsp ground turmeric (GI: 0)
- 1/4 tsp ground cumin (GI: 0)
- Salt and pepper to taste (optional)

Instructions:

1. **Prepare Cauliflower Rice:** Remove leaves and core from cauliflower. Pulse florets in a food processor until rice-like. Heat olive oil in a skillet over medium heat. Sauté cauliflower with turmeric, cumin, and salt for 5-7 minutes. Remove and keep warm.
2. **Cook Curry Base:** Heat oil in a pan. Sizzle cumin seeds for 1 minute. Add onion and sauté until golden, about 5 minutes. Stir in garlic and ginger for 1-2 minutes.
3. **Add Tomatoes and Spices:** Stir in diced tomatoes, coriander, turmeric, cinnamon, garam masala, and cayenne (if using). Cook for 5 minutes.
4. **Cook Chicken:** Add chicken pieces. Stir to coat with spices. Cook for 5-7 minutes until no longer pink.
5. **Finish Curry:** Lower heat. Stir in yogurt gradually, ensuring the curry doesn't boil. Simmer for 5 minutes until chicken is fully cooked. Adjust salt to taste.
6. **Serve:** Divide cauliflower rice into plates. Top with curry and garnish with cilantro. Serve with a cucumber-tomato salad for extra fiber.

Nutritional Information (Per Serving)

Calories: 280, Protein: 30g, Carbohydrates: 14g, Dietary Fiber: 5g, Sugars: 7g, Fat: 11g, Saturated Fat: 2g, Cholesterol: 70mg, Sodium: 350mg (less if salt is omitted), Potassium: 850mg

Middle Eastern Falafel with Tahini Sauce

Yield: 4 servings   Preparation Time: 15 minutes
Chilling Time: 30 minutes   Cooking Time: 20 minutes

Ingredients:

For the Falafel:
- 1 can (15 oz) chickpeas, drained and rinsed (GI: 28)
- 1/4 cup fresh parsley, chopped (GI: 0)
- 1/4 cup fresh cilantro, chopped (GI: 0)
- 1 small onion, chopped (GI: 10)
- 2 cloves garlic, minced (GI: 10)
- 2 tablespoons oat flour or almond flour (GI: 44 for oat flour, GI: 0 for almond flour)
- 1 teaspoon ground cumin (GI: 0)
- 1 teaspoon ground coriander (GI: 0)
- 1/2 teaspoon baking powder (GI: 0)
- 1/2 teaspoon salt (GI: 0)
- 1/4 teaspoon black pepper (GI: 0)
- 1/4 teaspoon cayenne pepper (optional) (GI: 0)
- 2 tablespoons olive oil (for cooking) (GI: 0)

For the Tahini Sauce:
- 1/4 cup tahini (GI: 0)
- 2 tablespoons lemon juice (GI: 20)
- 1 clove garlic, minced (GI: 10)
- 2 tablespoons water (or as needed for consistency) (GI: 0)
- Salt and pepper to taste (GI: 0)

Optional Ingredients for Serving:
- 1/2 cup chopped tomatoes (GI: 15)
- 1/2 cup chopped cucumbers (GI: 15)
- 4 whole-grain pita bread (GI: 57) or lettuce wraps for a low-carb option
- 1/4 cup pickled turnips or radishes (GI: 0)

Instructions:

1. **Prepare the Falafel Mixture:** Combine chickpeas, parsley, cilantro, onion, garlic, flour, spices, and baking powder in a food processor. Pulse until coarse but textured. Chill for 30 minutes.
2. **Shape and Cook Falafel:** Shape into 1.5-inch balls or patties. Heat olive oil in a skillet over medium heat. Cook falafel for 3-4 minutes per side until golden brown.
3. **Prepare Tahini Sauce:** Whisk tahini, lemon juice, garlic, and water until smooth. Adjust with water if necessary. Season with salt and pepper.
4. **Serve:** Serve falafel with tahini sauce, tomatoes, cucumbers, and pickled vegetables. Use whole-grain pita or lettuce wraps as desired.

Nutritional Information (Per Serving)

Calories: 280, Protein: 9g, Carbohydrates: 25g, Fat: 16g, Fiber: 8g, Cholesterol: 0mg, Sodium: 320mg, Potassium: 420mg

Vietnamese Pho with Tofu and Vegetables

Yield: 4 servings   Preparation Time: 15 minutes
Cooking Time: 30 minutes

Ingredients:

For the Broth:
- 8 cups low-sodium vegetable broth (GI: 0)
- 1 large onion, quartered (GI: 10)
- 3 cloves garlic, smashed (GI: 10)
- 3-inch piece of ginger, sliced (GI: 10)
- 2 cinnamon sticks (GI: 0)
- 4 whole star anise (GI: 0)
- 4 whole cloves (GI: 0)
- 1 tablespoon soy sauce (low sodium) (GI: 0)
- 1 tablespoon fish sauce (optional) (GI: 0)

For the Tofu and Vegetables:
- 14 oz firm tofu, drained and pressed, cut into cubes (GI: 15)
- 1 tablespoon olive oil (GI: 0)
- 2 cups broccoli florets (GI: 15)
- 1 cup carrots, julienned (GI: 39)
- 1 red bell pepper, sliced (GI: 15)
- 1 cup bean sprouts (GI: 25)

For the Noodles:
- 6 oz rice noodles (optional) (GI: 58)

Optional Toppings:
- 1/4 cup fresh cilantro, chopped (GI: 0)
- 1/4 cup fresh basil leaves (GI: 0)
- 1 lime, cut into wedges (GI: 20)
- 1 jalapeño, thinly sliced (GI: 15)

Instructions:

1. **Prepare the Broth:** Simmer vegetable broth, onion, garlic, ginger, cinnamon, star anise, and cloves for 20 minutes. Strain and add soy sauce and fish sauce (if using).
2. **Cook Tofu:** Heat olive oil in a skillet over medium-high heat. Cook tofu for 5-7 minutes until golden on all sides. Set aside.
3. **Cook Vegetables:** In the same skillet, sauté broccoli, carrots, and bell pepper for 3-4 minutes until tender.
4. **Prepare Noodles:** If using rice noodles, cook per package instructions. Drain and set aside.
5. **Assemble Pho:** Divide noodles (if using) among bowls. Ladle broth over noodles. Top with tofu, vegetables, and bean sprouts.
6. **Add Toppings:** Garnish with cilantro, basil, lime, and jalapeño. Serve with mixed greens or a light salad for additional fiber. For a lower-carb option, omit the rice noodles and add more vegetables.

Nutritional Information (Per Serving)

Calories: 220, Protein: 15g, Carbohydrates: 18g, Fat: 10g, Fiber: 5g, Cholesterol: 0mg, Sodium: 320mg, Potassium: 550mg

CHAPTER 8
SNACKS AND APPETIZERS
1. Healthy Snacking Tips

Greek Yogurt with Berries and Nuts

Yield: 2 servings   Preparation Time: 10 minutes
Cooking Time: None

Ingredients:

- 1 cup plain Greek yogurt (GI: 11) (unsweetened, full-fat or low-fat, depending on preference)
- 1/2 cup mixed berries (GI: 40) (such as blueberries, strawberries, and raspberries)
- 2 tablespoons chopped nuts (GI: 15) (such as almonds, walnuts, or pecans)
- 1 tablespoon chia seeds (GI: 1)
- 1 teaspoon vanilla extract (GI: 15)
- 1 tablespoon unsweetened shredded coconut (optional, GI: 42)
- 1/2 teaspoon ground cinnamon (optional, GI: 1)
- 1-2 teaspoons sugar-free sweetener (optional, such as stevia or erythritol, GI: 0)

Instructions:

1. **Prepare the Yogurt Base:** In a medium bowl, add 1 cup of plain Greek yogurt. Stir in the vanilla extract for flavor. Add 1-2 teaspoons of a sugar-free sweetener and mix well.
2. **Add Berries:** Gently wash and pat dry the mixed berries. Add 1/2 cup of mixed berries to the yogurt, gently folding them.
3. **Incorporate Nuts and Seeds:** Chop 2 tablespoons of nuts and sprinkle them over the yogurt. Add 1 tablespoon of chia seeds for additional fiber and protein.
4. **Enhance Flavor (Optional):** If desired, sprinkle 1 tablespoon of unsweetened shredded coconut and 1/2 teaspoon of ground cinnamon on top for added flavor and texture.
5. **Serve:** Divide the mixture evenly between two serving bowls or glasses. Serve immediately or refrigerate for up to 2 hours to allow the chia seeds to expand slightly, adding a creamy texture. Enjoy this dish as a quick breakfast or a satisfying snack. Pair it with a glass of water or herbal tea to stay hydrated.

Nutritional Information (Per Serving)

Calories: 220, Protein: 14g, Carbohydrates: 16g, Sugars: 8g, Fiber: 5g, Fats: 13g, Saturated Fat: 3g, Cholesterol: 10mg, Sodium: 70mg, Potassium: 300mg

Apple Slices with Almond Butter

Yield: 4 servings   Preparation Time: 10 minutes
Cooking Time: None

Ingredients:

- 1 medium apple (GI: 38) (such as Granny Smith or Gala)
- 4 tablespoons almond butter (GI: 35)
- 1 tablespoon chia seeds (GI: 1)
- 1 tablespoon unsweetened shredded coconut (optional, GI: 42)
- 1 teaspoon cinnamon (optional, GI: 1)
- 1 tablespoon crushed walnuts (optional, GI: 15)
- 1 teaspoon sugar-free sweetener (optional, such as stevia or erythritol, GI: 0)

Instructions:

1. **Prepare the Apple:** Wash and dry the apple thoroughly. Core the apple and slice it into thin, even wedges.
2. **Prepare the Almond Butter Spread:** Combine the almond butter with the optional sugar-free sweetener in a small bowl if you desire a sweeter taste. Mix until smooth and well combined.
3. **Assemble the Snack:** Spread approximately 2 tablespoons of almond butter evenly on each Serving of apple slices. Sprinkle 1/2 tablespoon of chia seeds evenly over the almond butter on each Serving.
4. **Optional Toppings:** For added texture and flavor, sprinkle unsweetened shredded coconut and ground cinnamon over the top. Optionally, add crushed walnuts for extra crunch and healthy fats.
5. **Serve:** Arrange the apple slices on a serving plate. Serve immediately for the freshest taste and texture. Pair with a cup of herbal tea or water for a balanced snack. Enjoy as a mid-morning or afternoon snack to keep energy levels steady

Nutritional Information (Per Serving)

Calories: 265, Protein: 7g, Carbohydrates: 27g, Sugars: 16g, Fiber: 8g, Fats: 17g, Saturated Fat: 1g, Cholesterol: 0mg, Sodium: 5mg, Potassium: 310mg

Carrot and Celery Sticks with Hummus

Yield: 4 servings   *Preparation Time: 10 minutes*   *Cooking Time: None*

Ingredients:

For the Hummus:
- 1 cup canned chickpeas (drained and rinsed) (GI: 28)
- 3 tablespoons tahini (GI: 5)
- 3 tablespoons fresh lemon juice (GI: 20)
- 2 tablespoons olive oil (GI: 0)
- 1 clove garlic (minced) (GI: 10)
- 1/2 teaspoon ground cumin (optional, GI: 1)
- Salt to taste (GI: 0)
- 2-4 tablespoons water (as needed to achieve desired consistency, GI: 0)
- 1/4 teaspoon paprika (optional for garnish, GI: 1)

For the Vegetables:
- 4 medium carrots (peeled and cut into sticks) (GI: 35)
- 4 celery stalks (cut into sticks) (GI: 15)

Instructions:

1. Prepare the Hummus:
- Place the drained and rinsed chickpeas, tahini, lemon juice, olive oil, minced garlic, cumin (if using), and a pinch of salt in a food processor.
- Process the mixture at high speed until it is smooth.
- Add water one tablespoon at a time to achieve the desired creamy consistency.
- Taste and adjust seasoning with more salt or lemon juice as needed.

2. Prepare the Vegetables:
- Wash and peel the carrots. Cut them into sticks about 4 inches long and 1/2 inch wide.
- Wash the celery stalks and cut them into similar-sized sticks.

3. Serve:
- Transfer the hummus to a serving bowl and sprinkle with paprika for garnish if desired.
- Arrange the carrot and celery sticks around the hummus bowl on a platter.
- Serve immediately, or refrigerate the hummus and veggies until ready to serve.

Nutritional Information (Per Serving)

Calories: 150, Protein: 4g, Carbohydrates: 16g, Sugars: 4g, Fiber: 5g, Fats: 8g, Saturated Fat: 1g, Cholesterol: 0mg, Sodium: 150mg, Potassium: 380mg

Cottage Cheese with Pineapple

Yield: 2 servings   *Preparation Time: 10 minutes*   *Cooking Time: None*

Ingredients:

- 1 cup low-fat cottage cheese (GI: 10)
- 1/2 cup fresh pineapple chunks (GI: 66)
- 1 tablespoon chia seeds (GI: 1)
- 1 tablespoon unsweetened shredded coconut (optional, GI: 42)
- 1 tablespoon chopped almonds or walnuts (optional, GI: 15)
- 1/2 teaspoon cinnamon (optional, GI: 1)
- 1 teaspoon sugar-free sweetener (optional, such as stevia or erythritol, GI: 0)

Instructions:

1. Prepare the Ingredients:
- If using fresh pineapple, peel and core it, then chop it into small chunks. If using canned pineapple, ensure it is unsweetened and drained well.
- Chop the almonds or walnuts if using.

2. Mix Cottage Cheese and Pineapple:
- Combine 1 cup of cottage cheese in a medium-sized bowl with 1/2 cup of pineapple chunks.
- Stir in 1 tablespoon of chia seeds for added fiber and texture.

3. Add Optional Ingredients:
- For added flavor and nutrition, add 1 tablespoon of unsweetened shredded coconut and 1 tablespoon of chopped almonds or walnuts.
- Sprinkle 1/2 teaspoon of cinnamon over the mixture for additional flavor.
- If you prefer a sweeter taste, mix in 1 teaspoon of a sugar-free sweetener.

4. Serve:
- Divide the mixture evenly between two serving bowls.
- Serve immediately, or refrigerate for an hour for a colder snack.

Nutritional Information (Per Serving)

Calories: 190, Protein: 14g, Carbohydrates: 18g, Sugars: 10g, Fiber: 5g, Fats: 7g, Saturated Fat: 2g, Cholesterol: 10mg, Sodium: 350mg, Potassium: 260mg

Mixed Nuts and Seeds

 Yield: 8 servings Preparation Time: 5 minutes
 Cooking Time: 10 minutes

Ingredients:

- 1 cup almonds, raw or lightly toasted (GI: 0)
- 1 cup walnuts, raw or lightly toasted (GI: 0)
- 1/2 cup pumpkin seeds (pepitas), raw or lightly toasted (GI: 0)
- 1/2 cup sunflower seeds, raw or lightly toasted (GI: 0) 1/4 cup chia seeds (GI: 1)
- 1/4 cup flaxseeds (GI: 0)
- 1 teaspoon cinnamon (optional) (GI: 0)
- 1 teaspoon sea salt (GI: 0)
- 2 tablespoons coconut oil, melted (optional, for additional flavor) (GI: 0)

Optional Ingredients:
- 1/4 cup dried cranberries or raisins (GI: 64) for a touch of sweetness
- 1 tablespoon honey or maple syrup (GI: 50-54) for extra sweetness
- 1/4 cup unsweetened coconut flakes (GI: 45) for added texture and flavor

Instructions:

1. **Preheat the Oven:** Preheat your oven to 350°F (175°C) if you toast the nuts and seeds for added flavor.
2. **Mix the Nuts and Seeds:** Combine the almonds, walnuts, pumpkin, sunflower, chia, and flaxseeds in a large mixing bowl. Add the mixture's optional coconut oil, cinnamon, and sea salt. Toss well to coat all the ingredients evenly.
3. **Toast the Mixture (Optional):** Spread the nut and seed mixture evenly on a baking sheet. Toast in the preheated oven for about 10 minutes, stirring halfway through, until the nuts and seeds are golden and fragrant. Watch closely to prevent burning.
4. **Add Optional Ingredients:** After toasting, mix in the dried cranberries, raisins, or coconut flakes to add a bit of sweetness and variety.
5. **Cool and Store:** Allow the mixture to cool completely. Store in an airtight container at room temperature for up to 2 weeks. Enjoy as a quick snack on its own. Sprinkle over yogurt or oatmeal for added texture and nutrients. Use as a topping for salads or smoothie bowls for extra crunch.

Nutritional Information (Per Serving)

Calories: 150, Protein: 4g, Carbohydrates: 16g, Sugars: 4g, Fiber: 5g, Fats: 8g, Saturated Fat: 1g, Cholesterol: 0mg, Sodium: 150mg, Potassium: 380mg

Bell Pepper Slices with Guacamole

 Yield: 4 servings Preparation Time: 10 minutes
Cooking Time: None

Ingredients:

For the Guacamole:
- 2 ripe avocados, peeled and pitted (GI: 15)
- 1 small lime, juiced (GI: 20)
- 1/4 cup red onion, finely chopped (GI: 10)
- 1 medium tomato, diced (GI: 15)
- 1 clove garlic, minced (GI: 10)
- 1/4 cup fresh cilantro, chopped (GI: 0)
- Salt and pepper to taste (GI: 0)
- 1/4 teaspoon cumin (optional) (GI: 0)
- 1/4 teaspoon cayenne pepper (optional) (GI: 0)

For the Bell Pepper Slices:
- 2 large bell peppers, any color, sliced into strips (GI: 15)

Optional Ingredients:
- 1 jalapeño, finely chopped, for extra spice (GI: 15)
- 1/4 cup crumbled feta cheese for added flavor (GI: 0)

Instructions:

1. **Prepare the Guacamole:** Mash the avocados with a fork until smooth but chunky in a medium bowl. Stir in the lime juice to prevent browning. Add the red onion, tomato, garlic, cilantro, salt, and pepper. Mix until well combined. For extra flavor, add cumin and cayenne pepper. Adjust seasoning to taste.
2. **Prepare the Bell Pepper Slices:** Wash and slice the bell peppers into strips. Arrange the bell pepper slices on a serving platter.
3. **Serve:** Serve the guacamole in a bowl alongside the bell pepper slices. Garnish with chopped jalapeño and crumbled feta cheese if using.

Nutritional Information (Per Serving)

Calories: 180, Protein: 3g, Carbohydrates: 12g, Fat: 15g, Fiber: 7g, Cholesterol: 0mg, Sodium: 90mg, Potassium: 530mg

Almond and Flaxseed Energy Bites

Yield: 12 servings (1 energy bite per Serving) *Preparation Time: 5 minutes* *Cooking Time: 10 minutes*

Ingredients:

- 1 cup Almonds, raw and unsalted (GI: 0)
- 1/4 cup Ground Flaxseed (GI: 35)
- 1/4 cup Chia Seeds (GI: 1)
- 1/4 cup Almond Butter, unsweetened (GI: 0)
- 2 tablespoons Sugar-Free Maple Syrup (GI: 0)
- 1/4 cup Unsweetened Shredded Coconut (GI: 45)
- 1 teaspoon Vanilla Extract (optional, GI: 0)
- 1/4 teaspoon Ground Cinnamon (optional, GI: 0)
  Pinch of Sea Salt (GI: 0)

Optional Add-ins for Flavor or Nutritional Benefits:

- 1/4 cup Dark Chocolate Chips (70% cocoa or higher) (GI: 23)
- 1 tablespoon Hemp Seeds (GI: 0)
- 1 tablespoon Pumpkin Seeds (GI: 0)

Instructions:

1. **Prepare the Almonds:** Pulse almonds in a food processor until finely ground but not pasty.
2. **Combine Dry Ingredients:** Mix ground almonds, flaxseed, chia seeds, shredded coconut, and optional seeds in a large bowl.
3. **Add Wet Ingredients:** Add almond butter, sugar-free maple syrup, vanilla extract, cinnamon, and salt. Mix until sticky.
4. **Form Energy Bites:** Roll into 12 balls (1 tablespoon each).
5. **Chill:** Refrigerate for 30 minutes (optional but recommended for firmness).
6. **Store:** Store in the refrigerator for up to one week or freeze for up to three months.

Nutritional Information (Per Serving)

Calories: 120, Protein: 4g, Carbohydrates: 5g, Fats: 9g, Fiber: 3g, Cholesterol: 0mg, Sodium: 18mg, Potassium: 125mg

Roasted Chickpeas with Sea Salt and Paprika

Yield: 4 servings *Preparation Time: 10 minutes* *Cooking Time: 30-35 minutes*

Ingredients:

- 1 can (15 oz) Chickpeas, drained and rinsed (GI: 28)
- 1 tablespoon Olive Oil (GI: 0)
- 1/2 teaspoon Sea Salt (GI: 0)
- 1 teaspoon Smoked Paprika (GI: 0)
- 1/2 teaspoon Garlic Powder (optional, GI: 0)
- 1/4 teaspoon Ground Cumin (optional, GI: 0)
- 1/4 teaspoon Black Pepper (optional, GI: 0)
- Pinch of Cayenne Pepper (optional, for a spicy kick, GI: 0)

Instructions:

1. **Preheat the Oven:** Preheat your oven to 400°F (200°C). Line a baking sheet with parchment paper or lightly grease it with olive oil.
2. **Prepare the Chickpeas:** Drain and rinse the chickpeas thoroughly under cold water. Pat them dry with a clean kitchen towel or paper towel. Removing as much moisture as possible is key to getting them crispy.
3. **Season the Chickpeas:** Toss the chickpeas with olive oil, sea salt, and smoked paprika in a large mixing bowl until they are evenly coated. If using optional spices like garlic powder, ground cumin, black pepper, or cayenne pepper, add them at this stage and mix well.
4. **Roast the Chickpeas:** Spread the seasoned chickpeas in a single layer on the prepared baking sheet. Roast in the preheated oven for 30-35 minutes, stirring or shaking the pan halfway through, until the chickpeas are golden brown and crispy. Watch closely during the last few minutes to prevent burning.
5. **Cool and Serve:** Remove the chickpeas from the oven and let them cool on the baking sheet. They will continue to crisp up as they cool down. Once cooled, serve immediately or store in an airtight container for up to 4 days.

Nutritional Information (Per Serving)

Calories: 180, Protein: 3g, Carbohydrates: 12g, Fat: 15g, Fiber: 7g, Cholesterol: 0mg, Sodium: 90mg, Potassium: 530mg

Greek Yogurt and Cucumber Dip with Veggie Sticks

Yield: 4 servings Preparation Time: 10 minutes
Cooking Time: None

Ingredients:

For the Greek Yogurt and Cucumber Dip:
- 1 cup Plain Greek Yogurt (non-fat or low-fat) (GI: 0)
- 1/2 medium Cucumber, grated and drained (GI: 15)
- 1 clove Garlic, minced (GI: 0)
- 1 tablespoon Fresh Lemon Juice (GI: 0)
- 1 tablespoon Fresh Dill, chopped (optional, GI: 0)
- 1 tablespoon Extra Virgin Olive Oil (optional, GI: 0)
- 1/4 teaspoon Sea Salt (GI: 0)
- 1/4 teaspoon Black Pepper (GI: 0)

For the Veggie Sticks:
- 1 medium Carrot, cut into sticks (GI: 35)
- 1 medium Red Bell Pepper, cut into sticks (GI: 10)
- 1 medium Cucumber, cut into sticks (GI: 15)
- 1 stalk Celery, cut into sticks (GI: 0)

Instructions:

1. **Prepare the Cucumber for the Dip:** Start by grating the cucumber using a box grater. Once grated, place the cucumber in a clean kitchen towel or cheesecloth and squeeze out as much excess water as possible. This step is crucial to prevent the dip from becoming too watery.
2. **Make the Greek Yogurt and Cucumber Dip:** In a medium mixing bowl, combine the plain Greek yogurt, grated cucumber, minced garlic, lemon juice, fresh dill (if using), and extra virgin olive oil (if using). Season with sea salt and black pepper to taste. Stir the ingredients until well combined.
3. **Taste and Adjust Seasoning:** Taste the dip and adjust the seasoning as needed. Add more lemon juice for extra tanginess or more dill for a more robust herb flavor.
4. **Prepare the Veggie Sticks:** While the dip is chilling, wash and prepare the vegetables. Cut the Carrot, red bell pepper, cucumber, and celery into sticks and arrange them on a serving platter.
5. **Serve:** Serve the chilled Greek yogurt and cucumber dip with the freshly prepared veggie sticks. This dip is perfect as a healthy snack or appetizer. You can also use it as a spread for sandwiches or wraps. Pair it with whole-grain crackers for an additional fiber boost.

Nutritional Information (Per Serving)

Calories: 78, Protein: 6g, Carbohydrates: 8g, Fats: 3g, Fiber: 2g, Cholesterol: 3mg, Sodium: 180mg, Potassium: 125mg

Celery Sticks with Cream Cheese and Walnuts

Yield: 4 servings Preparation Time: 10 minutes
Cooking Time: None

Ingredients:
- 4 large Celery Stalks (GI: 0)
- 1/2 cup Cream Cheese (low-fat or regular) (GI: 0)
- 1/4 cup Walnuts, chopped (GI: 0)
- 1 tablespoon Fresh Chives, chopped (optional, for garnish, GI: 0)
- 1/4 teaspoon Black Pepper (optional, for seasoning, GI: 0)

Optional Add-ins for Flavor or Nutritional Benefits:
- 1 tablespoon Ground Flaxseed (GI: 35)
- 1 tablespoon Sunflower Seeds (GI: 0)
- 1/2 teaspoon Smoked Paprika (optional, for a smoky flavor, GI: 0)

Instructions:

1. **Prepare the Celery Stalks:** Wash the celery stalks thoroughly under cold water. Trim the ends and cut each stalk into 3-inch pieces. This should yield approximately 12 celery sticks.
2. **Mix the Cream Cheese:** In a small bowl, soften the cream cheese by stirring it with a spoon. Mix any optional ingredients like ground flaxseed or smoked paprika into the cream cheese at this stage. You can also season the cream cheese with black pepper for added flavor.
3. **Assemble the Celery Sticks:** Using a butter knife or a small spoon, spread about 1-2 teaspoons of the cream cheese mixture into the groove of each celery stick.
4. **Top with Walnuts:** Sprinkle the chopped walnuts evenly over the cream cheese on each celery stick, pressing them gently into the cheese so they stick.
5. **Garnish:** If desired, sprinkle freshly chopped chives for flavor and color.
6. **Serve:** Arrange the celery sticks on a serving platter and serve immediately. These celery sticks make a great mid-morning or afternoon snack. They can also be served as an appetizer or a side dish for a light meal. Pair with a cup of herbal tea or an unsweetened beverage for a refreshing snack.

Nutritional Information (Per Serving)

Calories: 112, Protein: 4g, Carbohydrates: 5g, Fats: 10g, Fiber: 2g, Cholesterol: 15mg, Sodium: 100mg, Potassium: 180mg

2. Quick and Easy Snacks

Spicy Roasted Chickpeas

Yield: 4 servings *Preparation Time: 15 minutes*
Cooking Time: None

Ingredients:

- 1 can (15 oz) chickpeas, drained and rinsed (GI: 28)
- 1 tablespoon olive oil (GI: 0)
- 1 teaspoon smoked paprika (GI: 0)
- 1 teaspoon ground cumin (GI: 0)
- 1/2 teaspoon garlic powder (GI: 0)
- 1/2 teaspoon sea salt (GI: 0)
- 1/4 teaspoon black pepper (GI: 0)
- 1/4 teaspoon cayenne pepper (optional, for extra spice) (GI: 0)

Instructions:

1. **Preheat the Oven:** Preheat your oven to 400°F (200°C).
2. **Prepare the Chickpeas:** Drain and rinse the chickpeas thoroughly to remove any excess liquid. Spread the chickpeas on a clean kitchen towel and pat them dry to remove moisture. This step helps the chickpeas become crispy when roasted.
3. **Season the Chickpeas:** In a large mixing bowl, combine the chickpeas, olive oil, smoked paprika, ground cumin, garlic powder, salt, black pepper, and cayenne pepper (if using). Toss the chickpeas until they are evenly coated with the seasoning mixture.
4. **Roast the Chickpeas:** Spread the seasoned chickpeas in a single layer on a baking sheet. Roast in the preheated oven for about 25 minutes, stirring halfway through to ensure even cooking, until the chickpeas are golden brown and crispy.
5. **Cool and Serve:** Allow the roasted chickpeas to cool for a few minutes on the baking sheet before serving.
6. **Serve** as a healthy snack or as a crunchy topping for salads and soups. Enjoy this dish as a quick breakfast or a satisfying snack. Pair it with a glass of water or herbal tea to stay hydrated.

Nutritional Information (Per Serving)

Calories: 150, Protein: 7g, Carbohydrates: 22g, Fat: 5g, Fiber: 6g, Cholesterol: 0mg, Sodium: 290mg, Potassium: 200mg

Cucumber Slices with Hummus

Yield: 4 servings *Preparation Time: 10 minutes*
Cooking Time: None

Ingredients:

For the Hummus:
- 1 can (15 oz) chickpeas, drained and rinsed (GI: 28)
- 1/4 cup tahini (GI: 0)
- 2 tablespoons olive oil (GI: 0)
- 2 tablespoons lemon juice (GI: 20)
- 2 cloves garlic, minced (GI: 10)
- 1/2 teaspoon ground cumin (GI: 0)
- Salt and pepper to taste (GI: 0)
- 2-3 tablespoons water (as needed for consistency) (GI: 0)

For the Cucumber Slices:
- 2 large cucumbers, sliced into rounds (GI: 15)

Optional Ingredients:
- 1/4 teaspoon paprika or smoked paprika for garnish (GI: 0)
- 1 tablespoon chopped fresh parsley for garnish (GI: 0)
- 1/4 cup roasted red pepper, chopped, for added flavor (GI: 10)

Instructions:

1. **Prepare the Hummus:** In a food processor, combine chickpeas, tahini, olive oil, lemon juice, minced garlic, ground cumin, salt, and pepper. Blend until smooth, adding water as needed to achieve a creamy consistency.
2. **Prepare the Cucumber Slices:** Wash and slice the cucumbers into rounds approximately 1/4-inch thick. Arrange the cucumber slices on a serving platter.
3. **Assemble and Serve:** Transfer the hummus to a serving bowl and place it in the center of the cucumber platter. Garnish the hummus with a sprinkle of paprika and chopped parsley, if desired. Serve immediately, using the cucumber slices as dippers for the hummus. For variety, pair with other crunchy vegetables, such as carrot sticks or bell pepper strips. Serve as an appetizer at gatherings or as a healthy snack throughout the day.

Nutritional Information (Per Serving)

Calories: 150, Protein: 5g, Carbohydrates: 13g, Fat: 9g, Fiber: 4g, Cholesterol: 0mg, Sodium: 220mg, Potassium: 300mg

Cheese and Cherry Tomato Skewers

 Yield: 4 servings   Preparation Time: 10 minutes
 Cooking Time: None

Ingredients:

For the Greek Yogurt and Cucumber Dip:
- 1 cup Plain Greek Yogurt (non-fat or low-fat) (GI: 0)
- 1/2 medium Cucumber, grated and drained (GI: 15)
- 1 clove Garlic, minced (GI: 0)
- 1 tablespoon Fresh Lemon Juice (GI: 0)
- 1 tablespoon Fresh Dill, chopped (optional, GI: 0)
- 1 tablespoon Extra Virgin Olive Oil (optional, GI: 0)
- 1/4 teaspoon Sea Salt (GI: 0)
- 1/4 teaspoon Black Pepper (GI: 0)

For the Veggie Sticks:
- 1 medium Carrot, cut into sticks (GI: 35)
- 1 medium Red Bell Pepper, cut into sticks (GI: 10)
- 1 medium Cucumber, cut into sticks (GI: 15)
- 1 stalk Celery, cut into sticks (GI: 0)

Instructions:

1. **Prepare the Cucumber for the Dip:** Start by grating the cucumber using a box grater. Once grated, place the cucumber in a clean kitchen towel or cheesecloth and squeeze out as much excess water as possible. This step is crucial to prevent the dip from becoming too watery.
2. **Make the Greek Yogurt and Cucumber Dip:** In a medium mixing bowl, combine the plain Greek yogurt, grated cucumber, minced garlic, lemon juice, fresh dill (if using), and extra virgin olive oil (if using). Season with sea salt and black pepper to taste. Stir the ingredients until well combined.
3. **Taste and Adjust Seasoning:** Taste the dip and adjust the seasoning as needed. Add more lemon juice for extra tanginess or more dill for a more robust herb flavor.
4. **Prepare the Veggie Sticks:** While the dip is chilling, wash and prepare the vegetables. Cut the Carrot, red bell pepper, cucumber, and celery into sticks and arrange them on a serving platter.
5. **Serve:** Serve the chilled Greek yogurt and cucumber dip with the freshly prepared veggie sticks. This dip is perfect as a healthy snack or appetizer. You can also use it as a spread for sandwiches or wraps. Pair it with whole-grain crackers for an additional fiber boost.

Nutritional Information (Per Serving)

Calories: 78, Protein: 6g, Carbohydrates: 8g, Fats: 3g, Fiber: 2g, Cholesterol: 3mg, Sodium: 180mg, Potassium: 125mg

Mixed Nuts and Seeds Trail Mix

 Yield: 8 servings   Preparation Time: 5 minutes
Cooking Time: None

Ingredients:

- 1/2 cup raw almonds (GI: 0)
- 1/2 cup raw walnuts (GI: 0)
- 1/2 cup raw cashews (GI: 25)
- 1/4 cup pumpkin seeds (pepitas) (GI: 0)
- 1/4 cup sunflower seeds (GI: 0)
- 1/4 cup flaxseeds (GI: 0)
- 1/4 cup chia seeds (GI: 1)

Optional Ingredients:
- 1/4 cup unsweetened coconut flakes (GI: 45)
- 1/4 cup dried unsweetened cranberries (GI: 64) or raisins (GI: 64) for a touch of sweetness
- 1/4 teaspoon cinnamon (GI: 0) for added flavor
- 1/4 teaspoon sea salt (GI: 0) for seasoning

Instructions:

1. **Prepare the Ingredients:** Measure all the nuts and seeds according to the quantities listed above.
2. **Mix the Ingredients:** Combine almonds, walnuts, cashews, pumpkin seeds, sunflower seeds, flaxseeds, and chia seeds in a large bowl. Add optional ingredients like coconut flakes, dried cranberries, cinnamon, or sea salt if desired. Mix thoroughly until all the ingredients are evenly distributed.
3. **Store the Trail Mix:** Transfer the trail mix to an airtight container or individual snack bags for portion control. Store at room temperature for up to 2 weeks. Enjoy as a quick snack between meals. Sprinkle over yogurt or oatmeal for added texture and nutrients. Use as a topping for salads or smoothie bowls for extra crunch.

Nutritional Information (Per Serving)

Calories: 220, Protein: 6g, Carbohydrates: 8g, Fat: 19g, Fiber: 4g, Cholesterol: 0mg, Sodium: 3mg, Potassium: 200mg

Hard-Boiled Eggs with a Dash of Paprika

Yield: 4 servings *Preparation Time: 5 minutes* *Cooking Time: 10 minutes*

Ingredients:

- 4 large eggs (GI: 0)
- 1/4 teaspoon paprika (GI: 0)
- Salt and pepper to taste (GI: 0)

Optional Ingredients:
- 1 tablespoon fresh parsley, chopped (GI: 0) for garnish
- 1/4 teaspoon smoked paprika (GI: 0) for a smoky flavor
- 1 teaspoon Dijon mustard (GI: 0) for added tanginess

Instructions:

1. **Boil the Eggs:** Place the eggs in a saucepan and cover them with cold water by about an inch. Bring the water to a rolling boil over high heat. Once boiling, remove the saucepan from heat and cover it with a lid. Let the eggs sit in the hot water for about 10 minutes for hard-boiled eggs.
2. **Cool and Peel the Eggs:** After 10 minutes, transfer the eggs to a bowl of ice water or run them under cold water to stop cooking. Let them cool for at least 5 minutes. Peel the eggs once they are cool enough to handle.
3. **Prepare the Eggs:** Slice each egg in half lengthwise. Arrange the egg halves on a serving plate.
4. **Season the Eggs:** Sprinkle each egg half with a pinch of paprika. Season with salt and pepper to taste. For a smoky flavor, substitute regular paprika with smoked paprika if desired. If using, top with a dollop of Dijon mustard or sprinkle with fresh parsley for added flavor.
5. **Serve:** Serve immediately as a snack or as part of a meal. Pair with a small salad of mixed greens for a more filling snack. Enjoy as a high-protein addition to a breakfast or brunch spread.

Nutritional Information (Per Serving)

Calories: 70, Protein: 6g, Carbohydrates: 1g, Fat: 5g, Fiber: 0g, Cholesterol: 185mg, Sodium: 70mg, Potassium: 60mg

Edamame with Sea Salt

Yield: 4 servings *Preparation Time: 2 minutes* *Cooking Time: 10 minutes*

Ingredients:

- 2 cups frozen edamame in pods (GI: 18)
- 1 teaspoon sea salt (GI: 0)

Optional Ingredients:
- 1/2 teaspoon garlic powder (GI: 0) for added flavor
- 1/2 teaspoon red pepper flakes (GI: 0) for a spicy kick
- 1 tablespoon sesame seeds (GI: 0) for extra texture and flavor

Instructions:

1. **Boil the Edamame:** Bring a large pot of water to a boil. Add the frozen edamame pods to the boiling water. Cook for about 5 minutes until the edamame is tender and bright green.
2. **Drain and Season:** Drain the edamame in a colander and rinse briefly with cold water to stop the cooking process. Transfer the edamame to a bowl. Sprinkle with sea salt and toss to coat evenly.
3. **Optional Seasoning:** If desired, add garlic powder and red pepper flakes for additional flavor. Toss again to ensure the spices are evenly distributed. Sprinkle with sesame seeds before serving for extra texture.
4. **Serve:** Serve immediately as a healthy and satisfying snack. Enjoy as a snack on its own or as an appetizer before meals. Pair with a small side of sliced vegetables for added nutrients.

Nutritional Information (Per Serving)

Calories: 120, Protein: 11g, Carbohydrates: 10g, Fat: 5g, Fiber: 4g, Cholesterol: 0mg, Sodium: 300mg, Potassium: 340mg

Cottage Cheese and Tomato Stuffed Avocados

 Yield: 2 servings   Preparation Time: 10 minutes
 Cooking Time: None

Ingredients:

- 1 large Avocado, halved and pitted (GI: 15)
- 1/2 cup Cottage Cheese (low-fat or regular) (GI: 0)
- 1/2 cup Cherry Tomatoes, diced (GI: 15)
- 1 tablespoon Fresh Basil, chopped (optional, GI: 0)
- 1 tablespoon Red Onion, finely chopped (optional, GI: 10)
- 1 tablespoon Extra Virgin Olive Oil (optional, GI: 0)
- 1/4 teaspoon Sea Salt (GI: 0)
- 1/4 teaspoon Black Pepper (GI: 0)
- 1/4 teaspoon Balsamic Vinegar (optional, GI: 0)

Instructions:

1. **Prepare the Avocado Halves:** Cut the avocado in half lengthwise and remove the pit. If necessary, use a spoon to scoop out some of the flesh to create a larger cavity for the filling. Set aside the avocado halves.
2. **Prepare the Filling:** Combine the cottage cheese, diced cherry tomatoes, and optional ingredients like fresh basil and finely chopped red onion in a medium mixing bowl. Mix until well combined.
3. **Season the Filling:** Drizzle the olive oil over the filling mixture, and season with sea salt and black pepper. Stir to incorporate the seasonings evenly.
4. **Stuff the Avocados:** Mix the cottage cheese and tomato into each half of the avocado, generously filling the cavities. If desired, drizzle a small amount of balsamic vinegar over the stuffed avocados for extra flavor.
5. **Serve:** Serve the stuffed avocados immediately on a plate. They can be enjoyed as a light meal or a hearty snack. Serve these stuffed avocados as a quick snack, light lunch, or appetizer. Pair with a side of mixed greens for a more substantial meal. If you enjoy a bit of spice, sprinkle a pinch of red pepper flakes on top for extra flavor.

Nutritional Information (Per Serving)

Calories: 208, Protein: 8g, Carbohydrates: 9.6g, Fats: 17.6g, Fiber: 7.2g, Cholesterol: 9mg, Sodium: 240mg, Potassium: 620mg

Hard-Boiled Eggs with Hummus

 Yield: 2 servings   Preparation Time: 10 minutes (excluding boiling eggs)
 Cooking Time: None (after eggs are boiled)

Ingredients:

- 4 large Eggs, hard-boiled (GI: 0)
- 1/4 cup Hummus (GI: 6)
- 1 teaspoon Extra Virgin Olive Oil (optional, GI: 0)
- 1/4 teaspoon Paprika (optional, for garnish, GI: 0)
- 1/4 teaspoon Black Pepper (GI: 0)
- Fresh Parsley, chopped (optional, for garnish, GI: 0)

Optional Add-ins for Flavor or Nutritional Benefits:
- 1/2 teaspoon Ground Cumin (GI: 0)
- 1/2 teaspoon Lemon Zest (GI: 0)
- 1 tablespoon Crumbled Feta Cheese (optional, GI: 0)

Instructions:

1. **Prepare the Hard-Boiled Eggs:** If it still needs to be done, boil the eggs in cold water. Bring the water to a boil, then reduce to a simmer for 10 minutes. Remove from heat, drain, and transfer the eggs to an ice bath to cool. Once cool, peel the eggs.
2. **Slice the Eggs:** Slice each hard-boiled egg in half lengthwise. Arrange the egg halves on a serving plate with the cut side facing up.
3. **Top with Hummus:** Spoon about 1 teaspoon of hummus onto the top of each egg half, spreading it gently with the back of the spoon to cover the yolk area.
4. **Season and Garnish:** Drizzle the optional extra virgin olive oil over the hummus-topped eggs for added flavor and healthy fats. Sprinkle with black pepper, paprika, or other optional seasonings like ground cumin or lemon zest. Garnish with freshly chopped parsley if desired.
5. **Serve:** Serve immediately as a snack, appetizer, or part of a light meal. Pair with raw vegetable sticks such as carrots, cucumbers, or bell peppers for added crunch and fiber. These hummus-topped eggs can be enjoyed as a protein-packed snack between meals or a quick breakfast option.

Nutritional Information (Per Serving)

Calories: 200, Protein: 14g, Carbohydrates: 6g, Fats: 14g, Fiber: 2g, Cholesterol: 372mg, Sodium: 310mg, Potassium: 175mg

Rice Cake with Peanut Butter and Chia Seeds

Yield: 1 servings **Preparation Time:** 5 minutes **Cooking Time:** None

Ingredients:

- 1 Brown Rice Cake (unsalted) (GI: 55)
- 1 tablespoon Natural Peanut Butter (no added sugar) (GI: 14)
- 1 teaspoon Chia Seeds (GI: 1)
- 1/4 teaspoon Ground Cinnamon (optional, for flavor, GI: 0)
- 1 tablespoon Fresh Berries (optional, for added flavor and nutrition) (GI: varies, low)

Instructions:

1. **Prepare the Rice Cake:** Place the brown rice cake on a plate or flat surface.
2. **Spread the Peanut Butter:** Using a knife, spread the natural peanut butter evenly over the top of the rice cake.
3. **Add Chia Seeds and Optional Ingredients:** Sprinkle the chia seeds evenly over the peanut butter. If using, sprinkle ground cinnamon and flaxseed on top. For flavor and nutrition, you can add fresh berries to peanut butter and chia seeds.
4. **Serve:** The rice cake is ready to be enjoyed immediately. It can be served as a quick snack or a light breakfast option. Pair with a cup of unsweetened green or herbal tea for a satisfying snack. Add a drizzle of sugar-free maple syrup or honey for a touch of sweetness (if blood sugar levels allow).

Nutritional Information (Per Serving)

Calories: 185, Protein: 6g, Carbohydrates: 15g, Fats: 12g, Fiber: 5g, Cholesterol: 0mg, Sodium: 50mg, Potassium: 190mg

Zucchini Chips with Parmesan

Yield: 4 servings **Preparation Time:** 10 minutes **Cooking Time:** 20-25 minutes

Ingredients:

- 2 medium Zucchinis, thinly sliced (GI: 15)
- 1 tablespoon Olive Oil (GI: 0)
- 1/4 cup Grated Parmesan Cheese (GI: 0)
- 1/4 teaspoon Garlic Powder (optional, GI: 0)
- 1/4 teaspoon Paprika (optional, GI: 0)
- 1/4 teaspoon Sea Salt (GI: 0)
- 1/4 teaspoon Black Pepper (GI: 0)

Optional Add-ins for Flavor or Nutritional Benefits:

- 1 teaspoon Italian Seasoning (optional, GI: 0)
- 1/2 teaspoon Crushed Red Pepper Flakes (optional, for a spicy kick, GI: 0)

Instructions:

1. **Preheat the Oven:** Preheat your oven to 425°F (220°C). Line a baking sheet with parchment paper or lightly grease it with olive oil.
2. **Prepare the Zucchini Slices:** Wash and dry the zucchini. Slice them thinly using a mandoline or a sharp knife, aiming for about 1/8-inch thickness for even cooking.
3. **Season the Zucchini Slices:** Toss the zucchini slices with olive oil in a large bowl until they are evenly coated. In a separate bowl, mix the grated Parmesan cheese, garlic powder, paprika, sea salt, and black pepper (and any optional seasonings). Sprinkle this mixture over the zucchini slices and toss until they are well coated.
4. **Arrange on Baking Sheet:** Place the seasoned zucchini slices in a single layer on the prepared baking sheet. Ensure they do not overlap to cook evenly and crisp up.
5. **Bake the Zucchini Chips:** Bake in the preheated oven for 20-25 minutes or until the chips are golden brown and crispy. Keep an eye on them during the last few minutes to prevent burning, as thin slices can cook quickly.
6. **Cool and Serve:** Remove the zucchini chips from the oven and let them cool on the baking sheet for a few minutes. They will continue to crisp as they cool. Serve these zucchini chips as a healthy snack or as a side dish. Pair with a low-carb dip such as Greek yogurt or hummus for added flavor. Enjoy them on their own as a crunchy, savory treat.

Nutritional Information (Per Serving)

Calories: 200, Protein: 14g, Carbohydrates: 6g, Fats: 14g, Fiber: 2g, Cholesterol: 372mg, Sodium: 310mg, Potassium: 175mg

3. Appetizers for Entertaining

Smoked Salmon Cucumber Bites

🌿 Yield: 8 servings   🍲 Preparation Time: 15 minutes
🍽 Cooking Time: None

Ingredients:

- 2 large cucumbers (GI: 15)
- 4 oz smoked salmon, thinly sliced (GI: 0)
- 4 oz cream cheese, softened (GI: 0)
- 1 tablespoon fresh dill, chopped (GI: 0)
- 1 tablespoon capers, drained (optional) (GI: 0)
- 1 tablespoon lemon juice (GI: 20)
- 1/4 teaspoon black pepper (GI: 0)

Optional Ingredients:

- 1/4 teaspoon garlic powder (GI: 0) for added flavor
- 1 tablespoon chopped fresh chives (GI: 0) for garnish
- 1/4 teaspoon smoked paprika (GI: 0) for a smoky flavor

Instructions:

1. **Prepare the Cucumbers:** Wash cucumbers and pat dry. Slice into ½-inch thick rounds and arrange on a serving platter.
2. **Make the Cream Cheese Spread:** Combine softened cream cheese, lemon juice, black pepper, and garlic powder (if using) in a bowl. Stir until smooth. Add dill and capers (if using).
3. **Assemble the Cucumber Bites:** Spread a dollop of the cream cheese mixture on each cucumber slice. Top with a folded slice of smoked salmon.
4. **Garnish and Serve:** Garnish with dill, chives, or smoked paprika (optional). Serve immediately. Pair with other low-carb appetizers, such as deviled eggs or stuffed cherry tomatoes, for a complete party platter. Serve alongside a fresh green salad for a light and healthy meal.

Nutritional Information (Per Serving)

Calories: 80, Protein: 5g, Carbohydrates: 3g, Fat: 6g, Fiber: 1g, Cholesterol: 20mg, Sodium: 190mg, Potassium: 130mg

Caprese Salad Skewers

🌿 Yield: 8 servings   🍲 Preparation Time: 15 minutes
🍽 Cooking Time: None

Ingredients:

- 16 cherry tomatoes (GI: 15)
- 8 oz fresh mozzarella balls (bocconcini or ciliegine) (GI: 0)
- 16 fresh basil leaves (GI: 0)
- 2 tablespoons balsamic glaze (optional) (GI: 35)
- 2 tablespoons extra-virgin olive oil (GI: 0)
- Salt and pepper to taste (GI: 0)
- 16 small wooden skewers

Optional Ingredients:

- 1 teaspoon dried oregano or Italian seasoning (GI: 0)
- 1 tablespoon pine nuts, toasted (GI: 15) for added texture and flavor

Instructions:

1. **Prepare the Ingredients:** Wash and pat dry cherry tomatoes, basil leaves, and mozzarella balls.
2. **Assemble the Skewers:** Thread a cherry tomato, a folded basil leaf, and a mozzarella ball onto each skewer. Repeat until the skewer is filled (two sets per skewer).
3. **Season the Skewers:** Arrange on a serving platter. Drizzle lightly with olive oil and optional balsamic glaze. Sprinkle with salt, pepper, and oregano, if desired.
4. **Serve:** Serve immediately. Use lemon juice instead of balsamic glaze for a lower sugar option. Pair with other low-carb appetizers, such as smoked salmon cucumber bites or grilled vegetable skewers. Serve with a small bowl of mixed olives for a Mediterranean-themed platter.

Nutritional Information (Per Serving)

Calories: 150, Protein: 7g, Carbohydrates: 4g, Fat: 12g, Fiber: 1g, Cholesterol: 15mg, Sodium: 120mg, Potassium: 160mg

Stuffed Mini Bell Peppers with Cream Cheese

Yield: 8 servings *Preparation Time: 15 minutes* *Cooking Time: 5 minutes*

Ingredients:

- 16 mini bell peppers (GI: 15)
- 8 oz cream cheese, softened (GI: 0)
- 1/4 cup shredded mozzarella cheese (GI: 0)
- 1/4 cup chopped fresh parsley (GI: 0)
- 2 tablespoons chopped fresh chives (GI: 0)
- 1 tablespoon lemon juice (GI: 20)
- 1 clove garlic, minced (GI: 10)
- Salt and pepper to taste (GI: 0)

Optional Ingredients:
- 1/4 teaspoon smoked paprika (GI: 0) for a smoky flavor
- 1/4 cup chopped walnuts or almonds (GI: 0) for added crunch
- 1/4 cup sun-dried tomatoes, chopped (GI: 35) for additional flavor

Instructions:

1. **Prepare the Mini Bell Peppers:** Wash and pat dry. Slice in half lengthwise; remove seeds and membranes.
2. **Make the Cream Cheese Filling:** Combine cream cheese, mozzarella, parsley, chives, lemon juice, garlic, salt, and pepper in a bowl. Mix until smooth. Optional: Stir in smoked paprika or nuts.
3. **Stuff the Peppers:** Spoon about 1 tablespoon of the filling into each pepper half.
4. **Optional Broiling:** Preheat oven broiler. Place stuffed peppers on a baking sheet and broil for 3–5 minutes until slightly golden.
5. **Serve:** Arrange on a platter. For a fresh option, skip broiling and serve directly. For a varied spread, serve alongside other diabetic-friendly appetizers, such as cucumber slices with hummus or smoked salmon bites. Pair with a crisp white wine or sparkling water with lemon for a refreshing accompaniment.

Nutritional Information (Per Serving)
Calories: 120, Protein: 4g, Carbohydrates: 5g, Fat: 10g, Fiber: 1g, Cholesterol: 25mg, Sodium: 120mg, Potassium: 200mg

Zucchini and Feta Roll-Ups

Yield: 4 servings *Preparation Time: 15 minutes* *Cooking Time: 5 minutes*

Ingredients:

- 2 medium zucchinis (GI: 15)
- 4 oz feta cheese, crumbled (GI: 0)
- 2 tablespoons cream cheese, softened (GI: 0)
- 1/4 cup sun-dried tomatoes, chopped (GI: 35)
- 1/4 cup fresh basil leaves, chopped (GI: 0)
- 1 tablespoon olive oil (GI: 0)
- 1 clove garlic, minced (GI: 10)
- Salt and pepper to taste (GI: 0)

Optional Ingredients:
- 1/4 teaspoon dried oregano (GI: 0) for extra flavor
- 1 tablespoon pine nuts, toasted (GI: 15) for added texture
- 1 tablespoon lemon zest (GI: 20) for a refreshing twist

Instructions:

1. **Prepare the Zucchini:** Wash and trim ends. Slice into thin strips using a mandoline.
2. **Cook the Zucchini:** Heat olive oil in a skillet over medium-high heat. Sauté zucchini strips for 1–2 minutes per side. Remove and cool for 5 minutes.
3. **Make the Filling:** Combine feta, cream cheese, sun-dried tomatoes, basil, garlic, salt, and pepper. **Optional:** Add oregano, pine nuts, or lemon zest.
4. **Assemble the Roll-Ups:** Spread filling on each zucchini strip. Roll up tightly and secure with a toothpick.
5. **Serve:** Arrange on a platter. Optionally drizzle with olive oil or garnish with pine nuts. Pair with other low-carb appetizers, such as stuffed mini bell peppers or smoked salmon bites, for a complete spread. Serve with a light balsamic glaze for added flavor.

Nutritional Information (Per Serving)
Calories: 80, Protein: 4 g, Carbohydrates: 4g, Fat: 6g, Fiber: 1g, Cholesterol: 10mg, Sodium: 150mg, Potassium: 200mg

Guacamole with Veggie Sticks

Yield: 8 servings *Preparation Time: 15 minutes* *Cooking Time: None*

Ingredients:

For the Guacamole:
- 3 ripe avocados, peeled and pitted (GI: 15)
- 1 small lime, juiced (GI: 20)
- 1/4 cup red onion, finely chopped (GI: 10)
- 1 medium tomato, diced (GI: 15)
- 1-2 cloves garlic, minced (GI: 10)
- 1/4 cup fresh cilantro, chopped (GI: 0)
- Salt and pepper to taste (GI: 0)
- 1/4 teaspoon cumin (optional) (GI: 0)
- 1 jalapeño, seeded and minced (optional, for spice) (GI: 15)

For the Veggie Sticks:
- 2 large carrots, cut into sticks (GI: 41)
- 2 large cucumbers, cut into sticks (GI: 15)
- 2 bell peppers (any color), cut into sticks (GI: 15)
- 2 celery stalks, cut into sticks (GI: 15)

Optional Ingredients:
- 1 tablespoon olive oil (GI: 0) for extra flavor and healthy fats
- 1 tablespoon pumpkin seeds (pepitas) for a crunchy topping (GI: 0)

Instructions:

1. **Prepare the Guacamole:** Mash ripe avocados until smooth but slightly chunky. Stir in lime juice, red onion, tomato, garlic, cilantro, salt, and pepper. Optional: Add cumin and jalapeño for extra flavor.
2. **Prepare the Veggie Sticks:** Wash and cut carrots, cucumbers, bell peppers, and celery into uniform sticks (4–5 sticks per serving).
3. **Assemble and Serve:** Transfer guacamole to a serving bowl.
4. **Optional:** Drizzle with olive oil and sprinkle with pumpkin seeds. Arrange veggie sticks around the bowl. **Serve** immediately. Pair with whole-grain pita chips for a heartier snack. Serve alongside other diabetic-friendly appetizers, such as cheese, cherry tomato skewers, or smoked salmon bites.

Nutritional Information (Per Serving)

Calories: 160, Protein: 2g, Carbohydrates: 12g, Fat: 13g, Fiber: 6g, Cholesterol: 0mg, Sodium: 60mg, Potassium: 450mg

Almond-Crusted Mozzarella Sticks

Yield: 8 servings *Preparation Time: 20 minutes* *Cooking Time: 5 minutes*

Ingredients:

- 8 mozzarella string cheese sticks (part-skim) (GI: 0)
- 1/2 cup almond flour (GI: 0)
- 1/2 cup almonds, finely chopped or crushed (GI: 0)
- 2 large eggs (GI: 0)
- 1/4 teaspoon onion powder (GI: 0)
- 1/4 teaspoon dried oregano (GI: 0)
- 1/4 teaspoon salt (GI: 0)
- 1/4 teaspoon black pepper (GI: 0)
- Cooking spray or olive oil for baking (GI: 0)

Optional Ingredients:
- 1/4 teaspoon smoked paprika (GI: 0) for extra flavor
- 1 tablespoon chopped fresh parsley (GI: 0) for garnish
- Marinara sauce for dipping (GI: 45)

Instructions:

1. **Prepare the Mozzarella Sticks:** Cut mozzarella sticks in half. Freeze for 15 minutes to prevent melting during cooking.
2. **Prepare the Breading Station:** Mix almond flour, chopped almonds, garlic powder, onion powder, oregano, salt, and pepper in a shallow bowl. In another bowl, beat eggs.
3. **Coat the Mozzarella Sticks:** Dip each frozen stick in egg, then almond mixture. Repeat for a thicker coating. Freeze again for 10 minutes to set.
4. **Bake or Air Fry:** Preheat to 400°F (200°C). Bake on a parchment-lined tray for 12–15 minutes, turning halfway. *Air Fryer:* Preheat to 375°F (190°C). Air fry for 8–10 minutes, shaking halfway.
5. **Serve:** Serve hot with optional marinara sauce or fresh parsley. Pair with a fresh green salad or low-carb appetizers like cucumber slices with hummus or smoked salmon bites.

Nutritional Information (Per Serving)

Calories: 180, Protein: 10g, Carbohydrates: 4g, Fat: 15g, Fiber: 2g, Cholesterol: 45mg, Sodium: 250mg, Potassium: 80mg

Spinach and Artichoke Dip with Whole-Grain Crackers

 Yield: 8 servings   Preparation Time: 10 minutes
 Cooking Time: 20 minutes

Ingredients:

For the Spinach and Artichoke Dip:
- 1 cup Frozen Spinach, thawed and drained (GI: 15)
- 1 can (14 oz) Artichoke Hearts, drained and chopped (GI: 15)
- 1/2 cup Plain Greek Yogurt (non-fat or low-fat) (GI: 0)
- 1/2 cup Low-Fat Cream Cheese, softened (GI: 0)
- 1/4 cup Grated Parmesan Cheese (GI: 0)
- 1/2 cup Part-Skim Mozzarella Cheese, shredded (GI: 0)
- 1 clove Garlic, minced (GI: 0)
- 1 tablespoon Lemon Juice (GI: 0)
- 1/2 teaspoon Black Pepper (GI: 0)
- 1/4 teaspoon Sea Salt (GI: 0)
- 1/4 teaspoon Red Pepper Flakes (optional, for a bit of heat, GI: 0)

For Serving:
- 32 Whole-Grain Crackers (GI: 55)
- Fresh Veggie Sticks (optional, such as carrots, cucumbers, or bell peppers) (GI: varies, low)

Instructions:

1. **Preheat the Oven:** Preheat to 375°F (190°C). Grease a small baking dish.
2. **Prepare the Dip Mixture:** Combine spinach, artichoke hearts, Greek yogurt, cream cheese, Parmesan, mozzarella, garlic, lemon juice, salt, and pepper in a bowl. Mix well.
3. **Bake the Dip:** Spread mixture evenly in the baking dish. Bake for 20 minutes. Optional: Broil for 2 minutes for a golden top.
4. **Serve:** Serve warm with whole-grain crackers or celery sticks. Also this dip is perfect for entertaining as an appetizer or snack. Pair with a variety of veggie sticks for a low-carb dipping option. Serve alongside other diabetic-friendly appetizers like stuffed mushrooms or cucumber bites.

Nutritional Information (Per Serving)
Calories: 140, Protein: 8g, Carbohydrates: 12g, Fats: 7g, Fiber: 2g, Cholesterol: 20mg, Sodium: 320mg, Potassium: 220mg

Prosciutto-Wrapped Asparagus Spears

 Yield: 4 servings Preparation Time: 10 minutes
Cooking Time: 10-12 minutes

Ingredients:

- 8 mozzarella string cheese sticks (part-skim) (GI: 0)
- 1/2 cup almond flour (GI: 0)
- 1/2 cup almonds, finely chopped or crushed (GI: 0)
- 2 large eggs (GI: 0)
- 1/4 teaspoon onion powder (GI: 0)
- 1/4 teaspoon dried oregano (GI: 0)
- 1/4 teaspoon salt (GI: 0)
- 1/4 teaspoon black pepper (GI: 0)
- Cooking spray or olive oil for baking (GI: 0)

Optional Ingredients:
- 1/4 teaspoon smoked paprika (GI: 0) for extra flavor
- 1 tablespoon chopped fresh parsley (GI: 0) for garnish
- Marinara sauce for dipping (GI: 45)

Instructions:

1. **Prepare the Oven:** Preheat to 400°F (200°C). Line a baking sheet with parchment paper.
2. **Wrap the Asparagus:** Wash and trim asparagus. Wrap each spear with half a slice of prosciutto, spiraling from base to tip.
3. **Season and Bake:** Drizzle olive oil over asparagus. Sprinkle lightly with black pepper. Bake for 10–12 minutes until asparagus is tender and prosciutto is crispy.
4. **Garnish and Serve:** Garnish with Parmesan or balsamic glaze (use sparingly). Serve warm. Also these prosciutto-wrapped asparagus spears make a perfect appetizer or side dish for entertaining. Pair with other low-carb appetizers such as cheese platters or stuffed mushrooms. Serve with a lemon wedge for an extra burst of freshness.

Nutritional Information (Per Serving)
Calories: 85, Protein: 6g, Carbohydrates: 3g, Fats: 6g, Fiber: 2g, Cholesterol: 15mg, Sodium: 300mg, Potassium: 180mg

Garlic and Herb Stuffed Mushrooms

🌿 Yield: 4 servings (approximately 12 stuffed mushrooms)
🍲 Preparation Time: 15 minutes
🍽 Cooking Time: 20 minutes

Ingredients:

- 12 large White Mushrooms, stems removed and finely chopped (GI: 15)
- 1 tablespoon Olive Oil (GI: 0)
- 2 cloves Garlic, minced (GI: 0)
- 1/4 cup Onion, finely chopped (GI: 10)
- 1/4 cup Parmesan Cheese, grated (GI: 0)
- 1/4 cup Whole Wheat Breadcrumbs (GI: 45)
- 2 tablespoons Fresh Parsley, chopped (GI: 0)
- 1 tablespoon Fresh Thyme, chopped (optional, GI: 0)
- 1 tablespoon Fresh Basil, chopped (optional, GI: 0)
- 1/4 teaspoon Black Pepper (GI: 0)
- 1/4 teaspoon Sea Salt (optional, GI: 0)
- 1 tablespoon Lemon Juice (optional, for brightness, GI: 0)

- **Optional Add-ins for Flavor or Nutritional Benefits:**
- 1/4 cup Low-Fat Cream Cheese (optional, for a creamy texture, GI: 0)
- 1/4 teaspoon Red Pepper Flakes (optional, for a spicy kick, GI: 0)

Instructions:

1. **Preheat the Oven:** Preheat to 375°F (190°C). Line a baking sheet with parchment paper.
2. **Prepare the Mushrooms:** Clean mushrooms with a damp towel. Remove stems and finely chop.
3. **Make the Filling:** Sauté onion in olive oil for 2–3 minutes. Add mushroom stems and garlic; cook until soft. Remove from heat. Mix in breadcrumbs, Parmesan, parsley, thyme, basil, salt, pepper, and optional cream cheese or red pepper flakes.
4. **Stuff and Bake:** Fill mushroom caps with mixture. Bake for 15–20 minutes until golden.
5. **Serve:** Garnish with fresh herbs. Serve warm. Serve these stuffed mushrooms as an appetizer or side dish at your next gathering. Pair with a fresh green salad or grilled vegetables for a complete, low-carb meal. Garnish with additional fresh herbs or a sprinkle of grated Parmesan before serving.

Nutritional Information (Per Serving)

Calories: 95, Protein: 5g, Carbohydrates: 8g, Fats: 6g, Fiber: 2g, Cholesterol: 5mg, Sodium: 220mg, Potassium: 300mg

Shrimp Cocktail with Avocado Salsa

🌿 Yield: 4 servings
🍲 Preparation Time: 15 minutes
🍽 Cooking Time: 2 minutes

Ingredients:

For the Shrimp Cocktail:
- 1 lb Large Shrimp, peeled and deveined (GI: 0)
- 1 tablespoon Olive Oil (GI: 0)
- 1 clove Garlic, minced (GI: 0)
- 1/4 teaspoon Paprika (GI: 0)
- 1/4 teaspoon Black Pepper (GI: 0)
- 1/4 teaspoon Sea Salt (optional, GI: 0)
- Juice of 1/2 Lemon (GI: 0)

For the Avocado Salsa:
- 1 large Avocado, diced (GI: 15)
- 1/2 cup Cherry Tomatoes, diced (GI: 15)
- 1/4 cup Red Onion, finely chopped (GI: 10)
- 1/4 cup Fresh Cilantro, chopped (GI: 0)
- 1 tablespoon Fresh Lime Juice (GI: 0)
- 1 tablespoon Olive Oil (GI: 0)
- 1/2 teaspoon Ground Cumin (GI: 0)
- 1/4 teaspoon Sea Salt (optional, GI: 0)
- 1/4 teaspoon Black Pepper (GI: 0)
- 1/2 Jalapeño, finely chopped (optional, for a spicy kick) (GI: 15)

Instructions:

1. **Prepare the Shrimp:** Toss shrimp with olive oil, garlic, paprika, black pepper, and salt. Cook in a skillet over medium heat for 2–3 minutes per side. Squeeze lemon juice over shrimp; set aside.
2. **Make the Avocado Salsa:** Combine avocado, cherry tomatoes, red onion, cilantro, lime juice, olive oil, cumin, salt, and pepper.
3. **Optional:** Add jalapeño for spice.
4. **Assemble and Serve:** Plate salsa and arrange shrimp on top. Garnish with cilantro or lime wedges. Pair this shrimp cocktail with avocado salsa, mixed greens, or cucumber slices for a low-carb starter. Serve with whole-grain crackers or alongside a light gazpacho for a fuller meal.

Nutritional Information (Per Serving)

Calories: 210, Protein: 18g, Carbohydrates: 7g, Fats: 14g, Fiber: 4g, Cholesterol: 170mg, Sodium: 250mg, Potassium: 520mg

CHAPTER 9
DESSERTS AND TREATS
1. Low-Sugar Desserts

Berry Greek Yogurt Parfait

Yield: 4 servings   *Preparation Time: 10 minutes*
Cooking Time: None

Ingredients:

- 2 cups plain Greek yogurt, unsweetened (GI: 12)
- 1 cup fresh mixed berries (strawberries, blueberries, raspberries) (GI: 25)
- 1/4 cup chopped nuts (almonds, walnuts, or pecans) (GI: 0)
- 2 tablespoons chia seeds (GI: 1)
- 1 teaspoon vanilla extract (GI: 0)
- 2 tablespoons stevia or another sugar substitute (optional, to taste) (GI: 0)

Optional Ingredients:

- 1/4 cup unsweetened coconut flakes (GI: 45) for added texture
- 1/4 cup granola (low-sugar, high-fiber) (GI: 55) for crunch
- 1 tablespoon flaxseeds (GI: 0) for extra fiber

Instructions:

1. **Wash and pat dry the berries.** Chop nuts if needed.
2. **Combine** Greek yogurt, vanilla extract, and stevia (if using) in a bowl. Stir until smooth.
3. **Layer** yogurt, berries, chia seeds, and nuts in serving glasses. Repeat layers.
4. **Optionally** top with unsweetened coconut flakes, seeds, or granola in small amounts.
5. **Serve** immediately or chill for a refreshing dessert. Serve chilled for a refreshing dessert option. Pair with a cup of herbal or iced tea for a complete treat.

Nutritional Information (Per Serving)

Calories: 220, Protein: 18g, Carbohydrates: 18g, Fat: 10g, Fiber: 6g, Cholesterol: 10mg, Sodium: 50mg, Potassium: 300mg

Baked Apples with Cinnamon

Yield: 4 servings   *Preparation Time: 10 minutes*
Cooking Time: 35 minutes

Ingredients:

- 4 medium apples, such as Granny Smith or Gala (GI: 36-38)
- 1/4 cup chopped walnuts (optional, for added crunch) (GI: 0)
- 2 tablespoons raisins (optional, for natural sweetness) (GI: 64)
- 1 teaspoon ground cinnamon (GI: 0)
- 1 tablespoon granulated erythritol or another sugar substitute (GI: 0)
- 1/4 cup water (GI: 0)
- 1 teaspoon vanilla extract (GI: 0)

Optional Ingredients:

- 1/4 teaspoon ground nutmeg (GI: 0) for extra spice
- 1 tablespoon unsweetened shredded coconut (GI: 45) for added flavor

Instructions:

1. **Prepare the oven:** Preheat oven to 350°F (175°C). Prepare the apples: Core apples and place in a baking dish. Prepare the filling: Mix walnuts, raisins, cinnamon, erythritol, and nutmeg for filling.
2. **Stuff the apples:** Stuff apples and press mixture gently.
3. **Bake the apples:** Pour water into the dish, cover with foil, and bake for 20-25 minutes. Remove foil and bake another 10 minutes, checking for tenderness.
4. **Serve:** Drizzle with vanilla extract after baking. Serve warm. For a more indulgent treat, serve with a dollop of Greek yogurt or a scoop of sugar-free vanilla ice cream. Sprinkle with extra cinnamon before serving for enhanced flavor.

Nutritional Information (Per Serving)

Calories: 130, Protein: 1g, Carbohydrates: 23g, Fat: 5g, Fiber: 4g, Cholesterol: 0mg, Sodium: 2mg, Potassium: 180mg

Fresh Fruit Salad with Mint

 Yield: 4 servings   Preparation Time: 15 minutes
 Cooking Time: None

Ingredients:

- 1 cup strawberries, hulled and quartered (GI: 41)
- 1 cup blueberries (GI: 53)
- 1 cup raspberries (GI: 32)
- 1 cup diced cantaloupe (GI: 65)
- 1 tablespoon fresh mint leaves, finely chopped (GI: 0)
- 1 tablespoon lemon juice (GI: 20)
- 1 tablespoon stevia or another sugar substitute (optional, to taste) (GI: 0)

Optional Ingredients:

- 1/4 cup unsweetened shredded coconut (GI: 45) for added texture
- 1 tablespoon chia seeds (GI: 1) for added fiber and protein
- 1 tablespoon lime juice (GI: 20) for extra citrus flavor

Instructions:

1. **Prepare the fruits:** Wash and chop strawberries, blueberries, raspberries, and cantaloupe.
2. **Assemble the salad:** Toss fruit with lemon juice, mint, and stevia (if using).
3. **Add additional ingredients:** Sprinkle optional coconut or chia seeds for added texture.
4. **Cool and serve:** Chill for 10 minutes before serving. Serve with a dollop of Greek yogurt for added protein and creaminess. Pair with a light mint or herbal tea for a refreshing accompaniment.

Nutritional Information (Per Serving)

Calories: 70, Protein: 1g, Carbohydrates: 16g, Fat: 1g, Fiber: 4g, Cholesterol: 0mg, Sodium: 5mg, Potassium: 240mg

Chia Seed Pudding with Mango

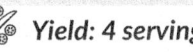 Yield: 4 servings   Preparation Time: 10 minutes
 Cooking Time: 4 hours

Ingredients:

- 1/2 cup chia seeds (GI: 1)
- 2 cups unsweetened almond milk (GI: 30)
- 1 teaspoon vanilla extract (GI: 0)
- 1-2 tablespoons stevia or another sugar substitute (optional, to taste) (GI: 0)
- 1 medium mango, peeled and diced (GI: 51)

Optional Ingredients:

- 1/4 teaspoon ground cinnamon (GI: 0) for added flavor
- 1 tablespoon unsweetened shredded coconut (GI: 45) for garnish
- 1 tablespoon chopped nuts (almonds, walnuts) (GI: 0) for added texture

Instructions:

1. **Mix ingredients:** Mix chia seeds, almond milk, vanilla extract, and stevia in a bowl. Stir well.
   Chill: Chill for 4+ hours, stirring after 30 minutes to prevent clumping.
2. **Prepare the mango:** Dice mango, limiting to 1/4 cup per serving.
3. **Layer and serve:** Layer pudding with mango and optional toppings (nuts, coconut, if using). Serve. Serve as a breakfast option or a refreshing dessert. Pair with a herbal tea or a light coconut drink for a complete treat.

Nutritional Information (Per Serving)

Calories: 180, Protein: 5g, Carbohydrates: 23g, Fat: 7g, Fiber: 9g, Cholesterol: 0mg, Sodium: 75mg, Potassium: 310mg

Strawberry Basil Sorbet

 Yield: 4 servings   Preparation Time: 15 minutes
Cooking Time: 3 hours

Ingredients:

- 3 cups fresh strawberries, hulled (GI: 41)
- 1/4 cup fresh basil leaves (GI: 0)
- 1/4 cup water (GI: 0)
- 1 tablespoon lemon juice (GI: 20)
- 2-3 tablespoons granulated erythritol or another sugar substitute (to taste) (GI: 0)

Optional Ingredients:

- 1/4 teaspoon vanilla extract (GI: 0) for added depth of flavor
- 1 tablespoon chia seeds (GI: 1) for added fiber
- Fresh basil leaves for garnish (GI: 0)

Instructions:

1. **Prepare and mix ingredients:** Blend strawberries, basil, lemon juice, water, and erythritol until smooth.
2. **Strain:** Strain through a sieve for smoother sorbet (optional).
3. **Freeze:** Freeze in a shallow container, stirring every 30 minutes for 2 hours.
4. **Serve:** Serve garnished with fresh basil leaves. Pair with fresh strawberries or a dollop of Greek yogurt for added creaminess. Enjoy as a light and refreshing dessert on a warm day.

Nutritional Information (Per Serving)

Calories: 50, Protein: 1g, Carbohydrates: 11g, Fat: 1g, Fiber: 1g, Cholesterol: 0mg, Sodium: 1mg, Potassium: 160mg

Orange and Almond Salad

 Yield: 4 servings   Preparation Time: 15 minutes
Cooking Time: None

Ingredients:

- 1/2 cup chia seeds (GI: 1)
- 2 cups unsweetened almond milk (GI: 30)
- 1 teaspoon vanilla extract (GI: 0)
- 1-2 tablespoons stevia or another sugar substitute (optional, to taste) (GI: 0)
- 1 medium mango, peeled and diced (GI: 51)

Optional Ingredients:

- 1/4 teaspoon ground cinnamon (GI: 0) for added flavor
- 1 tablespoon unsweetened shredded coconut (GI: 45) for garnish
- 1 tablespoon chopped nuts (almonds, walnuts) (GI: 0) for added texture

Instructions:

1. **Prepare the Salad Ingredients:** Wash and dry the salad greens thoroughly. Peel the oranges, segment them, and remove any seeds. Add the orange segments to a large salad bowl. Thinly slice the red onion and add to the bowl. Add the sliced almonds and crumbled feta cheese (if using).
2. **Make the Dressing:** In a small bowl, whisk together olive oil, balsamic vinegar, and lemon juice. Season with salt and pepper to taste.
3. **Assemble the Salad:** Drizzle the dressing over the salad ingredients. Toss gently to coat evenly.
4. **Garnish (Optional):** Sprinkle with fresh mint leaves and chia seeds for added flavor and nutrition.
5. **Serve:** Serve immediately as a light lunch or side dish. Pair with 3 oz of grilled chicken or fish for a complete meal.

Nutritional Information (Per Serving)

Calories: 175, Protein: 5g, Carbohydrates: 16g, Fat: 12 g, Fiber: 4 g, Cholesterol: 5 mg, Sodium: 90 mg, Potassium: 300 mg

Berry Chia Seed Jam

Yield: 16 servings (1 tablespoon per Serving)
Preparation Time: 5 minutes
Cooking Time: 10 minutes

Ingredients:

- 2 cups fresh or frozen mixed berries (strawberries, blueberries, raspberries) (GI: 25-40)
- 2 tablespoons chia seeds (GI: 1)
- 1-2 tablespoons granulated erythritol or another sugar substitute (to taste) (GI: 0)
- 1 teaspoon lemon juice (GI: 20)
- 1/2 teaspoon vanilla extract (optional) (GI: 0)

Optional Ingredients:
- 1/2 teaspoon ground cinnamon (GI: 0) for added warmth and flavor
- 1 tablespoon fresh mint leaves, chopped (GI: 0) for a refreshing twist

Instructions:

1. **Cook the Berries:** Combine the mixed berries and lemon juice in a medium saucepan. Cook over medium heat, stirring occasionally, for 5–7 minutes, until the berries break down and release their juices.
2. **Mash the Berries:** Use a fork or potato masher to mash the berries to your desired consistency. Leave some chunks for texture or make it smooth, as preferred.
3. **Add Chia Seeds and Sweetener:** Stir in the chia seeds and erythritol. Adjust sweetness to taste. Cook for 2–3 minutes, stirring occasionally, until the mixture thickens.
4. **Add Flavorings (Optional):** Stir in vanilla extract, ground cinnamon, or fresh mint leaves, if using, during the final minute of cooking.
5. **Cool the Jam:** Remove from heat and let the jam cool for 5 minutes. Transfer to a glass jar or airtight container and refrigerate for at least 1 hour to allow the jam to thicken further.
6. **Store and Serve:** Store in the refrigerator for up to 2 weeks. Serve 1 tablespoon as a spread for whole-grain toast, a topping for yogurt, or a filling for pastries. Use as a topping for oatmeal or pancakes. Mix into smoothies or as a filling for healthy crepes.

Nutritional Information (Per Serving)

Calories: 10, Protein: 1g, Carbohydrates: 2g, Fat: 1g, Fiber: 1g, Cholesterol: 0mg, Sodium: 0mg, Potassium: 30mg

Almond Butter Cookies

Yield: 16 servings
Preparation Time: 10 minutes
Cooking Time: 12-15 minutes

Ingredients:

- 1 cup almond butter, unsweetened and creamy (GI: 0)
- 1/4 cup granulated erythritol or another sugar substitute (GI: 0)
- 1 large egg (GI: 0)
- 1 teaspoon vanilla extract (GI: 0)
- 1/2 teaspoon baking soda (GI: 0)
- Pinch of salt (GI: 0)

Optional Ingredients:
- 1/4 cup sugar-free chocolate chips (GI: 0) for added flavor
- 1/4 cup chopped nuts (almonds, walnuts) (GI: 0) for extra crunch
- 1 teaspoon ground cinnamon (GI: 0) for a warm spice flavor

Instructions:

1. **Prepare the oven:** Preheat oven to 350°F (175°C).
2. **Mix ingredients:** Mix almond butter, erythritol, egg, vanilla, baking soda, and salt into a dough.
3. **Add ingredients:** Fold in optional chocolate chips or nuts. Shape the dough: Shape dough into 1-tbsp balls, flatten with a fork.
4. **Bake:** Bake 12-15 minutes or until edges are golden.
5. **Serve** as a light lunch or dinner option on its own. Pair with grilled chicken or fish for a complete meal.

Nutritional Information (Per Serving)

Calories: 110, Protein: 4g, Carbohydrates: 5g, Fat: 9g, Fiber: 2g, Cholesterol: 10mg, Sodium: 60mg, Potassium: 100mg

Coconut Flour Pancakes

 Yield: 4 servings (2 small pancakes per Serving) Preparation Time: 10 minutes Cooking Time: 10 minutes

Ingredients:

- 1/4 cup coconut flour (GI: 51)
- 4 large eggs (GI: 0)
- 1/4 cup unsweetened almond milk (GI: 30)
- 1 tablespoon coconut oil, melted (GI: 0)
- 1 tablespoon granulated erythritol or another sugar substitute (optional) (GI: 0)
- 1 teaspoon vanilla extract (GI: 0)
- 1/2 teaspoon baking powder (GI: 0)
- 1/4 teaspoon salt (GI: 0)
- 1/4 teaspoon ground cinnamon (optional) (GI: 0)

Optional Ingredients:
- 1 tablespoon chia seeds (GI: 1) for added fiber and omega-3s
- 1/4 cup fresh or frozen berries (GI: 25-40) for natural sweetness
- 1 tablespoon unsweetened shredded coconut (GI: 45) for extra texture

Instructions:

1. **Prepare the Batter:** In a large mixing bowl, whisk the eggs, almond milk, melted coconut oil, erythritol (if using), and vanilla extract until smooth.
2. **Mix Dry Ingredients:** Combine coconut flour, baking powder, salt, and cinnamon in another bowl. Mix well.
3. **Combine Ingredients:** Gradually add the dry ingredients to the wet ingredients, whisking continuously until the batter is smooth and thick.
4. **Add Optional Ingredients:** If using chia seeds or shredded coconut, add up to 1 tablespoon per serving to the batter.
5. **Cook the Pancakes:** Heat a non-stick skillet or griddle over medium heat and lightly grease with coconut oil. Pour about 2 tablespoons of batter per pancake onto the skillet. Spread gently with a spoon to form a round shape. Cook for 2–3 minutes on each side until edges are set and bubbles form on the surface. Flip and cook until golden brown.
6. **Serve:** Serve 2 pancakes per person with a dollop (1 tablespoon) of Greek yogurt and 1/4 cup of fresh berries. Use sugar-free syrup sparingly.

Nutritional Information (Per Serving)

Calories: 130, Protein: 7g, Carbohydrates: 8g, Fat: 9g, Fiber: 4g, Cholesterol: 110mg, Sodium: 210mg, Potassium: 100mg

Apple Cinnamon Chia Seed Pudding

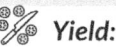 Yield: 4 servings Preparation Time: 10 minutes Cooking Time: 4 hours

Ingredients:

- 1/2 cup chia seeds (GI: 1)
- 2 cups unsweetened almond milk (GI: 30)
- 1 teaspoon vanilla extract (GI: 0)
- 1-2 tablespoons granulated erythritol or another sugar substitute (optional, to taste) (GI: 0)
- 1 teaspoon ground cinnamon (GI: 0)
- 1 medium apple, chopped into small pieces (GI: 36)
- 1 tablespoon lemon juice (GI: 20)

Optional Ingredients:
- 1/4 teaspoon ground nutmeg (GI: 0) for added warmth
- 1 tablespoon unsweetened shredded coconut (GI: 45) for texture
- 1 tablespoon chopped walnuts or almonds (GI: 0) for crunch

Instructions:

1. **Prepare the Chia Pudding:** Combine chia seeds, almond milk, vanilla extract, erythritol (if using), and cinnamon in a medium-sized bowl. Stir well until all ingredients are thoroughly mixed, and chia seeds are evenly distributed.
2. **Chill the Pudding:** Cover the bowl and refrigerate for at least 4 hours or overnight. Stir after the first 30 minutes to prevent clumping.
3. **Prepare the Apple Mixture:** Toss the chopped apple with lemon juice in a small bowl to prevent browning. Let sit for 5–10 minutes. Optionally, add ground nutmeg for flavor.
4. **Assemble the Pudding:** Divide the chilled chia pudding evenly among four serving glasses or bowls. Top each serving with 1/4 cup of the apple mixture.
5. **Optional Garnishes:** Sprinkle with 1 tablespoon unsweetened shredded coconut or chopped nuts per serving.
6. **Serve:** Serve immediately or keep refrigerated until ready to enjoy. Serve as a breakfast option, snack, or dessert. Pair with a cup of herbal tea for a complete treat.

Nutritional Information (Per Serving)

Calories: 190, Protein: 6g, Carbohydrates: 22g, Fat: 9g, Fiber: 10g, Cholesterol: 0mg, Sodium: 75mg, Potassium: 270mg

2. Baking with Sugar Substitutes

Almond Flour Chocolate Chip Cookies

Yield: 16 servings Preparation Time: 15 minutes
Cooking Time: 12-15 minutes

Ingredients:

- 2 cups almond flour (GI: 0)
- 1/4 cup granulated erythritol or another sugar substitute (GI: 0)
- 1/4 cup coconut oil or unsalted butter, melted (GI: 0)
- 1 large egg (GI: 0)
- 1 teaspoon vanilla extract (GI: 0)
- 1/2 teaspoon baking soda (GI: 0)
- 1/4 teaspoon salt (GI: 0)
- 1/3 cup sugar-free dark chocolate chips (GI: 0)

Optional Ingredients:

- 1/4 cup chopped walnuts or pecans (GI: 0) for added crunch
- 1 teaspoon ground cinnamon (GI: 0) for extra flavor

Instructions:

1. **Preheat oven:** Preheat your oven to 350°F (175°C) and line a baking sheet with parchment paper.
2. **Combine dry ingredients:** Combine almond flour, erythritol, baking soda, and salt in a medium bowl. Stir well.
3. **Combine wet ingredients:** Whisk coconut oil, egg, and vanilla extract in a separate bowl until smooth.
4. **Combine:** Mix the wet and dry ingredients until a dough forms. Fold in chocolate chips and optional ingredients.
5. **Form cookies:** Scoop 1 tablespoon of dough for each cookie, roll into balls, and flatten lightly on the baking sheet.
6. **Bake:** Bake for 12–15 minutes or until golden brown. Let cool before transferring to a wire rack.
7. **Serve:** Serve as a sweet snack paired with unsweetened almond milk. Pair with a glass of unsweetened almond milk or herbal tea. Enjoy it as a sweet treat on a balanced diet.

Nutritional Information (Per Serving)

Calories: 80, Protein: 5g, Carbohydrates: 3g, Fat: 6g, Fiber: 1g, Cholesterol: 20mg, Sodium: 190mg, Potassium: 130mg

Sugar-Free Banana Bread

Yield: 10 servings Preparation Time: 15 minutes
Cooking Time: 55 minutes

Ingredients:

- 1 1/2 cups almond flour (GI: 0)
- 1/2 cup coconut flour (GI: 51)
- 1 teaspoon baking soda (GI: 0)
- 1/4 teaspoon salt (GI: 0)
- 1 teaspoon ground cinnamon (GI: 0)
- 3 ripe medium bananas, mashed (GI: 51)
- 1/4 cup granulated erythritol or another sugar substitute (GI: 0)
- 3 large eggs (GI: 0)
- 1/4 cup unsweetened almond milk (GI: 30)
- 1 teaspoon vanilla extract (GI: 0)
- 1/4 cup melted coconut oil or unsalted butter (GI: 0)

Optional Ingredients:

- 1/4 cup chopped walnuts or pecans (GI: 0) for added texture
- 1/4 cup sugar-free chocolate chips (GI: 0) for extra flavor
- 1 tablespoon chia seeds (GI: 1) for added fiber

Instructions:

1. **Prepare the oven:** Preheat oven to 350°F (175°C). Grease a 9x5-inch loaf pan or line it with parchment paper.
2. **Mix the dry ingredients:** Combine almond flour, coconut flour, baking soda, salt, and cinnamon in a large bowl.
3. **Prepare the bananas and wet ingredients:** Mash bananas in another bowl. Add erythritol, eggs, almond milk, vanilla, and melted coconut oil. Mix well.
4. **Combine the batter:** Gradually fold the wet mixture into the dry ingredients until just combined. Add optional ingredients. Pour batter into the prepared loaf pan. Smooth the top with a spatula.
5. **Bake:** Bake for 50–55 minutes or until a toothpick comes out clean. Cool for 10 minutes before slicing.
6. **Serve:** Serve with Greek yogurt or unsweetened herbal tea.

Nutritional Information (Per Serving)

Calories: 180, Protein: 5g, Carbohydrates: 12g, Fat: 13g, Fiber: 4g, Cholesterol: 40mg, Sodium: 120mg, Potassium: 190mg

Low-Carb Lemon Bars

Yield: 16 servings Preparation Time: 20 minutes
Cooking Time: 50 minutes

Ingredients:

- 2 cups almond flour (GI: 0)
- 1/4 cup granulated erythritol or another sugar substitute (GI: 0)
- 1/4 cup coconut oil or unsalted butter, melted (GI: 0)
- 1 large egg (GI: 0)
- 1 teaspoon vanilla extract (GI: 0)
- 1/2 teaspoon baking soda (GI: 0)
- 1/4 teaspoon salt (GI: 0)
- 1/3 cup sugar-free dark chocolate chips (GI: 0)

Optional Ingredients:
- 1/4 cup chopped walnuts or pecans (GI: 0) for added crunch
- 1 teaspoon ground cinnamon (GI: 0) for extra flavor

Instructions:

1. **Preheat oven** to 350°F (175°C) and line an 8x8-inch pan with parchment paper.
2. **Combine dry ingredients:** Combine almond flour, erythritol, melted butter, and salt. Press into the pan to form the crust. Bake for 10–12 minutes.
3. **Combine wet ingredients:** In a bowl, whisk eggs and erythritol. Add lemon juice, almond flour, lemon zest, and turmeric (for color, optional). Whisk until smooth. Pour filling over the crust. Bake for 25–30 minutes or until set.
4. **Cool and serve:** Cool completely and refrigerate for 1 hour before slicing into 16 squares. Serve chilled with sugar-free whipped cream.

Nutritional Information (Per Serving)

Calories: 100, Protein: 3g, Carbohydrates: 4g, Fat: 8g, Fiber: 2g, Cholesterol: 35mg, Sodium: 40mg, Potassium: 25mg

Coconut Flour Brownies

Yield: 16 servings Preparation Time: 10 minutes
Cooking Time: 25-30 minutes

Ingredients:

- 1/2 cup coconut flour (GI: 51)
- 1/2 cup unsweetened cocoa powder (GI: 20)
- 1 cup granulated erythritol or another sugar substitute (GI: 0)
- 6 large eggs (GI: 0)
- 1/2 cup coconut oil or unsalted butter, melted (GI: 0)
- 1 teaspoon vanilla extract (GI: 0)
- 1/2 teaspoon baking powder (GI: 0)
- 1/4 teaspoon salt (GI: 0)
- 1/4 cup unsweetened almond milk (GI: 30)

Optional Ingredients:
- 1/4 cup sugar-free chocolate chips (GI: 0) for added richness
- 1/4 cup chopped walnuts or pecans (GI: 0) for extra crunch
- 1 tablespoon chia seeds (GI: 1) for added fiber

Instructions:

1. **Prepare oven:** Preheat oven to 350°F (175°C). Line an 8x8-inch pan with parchment paper.
2. **Prepare dry ingredients:** Sift coconut flour, cocoa powder, erythritol, baking powder, and salt in a bowl.
3. **Prepare wet ingredients:** Whisk eggs, almond milk, coconut oil, and vanilla in another bowl until smooth.
4. **To combine batter:** Combine wet and dry ingredients into a thick batter. Fold in optional ingredients like chocolate chips or nuts. Spread batter evenly in the pan.
5. **Bake:** Bake for 25–30 minutes, checking for moist crumbs on a toothpick.
6. **Serve:** Cool completely before slicing into 16 squares. Enjoy with a dollop of sugar-free whipped cream or Greek yogurt. Serve with a side of fresh berries for added sweetness and nutrition.

Nutritional Information (Per Serving)

Calories: 110, Protein: 4g, Carbohydrates: 10g, Fat: 8g, Fiber: 4g, Cholesterol: 60mg, Sodium: 60mg, Potassium: 100mg

Vanilla Almond Cupcakes

🌰 Yield: 12 servings 🍲 Preparation Time: 15 minutes
🍽 Cooking Time: 20-25 minutes

Ingredients:
- 2 cups almond flour (GI: 0)
- 1/4 cup coconut flour (GI: 51)
- 1/2 cup granulated erythritol or another sugar substitute (GI: 0)
- 1 teaspoon baking powder (GI: 0)
- 1/4 teaspoon salt (GI: 0)
- 3 large eggs (GI: 0)
- 1/4 cup unsweetened almond milk (GI: 30)
- 1/4 cup coconut oil, melted (GI: 0)
- 1 teaspoon vanilla extract (GI: 0)
- 2 tablespoons fresh lemon juice (GI: 20)
- 1 tablespoon lemon zest (GI: 20)
- 1 cup fresh or frozen blueberries (GI: 53)

Optional Ingredients:
- 1 tablespoon chia seeds (GI: 1) for added fiber
- 1/4 cup chopped walnuts (GI: 0) for extra crunch

Instructions:

1. Preheat Oven: Preheat your oven to 350°F (175°C) and line a 12-cup muffin tin with paper liners or lightly grease with coconut oil.

2. Mix Dry Ingredients: In a large bowl, mix sifted almond flour, coconut flour, erythritol, baking powder, and salt until well combined.

3. Mix Wet Ingredients: In a separate bowl, whisk together eggs, unsweetened almond milk, melted coconut oil, vanilla extract, fresh lemon juice, and lemon zest until smooth.

4. Combine Ingredients: Gradually add the dry mixture to the wet mixture, stirring gently until a thick batter forms. Avoid overmixing.

5. Fold in Blueberries: Fold in blueberries and optional ingredients such as chia seeds or chopped walnuts, if using.

6. Fill Muffin Cups: Divide the batter evenly among the prepared muffin cups, filling each about 3/4 full.

7. Bake: Bake for 20-25 minutes or until a toothpick inserted into the center comes out clean.

8. Cool and Serve: Allow the muffins to cool in the tin for 5 minutes, then transfer to a wire rack to cool completely before serving. Top with a dollop of sugar-free whipped cream or a sprinkle of sliced almonds for garnish. Pair with coffee or herbal tea for a satisfying snack or breakfast.

Nutritional Information (Per Serving)

Calories: 135, Protein: 4g, Carbohydrates: 8g, Fat: 11g, Fiber: 3g, Cholesterol: 30mg, Sodium: 70mg, Potassium: 100mg

Pumpkin Spice Muffins

🌰 Yield: 12 servings 🍲 Preparation Time: 10 minutes
🍽 Cooking Time: 20-25 minutes

Ingredients:
- 1 1/2 cups almond flour (GI: 0)
- 1/2 cup sugar-free canned pumpkin puree (GI: 65)
- 1/4 cup granulated erythritol or another sugar substitute (GI: 0)
- 3 large eggs (GI: 0)
- 1/4 cup unsweetened almond milk (GI: 30)
- 1/4 cup coconut oil, melted (GI: 0)
- 1 teaspoon vanilla extract (GI: 0)
- 1 tablespoon pumpkin pie spice (GI: 0)
- 1 teaspoon baking powder (GI: 0)
- 1/4 teaspoon salt (GI: 0)

Optional Ingredients:
- 1/4 cup chopped walnuts or pecans (GI: 0) for added texture
- 1 tablespoon chia seeds (GI: 1) for extra fiber
- 1/4 cup sugar-free chocolate chips (GI: 0) for added flavor

Instructions:

1. Preheat Oven: Preheat your oven to 350°F (175°C). Line a 12-cup muffin tin with paper liners or lightly grease with coconut oil.

2. Mix Dry Ingredients: In a medium bowl, combine sifted almond flour, pumpkin pie spice, erythritol, baking powder, and salt. Stir well to ensure an even mix.

3. Mix Wet Ingredients: In another bowl, whisk together unsweetened pumpkin puree, eggs, almond milk, melted coconut oil, and vanilla extract until smooth.

4. Combine Ingredients: Gradually fold the dry ingredients into the wet ingredients, stirring gently to avoid overmixing.

5. Add Optional Ingredients: If using, fold in chopped nuts, chia seeds, or sugar-free chocolate chips.

6. Fill Muffin Cups: Divide the batter evenly among the prepared muffin cups, filling each about 3/4 full.

7. Bake: Bake in the preheated oven for 20-25 minutes or until a toothpick inserted into the center of a muffin comes out clean.

8. Cool and Serve: Allow the muffins to cool in the tin for 5 minutes, then transfer to a wire rack to cool completely before serving. Serve with a spread of almond butter or sugar-free jam for extra flavor. Pair with coffee or herbal tea for a satisfying snack or breakfast.

Nutritional Information (Per Serving)

Calories: 120, Protein: 4g, Carbohydrates: 8g, Fat: 10g, Fiber: 3g, Cholesterol: 35mg, Sodium: 85 mg, Potassium: 95mg

Lemon Blueberry Muffins

Yield: 12 servings *Preparation Time: 10 minutes*
Cooking Time: 20-25 minutes

Ingredients:

- 2 cups almond flour (GI: 0)
- 1/4 cup granulated erythritol or another sugar substitute (GI: 0)
- 1/4 cup unsweetened almond milk (GI: 30)
- 1/4 cup coconut oil or unsalted butter, melted (GI: 0)
- 3 large eggs (GI: 0)
- 1 teaspoon vanilla extract (GI: 0)
- 1 teaspoon almond extract (GI: 0)
- 1 teaspoon baking powder (GI: 0)
- 1/4 teaspoon salt (GI: 0)

Optional Ingredients:
- 1/4 cup chopped almonds (GI: 0) for added texture
- 1 tablespoon chia seeds (GI: 1) for extra fiber

Instructions:

1. **Preheat Oven:** Preheat your oven to 350°F (175°C) and line a 12-cup muffin tin with cupcake liners.
2. **Mix Dry Ingredients:** In a large bowl, combine almond flour, erythritol, baking powder, and salt. Stir until evenly mixed.
3. **Mix Wet Ingredients:** In a separate bowl, whisk together eggs, unsweetened almond milk, melted coconut oil or unsalted butter, vanilla extract, and almond extract until smooth.
4. **Combine Ingredients:** Gradually add the dry ingredients to the wet ingredients, stirring until a smooth, thick batter forms. Avoid overmixing.
5. **Add Optional Ingredients:** If using, fold in chopped almonds or chia seeds.
6. **Fill Cupcake Liners:** Divide the batter evenly among the prepared cupcake liners, filling each about 3/4 full.
7. **Bake:** Bake in the preheated oven for 20-25 minutes or until a toothpick inserted into the center of a cupcake comes out clean.
8. **Cool and Serve:** Allow the cupcakes to cool in the tin for 5 minutes, then transfer to a wire rack to cool completely before serving. Top with a dollop of sugar-free whipped cream or a sprinkle of sliced almonds for garnish. Serve with a cup of herbal tea for a satisfying treat.

Nutritional Information (Per Serving)

Calories: 135, Protein: 4g, Carbohydrates: 7g, Fat: 11g, Fiber: 3g, Cholesterol: 30mg, Sodium: 75mg, Potassium: 70mg

Chocolate Almond Brownies

Yield: 16 servings *Preparation Time: 10 minutes*
Cooking Time: 25-30 minutes

Ingredients:

- 1 1/2 cups almond flour (GI: 0)
- 1/2 cup canned pumpkin puree (GI: 65)
- 1/4 cup granulated erythritol or another sugar substitute (GI: 0)
- 3 large eggs (GI: 0)
- 1/4 cup unsweetened almond milk (GI: 30)
- 1/4 cup coconut oil, melted (GI: 0)
- 1 teaspoon vanilla extract (GI: 0)
- 1 tablespoon pumpkin pie spice (GI: 0)
- 1 teaspoon baking powder (GI: 0)
- 1/4 teaspoon salt (GI: 0)

Optional Ingredients:
- 1/4 cup chopped walnuts or pecans (GI: 0) for added texture
- 1 tablespoon chia seeds (GI: 1) for extra fiber
- 1/4 cup sugar-free chocolate chips (GI: 0) for added flavor

Instructions:

1. **Preheat Oven:** Line an 8x8-inch baking sheet with parchment paper and set your oven temperature to 350°F (175°C).
2. **Mix Dry Ingredients:** Almond flour, cocoa powder, erythritol, baking powder, and salt. To make sure everything is incorporated equally, stir the items well.
3. **Mix Wet Ingredients:** In a separate dish, whisk together the wet ingredients: almond milk, eggs, melted coconut oil or butter, and vanilla essence.
4. **Combine Ingredients:** Gradually add the dry ingredients to the wet ingredients, stirring until a smooth, thick batter forms. Avoid overmixing.
5. **Add Optional Ingredients:** Combine the chopped almonds with the sugar-free chocolate chips or chia seeds, if desired.
6. **Prepare the dough:** Evenly distribute the batter into the baking pan that has been prepared.
7. **Bake:** Bake for 25 to 30 minutes, or until a toothpick with a few wet crumbs comes out from the middle.
8. **Cool and Serve:** After the brownies have cooled all in the pan, use the parchment paper to pull them out. Serve after cutting into 16 equal pieces. Enjoy a dollop of sugar-free whipped cream or a scoop of Greek yogurt. Serve with a side of fresh berries for added sweetness and nutrition.

Nutritional Information (Per Serving)

Calories: 130, Protein: 4 g, Carbohydrates: 6g, Fat: 11g, Fiber: 3g, Cholesterol: 40mg, Sodium: 85mg, Potassium: 50mg

Cinnamon Walnut Coffee Cake

Yield: 12 servings **Preparation Time:** 15 minutes **Cooking Time:** 30 minutes

Ingredients:

For the Cake:
- 2 cups almond flour (GI: 0)
- 1/4 cup coconut flour (GI: 51)
- 1/2 cup granulated erythritol or another sugar substitute (GI: 0)
- 1/4 cup unsweetened almond milk (GI: 30)
- 1/4 cup coconut oil or unsalted butter, melted (GI: 0)
- 3 large eggs (GI: 0)
- 1 teaspoon vanilla extract (GI: 0)
- 1 teaspoon baking powder (GI: 0)
- 1/2 teaspoon baking soda (GI: 0)
- 1/4 teaspoon salt (GI: 0)

For the Cinnamon Walnut Topping:
- 1/2 cup chopped walnuts (GI: 0)
- 2 tablespoons granulated erythritol or another sugar substitute (GI: 0)
- 1 tablespoon ground cinnamon (GI: 0)
- 2 tablespoons melted coconut oil or unsalted butter (GI: 0)

Optional Ingredients:
- 1 tablespoon chia seeds (GI: 1) for added fiber
- 1 teaspoon ground nutmeg (GI: 0) for extra spice

Instructions:

1. **Preheat Oven:** Preheat to 350°F (175°C). Line an 8x8-inch baking dish with parchment paper or lightly grease with cooking spray.
2. **Prepare Dry Ingredients:** In a large bowl, combine almond flour, coconut flour, erythritol, baking powder, baking soda, and salt. Stir until evenly mixed.
3. **Mix Wet Ingredients:** In another bowl, whisk together almond milk, eggs, melted coconut oil or butter, and vanilla extract until smooth.
4. **Make Batter:** Gradually add the dry ingredients to the wet ingredients, stirring gently until a batter forms. Do not overmix.
5. **Prepare Topping:** In a small bowl, mix walnuts, cinnamon, erythritol, and melted coconut oil or butter until crumbly.
6. **Assemble Cake:** Spread half the batter evenly into the prepared baking dish. Sprinkle half the topping over the batter. Repeat with the remaining batter and topping.
7. **Bake:** Bake for 25-30 minutes, or until a toothpick inserted into the center comes out clean.
8. **Cool and Serve:** Allow the cake to cool in the pan for 10 minutes, then transfer to a wire rack to cool completely. Slice into pieces and serve. Slice and serve with coffee, tea, or sugar-free whipped cream or Greek yogurt.

Nutritional Information (Per Serving)

Calories: 150, Protein: 5g, Carbohydrates: 8g, Fat: 12g, Fiber: 3g, Cholesterol: 40mg, Sodium: 80mg, Potassium: 80mg

Pumpkin Spice Bars

Yield: 16 servings **Preparation Time:** 10 minutes **Cooking Time:** 35 minutes

Ingredients:

- 1 1/2 cups almond flour (GI: 0)
- 1/4 cup coconut flour (GI: 51)
- 1/2 cup granulated erythritol or another sugar substitute (GI: 0)
- 1 cup canned pumpkin puree (GI: 65)
- 3 large eggs (GI: 0)
- 1/4 cup unsweetened almond milk (GI: 30)
- 1/4 cup coconut oil, melted (GI: 0)
- 1 teaspoon vanilla extract (GI: 0)
- 2 teaspoons pumpkin pie spice (GI: 0)
- 1 teaspoon baking powder (GI: 0)
- 1/4 teaspoon salt (GI: 0)

Optional Ingredients:
- 1/4 cup chopped walnuts or pecans (GI: 0) for added texture
- 1 tablespoon chia seeds (GI: 1) for extra fiber
- 1/4 cup sugar-free chocolate chips (GI: 0) for added flavor

Instructions:

1. **Preheat Oven:** Preheat your oven to 350°F (175°C) and line a 9x9-inch baking pan with parchment paper.
2. **Mix Dry Ingredients:** In a large bowl, combine almond flour, coconut flour, erythritol, pumpkin pie spice, baking powder, and salt. Stir to combine.
3. **Mix Wet Ingredients:** In another bowl, whisk together pumpkin puree, eggs, almond milk, melted coconut oil, and vanilla extract until smooth.
4. **Combine Ingredients:** Gradually add the dry mixture to the wet mixture, stirring gently until a thick batter forms. Do not overmix.
5. **Optional Add-Ins:** Fold in any optional ingredients like nuts, chia seeds, or sugar-free chocolate chips.
6. **Bake:** Spread the batter evenly into the prepared baking pan. Bake for 30-35 minutes, or until a toothpick inserted in the center comes out clean.
7. **Cool and Slice:** Allow the bars to cool completely in the pan before slicing into 16 squares. Enjoy a dollop of sugar-free whipped cream or a scoop of Greek yogurt. Serve with coffee or herbal tea for a satisfying snack or dessert.

Nutritional Information (Per Serving)

Calories: 120, Protein: 4g, Carbohydrates: 7g, Fat: 9g, Fiber: 3g, Cholesterol: 40mg, Sodium: 85mg, Potassium: 100mg

3. Special Occasion Treats

Dark Chocolate Covered Strawberries

Yield: 8 servings   Preparation Time: 20 minutes
Cooking Time: 10 minutes

Ingredients:

For the Cake:
- 16 large strawberries, washed and dried completely (GI: 41)
- 3.5 oz sugar-free dark chocolate (minimum 70% cacao) (GI: 23-25)
- 1 teaspoon coconut oil (GI: 0)

Optional Ingredients:
- 1 tablespoon unsweetened shredded coconut (GI: 45) for garnish
- 1 tablespoon finely chopped nuts, such as almonds or pistachios (GI: 0) for garnish
- 1 teaspoon freeze-dried strawberry powder for garnish

Instructions:

1. **Prepare Strawberries:** Wash and thoroughly dry the strawberries to prevent chocolate from sliding off.
2. **Melt Chocolate:** Break the dark chocolate into small pieces and place them in a microwave-safe bowl with the coconut oil. Microwave at medium power for 30 seconds. Stir and continue microwaving in 15-second intervals, stirring each time, until smooth (about 1–2 minutes).
3. **Dip Strawberries:** Hold each strawberry by the stem, dip into the melted chocolate, and swirl to coat evenly. Allow excess chocolate to drip off. Place coated strawberries on a parchment-lined baking sheet.
4. **Add Optional Garnishes:** If desired, sprinkle garnishes (coconut, nuts, or freeze-dried strawberry powder) before the chocolate sets.
5. **Chill:** Chill in the refrigerator for 20 minutes or until the chocolate sets.
6. **Serve:** Serve the strawberries chilled or at room temperature. Enjoy these as a dessert or a sweet treat for a special occasion. Pair with a cup of unsweetened herbal tea for a refreshing combination.

Nutritional Information (Per Serving)

Calories: 60, Protein: 1g, Carbohydrates: 4g, Fat: 4g, Fiber: 2g, Cholesterol: 0 mg, Sodium: 2mg, Potassium: 80 mg

Pumpkin Spice Cheesecake Bites

Yield: 16 servings   Preparation Time: 10 minutes
Cooking Time: 35 minutes   Total Time: 1 hour 30 minutes (includes chilling time)

Ingredients:

For the Crust:
- 1 cup almond flour (GI: 0)
- 2 tablespoons coconut flour (GI: 51)
- 2 tablespoons granulated erythritol or another sugar substitute (GI: 0)
- 2 tablespoons coconut oil, melted (GI: 0)
- 1/4 teaspoon salt (GI: 0)

For the Filling:
- 8 oz cream cheese, softened (GI: 0)
- 1/2 cup canned pumpkin puree (GI: 65)
- 1/4 cup granulated erythritol or another sugar substitute (GI: 0)1 teaspoon vanilla extract (GI: 0)
- 1 teaspoon pumpkin pie spice (GI: 0)
- 1/4 teaspoon ground cinnamon (GI: 0)

Optional Ingredients:
- 1 tablespoon chia seeds (GI: 1) for added fiber
- 1/4 cup chopped walnuts (GI: 0) for garnish
- Whipped cream, sugar-free (for topping)

Instructions:

1. **Prepare the Crust:** Preheat the oven to 350°F (175°C).
2. **Mix ingredients:** In a bowl, combine almond flour, coconut flour, erythritol, melted coconut oil, and salt until a crumbly dough forms.
3. **Bake:** Press of the crust mixture into each mini muffin tin cup. Flatten with a spoon. Bake for 5–7 minutes until lightly golden. Cool completely.
4. **Prepare the second part of the filling:** In a mixing bowl, beat cream cheese until smooth. Add pumpkin puree, erythritol, vanilla, pumpkin spice, and cinnamon. Beat until creamy and lump-free. Fold in chia seeds if using.
5. **Assemble the cheesecake:** Spoon the filling over cooled crusts, smoothing the tops.
6. **Cool and serve:** Chill for at least 1 hour to set. Garnish with walnuts or whipped cream, if desired. Serve these cheesecake bites chilled as a perfect treat for gatherings or festive occasions. Pair with a hot coffee or herbal tea for a delightful dessert experience.

Nutritional Information (Per Serving)

Calories: 90, Protein: 2g, Carbohydrates: 4g, Fat: 8g, Fiber: 1g, Cholesterol: 15mg, Sodium: 60mg, Potassium: 40mg

Low-Carb Coconut Panna Cotta

 Yield: 4 servings  Preparation Time: 20 minutes
 Chill Time: 2-3 hours Total Time: 2 hours 10 minutes

Ingredients:

- 1 1/2 cups full-fat coconut milk (low GI: 40)
- 1/4 cup unsweetened almond milk (optional, to lighten the texture, low GI: 30)
- 2 tbsp erythritol or stevia (to taste) (zero GI sweeteners)
- 1 tsp vanilla extract (optional)
- 1 tbsp gelatin or 2 tbsp chia seeds (low GI: 0 for gelatin, <1 for chia)
- Pinch of sea salt (optional)
- 1/4 cup mixed berries (optional garnish) (GI of berries: 25-40 depending on type)
- Fresh mint leaves (optional garnish)

Instructions:

1. **Prepare the Gelatin (if using):** If using gelatin, sprinkle it over 2 tbsp of cold water and let it bloom for 5 minutes. If using chia seeds, skip to step
2. **Heat the Coconut Mixture:** In a saucepan, combine coconut milk, almond milk, sweetener, and vanilla. Heat over medium until steaming (do not boil).
3. **Add Thickening Agent:** If using gelatin, remove the coconut mixture from heat and stir in the bloomed gelatin until fully dissolved. If using chia seeds, stir them into the heated mixture and let it sit for a few minutes to thicken.
4. **Pour and Chill:** Pour the panna cotta mixture into 4 small ramekins or glasses. If using gelatin, refrigerate for at least 2-3 hours until set. If using chia seeds, refrigerate for 30 minutes, then stir the mixture again to ensure the seeds are evenly distributed, and continue chilling until set (about 1-2 hours).
5. **Garnish and Serve:** Once set, top the panna cotta with a few fresh berries and a sprig of mint. You can also add a sprinkle of unsweetened coconut flakes or a drizzle of sugar-free chocolate sauce for extra indulgence. It pairs beautifully with fresh berries or a dash of cinnamon for added flavor. For a more decadent presentation, you can drizzle some sugar-free chocolate syrup or top it with a dollop of whipped coconut cream.
6. **Note:** The use of coconut milk and a sugar-free sweetener keeps this dessert light while chia seeds or gelatin help create the silky texture.

Nutritional Information (Per Serving)

Calories: 200, Protein: 5g, Carbohydrates: 7g, Fiber: 4g, Carbohydrates: 3g, Fat: 18g, Cholesterol: 0mg, Sodium: 35mg, Potassium: 250mg

Raspberry Lemon Tart

 Yield: 8 servings   Preparation Time: 20 minutes
 Cooking Time: 25 minutes

Ingredients:

- 1 1/2 cups almond flour (GI: 0)
- 1/4 cup coconut flour (GI: 51)
- 1/2 cup granulated erythritol or another sugar substitute (GI: 0)
- 3 large eggs (GI: 0)
- 1/4 cup unsweetened almond milk (GI: 30)
- 1/4 cup coconut oil, melted (GI: 0)
- 1 teaspoon vanilla extract (GI: 0)
- 2 teaspoons pumpkin pie spice (GI: 0)
- 1 teaspoon baking powder (GI: 0)
- 1/4 teaspoon salt (GI: 0)

Optional Ingredients:

- 1 cup fresh raspberries (GI: 25)
- Optional: fresh mint leaves for garnish (GI: 0)

Instructions:

1. **Preheat the Oven:** Preheat the oven to 350°F (175°C). Grease a 9-inch tart pan or line it with parchment paper.
2. **Prepare the Crust:** In a medium bowl, mix almond flour, coconut flour, erythritol, melted coconut oil, vanilla extract, and salt until the mixture resembles coarse crumbs.
3. **Shape and Bake the Crust:** Press the mixture evenly into the bottom and up the sides of the tart pan. Bake for 10–12 minutes until lightly browned. Remove from the oven and let cool.
4. **Prepare the Filling:** In a medium saucepan, whisk together eggs, lemon zest, erythritol, almond milk, and salt. Cook over medium heat, stirring constantly, until the mixture thickens enough to coat the back of a spoon (5–7 minutes).
5. **Assemble the Tart:** Pour the thickened lemon filling into the pre-baked crust, spreading it evenly with a spatula.
6. **Bake the Tart:** Bake for 12–15 minutes, or until the filling is set but slightly jiggly in the center. Remove from the oven and let cool to room temperature.
7. **Chill and Garnish:** Refrigerate the tart for at least 1 hour before serving. Garnish with fresh raspberries and optional mint leaves. Serve with coffee or herbal tea for a satisfying snack or dessert.

Nutritional Information (Per Serving)

Calories: 200, Protein: 5 g, Carbohydrates: 10 g, Sugars: 2 g, Fat: 17 g, Fiber: 4 g, Cholesterol: 55 mg, Sodium: 100 mg, Potassium: 100 mg

Chocolate Avocado Mousse

Yield: 4 servings   Preparation Time: 10 minutes   Cooking Time: None

Ingredients:

- 2 ripe avocados, peeled and pitted (GI: 15)
- 1/4 cup unsweetened cocoa powder (GI: 20)
- 1/4 cup unsweetened almond milk (GI: 30)
- 1/4 cup erythritol or monk fruit sweetener (GI: 0)
- 1 teaspoon vanilla extract (GI: 0)
- 1/8 teaspoon salt (GI: 0)
- 1 tablespoon chia seeds (optional, for added fiber) (GI: 1)
- Optional: 1 tablespoon natural almond butter (GI: 15)

Instructions:

1. **Prepare the Ingredients:** Scoop the avocado flesh into a food processor or blender.
2. **Blend the Base:** Add cocoa powder, almond milk, erythritol, vanilla extract, salt, and optional chia seeds. Blend until smooth and creamy, scraping down the sides as needed.
3. **Adjust Sweetness and Consistency:** Taste the mousse and add more erythritol if desired, blending after each addition. If too thick, add almond milk 1 tablespoon at a time until the desired consistency is reached.
4. **Optional Add-ins:** If using almond butter, whisk it into the mousse and blend until combined.
5. **Chill:** Spoon the mousse into serving dishes, cover, and refrigerate for at least 30 minutes to let the flavors meld.
6. **Serve:** Serve the mousse in small glass jars or dessert cups. Garnish with fresh berries, cocoa nibs, or slivered almonds or garnish with a dollop of unsweetened whipped cream and a mint leaf for a sophisticated touch. Serve chilled.

Nutritional Information (Per Serving)

Calories: 220, Protein: 3 g, Carbohydrates: 13 g, Sugars: 1 g, Fat: 21 g, Fiber: 8 g, Cholesterol: 0 mg, Sodium: 80 mg, Potassium: 450 mg

Carrot Cake with Cream Cheese Frosting

Yield: 12 servings   Preparation Time: 20 minutes   Cooking Time: 30 minutes

Ingredients:

For the Cake:
- 1 1/2 cups almond flour (GI: 0)
- 1/4 cup coconut flour (GI: 51)
- 1/4 cup erythritol or monk fruit sweetener (GI: 0)
- 1 teaspoon baking powder (GI: 0)
- 1/2 teaspoon baking soda (GI: 0)
- 1 teaspoon ground cinnamon (GI: 0)
- 1/2 teaspoon ground nutmeg (GI: 0)
- 1/4 teaspoon ground ginger (GI: 0)
- 1/4 teaspoon salt (GI: 0)
- 3 large eggs (GI: 0)
- 1/4 cup unsweetened applesauce (GI: 38)
- 1/4 cup coconut oil, melted (GI: 0)
- 1 teaspoon vanilla extract (GI: 0)
- 1 1/2 cups grated carrots (GI: 35)
- 1/2 cup chopped walnuts (optional, for added crunch) (GI: 15)
- 1/4 cup unsweetened shredded coconut (optional) (GI: 45)

For the Cream Cheese Frosting:
- 8 oz cream cheese, softened (GI: 0)
- 1/4 cup unsalted butter, softened (GI: 0)
- 1/4 cup erythritol or monk fruit sweetener, powdered (GI: 0)
- 1 teaspoon vanilla extract (GI: 0)
- 2 tablespoons Greek yogurt (GI: 0)

Instructions:

1. **Preheat the Oven:** Preheat to 350°F (175°C). Grease or line an 8-inch round cake pan.
2. **Mix Dry Ingredients:** Whisk almond flour, coconut flour, erythritol, baking powder, baking soda, cinnamon, nutmeg, ginger, and salt in a large bowl.
3. **Mix Wet Ingredients:** In another bowl, beat eggs, applesauce, coconut oil, and vanilla.
4. **Combine Ingredients:** Gradually mix wet ingredients into dry until combined. Fold in carrots, walnuts, and shredded coconut (if using).
5. **Bake:** Pour batter into the pan and bake for 25–30 minutes, or until a toothpick comes out clean. Cool for 10 minutes, then transfer to a wire rack.
6. **Prepare Frosting:** Beat cream cheese and butter until smooth. Gradually add powdered erythritol, then stir in Greek yogurt and vanilla until fluffy.
7. **Frost and Serve:** Spread frosting over the cooled cake. Cut into 12 slices. Serve immediately or refrigerate for up to 3 days.

Nutritional Information (Per Serving)

Calories: 240, Protein: 6 g, Carbohydrates: 11 g, Sugars: 3 g, Fat: 21 g, Fiber: 4 g, Cholesterol: 55 mg, Sodium: 150 mg, Potassium: 130 mg

Mini Berry Cheesecakes

Yield: 4 servings mini cheesecakes
Preparation Time: 10 minutes
Cooking Time: None
Chill Time: 1 hour

Ingredients:

For the Crust:
- 1 cup almond flour (GI: 0)
- 2 tablespoons coconut flour (GI: 51)
- 2 tablespoons erythritol or monk fruit sweetener (GI: 0)
- 3 tablespoons coconut oil, melted (GI: 0)
- 1/2 teaspoon vanilla extract (GI: 0)

For the Cheesecake Filling:
- 16 oz cream cheese, softened (GI: 0)
- 1/3 cup erythritol or monk fruit sweetener (GI: 0)
- 1 teaspoon vanilla extract (GI: 0)
- 2 large eggs (GI: 0)
- 1/4 cup Greek yogurt (GI: 0)
- 1 tablespoon lemon juice (GI: 20)

For the Topping:
- 1 cup mixed berries (e.g., raspberries, blueberries, strawberries) (GI: 25-40)
- Optional: 1 tablespoon chia seeds for added fiber (GI: 1)
- Optional: fresh mint leaves for garnish (GI: 0)

Instructions:

1. **Preheat the Oven:** Preheat the oven to 325°F (163°C). Line a 12-cup muffin pan with paper liners or silicone molds.
2. **Prepare the Crust:** In a bowl, mix almond flour, coconut flour, erythritol, melted coconut oil, and vanilla extract until crumbly.
3. **Bake the Crust:** Press 1 tablespoon of the crust mixture into the bottom of each muffin cup. Bake for 5 minutes, then let cool.
4. **Make the Filling:** Beat softened cream cheese and erythritol until smooth. Add vanilla extract, eggs, Greek yogurt, and lemon juice. Beat until creamy and well combined.
5. **Fill and Bake:** Divide the filling evenly among the muffin cups. Bake for 15–18 minutes, or until the centers are just set. Let cool in the pan to room temperature.
6. **Chill:** Refrigerate the cheesecakes for at least 1 hour.
7. **Top and Serve:** Mash berries with chia seeds (if using) to create a topping. Spoon over cheesecakes before serving. Garnish with mint leaves, if desired.

Nutritional Information (Per Serving)

Calories: 230, Protein: 3g, Carbohydrates: 13g, Sugars: 1g, Fat: 21g, Fiber: 8g, Cholesterol: 0mg, Sodium: 80mg, Potassium: 450mg

Dark Chocolate Coconut Truffles

Yield: 20 truffles
Preparation Time: 15 minutes
Chill Time: 1 hour

Ingredients:

For the Truffles:
- 1 cup unsweetened shredded coconut (GI: 45)
- 1/2 cup almond flour (GI: 0)
- 1/4 cup unsweetened cocoa powder (GI: 20)
- 1/4 cup erythritol or monk fruit sweetener (GI: 0)
- 1/4 cup coconut oil, melted (GI: 0)
- 1/2 teaspoon vanilla extract (GI: 0)
- 1/4 teaspoon salt (GI: 0)

For the Coating:
- 1 tablespoon chia seeds (optional, for added fiber) (GI: 1)
- 3 oz dark chocolate (70% or higher cocoa content) (GI: 23)
- 2 tablespoons unsweetened shredded coconut (GI: 45)
- Optional: 1 tablespoon chopped nuts (e.g., almonds, walnuts) (GI: 15)

Instructions:

1. **Make the Dough:** In a bowl, mix almond flour, cocoa powder, erythritol, shredded coconut, melted coconut oil, vanilla extract, salt, and optional chia seeds until a thick dough forms.
2. **Shape the Truffles:** Use a tablespoon to scoop the dough and roll into 1-inch balls. Place on a parchment-lined baking sheet.
3. **Chill:** Refrigerate the truffles for at least 30 minutes to firm up.
4. **Melt Chocolate:** Melt the dark chocolate in a microwave-safe bowl in 20-second intervals, stirring between each, or use a double boiler.
5. **Coat the Truffles:** Dip each truffle in the melted chocolate, letting excess drip off. Place back on the parchment-lined baking sheet.
6. **Add Toppings:** Before the chocolate sets, sprinkle with shredded coconut or chopped nuts (if desired).
7. **Set the Truffles:** Let the chocolate coating firm at room temperature or in the refrigerator.
8. **Serve:** Arrange on a tray or store in an airtight container in the refrigerator until ready to serve.

Nutritional Information (Per Serving)

Calories: 85, Protein: 2g, Carbohydrates: 5g, Sugars: 1g, Fat: 7g, Fiber: 2g, Cholesterol: 0mg, Sodium: 15mg, Potassium: 70mg

Almond Flour Lemon Bars

Yield: 16 bars *Preparation Time: 15 minutes*
Cooking Time: 30 minutes *Chill Time: 1 hour*

Ingredients:

For the Crust:
- 1 1/2 cups almond flour (GI: 0)
- 1/4 cup coconut flour (GI: 51)
- 1/4 cup erythritol or monk fruit sweetener (GI: 0)
- 1/4 teaspoon salt (GI: 0)
- 1/4 cup coconut oil, melted (GI: 0)
- 1 teaspoon vanilla extract (GI: 0)

For the Lemon Filling:
- 3 large eggs (GI: 0)
- 1/2 cup erythritol or monk fruit sweetener (GI: 0)
- 1/2 cup fresh lemon juice (GI: 20)
- 2 tablespoons lemon zest (GI: 0)
- 1/4 cup coconut flour (GI: 51)
- 1/4 teaspoon salt (GI: 0)

Instructions:

1. **Preheat the Oven:** Preheat to 350°F (175°C). Line an 8x8-inch baking pan with parchment paper, leaving an overhang for easy removal.
2. **Make the Crust:** Mix almond flour, coconut flour, erythritol, and salt in a bowl. Add melted coconut oil and vanilla extract, stirring until crumbly. Press into the pan.
3. **Bake the Crust:** Bake for 10–12 minutes, until lightly golden. Cool slightly.
4. **Make the Filling:** In a bowl, whisk eggs, erythritol, lemon juice, lemon zest, salt, and coconut flour until smooth.
5. **Assemble and Bake:** Pour the filling over the crust and bake for 18–20 minutes, or until the filling is set.
6. **Cool and Chill:** Let cool completely in the pan, then refrigerate for 1 hour.
7. **Cut and Serve:** Lift the bars using the parchment overhang, slice into 16 squares, and serve. Dust lightly with powdered erythritol, if desired.

Nutritional Information (Per Serving)
Calories: 110, Protein: 3g, Carbohydrates: 6g, Sugars: 1g, Fat: 9g, Fiber: 2g, Cholesterol: 40mg, Sodium: 60mg, Potassium: 45mg

Peanut Butter Chocolate Chip Cookies

Yield: 20 cookies *Preparation Time: 10 minutes*
Cooking Time: 10 minutes

Ingredients:

- 1 cup natural peanut butter (unsweetened, no added sugar) (GI: 14)
- 1/2 cup erythritol or monk fruit sweetener (GI: 0)
- 1 large egg (GI: 0)
- 1 teaspoon vanilla extract (GI: 0)
- 1/4 cup almond flour (GI: 0)
- 1/2 teaspoon baking soda (GI: 0)
- 1/4 teaspoon salt (GI: 0)
- 1/3 cup sugar-free dark chocolate chips (70% cocoa or higher) (GI: 23)
- Optional: 1 tablespoon chia seeds (for added fiber) (GI: 1)
- Optional: 1 tablespoon chopped walnuts or almonds (for added crunch) (GI: 15)

Instructions:

1. **Preheat the Oven:** Preheat the oven to 350°F (175°C). Line a baking sheet with parchment paper or a silicone baking mat.
2. **Mix Ingredients:** In a large bowl, mix the peanut butter and erythritol until smooth. Whisk in the egg and vanilla extract until fully combined. Add the almond flour, baking soda, and a pinch of salt (if using). Mix until a soft dough forms.
3. **Optional:** Gently fold in chocolate chips, nuts, or chia seeds if desired.
4. **Roll into balls:** Using a tablespoon, scoop the dough and roll into balls. Place them on the prepared baking sheet, spacing them 2 inches apart. Use a fork to flatten each ball slightly, creating a crisscross pattern on top.
5. **Bake:** Bake for 8–10 minutes, or until the edges are slightly browned and the cookies are set.
6. **Cool and serve:** Allow the cookies to cool on the baking sheet for 5 minutes before transferring them to a wire rack to cool completely. Store in an airtight container at room temperature for up to a week.

Nutritional Information (Per Serving)
Calories: 110, Protein: 4g, Carbohydrates: 6g, Sugars: 1g, Fat: 10g, Fiber: 2g, Cholesterol: 10mg, Sodium: 100mg, Potassium: 120mg

30-DAY MEAL PLAN

This 30-day meal plan is tailored for individuals with diabetes who seek to maintain optimal blood glucose levels while enjoying a nutritious and balanced diet. Each recipe has been meticulously chosen to ensure that the total daily caloric intake stays within the recommended limits for those with diabetes.

The meal plan includes a diverse selection of dishes that provide adequate amounts of protein, healthy fats, and low- glycemic index carbohydrates, all of which help stabilize blood sugar levels. This approach not only supports diabetes management but also fosters overall health and a balanced lifestyle.

Day	Breakfast	Lunch	Snack	Dinner	Dessert optional
Day 1	Breakfast Tostada (p. 14)	Quinoa and Black Bean Salad (p. 41)	Greek Yogurt with Berries and Nuts (p. 93)	Lemon Herb Grilled Chicken (p. 73)	Almond Flour Lemon Bars (p. 122)
Day 2	Overnight Oats with Chia Seeds (p.14)	Low-Carb Roast Beef Wrap with Mustard (p.48)	Apple Slices with Almond Butter (p. 93)	One-Pot Ratatouille (p. 87)	Berry Greek Yogurt Parfait (p. 108)
Day 3	Tomato and Basil Egg White Scramble (p. 32)	Chicken and Kale Soup (p.76)	Carrot and Celery Sticks with Hummus (p. 94)	Tofu and Vegetable Stir-Fry (p. 120)	Fresh Fruit Salad with Mint (p. 94)
Day 4	Avocado Toast with Tomato Slices Beet Salad (p. 15)	Kale and Roasted Beet Salad (p.43)	Mixed Nuts and Seeds Trail Mix (p.99)	Garlic Roasted Turkey Breast (p. 74)	Coconut Flour Brownies (p. 114)
Day 5	Apple Cinnamon Overnight Oats (p. 16)	Cauliflower Crust Margherita Pizza (p. 61)	Bell Pepper Slices with Guacamole (p.95)	Baked Turkey Meatballs (p. 75)	Strawberry Basil Sorbet (p. 110)
Day 6	Salad with Egg and Salsa Verde Vinaigrette (p.16)	Mediterranean Veggie and Hummus Wrap (p.47)	Mixed Nuts and Seeds (p. 95)	Moroccan Chicken Tagine with Vegetables (p. 90)	Lemon Blueberry Muffins (p. 116)
Day 7	Cottage Cheese with Pineapple Chunks (p.17)	Eggplant Mini Pizzas with Mozzarella (p. 63)	Almond and Flaxseed Energy Bites (p. 96)	Italian Stuffed Bell Peppers with Ground Turkey (p. 88)	Cinnamon Walnut Coffee Cake (p. 117)
Day 8	Creamy Scrambled Eggs with Smoked Salmon (p. 17)	Lentil and Feta Salad (p. 44)	Roasted Chickpeas with Sea Salt and Paprika (p. 96)	Balsamic Glazed Pork Tenderloin (p. 76)	Almond Butter Cookies (p. 111)
Day 9	Greek Yogurt with Fresh Berries and Nuts (p. 15)	Turkey and Avocado Whole Grain Wrap (p. 46)	Greek Yogurt and Cucumber Dip with Veggie Sticks (p. 97)	Herb-Rubbed Grilled Chicken Breasts (p. 77)	Coconut Flour Pancakes (p. 112)
Day 10	Avocado and Turkey Breakfast Roll-Ups (p. 18)	Tomato Basil Soup (p. 52)	Celery Sticks with Cream Cheese and Walnuts (p. 94)	Beef and Broccoli Stir-Fry with Cauliflower Rice (p. 81)	Apple Cinnamon Chia Seed Pudding (p. 112)

Day	Breakfast	Lunch	Snack	Dinner	Dessert optional
Day 11	Spinach and Mushroom Egg Scramble (p. 19)	Sardine and Avocado Stuffed Bell Peppers (p. 71)	Spicy Roasted Chickpeas (p. 98)	Spaghetti Squash Bolognese (p. 78)	Almond Flour Chocolate Chip Cookies (p. 113)
Day 12	Tofu and Veggie Breakfast Bowl (p. 19)	Salmon and Asparagus Salad (p. 45)	Cucumber Slices with Hummus (p. 98)	Slow Cooker Turkey Chili (p. 86)	Low-Carb Coconut Panna Cotta (p. 119)
Day 13	Smoked Salmon and Avocado Plate (p. 20)	Egg and Spinach Whole Wheat Sandwich (p. 47)	Cheese and Cherry Tomato Skewers (p. 99)	Zoodles with Pesto and Cherry Tomatoes (p. 79)	Low-Carb Lemon Bars (p. 114)
Day 14	Greek Yogurt with Almonds and Honey (p. 20)	Grilled Chicken Caesar Salad (p. 42)	Mixed Nuts and Seeds (p. 95)	Japanese Teriyaki Tofu with Broccoli (p. 90)	Chia Seed Pudding with Mango (p. 112)
Day 15	Cottage Cheese and Veggie Stuffed Bell Peppers (p. 22)	Split Pea Soup with Ham (p. 55)	Hard-Boiled Eggs with a Dash of Paprika (p. 100)	Beef and Broccoli Stir-Fry (p. 80)	Vanilla Almond Cupcakes (p. 115)
Day 16	Turkey Sausage and Egg Wrap (p. 21)	Broccoli Cheddar Soup (p. 51)	Edamame with Sea Salt (p. 100)	Herb-Roasted Chicken Thighs with Garlic and Vegetables (p. 80)	Carrot Cake with Cream Cheese Frosting (p. 120)
Day 17	Veggie and Cheese Frittata (p.24)	Tuna Salad Whole Grain Sandwich (p. 48)	Cottage Cheese and Tomato Stuffed Avocados (p. 101)	Lean Beef and Vegetable Stir-Fry (p. 77)	Orange and Almond Salad (p. 110)
Day 18	Chicken Sausage and Kale Breakfast Skillet (p. 23)	Butternut Squash Soup (p. 54)	Hard-Boiled Eggs with Hummus (p. 101)	Eggplant Lasagna (p. 81)	Chocolate Almond Brownies (p. 116)
Day 19	Cheese and HerbStuffed Omelette (p. 22)	Greek-Style Grilled Fish Tacos with Tzatziki (p. 69)	Rice Cake with Peanut Butter and Chia Seeds (p. 102)	Cauliflower Mashed Potatoes with Grilled Chicken (p. 82)	Berry Chia Seed Jam (p. 111)
Day 20	Cauliflower Hash Browns (p. 26)	Thai Peanut Chicken Salad (p. 44)	Zucchini Chips with Parmesan (p. 102)	Almond-Crusted Chicken Tenders (p. 82)	Pumpkin Spice Bars (p. 117)
Day 21	Egg and Cheese Breakfast Muffins (p. 21)	Smoked Salmon and Avocado Sandwich (p. 50)	Stuffed Mini Bell Peppers with Cream Cheese (p. 104)	Slow Cooker Chicken and Vegetable Stew (p. 83)	Dark Chocolate Covered Strawberries (p. 118)
Day 22	Low-Carb Pancakes with Berries (p. 24)	Lentil and Vegetable Soup (p. 51)	Caprese Salad Skewers (p. 103)	Garlic and Rosemary Grilled Pork Tenderloin (p. 76)	Pumpkin Spice Cheesecake Bites (p. 118)
Day 23	Zucchini and Tomato Omelette (p. 25)	Keto-Friendly Broccoli and Cheese Pizza (p. 65)	Smoked Salmon Cucumber Bites (p. 103)	Vietnamese Pho with Tofu and Vegetables (p. 92)	Sugar-Free Banana Bread (p. 113)

Day	Breakfast	Lunch	Snack	Dinner	Dessert optional
Day 24	Bacon-Wrapped Asparagus with Soft-Boiled Eggs (p. 28)	Mediterranean Chickpea Salad (p. 42)	Zucchini and Feta Roll-Ups (p. 104)	Stuffed Bell Peppers with Ground Turkey (p. 79)	Raspberry Lemon Tart (p. 119)
Day 25	Cottage Cheese and Cucumber Bowl (p.26)	Beef and Vegetable Stew (p. 54)	Guacamole with Veggie Sticks (p. 105)	Middle Eastern Falafel with Tahini Sauce (p. 92)	Chocolate Avocado Mousse (p. 120)
Day 26	Egg and Tofu Stir-Fry with Vegetables (p. 23)	Spicy Lentil Stew (p. 53)	Almond-Crusted Mozzarella Sticks (p. 105)	Chicken and Spinach Stuffed Portobello Mushrooms (p. 75)	Pumpkin Spice Muffins (p. 115)
Day 27	Yogurt Parfait with Nuts and Seeds (p. 27)	Roasted Veggie and Quinoa Bowl (p. 56)	Spinach and Artichoke Dip with Whole-Grain Crackers (p. 106)	Cauliflower Fried Rice with Chicken (p. 78)	Mini Berry Cheesecakes (p. 121)
Day 28	Zucchini Noodles with Poached Eggs (p. 27)	Low-Carb Salmon Patties with Cucumber Salad (p. 72)	Prosciutto Wrapped Asparagus Spears (p. 106)	Greek Lemon Chicken with Tzatziki (p. 88)	Dark Chocolate Coconut Truffles (p. 121)
Day 29	Chia Seed Pudding with Almond Milk (p. 25)	Cucumber and Cream Cheese Sandwich (p. 49)	Garlic and Herb Stuffed Mushrooms (p. 107)	Slow Cooker BBQ Pulled Pork (p. 86)	Baked Apples with Cinnamon (p. 108)
Day 30	Portobello Mushroom and Spinach Breakfast Bake (p. 28)	Grilled Veggie and Hummus Sandwich (p. 46)	Shrimp Cocktail with Avocado Salsa (p. 107)	Chicken and Broccoli Stir-Fry (p. 73)	Peanut Butter Chocolate Chip Cookies (p. 122)

RECIPE INDEX

ACTIVE DRY YEAST
Grilled Chicken and Spinach Alfredo Pizza, 62
Mushroom and Olive Pizza with Ricotta, 64
Whole Wheat Veggie Pizza with Pesto Sauce, 61

ALMOND BUTTER
Almond and Flaxseed Energy Bites, 96
Almond Butter Cookies, 111
Almond-Coconut Protein Smoothie, 36
Apple Slices with Almond Butter, 94
Greek Yogurt and Almond Protein Shake, 34
Chocolate Avocado Mousse, 120
Spinach Almond Butter Protein Smoothie, 34

ALMOND FLOR
Almond Flour Chocolate Chip Cookies, 113
Almond Flour Lemon Bars, 114
Almond-Crusted Chicken Tenders, 82
Almond-Crusted Mozzarella Sticks, 105
Baked Turkey Meatballs, 75
Carrot Cake with Cream Cheese Frosting, 120
Cauliflower Hash Browns, 26
Cinnamon Walnut Coffee Cake, 117
Chocolate Almond Brownies, 116
Dark Chocolate Coconut Truffles, 121
Lemon Blueberry Muffins, 116
Low-Carb Lemon Bars, 114
Low-Carb Salmon Patties with Cucumber Salad, 72
Middle Eastern Falafel with Tahini Sauce, 92
Mini Berry Cheesecakes, 121
Low-Carb Pancakes with Berries, 24
Peanut Butter Chocolate Chip Cookies, 122
Pumpkin Spice Bars, 117
Pumpkin Spice Cheesecake Bites, 118
Pumpkin Spice Muffins, 115
Raspberry Lemon Tart, 119
Sugar-Free Banana Bread, 113
Vanilla Almond Cupcakes, 115

ALMOND MILK
Pumpkin Spice Muffins, 115
Almond-Coconut Protein Smoothie, 36
Apple Cinnamon Chia Seed Pudding, 112
Apple Cinnamon Overnight Oats, 16
Avocado Berry Delight Smoothie, 30
Berry Bliss Smoothie with Chia Seeds, 31
Broccoli Cheddar Soup, 51
Cinnamon Walnut Coffee Cake, 117
Cheese and Herb-Stuffed Omelette, 22
Chia Seed Pudding with Almond Milk, 25
Chia Seed Pudding with Mango, 109
Chocolate Almond Brownies, 116
Chocolate Avocado Mousse, 120
Chocolate Banana Protein Smoothie, 33
Coconut Flour Brownies, 114
Coconut Flour Pancakes, 112
Creamy Avocado and Spinach Smoothie, 32
Creamy Scrambled Eggs with Smoked Salmon, 17
Cucumber Mint Green Smoothie, 30
Egg and Cheese Breakfast Muffins, 21
Greek Yogurt and Almond Protein Shake, 34
Kale and Green Apple Smoothie, 29
Lemon Blueberry Muffins, 116
Low-Carb Coconut Panna Cotta, 119
Overnight Oats with Chia Seeds, 15
Low-Carb Pancakes with Berries, 24
Peanut Butter and Greek Yogurt Power Shake, 35
Peanut Butter Berry Power Smoothie, 33
Pumpkin Spice Bars, 117
Raspberry Lemon Tart, 119
Spinach Almond Butter Protein Smoothie, 34
Spinach and Blueberry Blast Smoothie, 29
Strawberry Spinach Smoothie, 31
Sugar-Free Banana Bread, 113
Vanilla Almond Cupcakes, 115
Vanilla Strawberry Protein Smoothie, 35

ALMONDS
Greek Yogurt with Fresh Berries and Nuts, 15
Almond and Flaxseed Energy Bites, 96
Almond-Crusted Mozzarella Sticks, 105
Chocolate Almond Brownies, 116
Greek Yogurt and Almond Protein Shake, 34
Greek Yogurt with Almonds and Honey, 20
Mixed Nuts and Seeds, 94
Mixed Nuts and Seeds Trail Mix, 99
Orange and Almond Salad, 110
Yogurt Parfait with Nuts and Seeds, 27

APPLE
Apple Cinnamon Overnight Oats, 16
Apple Cinnamon Chia Seed Pudding, 112
Apple Slices with Almond Butter, 94
Baked Apples with Cinnamon, 108

APPLE SAUCE
Carrot Cake with Cream Cheese Frosting, 120

APRICOTS
Moroccan Chicken Tagine with Vegetables, 90

ARTICHOKE
Spinach and Artichoke Dip with Whole-Grain Crackers, 106

ASPARAGUS
Bacon-Wrapped Asparagus with Soft-Boiled Eggs, 28
Prosciutto-Wrapped Asparagus Spears, 106
Salmon and Asparagus Salad, 45
Seared Scallops with Asparagus and Lemon, 70

AVOCADO
Cottage Cheese and Cucumber Bowl, 26
Avocado and Turkey Breakfast Roll-Ups, 18
Avocado Berry Delight Smoothie, 30
Avocado Toast with Tomato Slices, 15
Bell Pepper Slices with Guacamole, 96
Berry Bliss Smoothie with Chia Seeds, 31
Breakfast Tostada, 14
Cobb Salad with Turkey and Avocado, 45
Cottage Cheese and Tomato Stuffed Avocados, 101
Creamy Avocado and Spinach Smoothie, 32
Creamy Scrambled Eggs with Smoked Salmon, 17
Cucumber Mint Green Smoothie, 30
Egg and Spinach Whole Wheat Sandwich, 47
Grilled Chicken Caesar Salad, 42
Grilled Salmon and Avocado Salad, 67
Guacamole with Veggie Sticks, 105
Chocolate Avocado Mousse, 120
Low-Carb Roast Beef Wrap with Mustard, 48

Quinoa and Black Bean Salad, 41
Salad with Egg and Salsa Verde Vinaigrette, 16
Salmon and Asparagus Salad, 45
Sardine and Avocado Stuffed Bell Peppers, 71
Shrimp Cocktail with Avocado Salsa, 107
Smoked Salmon and Avocado Plate, 20
Smoked Salmon and Avocado Sandwich, 50
Spicy Mackerel Salad with Cucumber and Tomato, 68
Strawberry Spinach Smoothie, 31
Sweet Potato and Black Bean Salad, 58
Tomato and Basil Egg White Scramble, 18
Tuna and Avocado Salad Bowl, 43
Tuna Salad Whole Grain Sandwich, 48
Turkey and Avocado Whole Grain Wrap, 46
Vegan Lentil Tacos, 56
Veggie and Tofu Wrap, 50

BACON
Bacon-wrapped asparagus with Soft-Boiled Eggs, 28

BANANA
Chocolate Banana Protein Smoothie, 33
Peanut Butter and Greek Yogurt Power Shake, 35
Sugar-Free Banana Bread, 113

BASIL
Caprese Salad Skewers, 103
Cauliflower Crust Margherita Pizza, 61
Cottage Cheese and Tomato Stuffed Avocados, 101
Eggplant Mini Pizzas with Mozzarella, 63
Garlic and Herb Stuffed Mushrooms, 107
Grilled Chicken and Spinach Alfredo Pizza, 62
Grilled Veggie and Hummus Sandwich, 46
Grilled Veggie Pizza with a Cauliflower Crust, 64
Herb-Rubbed Grilled Chicken Breasts, 77
Cheese and Herb-Stuffed Omelette, 22
Cheese and Cherry Tomato Skewers, 99
Keto-Friendly Broccoli and Cheese Pizza, 65
Lemon Basil Infused Water, 37
Low-Carb Zucchini Crust Pizza with Fresh Herbs, 62
Mushroom and Olive Pizza with Ricotta, 64
One-Pot Ratatouille, 87
Strawberry Basil Sorbet, 110
Stuffed Bell Peppers with Ground Turkey, 79
Tomato and Basil Egg White Scramble, 22
Tomato Basil Soup, 53
Whole Wheat Veggie Pizza with Pesto Sauce, 34
Zoodles with Pesto and Cherry Tomatoes, 58
Zucchini and Feta Roll-Ups, 104
Zucchini and Tomato Omelette, 25
Zucchini Noodles with Pesto and Cherry Tomatoes, 58
Zucchini Noodles with Pesto Shrimp, 69
Zucchini Noodles with Poached Eggs, 27

BBQ SAUCE Low-carb BBQ
Low-carb BBQ Chicken Pizza with Red Onion, 64

BEAN
Minestrone Soup, 53
One-pot Beef and Vegetable Chili, 83

BEAN SPROUTS
Vietnamese Pho with Tofu and Vegetables, 92

BEEF
Beef and Vegetable Stew, 54
Beef and Broccoli Stir-Fry, 80
Beef and Broccoli Stir-Fry with Cauliflower Rice, 81
Lean Beef and Vegetable Stir-Fry, 77
One-pot Beef and Vegetable Chili, 83
Slow Cooker Beef and Vegetable Soup, 84
Spaghetti Squash Bolognese, 78

BEEF BROTH
One-pot Beef and Vegetable Chili, 83
Slow Cooker Beef and Vegetable Soup, 84

BEETS
Kale and Roasted Beet Salad, 43

BELL PEPPER
Beef and Broccoli Stir-Fry, 80
Beef and Broccoli Stir-Fry with Cauliflower Rice, 81
Cauliflower Fried Rice with Chicken, 78
Cottage Cheese and Veggie Stuffed Bell Peppers, 22
Crispy Tilapia Lettuce Cups with Mango Salsa, 70
Egg and Cheese Breakfast Muffins 21
Egg and Tofu Stir-Fry with Vegetables, 23
Eggplant and Tomato Stew, 60
Greek Yogurt and Cucumber Dip with Veggie Sticks, 97
Grilled Veggie and Hummus Sandwich, 46Low-Carb Bell Pepper Crust Pizza with Fresh Herbs, 66
Guacamole with Veggie Sticks, 105
Chicken and Broccoli Stir-Fry, 73
Chicken Sausage and Kale Breakfast Skillet, 23
Italian Stuffed Bell Peppers with Ground Turkey, 88
Italian Stuffed Eggplant, 89
Lean Beef and Vegetable Stir-Fry, 77
Lentil and Vegetable Soup, 51
Low-Carb Roast Beef Wrap with Mustard, 48
Mediterranean Chickpea Salad, 42
Mexican Chicken Fajitas with Bell Peppers, 91
Minestrone Soup, 53
Moroccan Chicken Tagine with Vegetables, 90
Moroccan Chickpea Stew, 55
One-pot Beef and Vegetable Chili, 83
One-Pot Mexican Quinoa, 84
One-Pot Ratatouille, 87
Quinoa and Black Bean Salad, 41
Roasted Veggie and Quinoa Bowl, 56
Sardine and Avocado Stuffed Bell Peppers, 71
Slow Cooker Chicken and Vegetable Stew, 83
Slow Cooker Turkey Chili, 86
Spicy Lentil Stew, 53
Spinach and Mushroom Egg Scramble, 19
Stuffed Bell Peppers with Black Beans and Corn, 57
Stuffed Bell Peppers with Ground Turkey, 79
Stuffed Mini Bell Peppers with Cream Cheese, 104
Sweet Potato and Black Bean Salad, 58
Thai Peanut Chicken Salad, 44
Tofu and Vegetable Stir-Fry, 74
Tofu and Veggie Breakfast Bowl, 19
Tofu and Veggie Stir-Fry, 59
Turkey and Avocado Whole Grain Wrap, 46
Turkey and Spinach Wrap with Hummus, 49
Turkey Sausage and Egg Wrap, 21
Veggie and Cheese Frittata, 24
Veggie and Tofu Wrap, 50
Vietnamese Pho with Tofu and Vegetables, 92
Whole Wheat Veggie Pizza with Pesto Sauce, 61

BERRIES
Hibiscus Berry Iced Tea, 39
Berry Greek Yogurt Parfait, 108
Berry Chia Seed Jam, 111
Greek Yogurt with Almonds and Honey, 20
Greek Yogurt with Berries and Nuts, 15
Chia Seed Pudding with Almond Milk, 25
Peanut Butter Berry Power Smoothie, 33
Rice Cake with Peanut Butter and Chia Seeds, 102
Yogurt Parfait with Nuts and Seeds, 27

BLACK BEANS
Quinoa and Black Bean Salad, 41
Stuffed Bell Peppers with Black Beans and Corn, 57
Sweet Potato and Black Bean Salad, 58
One-Pot Mexican Quinoa, 84
Slow Cooker Turkey Chili, 86

BLACK OLIVES
Mushroom and Olive Pizza with Ricotta, 64
Whole Wheat Veggie Pizza with Pesto Sauce, 61

BLUE CHEESE
Cobb Salad with Turkey and Avocado, 45

BLUEBERRIES
Spinach and Blueberry Blast Smoothie, 29
Fresh Fruit Salad with Mint, 109
Lemon Blueberry Muffins, 116
Low-Carb Pancakes with Berries, 24

BROCCOLI
Egg and Tofu Stir-Fry with Vegetables, 23
Beef and Broccoli Stir-Fry, 80
Beef and Broccoli Stir-Fry with Cauliflower Rice, 81
Broccoli Cheddar Soup, 51
Chicken and Broccoli Stir-Fry, 73
Japanese Teriyaki Tofu with Broccoli, 90
Keto-Friendly Broccoli and Cheese Pizza, 65
Lean Beef and Vegetable Stir-Fry, 77
One-Pot Garlic Parmesan Chicken with Broccoli, 85
Roasted Veggie and Quinoa Bowl, 56
Tofu and Vegetable Stir-Fry, 74
Tofu and Veggie Stir-Fry, 59
Vietnamese Pho with Tofu and Vegetables, 92

BROWN RICE
Rice Cake with Peanut Butter and Chia Seeds, 102

BRUSSELS SPROUTS
Herb-Roasted Chicken Thighs with Garlic and Vegetables, 80

BUTTERNUT SQUASH
Butternut Squash Soup, 54

CABBAGE
Ginger-Lime Grilled Shrimp with Cabbage Slaw, 71

CANNED CHICKPEAS
Carrot and Celery Sticks with Hummus, 94

CANTALOUPE
Fresh Fruit Salad with Mint, 109

CAPERS
Smoked Salmon and Avocado Plate, 20
Smoked Salmon Cucumber Bites, 103
Smoked Salmon and Avocado Sandwich, 50

CARROT
Broccoli Cheddar Soup, 51
Beef and Vegetable Stew, 54
Carrot and Celery Sticks with Hummus, 94
Carrot Cake with Cream Cheese Frosting, 120
Cauliflower Fried Rice with Chicken, 78
Ginger-Lime Grilled Shrimp with Cabbage Slaw, 71
Greek Yogurt and Cucumber Dip with Veggie Sticks, 97
Guacamole with Veggie Sticks, 105
Chicken and Kale Soup, 52
Lentil and Vegetable Soup, 51
Minestrone Soup, 53
Moroccan Chicken Tagine with Vegetables, 90
Moroccan Chickpea Stew, 55
Slow Cooker Beef and Vegetable Soup, 84
Slow Cooker Chicken and Vegetable Stew, 83
Spaghetti Squash Bolognese, 78
Spicy Lentil Stew, 53
Split Pea Soup with Ham, 55
Thai Peanut Chicken Salad, 44
Tofu and Vegetable Stir-Fry, 74
Tofu and Veggie Breakfast Bowl, 19
Tofu and Veggie Stir-Fry, 59
Tomato Basil Soup, 53
Veggie and Tofu Wrap, 50
Vietnamese Pho with Tofu and Vegetables, 92

CASHEWS
Mixed Nuts and Seeds Trail Mix, 99

CAULIFLOWER
Cauliflower Hash Browns, 26
Beef and Broccoli Stir-Fry with Cauliflower Rice, 81
Blackened Fish and Cauliflower Rice Bowl, 72
Cauliflower Crust Margherita Pizza, 64
Cauliflower Fried Rice with Chicken, 78
Cauliflower Mashed Potatoes with Grilled Chicken, 82
Indian Chicken Curry with Cauliflower Rice, 91
Low-carb BBQ Chicken Pizza with Red Onion, 64
Spicy Shrimp and Garlic Pizza on a Cauliflower Crust, 63
Vegan Cauliflower Buffalo Wings, 59

CELERY
Tuna Salad Whole Grain Sandwich, 48
One-pot Beef and Vegetable Chili, 83
Slow Cooker Beef and Vegetable Soup, 84
Slow Cooker Chicken and Vegetable Stew, 83

CELERY STALK
Beef and Vegetable Stew, 54
Carrot and Celery Sticks with Hummus, 94
Celery Sticks with Cream Cheese and Walnuts, 97
Greek Yogurt and Cucumber Dip with Veggie Sticks, 97
Guacamole with Veggie Sticks, 105
Chicken and Kale Soup, 52
Lentil and Vegetable Soup, 51
Minestrone Soup, 53
Moroccan Chickpea Stew, 55
Spaghetti Squash Bolognese, 78
Spicy Lentil Stew, 53
Split Pea Soup with Ham, 55
Tomato Basil Soup, 53

CHEDDAR CHEESE
Broccoli Cheddar Soup, 51
Egg and Cheese Breakfast Muffins, 21
Spinach and Mushroom Egg Scramble, 19
Turkey Sausage and Egg Wrap, 21

CHERRY TOMATOES
Breakfast Tostada, 14
Caprese Salad Skewers, 103
Cauliflower Crust Margherita Pizza, 64

Cobb Salad with Turkey and Avocado, 45
Cottage Cheese and Cucumber Bowl, 26
Cottage Cheese and Tomato Stuffed Avocados, 101
Egg and Spinach Whole Wheat Sandwich, 47
Greek-Style Grilled Fish Tacos with Tzatziki, 69
Grilled Chicken Caesar Salad, 42
Grilled Salmon and Avocado Salad, 45
Lemon-Dill Shrimp and Quinoa Bowl, 67
Lentil and Feta Salad, 44
Low-Carb Zucchini Crust Pizza with Fresh Herbs, 65
Mediterranean Chickpea Salad, 42
Portobello Mushroom and Spinach Breakfast Bake, 28
Quinoa and Black Bean Salad, 41
Salad with Egg and Salsa Verde Vinaigrette, 16
Salmon and Asparagus Salad, 45
Sardine and Avocado Stuffed Bell Peppers, 71
Shrimp Cocktail with Avocado Salsa, 107
Spicy Mackerel Salad with Cucumber and Tomato, 68
Tofu and Veggie Breakfast Bowl, 19
Tomato and Basil Egg White Scramble, 22
Tuna and Avocado Salad Bowl, 43
Veggie and Cheese Frittata, 24
Whole Wheat Veggie Pizza with Pesto Sauce, 61
Zoodles with Pesto and Cherry Tomatoes, 58
Zucchini and Tomato Omelette, 25
Zucchini Noodles with Pesto and Cherry Tomatoes, 58
Zucchini Noodles with Poached Eggs, 27

BROWN RICE
Rice Cake with Peanut Butter and Chia Seeds, 102

BRUSSELS SPROUTS
Herb-Roasted Chicken Thighs with Garlic and Vegetables, 80

BUTTERNUT SQUASH
Butternut Squash Soup, 54

CABBAGE
Ginger-Lime Grilled Shrimp with Cabbage Slaw, 71

CANNED CHICKPEAS
Carrot and Celery Sticks with Hummus, 94

CANTALOUPE
Fresh Fruit Salad with Mint, 109

CAPERS
Smoked Salmon and Avocado Plate, 20
Smoked Salmon Cucumber Bites, 103
Smoked Salmon and Avocado Sandwich, 50

CARROT
Broccoli Cheddar Soup, 51
Beef and Vegetable Stew, 54
Carrot and Celery Sticks with Hummus, 94
Carrot Cake with Cream Cheese Frosting, 120
Cauliflower Fried Rice with Chicken, 78
Ginger-Lime Grilled Shrimp with Cabbage Slaw, 71
Greek Yogurt and Cucumber Dip with Veggie Sticks, 97
Guacamole with Veggie Sticks, 105
Chicken and Kale Soup, 52
Lentil and Vegetable Soup, 51
Minestrone Soup, 53
Moroccan Chicken Tagine with Vegetables, 90
Moroccan Chickpea Stew, 55
Slow Cooker Beef and Vegetable Soup, 84
Slow Cooker Chicken and Vegetable Stew, 83
Spaghetti Squash Bolognese, 78
Spicy Lentil Stew, 53
Split Pea Soup with Ham, 55
Thai Peanut Chicken Salad, 44
Tofu and Vegetable Stir-Fry, 74
Tofu and Veggie Breakfast Bowl, 19
Tofu and Veggie Stir-Fry, 59
Tomato Basil Soup, 53
Veggie and Tofu Wrap, 50
Vietnamese Pho with Tofu and Vegetables, 92

CASHEWS
Mixed Nuts and Seeds Trail Mix, 99

CAULIFLOWER
Cauliflower Hash Browns, 26
Beef and Broccoli Stir-Fry with Cauliflower Rice, 81
Blackened Fish and Cauliflower Rice Bowl, 72
Cauliflower Crust Margherita Pizza, 64
Cauliflower Fried Rice with Chicken, 78
Cauliflower Mashed Potatoes with Grilled Chicken, 82
Low-Carb Bell Pepper Crust Pizza with Fresh Herbs, 66
Indian Chicken Curry with Cauliflower Rice, 91
Low-carb BBQ Chicken Pizza with Red Onion, 64
Spicy Shrimp and Garlic Pizza on a Cauliflower Crust, 63
Vegan Cauliflower Buffalo Wings, 59

CELERY
Tuna Salad Whole Grain Sandwich, 48
One-pot Beef and Vegetable Chili, 83
Slow Cooker Beef and Vegetable Soup, 84
Slow Cooker Chicken and Vegetable Stew, 83

CELERY STALK
Beef and Vegetable Stew, 54
Carrot and Celery Sticks with Hummus, 94
Celery Sticks with Cream Cheese and Walnuts, 97
Greek Yogurt and Cucumber Dip with Veggie Sticks, 97
Guacamole with Veggie Sticks, 105
Chicken and Kale Soup, 52
Lentil and Vegetable Soup, 51
Minestrone Soup, 53
Moroccan Chickpea Stew, 55
Spaghetti Squash Bolognese, 78
Spicy Lentil Stew, 53
Split Pea Soup with Ham, 55
Tomato Basil Soup, 53

CHEDDAR CHEESE
Broccoli Cheddar Soup, 51
Egg and Cheese Breakfast Muffins, 21
Spinach and Mushroom Egg Scramble, 19
Turkey Sausage and Egg Wrap, 21

CHERRY TOMATOES
Breakfast Tostada, 14
Caprese Salad Skewers, 103
Cauliflower Crust Margherita Pizza, 64
Cobb Salad with Turkey and Avocado, 45
Cottage Cheese and Cucumber Bowl, 26
Cottage Cheese and Tomato Stuffed Avocados, 101
Egg and Spinach Whole Wheat Sandwich, 47
Greek-Style Grilled Fish Tacos with Tzatziki, 69
Grilled Chicken Caesar Salad, 42

Grilled Salmon and Avocado Salad, 45
Lemon-Dill Shrimp and Quinoa Bowl, 67
Lentil and Feta Salad, 44
Low-carb Zucchini Crust Pizza with Fresh Herbs, 65
Mediterranean Chickpea Salad, 42
Portobello Mushroom and Spinach Breakfast Bake, 28
Quinoa and Black Bean Salad, 41
Salad with Egg and Salsa Verde Vinaigrette, 16
Salmon and Asparagus Salad, 45
Sardine and Avocado Stuffed Bell Peppers, 71
Shrimp Cocktail with Avocado Salsa, 107
Spicy Mackerel Salad with Cucumber and Tomato, 68
Tofu and Veggie Breakfast Bowl, 19
Tomato and Basil Egg White Scramble, 22
Tuna and Avocado Salad Bowl, 43
Veggie and Cheese Frittata, 24
Whole Wheat Veggie Pizza with Pesto Sauce, 61
Zoodles with Pesto and Cherry Tomatoes, 58
Zucchini and Tomato Omelette, 25
Zucchini Noodles with Pesto and Cherry Tomatoes, 58
Zucchini Noodles with Poached Eggs, 27

CHIA SEEDS
Almond and Flaxseed Energy Bites, 96
Almond-Coconut Protein Smoothie, 36
Apple Cinnamon Chia Seed Pudding, 112
Apple Cinnamon Overnight Oats, 16
Apple Slices with Almond Butter, 94
Avocado Berry Delight Smoothie, 30
Berry Bliss Smoothie with Chia Seeds, 31
Berry Greek Yogurt Parfait, 108
Berry Chia Seed Jam, 111
Cottage Cheese with Pineapple Chunks, 17
Creamy Avocado and Spinach Smoothie, 32
Cucumber Lime Electrolyte Drink, 40
Cucumber Mint Green Smoothie, 30
Dark Chocolate Coconut Truffles, 121
Greek Yogurt and Almond Protein Shake, 34
Greek Yogurt with Almonds and Honey, 20
Greek Yogurt with Berries and Nuts, 15
Creek Yogurt with Fresh Berries and Nuts, 15
Chia Seed Pudding with Almond Milk, 25
Chia Seed Pudding with Mango, 109
Chocolate Avocado Mousse, 120
Chocolate Banana Protein Smoothie, 33
Kale and Green Apple Smoothie, 29
Low-Carb Coconut Panna Cotta, 119
Mixed Nuts and Seeds, 94
Mixed Nuts and Seeds Trail Mix, 99
Overnight Oats with Chia Seeds, 15
Peanut Butter and Greek Yogurt Power Shake, 35
Peanut Butter Berry Power Smoothie, 33
Rice Cake with Peanut Butter and Chia Seeds, 102
Smoked Salmon and Avocado Plate, 20
Spinach Almond Butter Protein Smoothie, 34
Spinach and Blueberry Blast Smoothie, 29
Strawberry Spinach Smoothie, 31
Vanilla Strawberry Protein Smoothie, 35
Yogurt Parfait with Nuts and Seeds, 27

CHICKEN
Almond-Crusted Chicken Tenders, 82
Cauliflower Fried Rice with Chicken, 78
Cauliflower Mashed Potatoes with Grilled Chicken, 82
Chicken and Kale Soup, 52
Chicken and Broccoli Stir-Fry, 73
Chicken and Spinach Stuffed Portobello Mushrooms, 75
Greek Lemon Chicken with Tzatziki, 88
Grilled Chicken and Spinach Alfredo Pizza, 62
Grilled Chicken Caesar Salad, 42
Herb-Roasted Chicken Thighs with Garlic and Vegetables, 80
Herb-Rubbed Grilled Chicken Breasts, 77
Indian Chicken Curry with Cauliflower Rice, 91
Lemon Herb Grilled Chicken, 73
Low-carb BBQ Chicken Pizza with Red Onion, 64
Mexican Chicken Fajitas with Bell Peppers, 91
Moroccan Chicken Tagine with Vegetables, 90
One-Pot Creamy Mushroom Chicken, 85
One-pot Garlic Parmesan Chicken with Broccoli, 85
Slow Cooker Chicken and Vegetable Stew, 83
Thai Peanut Chicken Salad, 44

CHICKEN BROTH
Chicken and Kale Soup, 52
Moroccan Chicken Tagine with Vegetables, 90
One-Pot Creamy Mushroom Chicken, 85
One-pot Garlic Parmesan Chicken with Broccoli, 85
Spaghetti Squash Bolognese, 78
Slow Cooker Chicken and Vegetable Stew, 83
Slow Cooker Turkey Chili, 86
Split Pea Soup with Ham, 55

CHICKEN SAUSAGE
Chicken Sausage and Kale Breakfast Skillet, 23

CHICKPEA FLOUR
Vegan Cauliflower Buffalo Wings, 59

CHICKPEAS
Mediterranean Chickpea Salad, 42
Moroccan Chickpea Stew, 55
Roasted Veggie and Quinoa Bowl, 56
Chickpea and Spinach Curry, 97
Indian Spiced Chickpea Stew, 92
Middle Eastern Falafel with Tahini Sauce, 92
Roasted Chickpeas with Sea Salt and Paprika, 96
Spicy Roasted Chickpeas, 96
Cucumber Slices with Hummus, 98

CHIVES
Stuffed Mini Bell Peppers with Cream Cheese, 104

CILANTRO
Breakfast Tostada, 14
Bell Pepper Slices with Guacamole, 95
Cauliflower Fried Rice with Chicken, 78
Crispy Tilapia Lettuce Cups with Mango Salsa, 70
Ginger-Lime Grilled Shrimp with Cabbage Slaw, 71
Grilled Salmon and Avocado Salad, 45
Guacamole with Veggie Sticks, 105
Chickpea and Spinach Curry, 97
Indian Chicken Curry with Cauliflower Rice, 91
Indian Spiced Chickpea Stew, 92
Lean Beef and Vegetable Stir-Fry, 77

Low-carb BBQ Chicken Pizza with Red Onion, 64
Mexican Chicken Fajitas with Bell Peppers, 91
Middle Eastern Falafel with Tahini Sauce, 92
Moroccan Chicken Tagine with Vegetables, 90
Moroccan Chickpea Stew, 55
One-Pot Mexican Quinoa, 84
Quinoa and Black Bean Salad, 41
Sardine and Avocado Stuffed Bell Peppers, 71
Shrimp Cocktail with Avocado Salsa, 107
Slow Cooker Lentil and Spinach Curry, 85
Slow Cooker Turkey Chili, 86
Spicy Lentil Stew, 53
Spicy Mackerel Salad with Cucumber and Tomato, 68
Sweet Potato and Black Bean Salad, 58
Thai Peanut Chicken Salad, 44
Tofu and Vegetable Stir-Fry, 74
Vegan Lentil Tacos, 59

COCOA POWDER
Dark Chocolate Coconut Truffles, 121
Chocolate Banana Protein Smoothie, 33
Coconut Flour Brownies, 114
Chocolate Almond Brownies, 116
Chocolate Avocado Mousse, 120

COCONUT FLAKES
Carrot Cake with Cream Cheese Frosting, 120
Dark Chocolate Coconut Truffles, 121
Yogurt Parfait with Nuts and Seeds, 27

COCONUT FLOUR
Almond Flour Lemon Bars, 114
Carrot Cake with Cream Cheese Frosting, 120
Cinnamon Walnut Coffee Cake, 117
Coconut Flour Brownies, 114
Coconut Flour Pancakes, 112
Lemon Blueberry Muffins, 116
Mini Berry Cheesecakes, 121
Low-Carb Pancakes with Berries, 24
Pumpkin Spice Bars, 117
Pumpkin Spice Cheesecake Bites, 118
Raspberry Lemon Tart, 119
Sugar-Free Banana Bread, 113

COCONUT MILK
Chickpea and Spinach Curry, 55
Slow Cooker Lentil and Spinach Curry, 85
Low-Carb Coconut Panna Cotta, 119

COCONUT OIL
Almond Flour Chocolate Chip Cookies, 113
Almond Flour Lemon Bars, 114
Carrot Cake with Cream Cheese Frosting, 120
Cinnamon Walnut Coffee Cake, 117
Coconut Flour Brownies, 114
Coconut Flour Pancakes, 112
Dark Chocolate Coconut Truffles, 121
Dark Chocolate Covered Strawberries, 120
Chocolate Almond Brownies, 116
Lemon Blueberry Muffins, 116
Mini Berry Cheesecakes, 121
Low-Carb Pancakes with Berries, 24
Pumpkin Spice Bars, 117
Pumpkin Spice Cheesecake Bites, 118
Pumpkin Spice Muffins, 115
Raspberry Lemon Tart, 119
Sugar-Free Banana Bread, 113
Vanilla Almond Cupcakes, 115

COD FILLETS
Baked Cod with Garlic Spinach, 69

CORN KERNELS
One-Pot Mexican Quinoa, 84
Stuffed Bell Peppers with Black Beans and Corn, 57

COTTAGE CHEESE
Carrot Cake with Cream Cheese Frosting, 120
Celery Sticks with Cream Cheese and Walnuts, 97
Cottage Cheese with Pineapple Chunks, 17
Cottage Cheese and Cucumber Bowl, 26
Cottage Cheese and Tomato Stuffed Avocados, 101
Creamy Scrambled Eggs with Smoked Salmon, 17
Cucumber and Cream Cheese Sandwich, 49
Mini Berry Cheesecakes, 121
Pumpkin Spice Cheesecake Bites, 118
Smoked Salmon Cucumber Bites, 103
Spinach and Artichoke Dip with Whole-Grain Crackers, 106
Stuffed Mini Bell Peppers with Cream Cheese, 104
Zucchini and Feta Roll-Ups, 104

CUCUMBER
Cobb Salad with Turkey and Avocado, 45
Cottage Cheese and Cucumber Bowl, 26
Cucumber and Cream Cheese Sandwich, 49
Cucumber Lime Electrolyte Drink, 40
Cucumber Mint Green Smoothie, 30
Cucumber Mint Infused Water, 30
Greek Yogurt and Cucumber Dip with Veggie Sticks, 97
Greek-Style Grilled Fish Tacos with Tzatziki, 69
Grilled Salmon and Avocado Salad, 45
Guacamole with Veggie Sticks, 105
Lemon-Dill Shrimp and Quinoa Bowl, 67
Lentil and Feta Salad, 44
Low-Carb Roast Beef Wrap with Mustard, 48
Low-Carb Salmon Patties with Cucumber Salad, 72
Mediterranean Chickpea Salad, 42
Mediterranean Veggie and Hummus Wrap, 46
Salad with Egg and Salsa Verde Vinaigrette, 16
Smoked Salmon and Avocado Plate, 20
Smoked Salmon and Avocado Sandwich, 50
Smoked Salmon Cucumber Bites, 103
Spicy Mackerel Salad with Cucumber and Tomato, 68
Turkey and Avocado Whole Grain Wrap, 46
Turkey and Spinach Wrap with Hummus, 49
Tuna and Avocado Salad Bowl, 43
Veggie and Tofu Wrap, 50

CULINARY LAVENDER
Lemon-Lavender Sparkling Water, 39

DARK CHOCOLATE
Almond Flour Chocolate Chip Cookies, 113
Dark Chocolate Covered Strawberries, 120
Dark Chocolate Coconut Truffles, 121

DIJON MUSTARD
Balsamic Glazed Pork Tenderloin, 76
Cobb Salad with Turkey and Avocado, 45
Garlic and Rosemary Grilled Pork Tenderloin, 76
Grilled Chicken Caesar Salad, 42
Grilled Salmon and Avocado Salad, 45
Kale and Roasted Beet Salad, 43
Lemon-Dill Shrimp and Quinoa Bowl, 67
Lentil and Feta Salad, 44
Low-Carb Roast Beef Wrap with Mustard, 48

Low-Carb Salmon Patties with Cucumber Salad, 72
Salmon and Asparagus Salad, 45
Slow Cooker BBQ Pulled Pork, 86
Spicy Mackerel Salad with Cucumber and Tomato, 68
Spinach and Strawberry Salad with Balsamic Vinaigrette, 43
Tuna Salad Whole Grain Sandwich, 48
Turkey and Avocado Whole Grain Wrap, 46

EDAMAME
Edamame with Sea Salt, 100

EGGPLANT
Eggplant and Tomato Stew, 60
Eggplant Lasagna, 81
Eggplant Mini Pizzas with Mozzarella, 63
Grilled Veggie and Hummus Sandwich, 46
Italian Stuffed Eggplant, 89
One-Pot Ratatouille, 87

EGGS
Almond Butter Cookies, 111
Almond Flour Chocolate Chip Cookies, 113
Almond Flour Lemon Bars, 114
Almond-Crusted Chicken Tenders, 82
Almond-Crusted Mozzarella Sticks, 105
Bacon-Wrapped Asparagus with Soft-Boiled Eggs, 27
Baked Turkey Meatballs, 75
Breakfast Tostada, 14
Carrot Cake with Cream Cheese Frosting, 120
Cauliflower Crust Margherita Pizza, 64
Cauliflower Fried Rice with Chicken, 78
Cauliflower Hash Browns, 26
Cinnamon Walnut Coffee Cake, 117
Cobb Salad with Turkey and Avocado, 45
Coconut Flour Brownies, 114
Coconut Flour Pancakes, 112
Creamy Scrambled Eggs with Smoked Salmon, 17
Egg and Cheese Breakfast Muffins, 21
Egg and Spinach Whole Wheat Sandwich, 47
Egg and Tofu Stir-Fry with Vegetables, 23
Eggplant Lasagna, 81
Grilled Veggie Pizza with a Cauliflower Crust, 66
Hard-Boiled Eggs with a Dash of Paprika, 100
Hard-Boiled Eggs with Hummus, 101
Cheese and Herb-Stuffed Omelette, 22
Chicken Sausage and Kale Breakfast Skillet, 23
Chocolate Almond Brownies, 116
Keto-Friendly Broccoli and Cheese Pizza, 65
Lemon Blueberry Muffins, 116
Low-Carb BBQ Chicken Pizza with Red Onion, 64
Low-Carb Lemon Bars, 114
Mini Berry Cheesecakes, 121
Low-Carb Pancakes with Berries, 24
Peanut Butter Chocolate Chip Cookies, 122
Portobello Mushroom and Spinach Breakfast Bake, 28
Pumpkin Spice Bars, 117
Pumpkin Spice Muffins, 115
Raspberry Lemon Tart, 119
Salad with Egg and Salsa Verde Vinaigrette, 16
Spicy Shrimp and Garlic Pizza on a Cauliflower Crust, 63
Spinach and Mushroom Egg Scramble, 19
Sugar-Free Banana Bread, 113
Tomato and Basil Egg White Scramble, 22
Turkey Sausage and Egg Wrap, 21
Vanilla Almond Cupcakes, 115
Veggie and Cheese Frittata, 24
Zucchini and Tomato Omelette, 25
Zucchini Noodles with Poached Eggs, 27

FETA CHEESE
Breakfast Tostada, 14
Greek-Style Grilled Fish Tacos with Tzatziki, 69
Low-Carb Bell Pepper Crust Pizza with Fresh Herbs, 66
Kale and Roasted Beet Salad, 43
Lemon-Dill Shrimp and Quinoa Bowl, 67
Lentil and Feta Salad, 44
Mediterranean Chickpea Salad, 42
Mediterranean Veggie and Hummus Wrap, 46
Orange and Almond Salad, 110
Portobello Mushroom and Spinach Breakfast Bake, 28
Roasted Veggie and Quinoa Bowl, 56
Salmon and Asparagus Salad, 45
Spinach and Strawberry Salad with Balsamic Vinaigrette, 43
Turkey and Avocado Whole Grain Wrap, 46
Whole Wheat Veggie Pizza with Pesto Sauce, 61
Zucchini and Feta Roll-Ups, 104

FIRM TOFU
Egg and Tofu Stir-Fry with Vegetables, 23
Japanese Teriyaki Tofu with Broccoli, 90
Tofu and Vegetable Stir-Fry, 74
Tofu and Veggie Stir-Fry, 59
Veggie and Tofu Wrap, 50
Vietnamese Pho with Tofu and Vegetables, 92

FLAXSEED
Almond and Flaxseed Energy Bites, 96
Avocado Berry Delight Smoothie, 30
Celery Sticks with Cream Cheese and Walnuts, 97
Cucumber Mint Green Smoothie, 30
Greek Yogurt with Almonds and Honey, 20
Greek Yogurt and Almond Protein Shake, 34
Greek Yogurt with Fresh Berries and Nuts, 15
Chocolate Banana Protein Smoothie, 33
Kale and Green Apple Smoothie, 29
Mixed Nuts and Seeds, 94
Mixed Nuts and Seeds Trail Mix, 99
Overnight Oats with Chia Seeds, 15
Peanut Butter Berry Power Smoothie, 33
Rice Cake with Peanut Butter and Chia Seeds, 102
Spinach Almond Butter Protein Smoothie, 34
Spinach and Blueberry Blast Smoothie, 29
Strawberry Spinach Smoothie, 31
Vanilla Strawberry Protein Smoothie, 35
Yogurt Parfait with Nuts and Seeds, 27

FRESH DILL
Greek Lemon Chicken with Tzatziki, 88
Greek Yogurt and Cucumber Dip with Veggie Sticks, 97
Greek-Style Grilled Fish Tacos with Tzatziki, 69

Lemon-Dill Shrimp and Quinoa Bowl, 67
Low-Carb Salmon Patties with Cucumber Salad, 72
Smoked Salmon Cucumber Bites, 103

GINGER
Lemon Basil Infused Water, 30
Ginger Lemon Herbal Tea, 30
Chickpea and Spinach Curry, 55
Tofu and Veggie Stir-Fry, 59
Ginger-Lime Grilled Shrimp with Cabbage Slaw, 71
Tofu and Vegetable Stir-Fry, 74
Cauliflower Fried Rice with Chicken, 78
Beef and Broccoli Stir-Fry, 80
Slow Cooker Lentil and Spinach Curry, 85
Indian Spiced Chickpea Stew, 92
Japanese Teriyaki Tofu with Broccoli, 90
Vietnamese Pho with Tofu and Vegetables, 92
Chicken and Broccoli Stir-Fry, 73
Lean Beef and Vegetable Stir-Fry, 77
Beef and Broccoli Stir-Fry with Cauliflower Rice, 81
Indian Chicken Curry with Cauliflower Rice, 91

GRAIN BREAD
Grilled Veggie and Hummus Sandwich, 46

GREEK YOGURT
Almond-Coconut Protein Smoothie, 36
Apple Cinnamon Overnight Oats, 16
Avocado Berry Delight Smoothie, 30
Berry Bliss Smoothie with Chia Seeds, 31
Berry Greek Yogurt Parfait, 108
Broccoli Cheddar Soup, 51
Butternut Squash Soup, 54
Carrot Cake with Cream Cheese Frosting, 120
Cauliflower Mashed Potatoes with Grilled Chicken, 82
Creamy Avocado and Spinach Smoothie, 32
Cucumber Mint Green Smoothie, 30
Greek Yogurt and Almond Protein Shake, 34
Greek Yogurt and Cucumber Dip with Veggie Sticks, 97
Greek Yogurt with Almonds and Honey, 20
Greek Yogurt with Fresh Berries and Nuts, 15
Greek-Style Grilled Fish Tacos with Tzatziki, 69
Grilled Chicken and Spinach Alfredo Pizza, 62
Grilled Chicken Caesar Salad, 42
Chocolate Banana Protein Smoothie, 33
Indian Chicken Curry with Cauliflower Rice, 91
Kale and Green Apple Smoothie, 29
Low-Carb Roast Beef Wrap with Mustard, 48
Mini Berry Cheesecakes, 121
One-Pot Creamy Mushroom Chicken, 85
Overnight Oats with Chia Seeds, 15
Low-Carb Pancakes with Berries, 24
Peanut Butter and Greek Yogurt Power Shake, 35
Peanut Butter Berry Power Smoothie, 33
Smoked Salmon and Avocado Sandwich, 50
Spinach Almond Butter Protein Smoothie, 34
Spinach and Artichoke Dip with Whole-Grain Crackers, 106
Spinach and Blueberry Blast Smoothie, 29
Strawberry Spinach Smoothie, 31
Tomato Basil Soup, 53
Tuna Salad Whole Grain Sandwich, 48
Turkey and Avocado Whole Grain Wrap, 46
Vanilla Strawberry Protein Smoothie, 35
Yogurt Parfait with Nuts and Seeds, 27

GREEN APPLE
Creamy Avocado and Spinach Smoothie, 32
Kale and Green Apple Smoothie, 29

GREEN BEANS
Beef and Vegetable Stew, 54
Slow Cooker Beef and Vegetable Soup, 84

GREEN OLIVES
Moroccan Chicken Tagine with Vegetables, 90

GREENS
Thai Peanut Chicken Salad, 44

HAM
Split Pea Soup with Ham, 55

HUMMUS
Grilled Veggie and Hummus Sandwich, 46
Hard-Boiled Eggs with Hummus, 101
Mediterranean Veggie and Hummus Wrap, 46
Turkey and Spinach Wrap with Hummus, 49
Veggie and Tofu Wrap, 50

JALAPENO
Crispy Tilapia Lettuce Cups with Mango Salsa, 70
Guacamole with Veggie Sticks, 105
Shrimp Cocktail with Avocado Salsa, 107
Spicy Mackerel Salad with Cucumber and Tomato, 68

KALAMATA OLIVES
Lentil and Feta Salad, 44
Mediterranean Chickpea Salad, 42

KALE
Chicken and Kale Soup, 52
Chicken Sausage and Kale Breakfast Skillet, 23
Kale and Green Apple Smoothie, 29
Kale and Roasted Beet Salad, 43

KETCHUP
Slow Cooker BBQ Pulled Pork, 86

KIDNEY BEANS
Minestrone Soup, 53
Slow Cooker Turkey Chili, 86

LEMON
Smoked Salmon and Avocado Plate, 20
Lemon Basil Infused Water, 30
Lemon-Lavender Sparkling Water, 39
Ginger Lemon Herbal Tea, 30
Greek-Style Grilled Fish Tacos with Tzatziki, 69

LEMON JUICE
Almond Flour Lemon Bars, 114
Apple Cinnamon Chia Seed Pudding, 112
Avocado Toast with Tomato Slices, 17
Baked Cod with Garlic Spinach, 69
Berry Chia Seed Jam, 111
Carrot and Celery Sticks with Hummus, 94
Cauliflower Mashed Potatoes with Grilled Chicken, 82
Cottage Cheese and Cucumber Bowl, 26
Crispy Tilapia Lettuce Cups with Mango Salsa, 70
Cucumber Mint Green Smoothie, 30

Cucumber Slices with Hummus, 98
Eggplant and Tomato Stew, 60
Fresh Fruit Salad with Mint, 109
Garlic and Herb Stuffed Mushrooms, 107
Garlic and Rosemary Grilled Pork Tenderloin, 76
Garlic Roasted Turkey Breast, 75
Ginger Lemon Herbal Tea, 30
Greek Lemon Chicken with Tzatziki, 88
Greek Yogurt and Cucumber Dip with Veggie Sticks, 97
Greek-Style Grilled Fish Tacos with Tzatziki, 69
Seared Scallops with Asparagus and Lemon, 70
Grilled Chicken Caesar Salad, 42
Grilled Salmon and Avocado Salad, 45
Herb-Roasted Chicken Thighs with Garlic and Vegetables, 80
Herb-Rubbed Grilled Chicken Breasts, 77
Hibiscus Berry Iced Tea, 39
Chicken and Spinach Stuffed Portobello Mushrooms, 75
Chickpea and Spinach Curry, 55
Indian Spiced Chickpea Stew, 92
Lemon Basil Infused Water, 30
Lemon Blueberry Muffins, 116
Lemon Herb Grilled Chicken, 73
Lemon-Dill Shrimp and Quinoa Bowl, 67
Lemon-Lavender Sparkling Water, 39
Lentil and Feta Salad, 44
Lentil and Vegetable Soup, 51
Low-Carb Lemon Bars, 114
Low-Carb Salmon Patties with Cucumber Salad, 72
Mediterranean Chickpea Salad, 42
Minestrone Soup, 53
Mini Berry Cheesecakes, 121
Moroccan Chicken Tagine with Vegetables, 90
Moroccan Chickpea Stew, 55
Mushroom and Barley Pilaf, 56
One-Pot Creamy Mushroom Chicken, 85
One-pot Garlic Parmesan Chicken with Broccoli, 85
Orange and Almond Salad, 110
Raspberry Lemon Tart, 119
Roasted Veggie and Quinoa Bowl, 56
Salmon and Asparagus Salad, 45
Sardine and Avocado Stuffed Bell Peppers, 71
Shrimp Cocktail with Avocado Salsa, 107
Smoked Salmon and Avocado Sandwich, 50
Smoked Salmon Cucumber Bites, 103

Spinach and Artichoke Dip with Whole Grain Crackers, 106
Strawberry Basil Sorbet, 110
Stuffed Mini Bell Peppers with Cream Cheese, 104
Tuna and Avocado Salad Bowl, 43
Tuna Salad Whole Grain Sandwich, 48
Turkey and Spinach Wrap with Hummus, 49
Whole Wheat Veggie Pizza with Pesto Sauce, 61
Zoodles with Pesto and Cherry Tomatoes, 58
Zucchini Noodles with Pesto and Cherry Tomatoes, 58
Zucchini Noodles with Pesto Shrimp, 69

LEMON ZEST
Almond Flour Lemon Bars, 114
Greek Lemon Chicken with Tzatziki, 88
Lemon Blueberry Muffins, 116
Lemon Herb Grilled Chicken, 73
Low-Carb Lemon Bars, 114
Prosciutto-Wrapped Asparagus Spears, 107
Raspberry Lemon Tart, 119
Seared Scallops with Asparagus and Lemon, 70

LENTILS
Lentil and Feta Salad, 44
Lentil and Vegetable Soup, 51
Slow Cooker Lentil and Spinach Curry, 85
Spicy Lentil Stew, 53
Vegan Lentil Tacos, 59

LETTUCE
Grilled Chicken Caesar Salad, 42
Greek-Style Grilled Fish Tacos with Tzatziki, 69
Low-Carb Roast Beef Wrap with Mustard, 48
Mediterranean Veggie and Hummus Wrap, 46
Vegan Lentil Tacos, 59

LIME
Breakfast Tostada, 14
Cucumber Lime Electrolyte Drink, 40
Guacamole with Veggie Sticks, 105

LIME JUICE
Bell Pepper Slices with Guacamole, 95
Cottage Cheese and Veggie Stuffed Bell Peppers, 22
Crispy Tilapia Lettuce Cups with Mango Salsa, 70
Ginger-Lime Grilled Shrimp with Cabbage Slaw, 71

Mexican Chicken Fajitas with Bell Peppers, 91
One-Pot Mexican Quinoa, 84
Quinoa and Black Bean Salad, 41
Shrimp Cocktail with Avocado Salsa, 107
Slow Cooker Lentil and Spinach Curry, 85
Slow Cooker Turkey Chili, 86
Spicy Mackerel Salad with Cucumber and Tomato, 68
Stuffed Bell Peppers with Black Beans and Corn, 57
Sweet Potato and Black Bean Salad, 58
Tofu and Veggie Stir-Fry, 59
Tofu and Vegetable Stir-Fry, 74
Vegan Lentil Tacos, 59
Watermelon Mint Cooler, 39

MACKEREL
Spicy Mackerel Salad with Cucumber and Tomato, 68

MANGO
Crispy Tilapia Lettuce Cups with Mango Salsa, 70
Chia Seed Pudding with Mango, 109

MAYONNAISE
Low-Carb Salmon Patties with Cucumber Salad, 72

MILK
Veggie and Cheese Frittata, 24
Zucchini and Tomato Omelette, 25

MINT
Cucumber Lime Electrolyte Drink, 40
Cucumber Mint Infused Water, 30
Fresh Fruit Salad with Mint, 109
Ginger Lemon Herbal Tea, 30
Lemon Basil Infused Water, 30
Lemon-Lavender Sparkling Water, 39
Lentil and Feta Salad, 44
Low-Carb Coconut Panna Cotta, 119
Raspberry Lemon Tart, 119
Watermelon Mint Cooler, 39

MIXED BERRIES
Avocado Berry Delight Smoothie, 30
Berry Bliss Smoothie with Chia Seeds, 31
Greek Yogurt with Fresh Berries and Nuts, 15
Low-Carb Coconut Panna Cotta, 119

Mini Berry Cheesecakes, 121
Overnight Oats with Chia Seeds, 15

MIXED GREENS
Cobb Salad with Turkey and Avocado, 45
Salad with Egg and Salsa Verde Vinaigrette, 16
Salmon and Asparagus Salad, 45
Tuna and Avocado Salad Bowl, 43
Tuna Salad Whole Grain Sandwich, 48
Turkey and Avocado Whole Grain Wrap, 46

MIXED SALAD GREENS
Grilled Salmon and Avocado Salad, 45
Orange and Almond Salad, 110
Spicy Mackerel Salad with Cucumber and Tomato, 68

MOZZARELLA CHEESE
Almond-Crusted Mozzarella Sticks, 105
Avocado and Turkey Breakfast Roll-Ups, 23
Caprese Salad Skewers, 103
Cauliflower Crust Margherita Pizza, 64
Cottage Cheese and Veggie Stuffed Bell Peppers, 22
Eggplant Lasagna, 81
Eggplant Mini Pizzas with Mozzarella, 63
Grilled Chicken and Spinach Alfredo Pizza, 62
Low-Carb Bell Pepper Crust Pizza with Fresh Herbs, 66
Cheese and Herb-Stuffed Omelette, 22
Cheese and Cherry Tomato Skewers, 99
Chicken and Spinach Stuffed Portobello Mushrooms, 75
Chicken Sausage and Kale Breakfast Skillet, 23
Italian Stuffed Bell Peppers with Ground Turkey, 88
Italian Stuffed Eggplant, 89
Keto-Friendly Broccoli and Cheese Pizza, 65
Low-carb BBQ Chicken Pizza with Red Onion, 64
Low-carb Zucchini Crust Pizza with Fresh Herbs, 65
Mushroom and Olive Pizza with Ricotta, 64
Portobello Mushroom and Spinach Breakfast Bake, 28
Spicy Shrimp and Garlic Pizza on a Cauliflower Crust, 63
Spinach and Artichoke Dip with Whole Grain Crackers, 106

Stuffed Mini Bell Peppers with Cream Cheese, 104
Veggie and Cheese Frittata, 24
Whole Wheat Veggie Pizza with Pesto Sauce, 61

MUSHROOMS
Egg and Cheese Breakfast Muffins, 21
Garlic and Herb Stuffed Mushrooms, 107
Cheese and Herb-Stuffed Omelette, 22
Mushroom and Barley Pilaf, 56
Mushroom and Olive Pizza with Ricotta, 64
One-Pot Creamy Mushroom Chicken, 85
Slow Cooker Beef and Vegetable Soup, 84
Spinach and Mushroom Egg Scramble, 19
Whole Wheat Veggie Pizza with Pesto Sauce, 61

NUTS
Berry Greek Yogurt Parfait, 108
Chia Seed Pudding with Almond Milk, 25
Greek Yogurt with Berries and Nuts, 15

ONION
Baked Turkey Meatballs, 75
Beef and Broccoli Stir-Fry, 80
Beef and Vegetable Stew, 54
Broccoli Cheddar Soup, 51
Butternut Squash Soup, 54
Cauliflower Fried Rice with Chicken, 78
Eggplant and Tomato Stew, 60
Eggplant Lasagna, 81
Garlic and Herb Stuffed Mushrooms, 107
Chicken and Kale Soup, 52
Chicken and Spinach Stuffed Portobello Mushrooms, 75
Chicken Sausage and Kale Breakfast Skillet, 23
Chickpea and Spinach Curry, 55
Indian Chicken Curry with Cauliflower Rice, 91
Indian Spiced Chickpea Stew, 92
Italian Stuffed Bell Peppers with Ground Turkey, 88
Italian Stuffed Eggplant, 89
Lentil and Vegetable Soup, 51
Mexican Chicken Fajitas with Bell Peppers, 91
Middle Eastern Falafel with Tahini Sauce, 92
Minestrone Soup, 53
Moroccan Chicken Tagine with Vegetables, 90
Moroccan Chickpea Stew, 55
Mushroom and Barley Pilaf, 56
One-pot Beef and Vegetable Chili, 83
One-Pot Creamy Mushroom Chicken, 85

One-Pot Mexican Quinoa, 84
One-Pot Ratatouille, 87
Slow Cooker BBQ Pulled Pork, 86
Slow Cooker Beef and Vegetable Soup, 84
Slow Cooker Chicken and Vegetable Stew, 83
Slow Cooker Lentil and Spinach Curry, 85
Slow Cooker Turkey Chili, 86
Spaghetti Squash Bolognese, 78
Spicy Lentil Stew, 53
Spinach and Mushroom Egg Scramble, 19
Split Pea Soup with Ham, 55
Stuffed Bell Peppers with Black Beans and Corn, 57
Stuffed Bell Peppers with Ground Turkey, 79
Tofu and Vegetable Stir-Fry, 74
Tofu and Veggie Stir-Fry, 59
Tomato Basil Soup, 53
Turkey Sausage and Egg Wrap, 21
Vegan Lentil Tacos, 59
Vietnamese Pho with Tofu and Vegetables, 92

ORANGES
Orange and Almond Salad, 110

OREGANO
Low-carb Zucchini Crust Pizza with Fresh Herbs, 65
Minestrone Soup, 53
Tomato Basil Soup, 53

PARMESAN CHEESE
Almond-Crusted Chicken Tenders, 82
Baked Turkey Meatballs, 75
Cauliflower Crust Margherita Pizza, 64
Cauliflower Hash Browns, 26
Cauliflower Mashed Potatoes with Grilled Chicken, 82
Eggplant Lasagna, 81
Eggplant Mini Pizzas with Mozzarella, 63
Garlic and Herb Stuffed Mushrooms, 107
Grilled Chicken and Spinach Alfredo Pizza, 62
Grilled Chicken Caesar Salad, 42Low-Carb Bell Pepper Crust Pizza with Fresh Herbs, 66
Chicken and Spinach Stuffed Portobello Mushrooms, 75
Italian Stuffed Eggplant, 89
Keto-Friendly Broccoli and Cheese Pizza, 65
Low-carb BBQ Chicken Pizza with Red Onion, 64
Low-carb Zucchini Crust Pizza with Fresh Herbs, 65

Mushroom and Olive Pizza with Ricotta, 64
One-Pot Creamy Mushroom Chicken, 85
One-pot Garlic Parmesan Chicken with Broccoli, 85
Spaghetti Squash Bolognese, 78
Spicy Shrimp and Garlic Pizza on a Cauliflower Crust, 63
Spinach and Artichoke Dip with Whole Grain Crackers, 106
Stuffed Bell Peppers with Ground Turkey, 57
Tomato and Basil Egg White Scramble, 22
Veggie and Cheese Frittata, 24
Whole Wheat Veggie Pizza with Pesto Sauce, 61
Zoodles with Pesto and Cherry Tomatoes, 58
Zucchini and Tomato Omelette, 25
Zucchini Chips with Parmesan, 99
Zucchini Noodles with Pesto and Cherry Tomatoes, 58
Zucchini Noodles with Pesto Shrimp, 69
Zucchini Noodles with Poached Eggs, 27

PARSLEY
Beef and Vegetable Stew, 54
Butternut Squash Soup, 54
Cheese and Herb-Stuffed Omelette, 22
Eggplant and Tomato Stew, 60
Eggplant Lasagna, 81
Garlic and Herb Stuffed Mushrooms, 107
Garlic and Rosemary Grilled Pork Tenderloin, 76
Garlic Roasted Turkey Breast, 75
Greek Lemon Chicken with Tzatziki, 88
Greek-Style Grilled Fish Tacos with Tzatziki, 69
Hard-Boiled Eggs with Hummus, 101
Herb-Roasted Chicken Thighs with Garlic and Vegetables, 80
Herb-Rubbed Grilled Chicken Breasts, 77
Chicken and Spinach Stuffed Portobello Mushrooms, 75
Italian Stuffed Bell Peppers with Ground Turkey, 88
Italian Stuffed Eggplant, 89
Lemon Herb Grilled Chicken, 73
Lentil and Feta Salad, 44
Low-Carb Salmon Patties with Cucumber Salad, 72
Low-Carb Zucchini Crust Pizza with Fresh Herbs, 65
Mediterranean Chickpea Salad, 42
Mediterranean Veggie and Hummus Wrap, 46
Middle Eastern Falafel with Tahini Sauce, 92
Minestrone Soup, 53

Mushroom and Barley Pilaf, 56
One-pot Beef and Vegetable Chili, 83
One-Pot Creamy Mushroom Chicken, 85
One-pot Garlic Parmesan Chicken with Broccoli, 85
One-Pot Ratatouille, 87
Roasted Veggie and Quinoa Bowl, 56
Seared Scallops with Asparagus and Lemon, 70
Slow Cooker Beef and Vegetable Soup, 84
Spaghetti Squash Bolognese, 78
Spicy Shrimp and Garlic Pizza on a Cauliflower Crust, 63
Split Pea Soup with Ham, 55
Stuffed Bell Peppers with Ground Turkey, 57
Stuffed Mini Bell Peppers with Cream Cheese, 104
Tuna and Avocado Salad Bowl, 43
Tuna Salad Whole Grain Sandwich, 48

PEANUT BUTTER
Peanut Butter Chocolate Chip Cookies, 122
Rice Cake with Peanut Butter and Chia Seeds, 102
Peanut Butter Berry Power Smoothie, 33
Peanut Butter and Greek Yogurt Power Shake, 35
Thai Peanut Chicken Salad, 44

PEANUTS
Thai Peanut Chicken Salad, 44

PEARL BARLEY
Mushroom and Barley Pilaf, 56

PEAS
Cauliflower Fried Rice with Chicken, 78
Split Pea Soup with Ham, 55

PINE NUTS
Zucchini Noodles with Pesto and Cherry Tomatoes, 58
Zoodles with Pesto and Cherry Tomatoes, 58
Zucchini Noodles with Pesto Shrimp, 69

PINEAPPLE
Cottage Cheese with Pineapple Chunks, 17

PORK
Balsamic Glazed Pork Tenderloin, 137
Garlic and Rosemary Grilled Pork Tenderloin, 136
Chicken and Spinach Stuffed Portobello Mushrooms, 134
Portobello Mushroom and Spinach Breakfast Bake, 42

Slow Cooker BBQ Pulled Pork, 86

PROSCIUTTO
Prosciutto-Wrapped Asparagus Spears, 107

PUMPKIN PUREE
Pumpkin Spice Muffins, 115
Pumpkin Spice Bars, 117
Pumpkin Spice Cheesecake Bites, 118

PUMPKIN SEEDS
Mixed Nuts and Seeds, 94
Mixed Nuts and Seeds Trail Mix, 99

QUINOA
Chicken and Kale Soup, 52
Italian Stuffed Bell Peppers with Ground Turkey, 88
Lemon-Dill Shrimp and Quinoa Bowl, 67
One-Pot Mexican Quinoa, 84
Quinoa and Black Bean Salad, 41
Roasted Veggie and Quinoa Bowl, 56
Stuffed Bell Peppers with Black Beans and Corn, 57
Stuffed Bell Peppers with Ground Turkey, 57

RAISINS
Baked Apples with Cinnamon, 109

RASPBERRIES
Fresh Fruit Salad with Mint, 109
Low-Carb Pancakes with Berries, 24
Raspberry Lemon Tart, 119

RED CABBAGE
Ginger-Lime Grilled Shrimp with Cabbage Slaw, 71
Thai Peanut Chicken Salad, 44

RED ONION
Bell Pepper Slices with Guacamole, 95
Breakfast Tostada, 14
Cobb Salad with Turkey and Avocado, 45
Cottage Cheese and Tomato Stuffed Avocados, 101
Cottage Cheese and Veggie Stuffed Bell Peppers, 22
Crispy Tilapia Lettuce Cups with Mango Salsa, 70
Egg and Spinach Whole Wheat Sandwich, 47
Greek-Style Grilled Fish Tacos with Tzatziki, 69
Grilled Chicken and Spinach Alfredo Pizza, 62
Grilled Chicken Caesar Salad, 42
Grilled Salmon and Avocado Salad, 45

Grilled Veggie and Hummus Sandwich, 46
Low-Carb Bell Pepper Crust Pizza with Fresh Herbs, 66
Guacamole with Veggie Sticks, 105
Herb-Roasted Chicken Thighs with Garlic and Vegetables, 80
Kale and Roasted Beet Salad, 43
Lemon-Dill Shrimp and Quinoa Bowl, 67
Lentil and Feta Salad, 44
Low-Carb BBQ Chicken Pizza with Red Onion, 64
Roast Beef Wrap with Mustard, 48
Low-Carb Salmon Patties with Cucumber Salad, 72
Low-Carb Zucchini Crust Pizza with Fresh Herbs, 65
Mediterranean Chickpea Salad, 42
Mediterranean Veggie and Hummus Wrap, 46
Orange and Almond Salad, 110
Quinoa and Black Bean Salad, 41
Roasted Veggie and Quinoa Bowl, 56
Salad with Egg and Salsa Verde Vinaigrette, 16
Salmon and Asparagus Salad, 45
Sardine and Avocado Stuffed Bell Peppers, 71
Shrimp Cocktail with Avocado Salsa, 107
Smoked Salmon and Avocado Sandwich, 50
Smoked Salmon and Avocado Plate, 20
Spicy Mackerel Salad with Cucumber and Tomato, 68
Spinach and Strawberry Salad with Balsamic Vinaigrette, 43
Sweet Potato and Black Bean Salad, 58
Tofu and Veggie Breakfast Bowl, 23
Tuna and Avocado Salad Bowl, 43
Tuna Salad Whole Grain Sandwich, 48
Turkey and Avocado Whole Grain Wrap, 46
Turkey and Spinach Wrap with Hummus, 49
Vegan Lentil Tacos, 59
Veggie and Cheese Frittata, 24
Whole Wheat Veggie Pizza with Pesto Sauce, 61

RICE NOODLES
Vietnamese Pho with Tofu and Vegetables, 92

RICOTTA CHEESE
Eggplant Lasagna, 81
Keto-Friendly Broccoli and Cheese Pizza, 65
Mushroom and Olive Pizza with Ricotta, 64

ROAST BEEF
Low-Carb Roast Beef Wrap with Mustard, 48

ROLLED OATS
Apple Cinnamon Overnight Oats, 16
Overnight Oats with Chia Seeds, 15

ROSEMARY
Garlic and Rosemary Grilled Pork Tenderloin, 76
Herb-Roasted Chicken Thighs with Garlic and Vegetables, 80

SALMON
Grilled Salmon and Avocado Salad, 45
Low-Carb Salmon Patties with Cucumber Salad, 72
Salmon and Asparagus Salad, 45
Sardine and Avocado Stuffed Bell Peppers, 71

SEA SCALLOPS
Seared Scallops with Asparagus and Lemon, 70

SESAME SEEDS
Japanese Teriyaki Tofu with Broccoli, 90
Tofu and Vegetable Stir-Fry, 74

SHREDDED COCONUT
Almond and Flaxseed Energy Bites, 96
Apple Slices with Almond Butter, 94
Almond-Coconut Protein Smoothie, 36
Cottage Cheese with Pineapple, 17

SHRIMP
Ginger-Lime Grilled Shrimp with Cabbage Slaw, 71
Lemon-Dill Shrimp and Quinoa Bowl, 67
Shrimp Cocktail with Avocado Salsa, 107
Spicy Shrimp and Garlic Pizza on a Cauliflower Crust, 63
Zucchini Noodles with Pesto Shrimp, 69

SMOKED SALMON
Creamy Scrambled Eggs with Smoked Salmon, 17
Smoked Salmon and Avocado Plate, 20
Smoked Salmon Cucumber Bites, 103
Smoked Salmon and Avocado Sandwich, 50

SNOW PEAS
Tofu and Veggie Stir-Fry, 59

SPAGHETTI SQUASH
Spaghetti Squash Bolognese, 78

SPINACH
Avocado and Turkey Breakfast Roll-Ups, 23
Baked Cod with Garlic Spinach, 69
Beef and Vegetable Stew, 54
Chicken and Spinach Stuffed Portobello Mushrooms, 75
Chickpea and Spinach Curry, 55
Cottage Cheese and Veggie Stuffed Bell Peppers, 22
Creamy Avocado and Spinach Smoothie, 32
Cucumber Mint Green Smoothie, 30
Egg and Cheese Breakfast Muffins, 21
Egg and Spinach Whole Wheat Sandwich, 47
Grilled Chicken and Spinach Alfredo Pizza, 62
Indian Spiced Chickpea Stew, 92
Lemon-Dill Shrimp and Quinoa Bowl, 67
Lentil and Vegetable Soup, 51
Mediterranean Veggie and Hummus Wrap, 46
Minestrone Soup, 53
Moroccan Chickpea Stew, 55
Mushroom and Barley Pilaf, 56
Portobello Mushroom and Spinach Breakfast Bake, 28
Slow Cooker Chicken and Vegetable Stew, 83
Slow Cooker Lentil and Spinach Curry, 85
Smoked Salmon and Avocado Plate, 20
Smoked Salmon and Avocado Sandwich, 50
Spicy Lentil Stew, 53
Spinach Almond Butter Protein Smoothie, 34
Spinach and Artichoke Dip with Whole-Grain Crackers, 106
Spinach and Blueberry Blast Smoothie, 29
Spinach and Mushroom Egg Scramble, 19
Spinach and Strawberry Salad with Balsamic Vinaigrette, 43
Strawberry Spinach Smoothie, 31
Tofu and Veggie Breakfast Bowl, 23
Turkey and Spinach Wrap with Hummus, 49
Turkey Sausage and Egg Wrap, 21
Veggie and Cheese Frittata, 24
Veggie and Tofu Wrap, 50
Whole Wheat Veggie Pizza with Pesto Sauce, 61

SQUASH
One-Pot Ratatouille, 87
Italian Stuffed Eggplant, 89

Turkey and Avocado Whole Grain Wrap, 46
Turkey and Spinach Wrap with Hummus, 49

TURKEY SAUSAGE
Turkey Sausage and Egg Wrap, 21

TURNIP
Beef and Vegetable Stew, 54
Split Pea Soup with Ham, 55

UNSALTED BUTTER
Cauliflower Mashed Potatoes with Grilled Chicken, 82
Carrot Cake with Cream Cheese Frosting, 120
Low-Carb Lemon Bars, 114

VANILLA EXTRACT
Almond Flour Lemon Bars, 114
Almond and Flaxseed Energy Bites, 94
Almond Butter Cookies, 105
Almond Flour Chocolate Chip Cookies, 110
Apple Cinnamon Chia Seed Pudding, 109
Berry Greek Yogurt Parfait, 108
Baked Apples with Cinnamon, 109
Berry Chia Seed Jam, 111
Carrot Cake with Cream Cheese Frosting, 120
Cinnamon Walnut Coffee Cake, 118
Coconut Flour Brownies, 113
Coconut Flour Pancakes, 108
Dark Chocolate Coconut Truffles, 119
Greek Yogurt with Berries and Nuts, 15
Chia Seed Pudding with Mango, 109
Chocolate Almond Brownies, 117
Chocolate Avocado Mousse, 120
Lemon Blueberry Muffins, 116
Low-Carb Coconut Panna Cotta, 119
Low-Carb Lemon Bars, 114
Mini Berry Cheesecakes, 121
Peanut Butter Chocolate Chip Cookies, 122
Pumpkin Spice Bars, 117
Pumpkin Spice Cheesecake Bites, 118
Pumpkin Spice Muffins, 115
Raspberry Lemon Tart, 119
Sugar-Free Banana Bread, 111
Vanilla Almond Cupcakes, 114

VANILLA WHEY PROTEIN POWDER
Greek Yogurt and Almond Protein Shake, 34
Peanut Butter Berry Power Smoothie, 33

Slow Cooker Turkey Chili, 86
Spaghetti Squash Bolognese, 78
Stuffed Bell Peppers with Ground Turkey, 57
Spinach Almond Butter Protein Smoothie, 34
Vanilla Strawberry Protein Smoothie, 35

VEGETABLE BROTH
Butternut Squash Soup, 54
Beef and Vegetable Stew, 54
Broccoli Cheddar Soup, 51
Eggplant and Tomato Stew, 60
Indian Spiced Chickpea Stew, 92
Lentil and Vegetable Soup, 51
Minestrone Soup, 53
Moroccan Chickpea Stew, 55
Mushroom and Barley Pilaf, 56
One-Pot Mexican Quinoa, 84
Roasted Veggie and Quinoa Bowl, 56
Slow Cooker Lentil and Spinach Curry, 85
Spicy Lentil Stew, 53
Spinach and Artichoke Dip with Whole Grain Crackers, 106
Tofu and Vegetable Stir-Fry, 74
Tomato Basil Soup, 53
Vegan Lentil Tacos, 59
Vietnamese Pho with Tofu and Vegetables, 92

WALNUTS
Apple Slices with Almond Butter, 94
Baked Apples with Cinnamon, 109
Carrot Cake with Cream Cheese Frosting, 120
Celery Sticks with Cream Cheese and Walnuts, 97
Cottage Cheese with Pineapple, 17
Kale and Roasted Beet Salad, 43
Mixed Nuts and Seeds, 94
Mixed Nuts and Seeds Trail Mix, 99
Spinach and Strawberry Salad with Balsamic Vinaigrette, 43
Whole Wheat Veggie Pizza with Pesto Sauce, 61
Yogurt Parfait with Nuts and Seeds, 27

WATERMELON
Watermelon Mint Cooler, 39

WHITEFISH
Blackened Fish and Cauliflower Rice Bowl, 70
Greek-Style Grilled Fish Tacos with Tzatziki, 69

WHOLE GRAIN BREAD
Avocado Toast with Tomato Slices, 17
Cucumber and Cream Cheese Sandwich, 50
Egg and Spinach Whole Wheat Sandwich, 47
Smoked Salmon and Avocado Sandwich, 50
Tuna Salad Whole Grain Sandwich, 48

WHOLE GRAIN CRACKERS
Spinach and Artichoke Dip with Whole Grain Crackers, 106

WHOLE GRAIN PASTA
Minestrone Soup, 53

WHOLE WHEAT BREADCRUMBS
Garlic and Herb Stuffed Mushrooms, 107

WHOLE WHEAT FLOUR
Crispy Tilapia Lettuce Cups with Mango Salsa, 70
Broccoli Cheddar Soup, 51
Grilled Chicken and Spinach Alfredo Pizza, 62
Mushroom and Olive Pizza with Ricotta, 64
Whole Wheat Veggie Pizza with Pesto Sauce, 61

WHOLE WHEAT TORTILLAS
Breakfast Tostada, 14
Greek-Style Grilled Fish Tacos with Tzatziki, 69
Mediterranean Veggie and Hummus Wrap, 46
Slow Cooker BBQ Pulled Pork, 86
Turkey and Avocado Whole Grain Wrap, 46
Turkey and Spinach Wrap with Hummus, 49
Turkey Sausage and Egg Wrap, 21
Veggie and Tofu Wrap, 50
Vegan Lentil Tacos, 59

ZUCCHINI
Chicken and Kale Soup, 52
Cottage Cheese and Veggie Stuffed Bell Peppers, 22
Egg and Tofu Stir-Fry with Vegetables, 23

CONCLUSION

Summarizing Key Takeaways As we reach the end of the "Diabetic Diet Cookbook After 50," it's important to reflect on the key lessons and insights you've gathered. You now understand how crucial it is to choose foods that stabilize blood sugar, how to incorporate healthy ingredients into your meals, and the importance of maintaining a balanced lifestyle. This book has provided practical recipes and meal plans that make managing diabetes more accessible and enjoyable without compromising taste or variety.

You've also learned about the benefits of low-glycemic foods, the role of portion control, and how to enjoy sweet flavors without added sugars. Each chapter has equipped you with the tools and knowledge to navigate the unique challenges of managing diabetes after 50, helping you live a healthier, more vibrant life.

Encouragement for Continued Healthy Living Your journey toward better health doesn't stop here—it's a lifelong commitment. Remember, the small, consistent changes you make today will profoundly impact your well-being. Continue to explore new recipes, stay physically active, and pay attention to your mental and emotional health. Healthy living is about enjoying the choices you make every day and finding balance in your life.

Stay proactive in managing your diabetes by regularly monitoring your blood sugar levels, working closely with your healthcare providers, and adjusting your diet as needed. Don't hesitate to experiment with new foods and flavors— this journey is about more than just following a diet; it's about discovering and enjoying the foods that nourish your body and delight your palate.

Final Reflections and Words of Encouragement By prioritizing your health and following the guidance in this book, you're already moving towards a healthier, more vibrant life. Managing diabetes can be challenging, but with the right attitude, resources, and support, you can reach your health goals and enjoy a life filled with energy, happiness, and purpose.

Keep in mind that progress is what truly counts—not perfection. Celebrate every victory, no matter how small, and treat setbacks as valuable lessons for growth. You have the ability to shape your future, and this book is just the start of your journey toward improved health.

Stay inspired, stay curious, and remain committed to your well-being. The best is yet to come; you have everything you need to make the most of each day.

Printed in Great Britain
by Amazon